PENGUIN BOOKS

Test Match Year 1996–1997

David Frith has written twenty books and has been a cricket magazine editor for twenty-five years. Founder of *Wisden Cricket Monthly* in 1979, he edited that journal for seventeen years. His life has been split between England and Australia, and he has reported on Test matches in eight of the nine countries. Two of his books, a biography of A. E. Stoddart (1970) and *Pageant of Cricket* (1987), have won Cricket Society Jubilee Literary Awards, and in 1988 he was chosen as British Magazine Sportswriter of the Year. He is currently striving to justify his forty-seventh playing season.

Warren Bagust is associate editor of *Test Match Year* and, like the editor, he used to play for the celebrated St George club in Sydney. A cricket aficionado with a weakness for statistics, this former legspinner, who settled in England in the 1950s, was the ideas man for *Test Match Year*, just as he was for the England v. Australia Test Records book, edited by David Frith in 1986.

Test Match Year

1996–1997

A Complete Record of Twelve Months
of Test Cricket Around the World

Edited by David Frith

PENGUIN BOOKS

Acknowledgements

The Editor wishes to acknowledge the support and assistance of the following:
contributors John Bishop, Gulu Ezekiel, Clayton Goodwin, Gideon Haigh,
Brian Murgatroyd and Terry Power; Dr Kim Baloch, Jeremy Malies,
Francis Payne; Adrian Murrell and Mark Goldsmith of Allsport Picture Agency;
the Indian Cricket Board; Diana Keen of BSkyB; Tony Lacey, Mark Handsley,
and Nicola Stanley of Penguin UK; and Warren Bagust.

PENGUIN BOOKS

Published by the Penguin Group
Penguin Books Ltd, 27 Wrights Lane, London w8 5tz, England
Penguin Books USA Inc., 375 Hudson Street, New York, New York 10014, USA
Penguin Books Australia Ltd, Ringwood, Victoria, Australia
Penguin Books Canada Ltd, 10 Alcorn Avenue, Toronto, Ontario, Canada m4v 3b2
Penguin Books (NZ) Ltd, 182–190 Wairau Road, Auckland 10, New Zealand

Penguin Books Ltd, Registered Offices: Harmondsworth, Middlesex, England

First published 1997
1 3 5 7 9 10 8 6 4 2

Editorial and statistical matter copyright © David Frith, 1997
Test match reports copyright © individual contributors, 1997
All rights reserved

The moral right of the author has been asserted

Set in 10/12pt Monotype Bembo
Designed in QuarkXpress on an Apple Macintosh
Printed in England by Clays Ltd, St Ives plc

Contents

Preface
by David Frith

'Anyone who says Test cricket's dead is a fool,' exclaimed Australia's captain Mark Taylor after the dramatic Port Elizabeth Test match in March. The remark would have been equally appropriate at the end of many of the other Tests played in the 1996–97 Test match year.

While the marketing zealots regard it as necessary to jazz up Test cricket alongside its gaudy spin-off, limited-overs cricket, the five-day game remains the 'real thing', the ultimate test of skill and strategy, in a sense the only pure and genuine form of cricket, where wickets have to be earned. The players have always known this. The limited-overs format is a big money-spinner and is often entertaining, sometimes predictable, sometimes anticlimactic. The key word is *limited*. The length of the innings is limited, bowlers' allocations of overs are limited, fielding positions are limited. Even memory's sweet recall is limited. While there is the occasionally duff Test match, most Tests remain in the forefront of memory.

Panic sometimes afflicts administrators when Test attendances are low, the reflex response being to lay on more one-day slogs to fill the stadiums and the coffers. Well, some of the finest things in life may need a spot of subsidising, but Test cricket, thanks in some part to television rights, stands on its own sturdy legs at the age of 120, having undergone inevitable change, but still recognisable, no doubt, to the ghosts from the past.

Evolution's Gifts

There are things which, presumably, those ghosts, together with many of us still living, might find hard to accept, like sponsors' logos spread across what ought to be sacred turf during Tests. They can do what they like to one-day cricket – 'crackit' as Bill O'Reilly used to call it – but the bounds of decency were broken when, in addition to the many accepted areas of commercial exposure, the first logo defaced the grass at straight-hit through the duration of a Test match. What next? The pitch area itself? It has been particularly intrusive on South Africa's Test fields. No amount of riches should be seen as compensation for such an intrusion.

Cricket's evolution has brought us protective helmets and players (probably sensibly) clad in sunglasses and smeared with sunblock facial cream. It has brought us fresh sets of jargon with each generation. It has seen, too, the wearing of wristwatches by bowlers, something for which offending 10-year-olds used to be scolded and sent from the field.

After wasted years when the dim and hopelessly reactionary could not be made to see its huge potential benefit, evolution has also brought us video replays, whereby a third umpire can determine the truth in a close-call run-out, stumping or boundary incident.

The Umpiring Problem

This raises the ongoing and apparently insoluble problem of fallible umpiring. Among the Test match narratives in this volume lurks a recurring lament at poor decisions, some of which altered the course of matches. The establishment of an international panel of umpires, with an overseas official serving with a local in each Test, has lessened the risk of accusations of bias, though only to a meagre degree. What it has not done is raise the quality of Test umpiring. Plans to improve performance by staging seminars are encouraging, as are suggestions that umpires might submit to brutally honest self-assessments after studying playbacks of their more woeful decisions. But the instinct for correctly judging matters such as wides and leg-befores cannot be implanted. You either have it or you don't. So very few umpires, unfortunately, seem to be adequately endowed. Indigestible as it is, allowances have to be made.

Where no allowance can be made is for the stubborn umpire who refuses to refer a close decision, thereby allowing a batsman who has narrowly been run out to continue batting – sometimes for several hours. It was just such an instance at Sydney in 1982–83, before replays were used, which persuaded some of us that television should be the judge. After all, it already *was* in the eyes of millions of viewers.

To campaign for video enlightenment was to fall foul of batsmen (who knew that they often benefited in tight run-out calls that were judged by the naked eye) and of umpires, more than one of whom took umbrage: 'Sounds like you want to get rid of us and just have a hat-stand out there for the bowler to hang his cap and sweater on!'

Well, it's beginning to seem more like a good idea. If what we see at Test level is the best umpiring to be found among the world fraternity, then the players and spectators will have to go on enduring the atrocities. We must continue to watch gnashingly as a bowler's boot comes down well over the popping crease, no-ball not having been called (perhaps the umpire is standing too far back), and the batsman succumbs to what – clearly to all viewers – was an illegal delivery. It happened with distressing frequency during the Test matches recorded here. The authorities are hardly in a position to ban replays. Why should they even try? It's often the best viewing of the day.

Dumb Bowlers

When they *are* called for front-foot no-balls – and it happens many more times than is professionally forgivable – bowlers glare at the crease, the umpire, the batsman, *anything* that might take the blame. The blame rests solely and squarely with the bowler. As a breed, they seem to share an unshakeable determination to plonk that front foot a millimetre from the limit, gaining total advantage in range from the batsman on strike – as if six inches would make any appreciable difference. This greed over distance, this blindness to logic, causes stacks of extras to be handed to the batting side, and can sometimes contribute towards defeat. The fault may be bred in the nets, where bowlers are often seen letting fly off 19 yards, even when the footholds are clear. No-balls not only stultify periods of play but can drag down the daily over rate, thus costing the fielding team money.

If it is all merely an unsubtle campaign to get the back-foot no-ball law restored, then let it fail, for an even greater blot on the game would be a return to the days where bowlers who drag as well as those with long legs would be letting go of the ball from well in front of the popping crease. That, as we saw in 1958–59, is a form of anarchy.

The Odd Tête-à-Tête

Match referees now preside as overall guardians of propriety at Test matches, and woe betide a player who even glances at his bat after a bad leg-before decision. The corruption of society and downturn in everyday behaviour have inevitably been partially reflected in cricket, and the advent of the game's own constabulary, sad commentary though it be, was another predestined piece of evolution.

But where matters have most lost balance is that while authority expects us to accept and absorb all the human failings of umpires, it is demanded of the players that they bottle up their emotions at all times. This dehumanises the game. Rotten decision; player explodes; referee fines him or bans him. Would that justice were so summarily dispensed in real life.

This extends to the perception of sledging – verbal abuse. A man whose name seems never far from this topic in historical terms is former Australian captain Ian Chappell, who observed in the Australian magazine *Inside Edge* that cultural differences mean that sledging is not clear-cut internationally. One of Test cricket's major fascinations stems from the variety of flavours attaching to cricket from country to country. South Africans have sledged in Afrikaans, Pakistanis in both Urdu and English, West Indians in patois on the subject of where the next bouncer will be aimed, Australians in florid expletives that are sometimes quite funny. And Parore v Cork in New Zealand earlier this year might have made an hilarious cassette. Like the less excusable slow over rates, sledging continues to cost the players money. But, as Chappell has clearmindedly pointed out, while batsmen are 'entitled to some peace on the field', 'the odd tête-à-tête is the source of much of the game's humour'. That has to be guarded at all costs.

Meanwhile, there seems little a match referee can do to stem the cries of 'Catch it!', that immoral and childish screech that comes from certain players whenever the ball bounces off a batsman's pad and sometimes even after he has played it straight onto the turf.

Who Are the Champions?

Our table on page xi gives one impression of a world Test championship. It is based on percentages of victories against losses. The current rankings will surprise. But the knowing will recognise that there is no completely reliable points scheme for determining such a fluid matter. Many have tried, and the latest round of urgings for a formal table embraces the idea that all countries should play against all others in a set period to show, by virtue of series successes, who are top dogs. Not only would this clog up the calendar (and what would the one-day cricket fiends feel if they suffered a cutback?) but there is something alien about coercion of nations. India and Pakistan would have to play on neutral ground, thanks to politics.

It would be even more absurd if, God forbid, but as one or two visionaries desire, more countries were elevated to Test status. Who needs expansion of the Test list? The existing countries are well content, most of them, to play among themselves. To expand would be to dilute.

So who are the supreme team in 1997? One of our contributors, Gideon Haigh, refers to 'the last days of the Caribbean Empire'. West Indies, by their own special means, were more clearly world champions in the 1980s than any country could claim to be at present. Australia have beaten all challengers of late, but keep letting the odd Test slip. If they were to play Pakistan when that team was 'on song', Australia would not necessarily be favourites. Then, too, India are almost unbeatable *at home*.

A beats B; B beats C; C beats A. What does this prove? Perhaps that Test competition today is tight, breeding inaccurate forecasting. And this, surely, is half the fun? It's the not knowing and it's the argument and speculation that fuel enthusiasm. A rigid, untrustworthy league table would spoil it all.

As for patriotic allegiance, if your particular country has not been doing very well of late, may we offer a suggestion? Spread your bets by adopting a second country. But choose wisely.

Annual Bundle

This first offering of a year's Test cricket contains more detail than has ever before been assembled. Nowhere else is it possible to find not only the basic scores of all Tests in a 12-month period but also the additional data relating to minutes batted, balls faced, boundaries hit, substitute catches, run-out details, third umpires' names, wides and no-balls per bowler. It may be assumed that all this material is easily come by. It isn't. Most of the national cricket boards have no such records and neither, surprisingly, does the International Cricket Council.

We've brought it to you as fast as production and distribution permit. And it is naturally hoped that public response will be great enough to ensure that *Test Match Year* becomes a regular annual which will enhance cricket at its supreme level.

Forty-one Tests were played on 37 grounds around the globe in the May-to-April period under review. Awesome batting and bowling feats are described, and an extensive 1996–97 analysis section has been constructed from it – all set against an in-depth Test records data-bank.

Oddities abound. The only South African not to register a duck all season was Brett Schultz, their No. 11 batsman. Less surprisingly, since they played most Tests (15), India provided the top two run-makers and top three wicket-takers: but two of those cricketers were new to Test cricket. The top score came from a New Zealander, while the best bowling figures came from another newcomer – who just happened to have become South Africa's fastest century-scorer as well. A world Test six-hitting record was broken and a partnership record too. And for the first time in Test cricket's 120 years, a batsman made two not-out centuries in a match. Uniquely, a Test was drawn with the scores level (and the umpiring, of course, was the subject of raging debate for days afterwards).

Our associate editor has chosen a World XI for 1996–97, based heavily on statistics. Some of the names will surprise:

Saeed Anwar	M. G. Bevan
M. A. Atherton	Wasim Akram
A. J. Stewart	S. K. Warne
S. Chanderpaul	A. A. Donald
R. S. Dravid	G. D. McGrath
S. R. Waugh	

No Lara. No Tendulkar. No Mark Waugh. No McMillan. No Mushtaq Ahmed. Try picking your own – or, even more fantastically, an Aesthetic XI.

And so another Test match year starts, with more debutants about to step into the arena and old favourites departing. Established giants will seek to reassert themselves on the major cricket grounds of the world. More thumping drives; more spilt catches; more shattered stumps. And more wobbly umpiring. 'Twas ever thus.

Analysis
1996–97

RESULTS COUNTRY BY COUNTRY 1996–97

	Tests	W	D	L	% won	% lost	Opponents (H: home; A: away)	No. of players
Pakistan	9	4	4	1	44.44	11.11	Eng. (3)^A Zim. (2)^H NZ (2)^H SL (2)^A	24
Australia	9	5	0	4	55.56	44.44	Ind. (1)^A WI (5)^H SA (3)^A	19
England	11	3	6	2	27.27	18.18	Ind. (3)^H Pak. (3)^H Zim. (2)^A NZ (3)^A	23
South Africa	9	4	1	4	44.44	44.44	Ind. (6)$^{3A}_{3H}$ Aus. (3)^H	17
New Zealand	7	3	1	3	42.86	42.86	Pak. (2)^A Eng. (3)^H SL (2)^H	17
Sri Lanka	6	2	2	2	33.33	33.33	Zim. (2)^H NZ (2)^A Pak. (2)^H	18
West Indies	10	3	4	3	30.00	30.00	Aus. (5)^A Ind. (5)^H	20
India	15	3	7	5	20.00	33.33	Eng. (3)^A Aus. (1)^H SA (6)$^{3H}_{3A}$ WI (5)^A	22
Zimbabwe	6	0	3	3	0.00	50.00	SL (2)^A Pak. (2)^A Eng. (2)^H	19
								179

Positions based on superiority of win percentage over loss percentage

---

SERIES RESULTS

Series Start	Home team	Visitors	Tests	Aus.	Eng.	Ind.	NZ	Pak.	SA	SL	WI	Zim.	Drawn
June '96	ENGLAND beat	India	3		1	0							2
July '96	England lost to	PAKISTAN	3		0			2					1
Sept '96	SRI LANKA beat	Zimbabwe	2							2		0	
Oct '96	INDIA beat	Australia	1	0		1							
Oct '96	PAKISTAN beat	Zimbabwe	2					1				0	1
Nov '96	INDIA beat	South Africa	3			2			1				
Nov '96	Pakistan drew with	New Zealand	2				1	1					
Nov '96	AUSTRALIA beat	West Indies	5	3							2		
Dec '96	Zimbabwe drew with	England	2		0							0	2
Dec '96	SOUTH AFRICA beat	India	3			0			2				1
Jan '97	New Zealand lost to	ENGLAND	3		2		0						1
Feb '97	South Africa lost to	AUSTRALIA	3	2					1				
March '97	WEST INDIES beat	India	5			0					1		4
March '97	NEW ZEALAND beat	Sri Lanka	2				2			0			
April '97	Sri Lanka drew with	Pakistan	2					0		0			2
			41	**5**	**3**	**3**	**3**	**4**	**4**	**2**	**3**	**0**	**14**

YEAR'S TEAM AVERAGES 1996–97

Batsmen	M	I	NO	R	HS	Av.	100	50	0	Ct	St
Australia	9	165	19	4075	214	27.91	5	18	25	95	0
England	11	178	23	5226	173	33.72	14	23	14	121	3
India	15	261	32	6224	201	27.18	11	27	22	125	2
New Zealand	7	141	15	3142	267★	24.94	3	20	14	67	1
Pakistan	9	137	21	4407	257★	37.99	11	22	13	61	4
South Africa	9	180	24	4262	153★	27.32	8	17	22	87	1
Sri Lanka	6	104	14	2984	168	33.16	7	15	13	59	2
West Indies	10	169	23	4104	137★	28.11	7	17	18	89	1
Zimbabwe	6	119	12	2208	112	20.64	3	12	17	42	2
	(41)	**1454**	**183**	**36632**	**267★**	**28.82**	**69**	**171**	**158**	**746**	**16**

Bowlers	O	M	R	W	Av.	BB	5w/i	10w/m
Australia	1370.1	365	3712	144	25.78	6–82	5	1
England	2126.2	528	5619	171	32.86	5–40	4	0
India	2557.4	565	7171	217	33.05	6–21	11	1
New Zealand	1126.4	283	3097	103	30.07	5–46	6	0
Pakistan	1628.3	349	4644	155	29.96	7–66	8	3
South Africa	1526.1	386	4136	150	27.57	8–64	4	0
Sri Lanka	1010.2	263	2566	86	29.84	6–98	3	0
West Indies	1609.2	344	4326	128	33.80	6–100	6	0
Zimbabwe	898.2	195	2513	65	38.66	5–106	3	0
	13853.3	**3278**	**37784**	**1219**	**31.00**	**8–64**	**50**	**5**

	Runs scored per 100 balls faced by batsmen	Balls per wicket taken by bowlers	Runs conceded by bowlers per 100 balls	Credit/debit account: batting avge ÷ bowling avge
Australia	43.67	57.09	45.15	1.08
England	42.81	74.61	44.04	1.03
India	41.41	70.72	46.73	0.82
New Zealand	42.78	65.63	45.81	0.83
Pakistan	48.16	63.04	47.53	1.27
South Africa	46.75	61.05	45.17	0.99
Sri Lanka	47.41	70.49	42.33	1.11
West Indies	45.38	75.44	44.80	0.83
Zimbabwe	37.30	82.92	46.62	0.53

HIGHEST TOTALS 1996–97 (350 upwards)

628 for 8 dec.	Australia v South Africa	Johannesburg	410	India v South Africa	Johannesburg
586 for 7 dec.	New Zealand v Sri Lanka	Dunedin	406	England v Zimbabwe	Bulawayo
564	England v India	Trent Bridge	400 for 7 dec.	India v South Africa	Kanpur
553	Pakistan v Zimbabwe	Sheikhupura	390	New Zealand v England	Auckland
529 for 7 dec.	South Africa v India	Cape Town	386 for 4 dec.	Sri Lanka v Pakistan	Colombo (Sinhalese)
521 for 8 dec.	Pakistan v England	The Oval	384	West Indies v Australia	Perth
521	India v England	Trent Bridge	384	South Africa v Australia	Centurion
521	England v New Zealand	Auckland	383	England v New Zealand	Wellington
517	Australia v West Indies	Adelaide	378	Pakistan v Sri Lanka	Colombo (Premadasa)
501	England v Pakistan	Headingley	376	Zimbabwe v England	Bulawayo
479	Australia v West Indies	Brisbane	375	Zimbabwe v Pakistan	Sheikhupura
448	Pakistan v England	Headingley	367 for 3 dec.	South Africa v India	Calcutta
436	India v West Indies	Port-of-Spain	361	India v Australia	Delhi
430	Pakistan v New Zealand	Rawalpindi	359	India v South Africa	Cape Town
429	India v England	Lord's	355	India v West Indies	Georgetown
428	South Africa v India	Calcutta	352 for 5 dec.	Pakistan v England	Lord's
427	West Indies v India	Kingston	350 for 8 dec.	Sri Lanka v Zimbabwe	Colombo (Sinhalese)
423 for 8	Sri Lanka v Pakistan	Colombo (Premadasa)			

LOWEST TOTALS 1996–97 (below 150)

66	India v South Africa	Durban
81	India v West Indies	Bridgetown
100	India v South Africa	Durban
105	South Africa v India	Ahmedabad
108	Australia v South Africa	Port Elizabeth
122	Australia v West Indies	Melbourne
124	New Zealand v England	Wellington
127	Zimbabwe v Sri Lanka	Colombo (Premadasa)
130	West Indies v Australia	Adelaide
130	South Africa v Australia	Johannesburg
135	Zimbabwe v Pakistan	Faisalabad

137	India v South Africa	Calcutta
140	West Indies v India	Bridgetown
141	Zimbabwe v Sri Lanka	Colombo (Sinhalese)
144	India v South Africa	Cape Town
145	Zimbabwe v Sri Lanka	Colombo (Premadasa)

Lowest innings totals by the other three countries were:

156	England v Zimbabwe	Harare
170	Sri Lanka v New Zealand	Hamilton
191	Pakistan v New Zealand	Lahore

BATSMEN

HIGHEST AGGREGATES 1996–97 (over 500 runs)

		Avge			*Avge*			*Avge*
1134	S.R. Tendulkar (Ind.)	47.25	687	B.C. Lara (WI)	40.41	622	Salim Malik (Pak.)	56.55
1039	R.S. Dravid (Ind.)	51.95	683	D.J. Cullinan (SA)	45.53	607	C.L. Hooper (WI)	40.47
1030	A.J. Stewart (Eng.)	68.67	676	N. Hussain (Eng.)	45.07	601	N.R. Mongia (Ind.)	25.04
787	S. Chanderpaul (WI)	52.47	669	G.P. Thorpe (Eng.)	41.81	572	G.S. Blewett (Aus.)	52.00
784	M.A. Atherton (Eng.)	49.00	655	Ijaz Ahmed (Pak.)	50.38	568	S.R. Waugh (Aus.)	51.64
768	S.C. Ganguly (Ind.)	42.67	648	B.A. Young (NZ)	54.00	541	G. Kirsten (SA)	30.06
701	Saeed Anwar (Pak.)	63.73	628	M.E. Waugh (Aus.)	39.25	506	S.P. Fleming (NZ)	42.17
691	M. Azharuddin (Ind.)	31.41						

Leading runmakers for the other two countries were: P.A. de Silva (SL) 492 (61.50); G.W. Flower (Zim.) 379 (34.45).

CENTURY PARTNERSHIPS (77)

First wicket

236	A.C. Hudson and G. Kirsten	SA v Ind., Calcutta
157	S.T. Jayasuriya and R.P. Arnold	SL v Pak., Colombo (Sinhalese)
136	Saeed Anwar and Shadab Kabir	Pak. v Eng., Lord's
130	M.A. Atherton and A.J. Stewart	Eng. v Ind., Trent Bridge
106	Saeed Anwar and Aamir Sohail	Pak. v Eng., Oval

Second wicket

262	Saeed Anwar and Ijaz Ahmed	Pak. v NZ, Rawalpindi
230	M.A. Atherton and N. Hussain (ret. injured when stand 192) and G.P. Thorpe	Eng. v Ind., Trent Bridge
212	G. Kirsten and D.J. Cullinan	SA v Ind., Calcutta
182	M.A. Atherton and A.J. Stewart	Eng. v NZ, Auckland
176	S.C. Williams and S. Chanderpaul	WI v Ind., Port-of-Spain
171	N.S. Sidhu and R.S. Dravid	Ind. v WI, Port-of-Spain
154	M.A. Atherton and A.J. Stewart	Eng. v Pak. Lord's
140	B.A. Young and M.J. Horne	NZ v SL, Dunedin
137	N.V. Knight and A.J. Stewart	Eng. v Zim., Bulawayo
133	Saeed Anwar and Ijaz Ahmed	Pak. v Eng., Oval
131	N.R. Mongia and S.C. Ganguly	Ind. v Aus., Delhi
127	G.W. Flower and A.D.R. Campbell	Zim. v Eng., Bulawayo
126	M.A. Taylor and R.T. Ponting	Aus. v WI, Brisbane
111	A.C. Hudson and A.M. Bacher	SA v Ind., Durban
107	A.J. Stewart and N. Hussain	Eng. v Pak., Headingley
102	A.M. Bacher and B.M. McMillan	SA v Aus., Centurion
102	Ramiz Raja and Ijaz Ahmed	Pak. v SL, Colombo (Premadasa)
101	A.D. Jadeja and R.S. Dravid	Ind. v WI, St John's

Third wicket

255	S.C. Ganguly and S.R. Tendulkar	Ind. v Eng., Trent Bridge
208	R.G. Samuels and B.C. Lara	WI v Aus., Perth
174	N.S. Sidhu and S.R. Tendulkar	Ind. v WI, Port-of-Spain
170	R.S. Dravid and S.R. Tendulkar	Ind. v WI, Bridgetown
164	M.L. Hayden and M.E. Waugh	Aus. v WI, Adelaide
163	R.S. Dravid and S.R. Tendulkar	Ind. v WI, Georgetown
142	M.T.G. Elliott (ret. injured when stand 76) and M.E. Waugh and M.G. Bevan	Aus. v WI, Sydney
130	Saeed Anwar and Inzamam-ul-Haq	Pak. v Eng., Lord's
129	P.A. de Silva and A. Ranatunga	SL v Pak., Colombo (Premadasa)
127	Ijaz Ahmed and Salim Malik	Pak. v SL, Colombo (Sinhalese)
122	S. Chanderpaul and B.C. Lara	WI v Ind., Kingston
117	Ijaz Ahmed and Salim Malik	Pak. v SL, Colombo (Premadasa)
114	G. Kirsten and D.J. Cullinan	SA v Ind., Cape Town
101	A.M. Bacher and D.J. Cullinan	SA v Aus., Centurion

Fourth wicket

172	C.L. Hooper and S. Chanderpaul	WI v Aus., Brisbane
147	B.C. Lara and C.L. Hooper	WI v Ind., Kingston
145	R.S. Dravid and S.C. Ganguly	Ind. v SA, Johannesburg
130	Ijaz Ahmed and Salim Malik	Pak. v Eng., Headingley
121	Salim Malik and Inzamam-ul-Haq	Pak. v SL, Colombo (Sinhalese)
118	Ijaz Ahmed and Inzamam-ul-Haq	Pak. v Eng., Lord's
117	C.L. Hooper and S. Chanderpaul	WI v Aus., Sydney
113	D.L. Houghton and A.D.R. Campbell	Zim. v Pak., Faisalabad
108	R.S. Dravid and S.C. Ganguly	Ind. v SA, Johannesburg
107	N. Hussain and G.P. Thorpe	Eng. v NZ, Wellington
106★	A.J. Stewart and G.P. Thorpe	Eng. v Zim., Harare
105	P.A. de Silva and A. Ranatunga	SL v Pak., Colombo (Sinhalese)

Fifth wicket

385	S.R. Waugh and G.S. Blewett	Aus. v SA, Johannesburg
148	N. Hussain and J.P. Crawley	Eng. v Zim., Bulawayo
142	B.C. Lara and R.I.C. Holder	WI v Ind., St John's
120	M.E. Waugh and M.G. Bevan	Aus. v WI, Perth
118	G.P. Thorpe and J.P. Crawley	Eng. v NZ, Wellington
114	A.P. Gurusinha and H.P. Tillekeratne	SL v Zim., Colombo (Sinhalese)
108	A.J. Stewart and N.V. Knight	Eng. v Pak., Headingley
102	S.R. Waugh and G.S. Blewett	Aus. v WI, Melbourne

Sixth wicket

222	S.R. Tendulkar and M. Azharuddin	Ind. v SA, Cape Town
165	M. Azharuddin and R.S. Dravid	Ind. v SA, Kanpur
165	G.S. Blewett and M.G. Bevan	Aus. v WI, Adelaide
142	A. Ranatunga and R.S. Kaluwitharana	SL v Zim., Colombo (Premadasa)
142	S.R. Waugh and I.A. Healy	Aus. v WI, Brisbane
141	S.P. Fleming and C.L. Cairns	NZ v Pak., Lahore
136	G.P. Thorpe and R.C. Russell	Eng. v Ind., Lord's
123	B.A. Young and C.L. Cairns	NZ v SL, Dunedin
118	S.P. Fleming and C.L. Cairns	NZ v Eng., Auckland
112	B.M. McMillan and S.M. Pollock	SA v Ind., Johannesburg

Seventh wicket

137	R.S. Kaluwitharana and V.P.U.J.C. Vaas	SL v NZ, Dunedin
131	G.W. Flower and P.A. Strang	Zim. v Pak., Sheikhupura
114	G.P. Thorpe and D.G. Cork	Eng. v NZ, Auckland
112	Asif Mujtaba and Moin Khan	Pak. v Eng., Headingley
101★	B.M. McMillan and S.M. Pollock	SA v Ind., Cape Town

Eighth wicket

313	Wasim Akram and Saqlain Mushtaq	Pak. v Zim., Sheikhupura
161	M. Azharuddin and A. Kumble	Ind. v SA, Calcutta
147★	B.M. McMillan and L. Klusener	SA v Ind., Cape Town
127	D.J. Cullinan and L. Klusener	SA v Ind., Johannesburg

Ninth wicket
No instance (highest: 87 P.A. Strang and B.C. Strang   Zim. v Pak., Sheikhupura)

Tenth wicket
106*   N.J. Astle and D.K. Morrison   NZ v Eng., Auckland

TOP AVERAGES (minimum of 6 innings)

78.00	Wasim Akram (Pak.)	51.64	S.R. Waugh (Aus.)	43.00	P.A. Strang (Zim)
68.67	A.J. Stewart (Eng.)	50.38	Ijaz Ahmed (Pak.)	42.67	S.C. Ganguly (Ind.)
63.73	Saeed Anwar (Pak.)	49.00	M.A. Atherton (Eng.)	42.17	S.P. Fleming (NZ)
61.50	P.A. de Silva (SL)	47.89	Moin Khan (Pak.)	41.81	G.P. Thorpe (Eng)
58.86	H.P. Tillekeratne (SL)	47.25	S.R. Tendulkar (Ind.)	41.00	S.T. Jayasuriya (SL)
56.88	J.P. Crawley (Eng.)	46.00	N.S. Sidhu (Ind.)	40.60	Saqlain Mushtaq (Pak.)
56.55	Salim Malik (Pak.)	45.53	D.J. Cullinan (SA)	40.47	C.L. Hooper (WI)
54.00	B.A. Young (NZ)	45.07	N. Hussain (Eng.)	40.44	R.S. Kaluwitharana (SL)
52.47	S. Chanderpaul (WI)	44.40	Inzamam-ul-Haq (Pak.)	40.43	D.L. Houghton (Zim.)
52.00	G.S. Blewett (Aus.)	43.27	B.M. McMillan (SA)	40.41	B.C. Lara (WI)
51.95	R.S. Dravid (Ind.)				

CENTURIES (69)

Australia

G.S. Blewett	214 v SA, Johannesburg
M.L. Hayden	125 v WI, Adelaide
I.A. Healy	161* v WI, Brisbane
M.E. Waugh	116 v SA, Port Elizabeth
S.R. Waugh	160 v SA, Johannesburg

England

M.A. Atherton (2)	160 v Ind., Trent Bridge
	118 v NZ, Christchurch
J.P. Crawley (2)	106 v Pak., Oval
	112 v Zim., Bulawayo
N. Hussain (3)	128 v Ind., Edgbaston
	107* v Ind., Trent Bridge
	113 v Zim., Bulawayo
N.V. Knight	113 v Pak., Headingley
R.C. Russell	124 v Ind., Lord's
A.J. Stewart (3)	170 v Pak., Headingley
	101* v Zim., Harare
	173 v NZ, Auckland
G.P. Thorpe (2)	119 v NZ, Auckland
	108 v NZ, Wellington

India

M. Azharuddin (3)	109 v SA, Calcutta
	163* v SA, Kanpur
	115 v SA, Cape Town
R.S. Dravid	148 v SA, Johannesburg
S.C. Ganguly (2)	131 v Eng., Lord's
	136 v Eng., Trent Bridge
N.R. Mongia	152 v Aus., Delhi
N.S. Sidhu	201 v WI, Port-of-Spain
S.R. Tendulkar (3)	122 v Eng., Edgbaston
	177 v Eng., Trent Bridge
	169 v SA, Cape Town

New Zealand

N.J. Astle	102* v Eng., Auckland

New Zealand (contd)

S.P. Fleming	129 v Eng., Auckland
B.A. Young	267* v SL, Dunedin

Pakistan

Ijaz Ahmed (3)	141 v Eng., Headingley
	125 v NZ, Rawalpindi
	113 v SL, Colombo (Premadasa)
Inzamam-ul-Haq	148 v Eng., Lord's
†Mohammad Wasim	109* v NZ, Lahore
Moin Khan	105 v Eng., Headingley
Saeed Anwar (2)	176 v Eng., Oval
	149 v NZ, Rawalpindi
Salim Malik (2)	100* v Eng., Oval
	155 v SL, Colombo (Sinhalese)
Wasim Akram	257* v Zim., Sheikhupura

South Africa

D.J. Cullinan (2)	153* v Ind., Calcutta
	122* v Ind., Johannesburg
A.C. Hudson	146 v Ind., Calcutta
G. Kirsten (3)	102 ⎱ v Ind., Calcutta
	133 ⎰
	102 v Ind., Cape Town
L. Klusener	102* v Ind., Cape Town
B.M. McMillan	103* v Ind., Cape Town

Sri Lanka

P.S. de Silva (3)	168 v Pak., Colombo (Premadasa)
	138* ⎱ v Pak., Colombo (Sinhalese)
	103* ⎰
S.T. Jayasuriya	113 v Pak., Colombo (Sinhalese)
R.S. Kaluwitharana	103 v NZ, Dunedin
H.P. Tillekeratne (2)	126* v Zim., Colombo (Sinhalese)
	103 v Pak., Colombo (Premadasa)

West Indies

S.L. Campbell	113 v Aus., Brisbane

†on Test debut

West Indies *(contd)*
S. Chanderpaul   137* v Ind., Bridgetown
C.L. Hooper (2)   102 v Aus., Brisbane
    129 v Ind., Kingston
B.C. Lara (2)   132 v Aus., Perth
    103 v Ind., St John's
S.C. Williams   128 v Ind., Port-of-Spain

Zimbabwe
A. Flower   112 v Eng., Bulawayo
G.W. Flower   110 v Pak., Sheikhupura
P.A. Strang   106* v Pak., Sheikhupura

The only score of 99 in the 1996–97 year was made by G.S. Blewett (v WI, Adelaide)

BOWLERS

MOST WICKETS 1996–97 (20 or more)

		Av.	Tests				Av.	Tests
55	B.K.V. Prasad (Ind.)	28.65	15		27	Waqar Younis (Pak.)	26.74	6
54	A. Kumble (Ind.)	33.54	15		27	P.R. Adams (SA)	28.89	7
46	J. Srinath (Ind.)	28.39	9		26	D. Gough (Eng.)	20.46	5
45	Mushtaq Ahmed (Pak.)	25.53	7		26	M. Muralitharan (SL)	20.54	5
41	A.A. Donald (SA)	19.15	8		25	P.A. Strang (Zim.)	29.20	6
41	G.D. McGrath (Aus.)	20.20	9		25	Saqlain Mushtaq (Pak.)	35.72	5
33	S.K. Warne (Aus.)	26.55	8		24	M.G. Bevan (Aus.)	18.38	8
32	I.R. Bishop (WI)	24.13	9		23	C.A. Walsh (WI)	36.61	9
31	S.B. Doull (NZ)	21.39	7		22	Wasim Akram (Pak.)	24.09	5
29	C.E.L. Ambrose (WI)	25.72	9		21	S.B. Joshi (Ind.)	31.76	9
29	D.G. Cork (Eng.)	38.03	9		21	L. Klusener (SA)	32.57	7
28	A.D. Mullally (Eng.)	33.11	9		20	R.D.B. Croft (Eng.)	23.25	5

FIVE OR MORE WICKETS IN AN INNINGS (50)

Australia
G.D. McGrath (2)   5–50 v WI, Melbourne
    6–86 v SA, Centurion
M.G. Bevan   6–82 v WI, Adelaide
J.N. Gillespie   5–54 v SA, Port Elizabeth
P.R. Reiffel   5–73 v WI, Perth

England
D.G. Cork   5–113 v Pak., Headingley
R.D.B. Croft   5–95 v NZ, Christchurch
D. Gough   5–40 v NZ, Wellington
C.C. Lewis   5–72 v Ind., Edgbaston

India
B.K.V. Prasad (5)   5–76 v Eng., Lord's
    6–104 v SA, Calcutta
    5–60 } v SA, Durban
    5–93 }
    5–82 v WI, Bridgetown
A. Kumble (3)   5–67 v Aus., Delhi
    5–120 v WI, Kingston
    5–104 v WI, Port-of-Spain
J. Srinath (2)   6–21 v SA, Ahmedabad
    5–104 v SA, Johannesburg
A. Kuruvilla   5–68 v WI, Bridgetown

New Zealand
S.B. Doull (3)   5–46 v Pak., Lahore
    5–75 v Eng., Wellington
    5–58 v SL, Dunedin
C.L. Cairns   5–137 v Pak., Rawalpindi
H.T. Davis   5–63 v SL, Hamilton
D.L. Vettori   5–84 v SL, Hamilton

Pakistan
Mushtaq Ahmed (4)   5–57 v Eng., Lord's
    6–78 v Eng., Oval
    6–84 v NZ, Lahore
    6–87 v NZ, Rawalpindi
†Mohammad Zahid   7–66 v NZ, Rawalpindi
Saqlain Mushtaq   5–89 v SL, Colombo (Premadasa)
Shahid Nazir   5–54 v Zim., Sheikhupura
Wasim Akram   6–48 v Zim., Faisalabad

South Africa
A.A. Donald (2)   5–40 v Ind., Durban
    5–36 v Aus., Centurion
P.R. Adams   6–55 v Ind., Kanpur
†L. Klusener   8–64 v Ind., Calcutta

Sri Lanka
M. Muralitharan (2)   5–33 v Zim., Colombo (Premadasa)
    6–98 v Pak., Colombo (Premadasa)
S.C. de Silva   5–85 v Pak., Colombo (Premadasa)

West Indies
C.E.L. Ambrose (3)   5–55 v Aus., Melbourne
    5–43 v Aus., Perth
    5–87 v Ind., Port-of-Spain
C.A. Walsh (2)   5–98 v Aus., Sydney
    5–74 v Aus., Perth
†F.A. Rose   6–100 v Ind., Kingston

Zimbabwe
P.A. Strang (3)   5–106 v SL, Colombo (Premadasa)
    5–212 v Pak., Sheikhupura
    5–123 v Eng., Bulawayo

†on Test debut

EIGHT OR MORE WICKETS IN A MATCH (24)

Australia
M.G. Bevan   10–113 (4–31, 6–82) v WI, Adelaide
J.N. Gillespie   8–103 (5–54, 3–49) v SA, Port Elizabeth
G.D. McGrath   8–91 (5–50, 3–41) v WI, Melbourne

England
D. Gough   9–92 (5–40, 4–52) v NZ, Wellington

India
A. Kumble   9–130 (4–63, 5–67) v Aus., Delhi
     8–196 (5–120, 3–76) v WI, Kingston
B.K.V. Prasad   10–153 (5–60, 5–93) v SA, Durban
     8–121 (5–82, 3–39) v WI, Bridgetown
J. Srinath   8–68 (2–47, 6–21) v SA, Ahmedabad

New Zealand
S.B. Doull   8–85 (5–46, 3–39) v Pak., Lahore
     8–140 (5–58, 3–82) v SL, Dunedin
D.L. Vettori   9–130 (4–46, 5–84) v SL, Hamilton

     †on Test debut

Pakistan
Mushtaq Ahmed   8–156 (2–78, 6–78) v Eng., Oval
     10–143 (4–59, 6–84) v NZ, Lahore
     8–139 (6–87, 2–52) v NZ, Rawalpindi
†Mohammad Zahid   11–130 (4–64, 7–66) v NZ, Rawalpindi
Saqlain Mushtaq   9–226 (5–89, 4–137) v SL, Colombo (Premadasa)
Waqar Younis   8–154 (4–69, 4–85) v Eng., Lord's
Wasim Akram   10–106 (6–48, 4–58) v Zim., Faisalabad

South Africa
A.A. Donald   9–54 (5–40, 4–14) v Ind., Durban
     8–96 (3–60, 5–36) v Aus., Centurion
P.R. Adams   8–139 (6–55, 2–84) v Ind., Kanpur
†L. Klusener   8–139 (0–75, 8–64) v Ind., Calcutta

Sri Lanka   No instance

West Indies
C.E.L. Ambrose   9–72 (5–55, 4–17) v Aus., Melbourne

Zimbabwe   No instance

BEST STRIKE RATES (Balls needed per wicket taken; all bowlers who took 15 or more wickets)

Rate	Wkts		Rate	Wkts	
34.63	24	M.G. Bevan (Aus.)	60.07	55	B.K.V. Prasad (Ind.)
44.18	17	P.R. Reiffel (Aus.)	61.94	18	D.L. Vettori (NZ)
44.19	26	D. Gough (Eng.)	63.19	21	L. Klusener (SA)
44.59	41	A.A. Donald (SA)	63.85	33	S.K. Warne (Aus.)
46.00	16	K.J. Silva (SL)	65.07	29	C.E.L. Ambrose (WI)
46.16	31	S.B. Doull (NZ)	65.74	19	W.P.U.J.C. Vaas (SL)
47.06	18	F.A. Rose (WI)	68.95	20	R.D.B. Croft (Eng.)
49.56	27	Waqar Younis (Pak.)	68.96	25	P.A. Strang (Zim.)
51.00	41	G.D. McGrath (Aus.)	72.52	29	D.G. Cork (Eng.)
51.25	16	J.N. Gillespie (Aus.)	72.76	21	S.B. Joshi (Ind.)
52.19	27	P.R. Adams (SA)	76.00	16	C.C. Lewis (Eng.)
53.09	32	I.R. Bishop (WI)	78.72	25	Saqlain Mushtaq (Pak.)
54.45	22	Wasim Akram (Pak.)	79.35	54	A. Kumble (Ind.)
55.27	26	M. Muralitharan (SL)	81.35	23	C.A. Walsh (WI)
55.80	46	J. Srinath (Ind.)	84.96	28	A.D. Mullally (Eng.)
58.58	45	Mushtaq Ahmed (Pak.)			

WICKETKEEPERS

MOST DISMISSALS IN THE YEAR 1996–97

43	(41ct/2st)	*N.R. Mongia (Ind.)	15 Tests		11	(9/2)	R.S. Kaluwitharana (SL)	6 Tests
28	(27/1)	D.J. Richardson (SA)	9 Tests		10	(10ct)	A.C. Parore (NZ)	3 Tests
27	(27ct)	I.A. Healy (Aus.)	9 Tests		7	(6/1)	L.K. Germon (NZ)	4 Tests
25	(25ct)	C.O. Browne (WI)	6 Tests		7	(6/1)	J.R. Murray (WI)	4 Tests
23	(20/3)	A.J. Stewart (Eng.)	6 Tests		3	(3ct)	Rashid Latif (Pak.)	1 Test
17	(17ct)	R.C. Russell (Eng.)	5 Tests		1	(1ct)	†Salim Elahi (Pak.)	1 Test
15	(12/3)	Moin Khan (Pak.)	8 Tests					
13	(11/2)	A. Flower (Zim.)	6 Tests					

*Injured in one match and did not keep wicket
†Kept wicket in one innings when Moin injured

FIVE OR MORE DISMISSALS IN A TEST

8ct	N.R. Mongia	Ind. v SA, Durban	5ct	C.O. Browne	WI v Aus., Brisbane
7ct	I.A. Healy	Aus. v SA, Johannesburg	5ct	C.O. Browne	WI v Ind., Bridgetown
6ct	C.O. Browne	WI v Aus., Perth	5ct	I.A. Healy	Aus. v WI, Adelaide
6(5ct/1st)	D.J. Richardson	SA v Ind., Cape Town	5ct	R.C. Russell	Eng. v Pak., Headingley
6ct	D.J. Richardson	SA v Aus., Centurion	5(4ct/1st)	A.J. Stewart	Eng. v NZ, Auckland
6ct	A.J. Stewart	Eng. v NZ, Wellington	5(4ct/1st)	A.J. Stewart	Eng. v NZ, Christchurch

FOUR OR MORE DISMISSALS IN AN INNINGS

5ct	I.A. Healy	Aus. v SA, Johannesburg	4ct	I.A. Healy	Aus. v WI, Perth
5ct	N.R. Mongia	Ind. v SA, Durban	4ct	N.R. Mongia	Ind. v SA, Cape Town
4ct	C.O. Browne	WI v Aus., Perth	4(3ct/1st)	D.J. Richardson	SA v Ind., Cape Town
4ct	C.O. Browne	WI v Ind., Bridgetown	4ct	D.J. Richardson	SA v Aus., Port Elizabeth
4ct	C.O. Browne	WI v Ind., Georgetown	4ct	D.J. Richardson	SA v Aus., Centurion
4ct	A. Flower	Zim. v Pak., Faisalabad	4ct	A.J. Stewart	Eng. v NZ, Auckland
4ct	I.A. Healy	Aus. v WI, Adelaide	4ct	A.J. Stewart	Eng. v NZ, Wellington

FIELDSMEN

MOST CATCHES IN THE YEAR 1996–97

Ct	Tests		Ct	Tests		Ct	Tests	
19	15	M. Azharuddin (Ind.)	13	8	B.M. McMillan (SA)	12	10	N. Hussain (Eng.)
16	4	R.S. Mahanama (SL)	13	9	M.E. Waugh (Aus.)	12	10	B.C. Lara (WI)
16	9	N.V. Knight (Eng.)	12	6	V.S. Rathore (Ind.)	11	15	S.R. Tendulkar (Ind.)
16	14	R.S. Dravid (Ind.)	12	9	M.A. Taylor (Aus.)	10	7	B.A. Young (NZ)
13	7	S.P. Fleming (NZ)	12	10	C.L. Hooper (WI)			

FOUR OR MORE CATCHES IN A TEST

5	C.L. Hooper	WI v Aus., Melbourne	4 *(contd)*	N.V. Knight	Eng. v NZ, Wellington
	R.S. Mahanama	SL v Zim., Colombo (Premadasa)		N.V. Knight	Eng. v NZ, Christchurch
4	M. Azharuddin	Ind. v WI, Port-of-Spain		B.C. Lara	WI v Aus., Sydney
	A.D.R. Campbell	Zim. v Eng., Harare		R.S. Mahanama	SL v NZ, Dunedin
	J.P. Crawley	Eng. v Zim., Bulawayo		R.S. Mahanama	SL v NZ, Hamilton
	N. Hussain	Eng. v NZ, Christchurch		Salim Elahi	Pak. v SL, Colombo (Sinhalese)
	N.V. Knight	Eng. v Ind., Edgbaston		M.A. Taylor	Aus. v WI, Adelaide

FOUR CATCHES IN AN INNINGS

N.V. Knight	Eng. v NZ, Christchurch
R.S. Mahanama	SL v Zim., Colombo (Premadasa)
R.S. Mahanama	SL v NZ, Dunedin
Salim Elahi	Pak. v SL, Colombo (Sinhalese)

ALLROUNDERS

VALUE QUOTIENT (batting average divided by bowling average)
(Minimum performance: 200 runs and 10 wickets)

		Runs	Av.	Wkts	Av.			Runs	Av.	Wkts	Av.
3.24	Wasim Akram (Pak.)	390	78.00	22	24.09	1.23	S.M. Pollock (SA)	211	30.14	14	24.43
2.01	M.G. Bevan (Aus.)	406	36.91	24	18.38	1.14	Saqlain Mushtaq (Pak.)	203	40.60	25	35.72
1.53	S.C. Ganguly (Ind.)	768	42.67	10	27.90	0.96	L. Klusener (SA)	282	31.33	21	32.57
1.47	P.A. Strang (Zim.)	301	43.00	25	29.20	0.57	A. Kumble (Ind.)	361	19.00	54	33.54
1.25	B.M. McMillan (SA)	476	43.27	13	34.54	0.52	D.G. Cork (Eng.)	216	19.64	29	38.03

FINAL AVERAGES
May 1 1996 to April 30 1997

AUSTRALIA
9 Tests: 1 in India, 5 v West Indies, 3 in South Africa
19 players used

Batting:	M	I	NO	R	HS	Av.	100	50	0	Ct/st
G.S. Blewett	7	12	1	572	214	52.00	1	3	2	6
S.R. Waugh	8	13	2	568	160	51.64	1	5	2	5
M.E. Waugh	9	16	0	628	116	39.25	1	4	1	13
M.T.G. Elliott	5	9	1	310	85	38.75	0	2	1	3
M.G. Bevan	8	14	3	406	87★	36.91	0	3	2	2
I.A. Healy	9	16	4	442	161★	36.83	1	0	1	27/0
M.L. Hayden	6	10	0	241	125	24.10	1	0	4	7
R.T. Ponting	3	6	0	137	88	22.83	0	1	0	5
M.J. Slater	1	2	0	44	44	22.00	0	0	1	0
P.E. McIntyre	1	2	1	22	16	22.00	0	0	0	0
M.A. Taylor	9	16	0	297	43	18.56	0	0	0	12
J.N. Gillespie	5	7	5	29	16★	14.50	0	0	1	0
S.K. Warne	8	12	0	170	30	14.17	0	0	1	9
M.S. Kasprowicz	2	2	0	27	21	13.50	0	0	0	0
A.J. Bichel	2	3	0	40	18	13.33	0	0	0	0
J.L. Langer	2	3	0	31	19	10.33	0	0	1	0
P.R. Reiffel	4	8	0	57	20	7.13	0	0	2	2
G.D. McGrath	9	12	2	49	24	4.90	0	0	6	4
G.B. Hogg	1	2	0	5	4	2.50	0	0	0	0
	99	165	19	4075	214	27.91	5	18	25	95/0

Bowling:	O	M	R	W	Av.	BB	5w/i	10w/m
R.T. Ponting	1.5	1	0	1	00.00	1–0	0	0
M.G. Bevan	138.3	20	441	24	18.38	6–82	1	1
G.D. McGrath	348.3	111	828	41	20.20	6–86	2	0
P.R. Reiffel	125.1	31	364	17	21.41	5–73	1	0
J.N. Gillespie	136.4	46	381	16	23.81	5–54	1	0
S.K. Warne	351.1	104	876	33	26.55	4–43	0	0
P.E. McIntyre	38	7	107	3	35.67	3–103	0	0
S.R. Waugh	46.4	13	108	3	36.00	1–4	0	0
M.E. Waugh	34	2	131	2	65.50	1–34	0	0
G.S. Blewett	47.2	12	138	2	69.00	1–13	0	0
G.B. Hogg	17	3	69	1	69.00	1–69	0	0
A.J. Bichel	37.2	6	143	1	143.00	1–31	0	0
M.S. Kasprowicz	48	9	126	0	—	—	0	0
	1370.1	365	3712	144	25.78	6–82	5	1

ENGLAND
11 Tests: 3 v India, 3 v Pakistan, 2 in Zimbabwe, 3 in New Zealand
23 players used

Batting:	M	I	NO	R	HS	Av.	100	50	0	Ct/st
A.J. Stewart	10	16	1	1030	173	68.67	3	6	0	24/3
J.P. Crawley	7	10	2	455	112	56.88	2	2	0	8
M.A. Atherton	11	18	2	784	160	49.00	2	4	1	8
N. Hussain	10	16	1	676	128	45.07	3	2	1	12
G.P. Thorpe	11	18	2	669	119	41.81	2	4	0	9
R.C. Russell	5	7	1	213	124	35.50	1	0	2	17
N.V. Knight	9	15	0	484	113	32.27	1	3	0	16
M.A. Ealham	2	3	0	81	51	27.00	0	1	0	1
R.C. Irani	2	3	0	76	41	25.33	0	0	0	0
P.C.R. Tufnell	5	5	3	49	19*	24.50	0	0	0	1
M.M. Patel	2	2	0	45	27	22.50	0	0	0	2
D.G. Cork	9	13	2	216	59	19.64	0	1	2	8
I.D.K. Salisbury	2	4	1	50	40	16.67	0	0	0	0
C.C. Lewis	5	7	1	96	31	16.00	0	0	1	2
P.J. Martin	1	2	0	27	23	13.50	0	0	0	0
R.D.B. Croft	5	6	1	63	31	12.60	0	0	1	5
S.J.E. Brown	1	2	1	11	10*	11.00	0	0	0	1
A.R. Caddick	3	4	0	43	20	10.75	0	0	0	1
A.D. Mullally	9	12	4	79	24	9.88	0	0	3	1
G.A. Hick	4	6	0	43	20	7.17	0	0	0	3
D. Gough	5	6	1	27	18	5.40	0	0	1	1
C. White	2	2	0	9	9	4.50	0	0	1	0
C.E.W. Silverwood	1	1	0	0	0	0.00	0	0	1	1
	121	**178**	**23**	**5226**	**173**	**33.72**	**14**	**23**	**14**	**121/3**

Bowling:	O	M	R	W	Av.	BB	5w/i	10w/m
C.E.W. Silverwood	25	8	71	4	17.75	3–63	0	0
M.A. Atherton	7	1	20	1	20.00	1–20	0	0
D. Gough	191.3	47	532	26	20.46	5–40	1	0
R.D.B. Croft	229.5	63	465	20	23.25	5–95	1	0
A.R. Caddick	145.1	35	339	14	24.21	4–45	0	0
M.A. Ealham	80	22	192	7	27.43	4–21	0	0
P.C.R. Tufnell	214.5	66	434	14	31.00	4–61	0	0
A.D. Mullally	396.3	114	927	28	33.11	3–44	0	0
R.C. Irani	21	7	74	2	37.00	1–22	0	0
D.G. Cork	350.3	70	1103	29	38.03	5–113	1	0
C.C. Lewis	202.4	43	620	16	38.75	5–72	1	0
C. White	41	9	118	3	39.33	2–51	0	0
S.J.E. Brown	33	4	138	2	69.00	1–60	0	0
P.J. Martin	34	10	70	1	70.00	1–70	0	0
G.A. Hick	32	8	93	1	93.00	1–26	0	0
I.D.K. Salisbury	61.2	8	221	2	110.50	1–42	0	0
M.M. Patel	46	8	180	1	180.00	1–101	0	0
G.P. Thorpe	15	5	22	0	–	–	0	0
	2126.2	**528**	**5619**	**171**	**32.86**	**5–40**	**4**	**0**

INDIA

15 Tests: 3 in England, 1 v Australia, 3 v South Africa, 3 in South Africa, 5 in West Indies
22 players used

Batting:	M	I	NO	R	HS	Av.	100	50	0	Ct/st
R.S. Dravid	14	23	3	1039	148	51.95	1	8	0	16
S.R. Tendulkar	15	25	1	1134	177	47.25	3	5	1	11
N.S. Sidhu	4	6	0	276	201	46.00	1	0	1	1
S.C. Ganguly	12	19	1	768	136	42.67	2	3	2	2
M. Azharuddin	15	24	2	691	163*	31.41	3	1	1	19
P.L. Mhambrey	2	3	1	58	28	29.00	0	0	0	1
V.V.S. Laxman	8	13	2	289	64	26.27	0	3	1	5
N.R. Mongia	15	24	0	601	152	25.04	1	2	1	41/2
S.V. Manjrekar	3	6	0	144	53	24.00	0	1	0	3
A.D. Jadeja	4	5	0	120	96	24.00	0	1	1	1
A.R. Kapoor	2	3	1	39	22	19.50	0	0	0	0
A. Kumble	15	23	4	361	88	19.00	0	1	1	4
S.B. Joshi	9	13	1	181	43	15.08	0	0	1	3
W.V. Raman	3	6	0	81	57	13.50	0	1	1	1
V.S. Rathore	6	10	0	131	44	13.10	0	0	0	12
J. Srinath	9	15	0	184	52	12.27	0	1	2	3
D. Ganesh	4	7	3	26	8	6.50	0	0	0	0
B.K.V. Prasad	15	22	9	67	15	5.15	0	0	5	2
N.D. Hirwani	2	4	2	9	9	4.50	0	0	1	0
D. Johnson	2	3	1	8	5	4.00	0	0	0	0
A. Kuruvilla	5	5	0	16	9	3.20	0	0	2	0
S.L.V. Raju	1	2	1	1	1*	1.00	0	0	1	0
	165	261	32	6224	201	27.18	11	27	22	125/2

Bowling:	O	M	R	W	Av.	BB	5w/i	10w/m
A.R. Kapoor	53	18	101	5	20.20	2–19	0	0
S.C. Ganguly	96.5	19	279	10	27.90	3–71	0	0
J. Srinath	427.5	104	1306	46	28.39	6–21	2	0
B.K.V. Prasad	550.4	125	1576	55	28.65	6–104	5	1
S.B. Joshi	254.4	59	667	21	31.76	4–43	0	0
A. Kumble	714.1	154	1811	54	33.54	5–67	3	0
A. Kuruvilla	172	34	480	13	36.92	5–68	1	0
D. Johnson	40	6	143	3	47.67	2–52	0	0
D. Ganesh	76.5	15	287	5	57.40	2–28	0	0
N.D. Hirwani	40	6	129	2	64.50	2–38	0	0
P.L. Mhambrey	43	6	148	2	74.00	1–43	0	0
S.L.V. Raju	43	12	76	1	76.00	1–76	0	0
V.V.S. Laxman	15	3	49	0	–	–	0	0
S.R. Tendulkar	15.4	3	56	0	–	–	0	0
W.V. Raman	15	1	63	0	–	–	0	0
	2557.4	565	7171	217	33.05	6–21	11	1

NEW ZEALAND

7 Tests: 2 in Pakistan, 2 v England, 2 v Sri Lanka
17 players used

Batting:	M	I	NO	R	HS	Av.	100	50	0	Ct/st
B.A. Young	7	13	1	648	267*	54.00	1	3	0	10
S.P. Fleming	7	13	1	506	129	42.17	1	5	1	13
B.A. Pocock	5	9	0	292	85	32.44	0	3	1	2
M.J. Horne	3	5	0	158	66	31.60	0	1	0	2
C.L. Cairns	7	13	0	409	93	31.46	0	5	0	4
N.J. Astle	7	13	1	266	102*	22.17	1	1	2	2
A.C. Parore	7	13	0	232	59	17.85	0	1	0	10
D.L. Vettori	4	7	3	70	29*	17.50	0	0	0	2
L.K. Germon	4	8	0	114	55	14.25	0	1	2	6/1
S.B. Doull	7	12	3	128	26	14.22	0	0	2	6
D.N. Patel	6	11	1	139	45	13.90	0	0	5	4
M.J. Greatbatch	2	4	0	40	19	10.00	0	0	0	0
J.T.C. Vaughan	3	6	0	58	27	9.67	0	0	0	1
H.T. Davis	3	4	2	19	8*	9.50	0	0	0	3
C.Z. Harris	2	4	0	31	16	7.75	0	0	1	1
G.I. Allott	2	4	1	12	8*	4.00	0	0	0	1
D.K. Morrison	1	2	2	20	14*	–	0	0	0	0
	77	**141**	**15**	**3142**	**267***	**24.94**	**3**	**20**	**14**	**67/1**

Bowling:	O	M	R	W	Av.	BB	5w/i	10w/m
S.B. Doull	238.3	63	663	31	21.39	5–46	3	0
D.L. Vettori	185.5	56	429	18	23.83	5–84	1	0
H.T. Davis	114.2	23	304	11	27.64	5–63	1	0
N.J. Astle	104	27	254	8	31.75	2–26	0	0
J.T.C. Vaughan	79.5	18	204	6	34.00	4–27	0	0
D.K. Morrison	24.4	4	104	3	34.67	3–104	0	0
G.I. Allott	61.4	11	197	5	39.40	4–74	0	0
C.Z. Harris	31	9	80	2	40.00	2–57	0	0
D.N. Patel	157.1	42	406	10	40.60	4–36	0	0
C.L. Cairns	117.4	23	424	9	47.11	5–137	1	0
B.A. Pocock	2	0	10	0	–	–	0	0
M.J. Horne	10	7	22	0	–	–	0	0
	1126.4	**283**	**3097**	**103**	**30.07**	**5–46**	**6**	**0**

PAKISTAN
9 Tests: 3 in England, 2 v Zimbabwe, 2 v New Zealand, 2 in Sri Lanka
24 players used

Batting:	M	I	NO	R	HS	Av.	100	50	0	Ct/st
Wasim Akram	5	7	2	390	257*	78.00	1	0	0	2
Saeed Anwar	7	12	1	701	176	63.73	2	5	1	5
Mohammad Wasim	2	3	1	114	109*	57.00	1	0	1	3
Salim Malik	9	13	2	622	155	56.55	2	4	0	5
Ijaz Ahmed	9	14	1	655	141	50.38	3	3	0	2
Moin Khan	8	10	1	431	105	47.89	1	3	1	12/3
Rashid Latif	1	1	0	45	45	45.00	0	0	0	3
Inzamam-ul-Haq	7	11	1	444	148	44.40	1	3	1	4
Saqlain Mushtaq	5	7	2	203	79	40.60	0	2	1	1
Aamir Sohail	4	6	2	143	46	35.75	0	0	0	1
Ramiz Raja	2	3	0	86	50	28.67	0	1	1	2
Asif Mujtaba	4	6	0	166	51	27.67	0	1	0	2
Hassan Raza	1	1	0	27	27	27.00	0	0	0	0
Shadab Kabir	3	5	0	89	35	17.80	0	0	0	4
Mushtaq Ahmed	7	10	1	153	42	17.00	0	0	0	4
Azam Khan	1	1	0	14	14	14.00	0	0	0	0
Zahoor Elahi	2	3	0	30	22	10.00	0	0	0	1
Waqar Younis	6	7	1	37	23	6.17	0	0	1	1
Shahid Nazir	6	7	2	27	13*	5.40	0	0	1	2
Salim Elahi	2	3	0	14	14	4.67	0	0	2	6/1
Mohammad Zahid	3	3	1	6	6*	3.00	0	0	2	0
Mohammad Hussain	1	1	0	0	0	0.00	0	0	1	1
Ata-ur-Rehman	2	2	2	10	10*	–	0	0	0	0
Mohammad Akram	2	1	1	0	0*	–	0	0	0	0
	99	137	21	4407	257*	37.99	11	22	13	61/4

Bowling:	O	M	R	W	Av.	BB	5w/i	10w/m
Mohammad Hussain	10	4	21	1	21.00	1–7	0	0
Mohammad Zahid	81	12	278	13	21.38	7–66	1	1
Wasim Akram	199.4	50	530	22	24.09	6–48	1	1
Mushtaq Ahmed	439.2	94	1149	45	25.53	6–78	4	1
Waqar Younis	223	49	722	27	26.74	4–48	0	0
Shahid Nazir	135.5	29	436	14	31.14	5–54	1	0
Ata-ur-Rehman	48.4	6	173	5	34.60	4–50	0	0
Saqlain Mushtaq	328	71	893	25	35.72	5–89	1	0
Asif Mujtaba	67	15	151	2	75.50	1–23	0	0
Mohammad Akram	41	7	130	1	130.00	1–41	0	0
Shadab Kabir	1	0	9	0	–	–	0	0
Ijaz Ahmed	5	0	18	0	–	–	0	0
Aamir Sohail	28	9	58	0	–	–	0	0
Salim Malik	21	3	76	0	–	–	0	0
	1628.3	349	4644	155	29.96	7–66	8	3

SOUTH AFRICA
9 Tests: 3 in India, 3 v India, 3 v Australia
17 players used

Batting:	M	I	NO	R	HS	Av.	100	50	0	Ct/st
D.J. Cullinan	9	18	3	683	153*	45.53	2	2	2	8
B.M. McMillan	8	16	5	476	103*	43.27	1	4	1	13
A.C. Hudson	7	14	1	476	146	36.62	1	3	2	9
W.J. Cronje	9	17	2	496	79*	33.07	0	3	1	2
L. Klusener	7	12	3	282	102*	31.33	1	0	1	6
A.M. Bacher	5	10	0	302	96	30.20	0	2	1	4
S.M. Pollock	5	10	3	211	79	30.14	0	1	2	1
G. Kirsten	9	18	0	541	133	30.06	3	0	2	4
P.S. de Villiers	2	4	1	75	67*	25.00	0	1	1	2
D.J. Richardson	9	15	3	267	72*	22.25	0	1	1	27/1
P.L. Symcox	4	6	1	95	32	19.00	0	0	1	0
H.H. Gibbs	4	8	0	125	31	15.63	0	0	1	1
J.N. Rhodes	2	4	0	44	22	11.00	0	0	1	2
J.H. Kallis	3	5	0	49	39	9.80	0	0	1	0
A.A. Donald	8	12	1	101	26	9.18	0	0	2	1
P.R. Adams	7	10	1	37	15	4.11	0	0	2	6
B.N. Schultz	1	1	0	2	2	2.00	0	0	0	1
	99	**180**	**24**	**4262**	**153***	**27.32**	**8**	**17**	**22**	**87/1**

Bowling:	O	M	R	W	Av.	BB	5w/i	10w/m
B.N. Schultz	37	8	91	6	15.17	4–52	0	0
A.A. Donald	304.4	90	785	41	19.15	5–36	2	0
S.M. Pollock	134	27	342	14	24.43	3–25	0	0
J.H. Kallis	58.4	16	134	5	26.80	3–29	0	0
W.J. Cronje	128.4	51	256	9	28.44	2–11	0	0
P.R. Adams	234.5	41	780	27	28.89	6–55	1	0
L. Klusener	221.1	46	684	21	32.57	8–64	1	0
B.M. McMillan	183.1	50	449	13	34.54	2–27	0	0
P.S. de Villiers	74	26	176	5	35.20	2–55	0	0
P.L. Symcox	149	31	435	9	48.33	2–47	0	0
A.M. Bacher	1	0	4	0	–	–	0	0
	1526.1	**386**	**4136**	**150**	**27.57**	**8–64**	**4**	**0**

SRI LANKA
6 Tests: 2 v Zimbabwe, 2 in New Zealand, 2 v Pakistan
18 players used

Batting:	M	I	NO	R	HS	Av.	100	50	0	Ct/st
A.P. Gurusinha	2	2	0	140	88	70.00	0	2	0	3
P.A. de Silva	6	10	2	492	168	61.50	3	0	1	4
H.D.P.K. Dharmasena	3	5	3	119	42★	59.50	0	0	0	3
H.P. Tillekeratne	6	10	3	412	126★	58.86	2	2	0	3
S.T. Jayasuriya	6	11	1	410	113	41.00	1	3	2	1
R.S. Kaluwitharana	6	9	0	364	103	40.44	1	2	0	9/2
A. Ranatunga	6	10	0	322	75	32.20	0	3	0	7
R.P. Arnold	2	4	0	126	50	31.50	0	1	0	3
R.S. Mahanama	4	7	1	176	65	29.33	0	1	0	16
K.R. Pushpakumara	1	1	0	23	23	23.00	0	0	0	0
G.P. Wickremasinghe	1	2	0	43	43	21.50	0	0	1	1
W.P.U.J.C. Vaas	6	9	0	172	57	19.11	0	1	0	5
M.S. Atapattu	3	6	0	90	25	15.00	0	0	1	2
D.N.T. Zoysa	3	5	1	43	16★	10.75	0	0	2	1
M. Muralitharan	5	7	2	47	26	9.40	0	0	2	1
R.S. Kalpage	1	1	0	5	5	5.00	0	0	0	0
S.C. de Silva	2	3	1	0	0★	0.00	0	0	2	0
K.J. Silva	3	2	0	0	0	0.00	0	0	2	1
	66	104	14	2984	168	33.16	7	15	13	60/2

Bowling:	O	M	R	W	Av.	BB	5w/i	10w/m
M.S. Atapattu	4	0	9	1	9.00	1–9	0	0
K.J. Silva	122.4	47	262	16	16.38	4–16	0	0
M. Muralitharan	239.3	63	534	26	20.54	6–98	2	0
K.R. Pushpakumara	19	3	58	2	29.00	1–24	0	0
W.P.U.J.C. Vaas	208.1	46	557	19	29.32	4–60	0	0
S.T. Jayasuriya	23	6	71	2	35.50	2–16	0	0
D.N.T. Zoysa	90.4	16	267	7	38.14	3–47	0	0
H.D.P.K. Dharmasena	121.5	41	249	6	41.50	2–75	0	0
A. Ranatunga	12.1	2	42	1	42.00	1–29	0	0
S.C. de Silva	68.2	13	223	5	44.60	5–85	1	0
G.P. Wickremasinghe	25	4	117	1	117.00	1–117	0	0
H.P. Tillekeratne	2	1	3	0	–	–	0	0
A.P. Gurusinha	5	1	7	0	–	–	0	0
R.P. Arnold	13	4	31	0	–	–	0	0
P.A. de Silva	13	2	34	0	–	–	0	0
R.S. Kalpage	43	14	102	0	–	–	0	0
	1010.2	263	2566	86	29.84	6–98	3	0

WEST INDIES
10 Tests: 5 in Australia, 5 v India
20 players used

Batting:	M	I	NO	R	HS	Av.	100	50	0	Ct/st
S. Chanderpaul	10	17	2	787	137★	52.47	1	6	0	3
C.L. Hooper	10	17	2	607	129	40.47	2	2	0	12
B.C. Lara	10	17	0	687	132	40.41	2	3	0	12
R.I.C. Holder	5	7	1	212	91	35.33	0	2	0	6
R.G. Samuels	4	8	1	231	76	33.00	0	1	0	4
S.C. Williams	5	8	0	263	128	32.88	1	0	2	2
J.R. Murray	4	6	1	136	53	27.20	0	1	0	6/1
S.L. Campbell	10	17	1	420	113	26.25	1	1	2	4
F.A. Rose	5	4	1	63	34	21.00	0	0	0	0
J.C. Adams	5	9	2	140	74★	20.00	0	1	2	3
C.O. Browne	6	9	3	113	39★	18.83	0	0	2	25/0
C.E.L. Ambrose	9	12	2	165	37	16.50	0	0	2	1
P.I.C. Thompson	1	2	1	16	10★	16.00	0	0	0	0
I.R. Bishop	9	12	0	137	48	11.42	0	0	4	3
M.V. Dillon	2	3	1	21	21	10.50	0	0	1	0
C.A. Walsh	9	11	4	56	21	8.00	0	0	2	4
A.F.G. Griffith	1	2	0	14	13	7.00	0	0	0	0
K.C.G. Benjamin	3	5	0	31	11	6.20	0	0	0	1
C.E. Cuffy	1	2	1	5	3★	5.00	0	0	0	0
P.V. Simmons	1	1	0	0	0	0.00	0	0	1	3
	110	**169**	**23**	**4104**	**137★**	**28.11**	**7**	**17**	**18**	**89/1**

Bowling:	O	M	R	W	Av.	BB	5w/i	10w/m
F.A. Rose	141.1	27	402	18	22.33	6–100	1	0
I.R. Bishop	283.1	55	772	32	24.13	4–22	0	0
C.E.L. Ambrose	314.3	79	746	29	25.72	5–43	3	0
C.A. Walsh	311.5	65	842	23	36.61	5–74	2	0
M.V. Dillon	54	11	148	4	37.00	3–92	0	0
K.C.G. Benjamin	117.5	22	362	9	40.22	3–34	0	0
C.E. Cuffy	33	4	116	2	58.00	2–116	0	0
J.C. Adams	18.5	1	59	1	59.00	1–11	0	0
P.V. Simmons	23	5	67	1	67.00	1–58	0	0
S. Chanderpaul	68	14	158	2	79.00	1–2	0	0
P.I.C. Thompson	16	0	80	1	80.00	1–80	0	0
C.L. Hooper	222	61	539	6	89.83	3–34	0	0
B.C. Lara	3	0	16	0	–	–	0	0
S.C. Williams	3	0	19	0	–	–	0	0
	1609.2	**344**	**4326**	**128**	**33.80**	**6–100**	**6**	**0**

ZIMBABWE

6 Tests: 2 in Sri Lanka, 2 in Pakistan, 2 v England

19 players used

Batting:	M	I	NO	R	HS	Av.	100	50	0	Ct/st
P.A. Strang	6	11	4	301	106*	43.00	1	1	0	2
D.L. Houghton	4	7	0	283	74	40.43	0	2	0	4
G.W. Flower	6	11	0	379	110	34.45	1	2	3	3
A.H. Shah	1	2	0	63	62	31.50	0	1	0	0
A.D.R. Campbell	6	11	0	296	84	26.91	0	2	0	7
A. Flower	6	11	0	281	112	25.55	1	1	1	11/2
A.C. Waller	2	3	0	69	50	23.00	0	1	0	1
H.H. Streak	3	5	3	37	19	18.50	0	0	0	1
G.J. Whittall	6	11	0	160	56	14.55	0	1	3	1
B.C. Strang	4	7	2	68	42	13.60	0	0	0	2
C.B. Wishart	4	8	0	98	51	12.25	0	1	2	2
M.H. Dekker	5	9	0	100	20	11.11	0	0	1	2
E.A. Brandes	1	1	0	9	9	9.00	0	0	0	0
E. Matambanadzo	1	2	1	7	7	7.00	0	0	0	0
A.R. Whittall	3	6	1	27	12	5.40	0	0	1	2
C.N. Evans	1	2	0	10	9	5.00	0	0	0	1
H.K. Olonga	5	8	1	14	7	2.00	0	0	4	1
S.V. Carlisle	1	2	0	4	4	2.00	0	0	1	2
M. Mbangwa	1	2	0	2	2	1.00	0	0	1	0
	66	119	12	2208	112	20.64	3	12	17	42/2

Bowling:	O	M	R	W	Av.	BB	5w/i	10w/m
H.H. Streak	109.1	26	294	11	26.73	4–43	0	0
P.A. Strang	287.2	61	730	25	29.20	5–106	3	0
G.J. Whittall	103	27	244	8	30.50	4–18	0	0
B.C. Strang	79.5	20	224	6	37.33	3–53	0	0
M. Mbangwa	24	4	81	2	40.50	2–67	0	0
E. Matambanadzo	16	0	89	2	44.50	2–62	0	0
H.K. Olonga	106.4	18	375	8	46.88	3–90	0	0
G.W. Flower	40	10	108	1	108.00	1–4	0	0
A.R. Whittall	89.2	17	261	2	130.50	2–146	0	0
C.N. Evans	6	0	27	0	–	–	0	0
E.A. Brandes	37	12	80	0	–	–	0	0
	898.2	195	2513	65	38.66	5–106	3	0

CAREER RECORDS
to June 1 1997

AUSTRALIA

Batting:	M	I	NO	R	HS	Av.	100	50	Ct	St
M.G. Bevan	14	24	3	730	91	34.76	0	6	7	0
‡A.J. Bichel	2	3	0	40	18	13.33	0	0	0	0
G.S. Blewett	16	27	2	1040	214	41.60	3	5	17	0
‡M.T.G. Elliott	5	9	1	310	85	38.75	0	2	3	0
‡J.N. Gillespie	5	7	5	29	16*	14.50	0	0	0	0
M.L. Hayden	7	12	0	261	125	21.75	1	0	8	0
I.A. Healy	88	133	18	3245	161*	28.22	3	17	282	20
‡G.B. Hogg	1	2	0	5	4	2.50	0	0	0	0
‡M.S. Kasprowicz	2	2	0	27	21	13.50	0	0	0	0
J.L. Langer	8	12	0	272	69	22.67	0	3	2	0
G.D. McGrath	28	32	7	81	24	3.24	0	0	6	0
P.E. McIntyre	2	4	1	22	16	7.33	0	0	0	0
R.T. Ponting	6	10	0	330	96	33.00	0	3	9	0
P.R. Reiffel	25	35	9	469	56	18.04	0	2	13	0
M.J. Slater	34	59	3	2655	219	47.41	7	10	11	0
M.A. Taylor	81	145	9	5799	219	42.64	14	33	117	0
S.K. Warne	52	70	9	839	74*	13.75	0	1	39	0
M.E. Waugh	63	102	4	4255	140	43.42	11	26	81	0
S.R. Waugh	89	138	28	5570	200	50.64	12	33	66	0

Bowling:	O	M	R	W	Av.	BB	5w/i	10w/m
M.G. Bevan	153.3	21	508	25	20.32	6-82	1	1
‡A.J. Bichel	37.2	6	143	1	143.00	1-31	0	0
G.S. Blewett	87.2	25	260	4	65.00	2-25	0	0
‡J.N. Gillespie	136.4	46	381	16	23.81	5-54	1	0
‡G.B. Hogg	17	3	69	1	69.00	1-69	0	0
‡M.S. Kasprowicz	48	9	126	0	–	–	0	0
G.D. McGrath	1105.4	289	2935	119	24.66	6-47	6	0
P.E. McIntyre	65.3	10	194	5	38.80	3-103	0	0
R.T. Ponting	5.5	3	8	2	4.00	1-0	0	0
P.R. Reiffel	770	194	2108	80	26.35	6-71	4	0
S.K. Warne	2537.3	840	5746	240	23.94	8-71	10	3
M.E. Waugh	522	123	1473	40	36.83	5-40	1	0
S.R. Waugh	1065.5	278	2818	80	35.23	5-28	3	0

‡Debutant 1996-97

ENGLAND

Batting:	M	I	NO	R	HS	Av.	100	50	Ct	St
M.A. Atherton	67	122	4	4986	185★	42.25	11	31	47	0
‡S.J.E. Brown	1	2	1	11	10★	11.00	0	0	1	0
A.R. Caddick	11	18	2	213	29★	13.31	0	0	5	0
D.G. Cork	19	27	4	482	59	20.96	0	2	10	0
J.P. Crawley	17	26	3	785	112	34.13	2	5	18	0
‡R.D.B. Croft	5	6	1	63	31	12.60	0	0	5	0
‡M.A. Ealham	2	3	0	81	51	27.00	0	1	1	0
D. Gough	17	24	4	346	65	17.30	0	2	8	0
G.A. Hick	46	80	6	2672	178	36.11	4	15	62	0
N. Hussain	17	29	3	960	128	36.92	3	3	15	0
‡R.C. Irani	2	3	0	76	41	25.33	0	0	0	0
N.V. Knight	11	19	0	573	113	30.16	1	4	21	0
C.C. Lewis	32	51	3	1105	117	23.02	1	4	25	0
P.J. Martin	7	11	0	92	29	8.36	0	0	5	0
‡A.D. Mullally	9	12	4	79	24	9.88	0	0	1	0
‡M.M. Patel	2	2	0	45	27	22.50	0	0	2	0
R.C. Russell	49	77	15	1807	128★	29.15	2	6	141	11
I.D.K. Salisbury	9	17	2	255	50	17.00	0	1	3	0
‡C.E.W. Silverwood	1	1	0	0	0	0.00	0	0	1	0
A.J. Stewart	63	111	7	4433	190	42.63	10	22	89	7
G.P. Thorpe	37	67	6	2511	123	41.16	4	19	31	0
P.C.R. Tufnell	27	37	20	111	22★	6.53	0	0	11	0
C. White	8	12	0	166	51	13.83	0	1	3	0

Bowling:	O	M	R	W	Av.	BB	5w/i	10w/m
M.A. Atherton	68	12	302	2	151.00	1–20	0	0
‡S.J.E. Brown	33	4	138	2	69.00	1–60	0	0
A.R. Caddick	468.3	93	1372	37	37.08	6–65	2	0
D.G. Cork	724.1	148	2249	74	30.39	7–43	3	0
‡R.D.B. Croft	229.5	63	465	20	23.25	5–95	1	0
‡M.A. Ealham	80	22	192	7	27.43	4–21	0	0
D. Gough	611.4	118	1890	69	27.39	6–49	2	0
G.A. Hick	495.3	128	1247	22	56.68	4–126	0	0
‡R.C. Irani	21	7	74	2	37.00	1–22	0	0
C.C. Lewis	1142	222	3490	93	37.53	6–111	3	0
P.J. Martin	223	68	529	17	31.12	4–60	0	0
‡A.D. Mullally	396.3	114	927	28	33.11	3–44	0	0
‡M.M. Patel	46	8	180	1	180.00	1–101	0	0
I.D.K. Salisbury	295.3	32	1154	18	64.11	4–163	0	0
‡C.E.W. Silverwood	25	8	71	4	17.75	3–63	0	0
G.P. Thorpe	23	7	37	0	–	–	0	0
P.C.R. Tufnell	1277.5	343	3105	82	37.87	7–47	4	1
C. White	135.1	26	452	11	41.09	3–18	0	0

‡Debutant 1996–97

INDIA

Batting:

	M	I	NO	R	HS	Av.	100	50	Ct	St
M. Azharuddin	83	120	6	5011	199	43.96	17	16	88	0
‡R.S. Dravid	14	23	3	1039	148	51.95	1	8	16	0
‡D. Ganesh	4	7	3	26	8	6.50	0	0	0	0
‡S.C. Ganguly	12	19	1	768	136	42.67	2	3	2	0
N.D. Hirwani	17	22	12	54	17	5.40	0	0	5	0
A.D. Jadeja	10	14	1	399	96	30.69	0	3	3	0
‡D. Johnson	2	3	1	8	5	4.00	0	0	0	0
‡S.B. Joshi	9	13	1	181	43	15.08	0	0	3	0
A.R. Kapoor	4	6	1	97	42	19.40	0	0	1	0
A. Kumble	38	46	9	618	88	16.70	0	2	15	0
‡A. Kuruvilla	5	5	0	16	9	3.20	0	0	0	0
‡V.V.S. Laxman	8	13	2	289	64	26.27	0	3	5	0
S.V. Manjrekar	37	61	6	2043	218	37.15	4	9	25	1
‡P.L. Mhambrey	2	3	1	58	28	29.00	0	0	1	0
N.R. Mongia	25	37	2	989	152	28.26	1	3	61	4
‡B.K.V. Prasad	15	22	9	67	15	5.15	0	0	2	0
S.L.V. Raju	24	30	10	229	31	11.45	0	0	5	0
W.V. Raman	11	19	1	448	96	24.89	0	4	6	0
‡V.S. Rathore	6	10	0	131	44	13.10	0	0	12	0
N.S. Sidhu	40	60	2	2363	201	40.74	7	10	9	0
J. Srinath	27	38	12	432	60	16.62	0	3	11	0
S.R. Tendulkar	53	80	8	3617	179	50.24	11	18	42	0

Bowling:

	O	M	R	W	Av.	BB	5w/i	10w/m
‡D. Ganesh	76.5	15	287	5	57.40	2–28	0	0
‡S.C. Ganguly	96.5	19	279	10	27.90	3–71	0	0
N.D. Hirwani	716.2	155	1987	66	30.11	8–61	4	1
‡D. Johnson	40	6	143	3	47.67	2–52	0	0
‡S.B. Joshi	254.4	59	667	21	32.05	4–43	0	0
A.R. Kapoor	107	26	255	6	42.50	2–19	0	0
A. Kumble	1882	484	4473	163	27.44	7–59	9	1
‡A. Kuruvilla	172	34	480	13	36.92	5–68	1	0
‡V.V.S. Laxman	15	3	49	0	–	–	0	0
S.V. Manjrekar	2.5	0	15	0	–	–	0	0
‡P.L. Mhambrey	43	6	148	2	74.00	1–43	0	0
‡B.K.V. Prasad	550.4	125	1576	55	28.65	6–104	5	1
S.L.V. Raju	1100	325	2439	85	28.69	6–12	5	1
W.V. Raman	58	20	129	2	64.50	1–7	0	0
N.S. Sidhu	1	0	9	0	–	–	0	0
J. Srinath	1051.5	241	2936	92	31.91	6–21	2	0
S.R. Tendulkar	87.4	22	247	4	61.75	2–10	0	0

‡Debutant 1996–97

NEW ZEALAND

Batting:	M	I	NO	R	HS	Av.	100	50	Ct	St
G.I. Allott	4	6	2	12	8*	3.00	0	0	1	0
N.J. Astle	11	21	1	633	125	31.65	3	2	8	0
C.L. Cairns	23	39	0	1084	120	27.79	1	9	11	0
H.T. Davis	4	6	4	19	8*	9.50	0	0	3	0
S.B. Doull	18	30	5	338	31*	13.52	0	0	14	0
S.P. Fleming	27	47	2	1649	129	36.64	1	13	32	0
L.K. Germon	12	21	3	382	55	21.22	0	1	27	2
M.J. Greatbatch	41	71	5	2021	146*	30.62	3	10	27	0
C.Z. Harris	9	18	1	191	56	11.24	0	1	4	0
‡M.J. Horne	3	5	0	158	66	31.60	0	1	2	0
D.K. Morrison	48	71	26	379	42	8.42	0	0	14	0
A.C. Parore	34	59	6	1304	100*	24.60	1	7	69	2
D.N. Patel	37	66	8	1200	99	20.69	0	5	15	0
B.A. Pocock	11	21	0	427	85	20.33	0	3	3	0
J.T.C. Vaughan	6	12	1	201	44	18.27	0	0	4	0
‡D.L. Vettori	4	7	3	70	29*	17.50	0	0	2	0
B.A. Young	25	49	2	1700	267*	36.17	2	11	39	0

Bowling:	O	M	R	W	Av.	BB	5w/i	10w/m
G.I. Allott	127.4	26	406	9	45.11	4–74	0	0
N.J. Astle	109	28	264	8	33.00	2–26	0	0
C.L. Cairns	655.5	136	2206	60	36.77	6–52	3	0
H.T. Davis	135.2	23	397	12	33.08	5–63	1	0
S.B. Doull	573.3	133	1740	64	27.19	5–46	5	0
C.Z. Harris	126	37	375	7	53.57	2–57	0	0
‡M.J. Horne	10	7	22	0	—	—	0	0
D.K. Morrison	1677.2	313	5549	160	34.68	7–89	10	0
D.N. Patel	1099	256	3154	75	42.05	6–50	3	0
B.A. Pocock	4	0	20	0	—	—	0	0
J.T.C. Vaughan	173.2	41	450	11	40.91	4–27	0	0
‡D.L. Vettori	185.5	56	429	18	23.83	5–84	1	0

‡Debutant 1996–97

PAKISTAN

Batting:	M	I	NO	R	HS	Av.	100	50	Ct	St
Aamir Sohail	34	62	3	2103	205	35.64	2	13	31	0
Asif Mujtaba	25	41	3	928	65*	24.42	0	8	19	0
Ata-ur-Rehman	13	15	6	76	19	8.44	0	0	2	0
‡Azam Khan	1	1	0	14	14	14.00	0	0	0	0
‡Hassan Raza	1	1	0	27	27	27.00	0	0	0	0
Ijaz Ahmed	36	54	2	2034	141	39.12	7	9	22	0
Inzamam-ul-Haq	37	63	8	2491	148	45.29	5	17	36	0
Mohammad Akram	6	9	3	8	5	1.33	0	0	4	0
‡Mohammad Hussain	1	1	0	0	0	0.00	0	0	1	0
‡Mohammad Wasim	2	3	1	114	109*	57.00	1	0	3	0
‡Mohammad Zahid	3	3	1	6	6*	3.00	0	0	0	0
Moin Khan	26	38	5	1055	117*	31.97	3	5	55	7
Mushtaq Ahmed	28	42	7	355	42	10.14	0	0	10	0
Ramiz Raja	57	94	5	2833	122	31.83	2	22	34	0
Rashid Latif	19	29	4	623	68*	24.92	0	3	58	8
Saeed Anwar	21	37	1	1739	176	48.31	4	13	12	0
Salim Elahi	4	7	0	57	17	8.14	0	0	7	1
Salim Malik	96	142	21	5528	237	45.69	15	28	62	0
Saqlain Mushtaq	9	14	4	256	79	25.60	0	2	4	0
‡Shadab Kabir	3	5	0	89	35	17.80	0	0	4	0
‡Shahid Nazir	6	7	2	27	13*	5.40	0	0	2	0
Waqar Younis	44	57	11	429	34	9.33	0	0	6	0
Wasim Akram	72	100	13	1944	257*	22.34	2	4	27	0
‡Zahoor Elahi	2	3	0	30	22	10.00	0	0	1	0

Bowling:	O	M	R	W	Av.	BB	5w/i	10w/m
Aamir Sohail	268.5	57	710	17	41.76	4–54	0	0
Asif Mujtaba	111	26	303	4	75.75	1–0	0	0
Ata-ur-Rehman	328.5	62	1071	31	34.55	4–50	0	0
Ijaz Ahmed	14	0	36	1	36.00	1–9	0	0
Mohammad Akram	172.1	32	522	10	52.20	3–39	0	0
‡Mohammad Hussain	10	4	21	1	21.00	1–7	0	0
‡Mohammad Zahid	81	12	278	13	21.38	7–66	1	1
Mushtaq Ahmed	1195.2	242	3309	117	28.28	7–56	7	2
Rashid Latif	2	0	10	0	–	–	0	0
Saeed Anwar	3	2	4	0	–	–	0	0
Salim Malik	91.2	19	322	5	64.40	1–3	0	0
Saqlain Mushtaq	507.3	118	1386	38	36.47	5–89	1	0
‡Shadab Kabir	1	0	9	0	–	–	0	0
‡Shahid Nazir	135.5	29	436	14	31.14	5–54	1	0
Waqar Younis	1511.5	299	4844	227	21.34	7–76	19	4
Wasim Akram	2744	635	7054	311	22.68	7–119	21	4

‡Debutant 1996–97

SOUTH AFRICA

Batting:	M	I	NO	R	HS	Av.	100	50	Ct	St
P.R. Adams	9	13	2	66	29	6.00	0	0	8	0
‡A.M. Bacher	5	10	0	302	96	30.20	0	2	4	0
W.J. Cronje	36	63	7	2012	135	35.93	5	7	12	0
D.J. Cullinan	28	49	5	1778	153★	40.41	3	11	21	0
P.S. de Villiers	16	23	6	305	67★	17.94	0	2	9	0
A.A. Donald	33	44	18	334	33	12.85	0	0	8	0
‡H.H. Gibbs	4	8	0	125	31	15.63	0	0	1	0
A.C. Hudson	32	58	3	1920	163	34.91	4	13	33	0
J.H. Kallis	5	7	0	57	39	8.14	0	0	1	0
G. Kirsten	29	53	2	1806	133★	35.41	4	9	22	0
‡L. Klusener	7	12	3	282	102★	31.33	1	0	6	0
B.M. McMillan	31	51	11	1702	113	42.55	3	11	41	0
S.M. Pollock	10	16	4	344	79	28.67	0	1	3	0
J.N. Rhodes	29	47	5	1267	101★	30.17	1	7	16	0
D.J. Richardson	37	56	7	1273	109	25.98	1	8	134	1
B.N. Schultz	8	7	2	8	6	1.60	0	0	1	0
P.L. Symcox	10	13	1	259	50	21.58	0	1	0	0

Bowling:	O	M	R	W	Av.	BB	5w/i	10w/m
P.R. Adams	342	78	1011	35	28.89	6–55	1	0
‡A.M. Bacher	1	0	4	0	–	–	0	0
W.J. Cronje	401.5	158	768	17	45.18	2–11	0	0
P.S. de Villiers	742.1	207	1909	75	25.45	6–43	4	2
A.A. Donald	1268.1	316	3621	155	23.36	8–71	8	2
J.H. Kallis	62.4	18	136	5	27.20	3–29	0	0
‡L. Klusener	221.1	46	684	21	32.57	8–64	1	0
B.M. McMillan	890	234	2238	73	30.66	4–65	0	0
S.M. Pollock	283.5	71	719	30	23.97	5–32	1	0
B.N. Schultz	273.5	78	691	36	19.19	5–48	2	0
P.L. Symcox	313.5	68	861	18	47.83	3–75	0	0

‡Debutant 1996–97

SRI LANKA

Batting:	M	I	NO	R	HS	Av.	100	50	Ct	St
‡R.P. Arnold	2	4	0	126	50	31.50	0	1	3	0
M.S. Atapattu	6	12	0	91	25	7.58	0	0	0	0
P.A. de Silva	59	103	6	3668	267	37.81	11	13	27	0
‡S.C. de Silva	2	3	1	0	0★	0.00	0	0	2	0
H.D.P.K. Dharmasena	13	23	4	426	62★	22.42	0	2	7	0
A.P. Gurusinha	41	70	7	2452	143	38.92	7	8	33	0
S.T. Jayasuriya	23	38	6	1181	113	36.91	2	7	18	0
R.S. Kalpage	9	15	1	270	63	19.29	0	2	6	0
R.S. Kaluwitharana	12	19	1	714	132★	39.67	2	4	21	2
R.S. Mahanama	41	70	1	2014	153	29.19	3	10	42	0
M. Muralitharan	28	39	19	252	26	12.60	0	0	14	0
K.R. Pushpakumara	8	13	6	68	23	9.71	0	0	4	0
A. Ranatunga	67	114	6	3793	135★	35.12	4	26	32	0
K.J. Silva	4	4	1	6	6★	2.00	0	0	1	0
H.P. Tillekeratne	42	71	11	2578	126★	42.97	6	14	72	0
W.P.U.J.C. Vaas	18	30	2	492	57	17.57	0	2	6	0
G.P. Wickremasinghe	24	39	4	323	43	9.23	0	0	9	0
‡D.N.T. Zoysa	3	5	1	43	16★	10.75	0	0	1	0

Bowling:	O	M	R	W	Av.	BB	5w/i	10w/m
‡R.P. Arnold	13	4	31	0	–	–	0	0
M.S. Atapattu	4	0	9	1	9.00	1–9	0	0
P.A. de Silva	204.3	24	639	17	37.59	3–39	0	0
‡S.C. de Silva	68.2	13	223	5	44.60	5–85	1	0
H.D.P.K. Dharmasena	554.1	134	1295	29	44.66	6–99	1	0
A.P. Gurusinha	234.4	47	681	20	34.05	2–7	0	0
S.T. Jayasuriya	131	21	457	6	76.17	2–16	0	0
R.S. Kalpage	195.5	38	507	6	84.50	2–27	0	0
R.S. Mahanama	6	0	30	0	–	–	0	0
M. Muralitharan	1256	286	3279	107	30.64	6–98	7	0
K.R. Pushpakumara	198.4	27	749	20	37.45	7–116	1	0
A. Ranatunga	372.3	103	984	15	65.60	2–17	0	0
K.J. Silva	157.4	52	382	17	22.47	4–16	0	0
H.P. Tillekeratne	5.4	1	14	0	–	–	0	0
W.P.U.J.C. Vaas	675	158	1674	67	24.99	6–87	4	1
G.P. Wickremasinghe	750.5	138	2337	47	49.72	5–73	1	0
‡D.N.T. Zoysa	90.4	16	267	7	38.14	3–47	0	0

‡Debutant 1996–97

WEST INDIES

Batting:	M	I	NO	R	HS	Av.	100	50	Ct	St
J.C. Adams	29	46	11	1991	208★	56.89	5	9	30	0
C.E.L. Ambrose	70	99	21	1015	53	13.01	0	1	14	0
K.C.G. Benjamin	24	32	7	215	43★	8.60	0	0	2	0
I.R. Bishop	35	51	9	493	48	11.74	0	0	7	0
C.O. Browne	11	17	6	250	39★	22.73	0	0	48	1
S.L. Campbell	21	35	2	1305	208	39.55	2	7	17	0
S. Chanderpaul	21	33	6	1454	137★	53.85	1	14	9	0
C.E. Cuffy	3	5	2	6	3★	2.00	0	0	1	0
‡M.V. Dillon	2	3	1	21	21	10.50	0	0	0	0
‡A.F.G. Griffith	1	2	0	14	13	7.00	0	0	0	0
‡R.I.C. Holder	5	7	1	212	91	35.33	0	2	6	0
C.L. Hooper	62	104	9	3155	178★	33.21	7	14	69	0
B.C. Lara	43	72	2	3884	375	55.49	9	20	57	0
J.R. Murray	28	37	4	848	101★	25.70	1	3	92	3
‡F.A. Rose	5	4	1	63	34	21.00	0	0	0	0
R.G. Samuels	6	12	2	372	125	37.20	1	1	8	0
P.V. Simmons	25	45	2	1000	110	23.26	1	4	26	0
P.I.C. Thompson	2	3	1	17	10★	8.50	0	0	0	0
C.A. Walsh	91	119	36	768	30★	9.25	0	0	16	0
S.C. Williams	17	27	2	649	128	25.96	1	1	16	0

Bowling:	O	M	R	W	Av.	BB	5w/i	10w/m
J.C. Adams	199.3	31	654	15	43.60	5–17	1	0
C.E.L. Ambrose	2701	700	6404	295	21.71	8–45	17	3
K.C.G. Benjamin	792.2	144	2619	89	29.43	6–66	4	1
I.R. Bishop	1240.1	266	3337	149	22.40	6–40	6	0
S. Chanderpaul	171	32	490	4	122.50	1–2	0	0
C.E. Cuffy	85.2	14	306	7	43.71	3–80	0	0
‡M.V. Dillon	54	11	148	4	37.00	3–92	0	0
C.L. Hooper	1232	261	3211	57	56.33	5–40	2	0
B.C. Lara	10	1	28	0	–	–	0	0
‡F.A. Rose	141.1	27	402	18	22.33	6–100	1	0
P.V. Simmons	102	27	248	4	62.00	2–34	0	0
P.I.C. Thompson	38	1	215	5	43.00	2–58	0	0
C.A. Walsh	3241.3	694	8560	332	25.84	7–37	13	2
S.C. Williams	3	0	19	0	–	–	0	0

‡Debutant 1996–97

ZIMBABWE

Batting:	M	I	NO	R	HS	Av.	100	50	Ct	St
E.A. Brandes	9	13	2	111	39	10.09	0	0	4	0
A.D.R. Campbell	22	38	1	1115	99	30.14	0	9	17	0
S.V. Carlisle	6	10	1	175	58	19.44	0	1	10	0
M.H. Dekker	14	22	1	333	68*	15.86	0	2	12	0
‡C.N. Evans	1	2	0	10	9	5.00	0	0	1	0
A. Flower	22	37	5	1330	156	41.56	3	9	50	4
G.W. Flower	22	38	1	1175	201*	31.76	2	6	11	0
D.L. Houghton	20	32	2	1396	266	46.53	4	4	15	0
‡E. Matambanadzo	1	2	1	7	7	7.00	0	0	0	0
‡M. Mbangwa	1	2	0	2	2	1.00	0	0	0	0
H.K. Olonga	7	9	1	14	7	1.75	0	0	4	0
A.H. Shah	3	5	0	122	62	24.40	0	1	0	0
B.C. Strang	9	15	5	117	42	11.70	0	0	6	0
P.A. Strang	13	21	5	505	106*	31.56	1	1	6	0
H.H. Streak	15	22	5	225	53	13.24	0	1	5	0
‡A.C. Waller	2	3	0	69	50	23.00	0	1	1	0
‡A.R. Whittall	3	6	1	27	12	5.40	0	0	2	0
G.J. Whittall	18	30	2	642	113*	22.93	1	3	7	0
C.B. Wishart	6	12	1	154	51	14.00	0	1	3	0

Bowling:	O	M	R	W	Av.	BB	5w/i	10w/m
E.A. Brandes	311.4	64	886	22	40.27	3–45	0	0
‡C.N. Evans	6	0	27	0	–	–	0	0
G.W. Flower	112	23	322	3	107.33	1–4	0	0
‡E. Matambanadzo	16	0	89	2	44.50	2–62	0	0
‡M. Mbangwa	24	4	81	2	40.50	2–67	0	0
H.K. Olonga	133.4	21	487	10	48.70	3–90	0	0
B.C. Strang	296	101	661	24	27.54	5–101	1	0
P.A. Strang	482.2	101	1278	32	39.94	5–106	3	0
H.H. Streak	606.5	153	1551	69	22.48	6–90	3	0
‡A.R. Whittall	89.2	17	261	2	130.50	2–146	0	0
G.J. Whittall	369	98	919	27	34.04	4–18	0	0

‡Debutant 1996–97

England v India
First Test: Edgbaston
June 6–9 1996

Heaven-Sent Hussain and Another Tendulkar Masterpiece

Desperate for success to blot out the disappointing winter in South Africa, England beat India with some ease inside four days in the opening Test of 1996. Ray Illingworth, in his final season as chairman of selectors, and indignantly facing a disciplinary charge by the TCCB over the contents of his latest book (he was fined £2000, but the decision was reversed upon appeal), led his panel to the choice of three new caps, while dropping Alec Stewart (53 Tests) and recalling Nasser Hussain.

India, markedly less successful overseas than at home in recent years, had had to endure a cold English spring as well as the walk-out by opening batsman Navjot Singh Sidhu, who took exception to his omission from the team for the third one-day international. For the first time since 1947–48 (Brisbane) India fielded four debutants.

England's rejuvenation was quickly expressed. The four-man seam attack disposed of India inside 70 overs, and England were 60 without loss at the close. Their catching – apart from Hussain's missing of Rathore at square cover – had been sharp, Knight's three takes including a fine, twisting effort at short midwicket to dismiss Azharuddin, while Atherton clung to one at gully which was screaming towards his shoulder. This was from Manjrekar's bat, after he had resumed following treatment for a twisted ankle. Cork was the fieriest of the bowlers, and gained the prize of Tendulkar, who drove carelessly and missed. Mullally, the 6ft 5in English-born, Australian-raised left-armer, was also impressive. Almost 27, he could scarcely have envisaged a Test debut when, a few months earlier, he lay desperately ill after having been bitten by a lethal redback spider in Perth, WA.

A defiant top-score 52 by Srinath, who was supported by Mhambrey, lifted India out of the depths, but the gremlins in the pitch and the loose strokeplay by most of the top order rendered it a bad day for the visitors. Lewis, given a fresh chance, bowled with some imagination, and Irani took a wicket with his fifth ball in Test cricket. It was then time to see whether India's estimable opening attack of Srinath and Prasad could make inroads through the England batting.

Atherton and Knight gave them a sturdy launch but India's two fast men got life from the pitch on the second day, and with Knight falling without addition, and Atherton forced into near-immobility, the innings became desperately hard work, seven wickets being lost before India's 214 was passed.

The saviour was Hussain, now much more mature at 28, neat of method and highly watchable, and in the early stages of this innings quite lucky. He was missed twice on the leg side off Srinath, and then, on 14, umpire Hair refused a roaring appeal for a leg-side catch by the wicketkeeper off another waspish lifter. The Indians were inconsolable. After Thorpe had played on and Hick had limply got out to the hook, Hussain's first reassuring support came from Irani, an extrovert cricketer, who

Adrian Murrell/Allsport

clattered 34 runs off as many balls. Russell and Lewis, however, recorded ducks, Cork only 4, and it fell to Patel and Mullally to see England's hoodoo-breaking No.3 past his century. Hussain was 93 when last-man Mullally joined him, and when, after 275 minutes at the crease, he ran the ball to third man and reached his hundred, his celebrations were heartfelt, midst the glowering of the fieldsmen.

Time had been lost to drizzle before lunch, and now the weather deteriorated, ending play 15 overs early, with India 5 without loss in their second innings, still 94 in arrears. And their ill-luck stretched into Saturday, when Rathore was given out to a slip catch that slow-motion television showed to have bounced fractionally before entering the fielder's hands. It gave Cork his 50th Test wicket and precipitated a slide to 68 for 5 before Tendulkar and the injured Manjrekar arrested it with a stand of 59. England were insistent on this capricious surface, this time with Lewis as the most hostile of the bowlers. For only the third time in 28 Tests he secured five wickets in an innings, and but for Tendulkar's glorious 122, it would have been a rout. The 23-year-old Indian vice-captain was in a class of his own, his strokeplay judicious and crisp, his calmness shining from the surrounding sense of emergency and, sometimes, despair. Tendulkar reached his century with a memorable six off Patel, only the 139th ball bowled to him. It was his ninth hundred in his 39 Tests.

Inspired by coach David Lloyd's music-backed match videos, the bowlers were patently keen, none more so than Mullally, who took the key wicket of Azharuddin (0) by bowling him round his legs. Manjrekar's studious approach was not capitalized upon, and of the rest only Kumble dropped anchor, until smart fielding by Knight ended his stay.

It left England needing 121, and the opening forays of Srinath and Prasad were weathered for an overnight score of 73 for 1. Hussain was caught off the hook next morning, but Atherton steered his side home, with the trusty Thorpe, who somehow had survived a close lbw shout the previous evening. Little more than an hour was needed, the quality of the Edgbaston pitch emerging as the joint major talking-point alongside England's exciting youth-based re-emergence.   **David Frith**

Nasser Hussain, on his way to his first Test century, is given 'not out' at 14 to what the Indians were convinced was a leg-side catch to the keeper

FIRST TEST MATCH

Edgbaston, Birmingham

June 6, 7, 8, 9 1996

Toss: India

INDIA

			Mins	Balls	Fours			Mins	Balls	Fours
V.S. Rathore	c Knight b Cork	20	66	52	1	c Hick b Cork	7	21	11	1
A.D. Jadeja	c Atherton b Lewis	0	17	9	0	c Russell b Lewis	6	38	27	1
S.V. Manjrekar	c Atherton b Lewis	23	68	47	4	(7) c Knight b Lewis	18	98	64	2
S.R. Tendulkar	b Cork	24	70	41	4	c Thorpe b Lewis	122	262	176	19‡
*M. Azharuddin	c Knight b Irani	13	30	27	3	b Mullally	0	5	3	0
†N.R. Mongia	b Mullally	20	48	39	4	(3) c Hussain b Cork	9	49	36	1
S.B. Joshi	c Thorpe b Mullally	12	93	64	1	(6) c Russell b Mullally	12	20	15	1
A. Kumble	c Knight b Cork	5	13	8	1	run out (*Knight/Hick*)	15	70	54	2
J. Srinath	c Russell b Mullally	52	92	65	9	lbw b Lewis	1	18	14	0
P.L. Mhambrey	c Thorpe b Cork	28	76	49	4	b Lewis	15	29	20	2
B.K.V. Prasad	not out	0	25	18	0	not out	0	16	6	0
Extras:	b3 lb10 nb4	17				b4 lb9 nb1	14			
Total:		214					219			‡ plus 1 six

Fall: 8, 41, 64, 93, 103, 118, 127, 150, 203

15, 17, 35, 36, 68, 127, 185, 193, 208

Manjrekar retired injured when 10 (40 for 1) and returned at 103 for 5

Bowling:

Lewis	18–2–44–2 3nb	Lewis	22.4–6–72–5
Cork	20.1–5–61–4	Cork	19–5–40–2
Mullally	22–7–60–3 1nb	Mullally	15–4–43–2 1nb
Irani	7–4–22–1	Irani	2–0–21–0
Patel	2–0–14–0	Patel	8–3–18–0
		Hick	4–1–12–0

ENGLAND

			Mins	Balls	Fours			Mins	Balls	Fours
N.V. Knight	c Mongia b Srinath	27	79	48	4	lbw b Prasad	14	40	29	1
*M.A. Atherton	c Rathore b Mhambrey	33	123	98	5	not out	53	154	100	3
N. Hussain	c sub (*R.S. Dravid*) b Srinath	128	309	227	18‡	c Srinath b Prasad	19	53	44	2
G.P. Thorpe	b Srinath	21	45	30	2‡	not out	17	59	36	2
G.A. Hick	c Mhambrey b Prasad	8	41	29	2					
R.C. Irani	c Mongia b Srinath	34	41	34	7					
†R.C. Russell	b Prasad	0	23	14	0					
C.C. Lewis	c Rathore b Prasad	0	1	1	0					
D.G. Cork	c Jadeja b Prasad	4	8	9	0					
M.M. Patel	lbw b Kumble	18	52	35	2					
A.D. Mullally	not out	14	47	25	3					
Extras:	b16 lb3 nb7	26				b8 lb7 w1 nb2	18			
Total:		313		‡ plus 1 six			2 wkts 121			

Fall: 60, 72, 109, 149, 195, 205, 205, 215, 264

37, 77

Bowling:

Srinath	28.2–5–103–4 5nb	Srinath	14.5–3–47–0 5nb 1w
Prasad	28–9–71–4	Prasad	14–0–50–2
Kumble	24–4–77–1	Kumble	5–3–9–0
Mhambrey	10–0–43–1 3nb		

Umpires: D.B. Hair (Aus.) & D.R. Shepherd (Eng.). *Third umpire:* A.A. Jones (Eng.). *Referee:* C.W. Smith (WI).
Debuts: R.C. Irani, A.D. Mullally, M.M. Patel (Eng.); S.B. Joshi, P.L. Mhambrey, B.K.V. Prasad, V.S. Rathore (Ind.).
Man of the Match: N. Hussain

England won by 8 wickets

England v India

Second Test: Lord's

June 20–24 1996

Bird Flies Away As New Indian Star Lands

Markedly lacking in prolonged tension, the Lord's Test began with a weepy umpire and ended with an Indian surge for victory that was repelled by stout lower-order batting by England. Only on the opening day did the ball move around dangerously, fully justifying Azharuddin's decision to put England in, and England had the worst of starts when Atherton was leg-before to the fifth ball. This at least demonstrated that umpire H. D. 'Dickie' Bird had finally controlled his emotions following the mighty reception which greeted his entry onto the field for his record 66th, and final, Test appearance.

Stewart seemed to be similarly plumb, but received the benefit of Bird's judgment, and batted a further two hours, though never convincingly in this comeback opportunity afforded by Knight's finger injury. Beneath a heavily clouded sky, India's pace duo of Srinath and Prasad might easily have picked up three wickets apiece before lunch after the delayed start. From 39 for 1 at the interval, England lost four wickets in the next session, with Stewart yorked, Hussain edging an ambitious drive at Ganguly's seventh ball in Test cricket, Hick driving the same bowler meekly to mid-off, and Irani leaving his leg stump exposed. Azharuddin used Kumble extensively throughout the match, but only towards its conclusion did he seem able to regain the rhythm of old. Thus, as the fast men tired, England were able doggedly to stay in the match.

The fifth wicket fell at 107, but Thorpe and fellow left-hander Russell fought hard and lifted the score to 238 when poor light intervened at 6.25 pm, with 10 overs still to be bowled. Thorpe, who was hit on the helmet by one of Tendulkar's darting deliveries as he tried to hook, was 85 at the close, Russell a grim 69, both having had to cope with changes of direction not only off the bowler-friendly pitch but from the constant switches in the attack from over to around the wicket and back again.

With only five added, England lost Thorpe on a sunny second morning, but India were held off by Russell still and now Lewis, whose 2½-hour 31 made for a seventh-wicket stand of 83. Russell exploded with joy as he reached his second Test century (234 mins), and thereafter went even further into his shell, his last 24 runs taking two hours, wickets sinking at the other end. Cork's duck spanned 24 balls. It was a satisfactory total, 344, Prasad securing the outstanding bowling figures, and India soon found runmaking no less difficult. They lost Rathore, smartly taken at slip, and makeshift opener Mongia, a shade unluckily lbw after two hours' defiance.

From 83 for 2 India advanced on the Saturday to 324 for 6, the day belonging to Sourav Ganguly, 23, the slender left-hander on his Test debut. It had been suggested in some quarters in his homeland that he was a 'token' Bengal player and that his wealthy background had advanced his progress. But he showed here at Lord's that he was actually close to world-class. Unruffled, eager always to punish lesser deliveries, and attractive in his strokeplay on both sides of the wicket, Ganguly reached his half-century off 108 balls and drove Cork to the boundary to bring up his hundred after 340 minutes. Only Harry Graham of Australia (1893) and John Hampshire of England (1969) had previously scored a century at Lord's on a Test debut. Ganguly was the 10th batsman to make a debut hundred for India, the third left-hander.

The key wicket of Tendulkar was taken by Lewis, whose legcutter up the slope removed his off stump, soon after Hick had dropped him at slip. Out-of-form Azharuddin flicked fatally at Mullally, and Jadeja's 10 lasted 95 minutes, but Rahul Dravid, another debutant, supported Ganguly in a crucial sixth-wicket stand of 94 before the No.3 fell to Mullally after more than seven hours at the crease. Dravid then supervised India's progress to a first-innings lead, coming close in the process to emulating Ganguly. A century seemed there for the taking when the elegant 23-year-old from Karnataka, having frozen on 79 for 10 overs, now, at 95, played somewhat mechanically at Lewis and got a thin edge to the new ball after lunch on the fourth day: 419 for 9. He had been missed by Hussain at point when 47, but his wristy play, allied with that of Ganguly, made the India innings a notable and refreshing event. Kumble, Srinath and Mhambrey all served their side well with the bat, but the sameness of England's bowling slowly tempered the optimism which had sprung from the victory in the previous Test. It was now up to their batsmen to hold the fort in the 4½ sessions remaining.

Atherton somehow avoided a 'pair' and not until 49 was on the board did he fall to a perfect Kumble legspinner. The arrears of 85 were wiped off, but India's big effort was rewarded just before the close when Hussain tried to pull out of a hook and merely spooned a catch to point. At 113 for 2, England slept slightly uneasily.

Martin served his team well as nightwatchman, hanging on for two hours, but Stewart, having been at his best, timing sweetly, always watchful, played on after adding only one run. There were four casualties before lunch, Thorpe parrying a ball from Kumble which leapt at him, Rathore holding a marvellous catch, and Hick edging a Prasad legcutter, and at the break England, six down, were only 85 ahead. It was an afternoon of continuous mathematical calculations. Irani's apparently nerveless approach and Russell's intense watchfulness saw England through all but a few minutes of the second session, and by the time the wicketkeeper succumbed to a Ganguly in-swinger he had batted for 9½ hours in the match. Lewis again got his head down, and the balance of the match at the end, with the pitch allowing uneven bounce, left regrets that there was not a sixth day.

Only 29 wickets had fallen in the five days, but it had been no run-feast. After 40 Tests on English soil since 1932, India still had only three victories to their credit. If anything, England's players were even more aggrieved, for their lucklustre bowling had also proved costly in its over rate: each man was docked £1300. All the same it was not the least historic of Tests, for it marked the departure of a popular umpire and the arrival of two exciting new Subcontinental batsmen. **David Frith**

Graham Chadwick/Allsport

A golden moment for Sourav Ganguly: a Test-debut hundred at Lord's. Also in the picture is Rahul Dravid, who scored 95 on debut

England v India

SECOND TEST MATCH
Lord's

June 20, 21, 22, 23, 24 1996
Toss: India

ENGLAND			Mins	Balls	Fours			Mins	Balls	Fours
*M.A. Atherton	lbw b Srinath	0	2	5	0	b Kumble	17	72	51	2
A.J. Stewart	b Srinath	20	126	81	3	b Srinath	66	193	136	8
N. Hussain	c Rathore b Ganguly	36	170	110	5	c Dravid b Srinath	28	95	69	3
G.P. Thorpe	b Srinath	89	239	178	10	(5) c Rathore b Kumble	21	55	49	3
G.A. Hick	c Srinath b Ganguly	1	10	9	0	(6) c Mongia b Prasad	6	36	24	1
R.C. Irani	b Prasad	1	4	2	0	(7) b Mhambrey	41	138	100	3
†R.C. Russell	c Tendulkar b Prasad	124	372	261	13	(8) lbw b Ganguly	38	195	136	2
C.C. Lewis	c Mongia b Prasad	31	156	118	3	(9) not out	26	81	61	2
D.G. Cork	c Mongia b Prasad	0	23	24	0	(10) c Azharuddin b Kumble	1	5	2	0
P.J. Martin	c Tendulkar b Prasad	4	9	8	1	(4) c Rathore b Prasad	23	124	97	3
A.D. Mullally	not out	0	6	3	0	not out	0	11	6	0
Extras:	b13 lb11 nb14	38				b1 lb5 nb5	11			
Total:		344				9 wkts dec.	278			

Fall: 0, 67, 98, 102, 107, 243, 326, 337, 343

Fall: 49, 109, 114, 154, 167, 168, 228, 274, 275

Bowling:

Srinath	33–9–76–3 *4nb*		Srinath	29–8–76–2 *3nb*
Prasad	33.3–10–76–5 *1nb*		Prasad	24–8–54–2
Mhambrey	19–3–58–0 *8nb*		Kumble	51–14–90–3
Kumble	28–9–60–0		Ganguly	3–0–5–1 *1nb*
Ganguly	15–2–49–2 *3nb*		Mhambrey	14–3–47–1 *1nb*
Tendulkar	2–1–1–0			

INDIA			Mins	Balls	Fours
V.S. Rathore	c Hussain b Cork	15	49	31	2
†N.R. Mongia	lbw b Lewis	24	123	95	3
S.C. Ganguly	b Mullally	131	436	300	20
S.R. Tendulkar	b Lewis	31	82	59	5
*M. Azharuddin	c Russell b Mullally	16	53	34	2
A.D. Jadeja	b Irani	10	95	55	1
R.S. Dravid	c Russell b Lewis	95	363	268	6
A. Kumble	lbw b Martin	14	115	80	1
J. Srinath	b Mullally	19	62	47	2
P.L. Mhambrey	not out	15	74	42	2
B.K.V. Prasad	c Stewart b Cork	4	17	16	0
Extras:	b11 lb25 w10 nb9	55			
Total:		429			

Fall: 25, 59, 123, 154, 202, 296, 351, 388, 419

Bowling:

Lewis	40–11–101–3
Cork	42.3–10–112–2 *6nb 1w*
Mullally	39–14–71–3 *3nb 2w*
Martin	34–10–70–1
Irani	12–3–31–1
Hick	2–0–8–0

Umpires: H.D. Bird (Eng.) & D.B. Hair (Aus.). *Third umpire:* A.G.T. Whitehead (Eng.). *Referee:* C.W. Smith (WI).
Debuts: R.S.Dravid, S.C. Ganguly (Ind.). *Man of the Match:* R.C. Russell

---

Match drawn

England v India
Third Test: Trent Bridge
July 4–9 1996

Centurions' Display-Cabinet

By matching India's large first innings, England drew to win the three-match series, though had the fortunes of spilled catches not been spread evenly it might have been a different tale. By the first evening, India were soundly placed at 287 for 2, having lost both openers cheaply after Azharuddin's third success with the toss. But Atherton missed Tendulkar at gully off Lewis before he had scored, and the young Indian master was to bat for almost eight hours for his sparkling 177, confirming the view recently expressed by the 87-year-old Australian champion himself that his method came closest to that of Don Bradman.

England's culprit, a batsman of a different kind, by chance was also given fateful reprieves when his turn came to bat, allowing him to play an innings as lengthy as Tendulkar's that helped his side to safety and restored his reputation.

Of the four centuries on this placid Nottingham pitch Ganguly's was marginally the most note-worthy in that it gave him hundreds in each of his first two Test innings (emulating Lawrence Rowe and Alvin Kallicharran). He and Tendulkar, both delights to the eye, batted for the rest of the opening day, under threatening dark clouds, making India's first-ever centuries at Trent Bridge while putting on 254, a record for any Indian wicket in Tests in England. But with only one run added next day, Ganguly, having been rapped on the glove by Mullally, edged the next ball to third slip. Manjrekar, back after injury, contributed a workmanlike half-century, and with the large video screen provocatively replaying the marginal lbw appeals England's frustration grew. With Cork showing signs of being jaded, and Patel posing no discernible threat, and the other three seamers bowling capably but no more, critics wondered if this new-look attack was the one to carry England into a brighter era. Gough might, at this stage, have been the only constructive substitution.

Azharuddin fell into a preconceived trap, caught on the leg side off a lifting ball, following Tendulkar's mis-hit pull which gave Ealham his maiden Test wicket. But Dravid was again impressive, overseeing the finishing touches to the bulky Indian innings with an 84 to follow his first Test innings of 95 at Lord's. Prasad helped him add 60 for the ninth wicket, and soon it was time to test England's batting fibre once more.

That evening, Atherton was missed on 0 by Dravid at third slip off Srinath as England made 32 without loss off 11 overs. And on the third day, the captain had another let-off at 34, when Azharuddin jumped at slip and merely fingered a flashing chance off the same bowler. Thereafter, the spirit of Johannesburg was recaptured, with Atherton batting with the same resolution as when he and Russell saved that 'unsaveable' Test against South Africa seven months earlier.

Atherton and Stewart posted 130 for the first wicket with growing assurance, only for the Surrey man to be given out caught at the wicket when the evidence was otherwise. But Hussain entered to score a century even higher in quality than his first, in the opening Test. By the close, England were 322 for the loss of only Stewart, the follow-on also having been averted. Atherton, a mass of concentration in the Boycott mould, and Hussain, full of flair and confidence, had an unbeaten partnership of 192 by the close, but minutes from the end Hussain sustained a hairline fracture on his right index finger and could not continue after the rest day.

This seriously interfered with England's momentum, to the extent that, although they occupied the wicket all through the fourth day, only 228 runs accrued in 92 overs, poor fare for another sub-capacity attendance. Atherton's 10th Test century (his fourth at Trent Bridge) ended with a catch to third slip, and India's seam and spin merchants kept a tight hold on matters thereafter. Thorpe looked for runs, but Hick, fighting to retain his place in the XI, froze on four for just short of an hour.

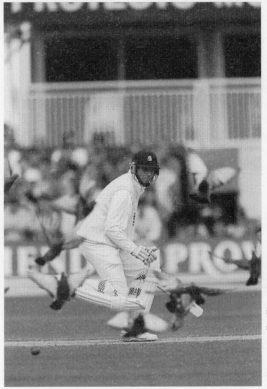

Adrian Murrell/Allsport

Ganguly had Thorpe (who passed 2000 Test runs) leg-before and Hick edged left-arm spinner Raju, trying to hit to midwicket when the ball pitched into the rough. Ealham then restored England's direction with a worthy 2½-hour fifty in his first Test innings, and although Russell went for 0, there was enough determination – and good fortune – in the tail to secure England a first-innings lead, with umpire Francis at the centre of criticism for several of his decisions.

From 550 for 7, England reached 564 on the final day, 43 ahead. And with Rathore unable to bat after dislocating a shoulder while throwing, and Manjrekar (another to reach 2000 Test runs) soon caught off the glove as he took evasive action against Lewis, thoughts of squeezing victory out of this near-stalemate will have crossed English minds. But India had stacked their side with batting, and the stubborn Mongia steadied the innings in company with Ganguly, who had the chance of a third century in as many Test innings. From the way he hammered Patel, the chances seemed good. But he played on to Cork for 48, and Mullally had Mongia caught at cover. Dravid registered his first failure, taken at slip off Mullally, and Azharuddin's wretched series ended when he became the first victim earned in a 4 for 3 spell by Ealham's clever medium-pace variations. The captain had not fielded through most of England's long innings after a blow on the ankle while fielding at silly point.

Through it all, and again like a superior breed of batsman, Sachin Tendulkar almost did as he chose with the bowling, and was on course for his second century of the match when, at 74, he again mistimed a pull and was caught. In 14 Test innings against England, Tendulkar had now scored 975 runs at 81.25, quite Bradmanesque.

The draw gave England a rare series victory, but neither captain, manager, coach nor any of the players allowed the glow of satisfaction to blind them to the reality that Pakistan would be providing a sterner Test in the second half of the summer.   **David Frith**

*England's skipper, Mike Atherton, raised the nation's spirits – as well as the grazing
pigeons – with a long century at Nottingham, where luck was also on his side*

THIRD TEST MATCH

Trent Bridge, Nottingham

July 4, 5, 6, 8, 9 1996
Toss: India

INDIA			Mins	Balls	Fours			Mins	Balls	Fours
V.S. Rathore	c Russell b Cork	4	13	7	0	absent injured		–	–	–	–
†N.R. Mongia	c Russell b Lewis	9	38	24	1	(1) c Lewis b Mullally	45	198	153	4
S.C. Ganguly	c Hussain b Mullally	136	361	268	17§	b Cork	48	120	86	8
S.R. Tendulkar	c Patel b Ealham	177	462	360	26	c Stewart b Lewis	74	112	97	11‡
S.V. Manjrekar	c Hick b Patel	53	217	144	5‡	(2) c Stewart b Lewis	11	36	33	2
*M. Azharuddin	c Patel b Lewis	5	17	11	0	c Cork b Ealham	8	36	14	0
R.S. Dravid	c Russell b Ealham	84	176	149	12	(5) c Thorpe b Mullally	8	25	21	1
A. Kumble	lbw b Mullally	0	4	6	0	(7) lbw b Ealham	2	12	6	0
J. Srinath	c Cork b Lewis	1	7	9	0	(8) c Thorpe b Ealham	3	14	8	0
B.K.V. Prasad	run out (*Stewart*)	13	79	32	0	(9) not out	0	14	3	0
S.L.V. Raju	not out	1	10	8	0	(10) c sub (*N.A. Gie*) b Ealham	0	5	4	0
Extras:	b6 lb12 w7 nb13	38		§ plus 2 sixes		b1 lb1 w1 nb9	12			‡ plus 1 six
Total:		521		‡ plus 1 six			211			

Fall: 7, 33, 288, 377, 385, 446, 447, 453, 513

17, 103, 140, 160, 204, 208, 208, 211, 211

Bowling:

Lewis	37–10–89–3 9nb 4w	Lewis	14–4–50–2 1nb 1w
Cork	32–6–124–1 4nb	Cork	7–0–32–1 3nb
Mullally	40–12–88–2 1nb 1w	Mullally	13–3–36–2 6nb
Ealham	29–9–90–2	Ealham	14–5–21–4
Patel	24–2–101–1 2nb	Patel	12–3–47–0 1nb
Hick	4–1–8–0	Hick	9–4–23–0
Thorpe	1–0–3–0 2w		

ENGLAND		Mins	Balls	Fours
*M.A. Atherton	c Manjrekar b Prasad	160	467	376	20
A.J. Stewart	c Mongia b Srinath	50	170	115	6
N. Hussain	retired injured	107	239	180	12
G.P. Thorpe	lbw b Ganguly	45	126	92	5
G.A. Hick	c Srinath b Raju	20	140	83	3
M.A. Ealham	c sub (*A.D. Jadeja*) b Srinath	51	151	120	3
†R.C. Russell	c Mongia b Prasad	0	6	5	0
C.C. Lewis	lbw b Kumble	21	66	60	2
D.G. Cork	not out	32	110	96	2
M.M. Patel	c Manjrekar b Ganguly	27	88	77	2
A.D. Mullally	c Mongia b Ganguly	1	14	9	0
Extras:	b18 lb18 nb14	50		
Total:		564		

Fall: 130, 360, 396, 444, 444, 491, 497, 558, 564
Hussain retired injured at the end of the third day at 322 for 1

Bowling:

Srinath	47–12–131–2 5nb
Prasad	43–12–124–2 7nb
Kumble	39–6–98–1 3nb
Raju	43–12–76–1
Ganguly	19.5–2–71–3 3nb
Tendulkar	7–0–28–0

Umpires: K.T. Francis (SL) & G. Sharp (Eng.). *Third umpire:* D.J. Constant (Eng.). *Referee:* C.W. Smith (WI).
Debut: M.A. Ealham (Eng.). *Man of the Match:* S.C. Ganguly. *Man of the Series:* N. Hussain (Eng.); S.C. Ganguly (Ind.).

Match drawn

SERIES AVERAGES

ENGLAND

Batting:

	M	I	NO	R	HS	Av.	100	50	Ct/st
N. Hussain	3	5	1	318	128	79.50	2	0	3
M.A. Atherton	3	5	1	263	160	65.75	1	1	2
M.A. Ealham	1	1	0	51	51	51.00	0	1	0
G.P. Thorpe	3	5	1	193	89	48.25	0	1	5
A.J. Stewart	2	3	0	136	66	45.33	0	2	3
R.C. Russell	3	4	0	162	124	40.50	1	0	8
C.C. Lewis	3	4	1	78	31	26.00	0	0	1
R.C. Irani	2	3	0	76	41	25.33	0	0	0
M.M. Patel	2	2	0	45	27	22.50	0	0	2
N.V. Knight	1	2	0	41	27	20.50	0	0	4
A.D. Mullally	3	4	3	15	14*	15.00	0	0	0
P.J. Martin	1	2	0	27	23	13.50	0	0	0
D.G. Cork	3	4	1	37	32*	12.33	0	0	2
G.A. Hick	3	4	0	35	20	8.75	0	0	2

Substitute catch was held by N.A. Gie

Bowling:

	O	M	R	W	Av.	BB	5w/i
M.A. Ealham	43	14	111	6	18.50	4–21	0
C.C. Lewis	131.4	33	356	15	23.73	5–72	1
A.D. Mullally	129	40	298	12	24.83	3–60	0
D.G. Cork	120.4	26	369	10	36.90	4–61	0
R.C. Irani	21	7	74	2	37.00	1–22	0
P.J. Martin	34	10	70	1	70.00	1–70	0
M.M. Patel	46	8	180	1	180.00	1–101	0
G.P. Thorpe	1	0	3	0	–	–	0
G.A. Hick	19	6	51	0	–	–	0

INDIA

Batting:

	M	I	NO	R	HS	Av.	100	50	Ct/st
S.C. Ganguly	2	3	0	315	136	105.00	2	0	0
S.R. Tendulkar	3	5	0	428	177	85.60	2	1	2
R.S. Dravid	2	3	0	187	95	62.33	0	2	1
P.L. Mhambrey	2	3	1	58	28	29.00	0	0	1
S.V. Manjrekar	2	4	0	105	53	26.25	0	1	2
N.R. Mongia	3	5	0	107	45	21.40	0	0	8
J. Srinath	3	5	0	76	52	15.20	0	1	3
S.B. Joshi	1	2	0	24	12	12.00	0	0	0
V.S. Rathore	3	4	0	46	20	11.50	0	0	5
B.K.V. Prasad	3	5	3	17	13	8.50	0	0	0
M.Azharuddin	3	5	0	42	16	8.40	0	0	1
A. Kumble	3	5	0	36	15	7.20	0	0	0
A.D. Jadeja	2	3	0	16	10	5.33	0	0	1
S.L.V. Raju	1	2	1	1	1*	1.00	0	0	0

Substitute catches were held by R.S. Dravid (1) and A.D. Jadeja (1)

Bowling:

	O	M	R	W	Av.	BB	5w/i
S.C. Ganguly	37.5	4	125	6	20.83	3–71	0
B.K.V. Prasad	142.3	39	375	15	25.00	5–76	1
J. Srinath	152.1	37	433	11	39.36	4–103	0
A. Kumble	147	36	334	5	66.80	3–90	0
P.L. Mhambrey	43	6	148	2	74.00	1–43	0
S.L.V. Raju	43	12	76	1	76.00	1–76	0
S.R. Tendulkar	9	1	29	0	–	–	0

England v Pakistan

First Test: Lord's

July 25–29 1996

Talented Pakistan Dash England's Renewed Hopes

The first England v Pakistan Test for four years began against a background of administrative anxiety that relations between the two sides should be harmonious, for the 1992 allegations of ball-tampering and incompetent umpiring had added grievously to the earlier history of animosity between these two sides. Pakistan were keen to assert their position in world Test rankings, while England needed to do something about their dismal record against these opponents, whom they had managed to defeat only once in the previous 16 Tests since 1982.

The home side, who lacked Hussain and Lewis through injury and whose five bowlers boasted only 24 Tests between them, started well, left-armer Brown soon trapping Sohail (padding away) and Cork bowling Ijaz as he walked across the crease and got into a tangle. Saeed Anwar and Inzamam then embarked on a steadying stand of 130, the left-hander batting with poise and maturity, Inzamam, bulky and phlegmatic, building his fifth Test century, his highest, with pounding drives. Mullally held them in check, and Ealham bowled with skill and teasing variety. But there was little here to embarrass the batsmen, not even from recalled legspinner Salisbury when the pitch began to wear on the fourth day.

Hick effected the breakthrough, Russell holding a rebound catch, and Malik was run out seeking a futile second run off Inzamam's stroke to midwicket. The No.4, however, continued to drive with the power of a Walcott, and reached his hundred with a six over long-on off Hick. Newcomer Shadab was the first of five wickets to slide after tea, Mullally moving the old ball from leg and taking the last three, starting with Inzamam, who batted five hours.

From 290 for 9, Latif, with the last man, created 50 more runs on the second morning, and England were unfortunate to lose Atherton before lunch, lbw in umpire Willey's opinion, when most others thought the ball would have missed off stump by some distance. Two more leg-befores came with the second session, Knight (51) also appearing to be rather unlucky. England's troubles deepened when Hick was yorked by Waqar Younis after tea, Thorpe and Ealham rallying the innings with a stand of 64 as the light deteriorated, only for Ealham, who was not alone in being blind to Mushtaq's googly, to flick at a lifting legcutter from Ata-ur-Rehman. As the evening sunlight returned, Thorpe was let off at 43, striking a ball from the suffering Mushtaq at Shadab's midriff at square short leg. But the closing score was a miserable 200 for 5.

There was a further reprieve for Thorpe on 73, Latif leaping and probably depriving first slip of the catch. But soon the Surrey left-hander was gone after a diligent four-hour 77, and Russell shouldered the remaining responsibility, dragging England to within 55 of Pakistan, whose fast bowlers moved the ball about and met their captain's needs.

Having lost their last five wickets for a dismal 25, England now had little with which to trouble the Pakistan openers, who sailed to 136 before Anwar, who had driven Salisbury for six and survived a justified appeal for a catch off the glove from the same bowler, finally touched a good lifter from Mullally. Shadab, his partner, gloved a nasty ball from Cork at the same total, having been hurt by a similar delivery, with the light now poor. And when nightwatchman Mushtaq was taken at slip after Ijaz had pulled Salisbury for six, Pakistan were 216 ahead with seven wickets remaining.

Adrian Murrell/Allsport

At lunch on the Sunday that advantage had swelled decisively to 307 without further loss of wicket, and Lord's, little more than half-full, was a comparatively quiet and subdued sporting venue. Cork three times in one over came close to dismissing Inzamam, but the batsman unemotionally cruised towards another century, hobbling from a leg injury but still getting well into position. He had reached 70 after lunch when mid-off held a thumping drive above his head.

Before that, Ijaz, having extended his brilliant form from the tour of Australia, had also seemed set for three figures, until Cork cut one back at him. The Reader ball had to be changed yet again after going out of shape, but the shape of the match was well enough defined when Pakistan declared on the stroke of tea, leaving England to score 408 for victory in four sessions. They lost Knight, back on his stumps, but had 74 runs on the board by the close, Atherton 'freezing' on 24 for the final 50 minutes, having weathered a blow on the chest and a bouncer past his face from Younis and having strolled up the pitch to register his displeasure to the umpire at substitute Moin's 'verbals'.

An astonishing collapse on the final day cast ridicule over the usual early-morning pronouncements and forecasts as England contemplated a remaining target of 334. What rendered it all surreal was the lunchtime score: 152 for 1. From there, a good second session could have set up an explosive run-chase in the final overs. Mushtaq had spun beautifully and conceded little more than one run per over, while Younis's roundarm inswingers had needed close watching and Wasim Akram's frequent bouncers had both batsmen hopping about.

Stewart, in his 100th Test innings, had moved to 88, and the stand to 154, when he lost his captain, Atherton edging Mushtaq to slip. It was the first of eight wickets to fall (five to Mushtaq, three to Younis) for 40 runs, Salisbury and Brown then salvaging 35 more for the last wicket while the tea interval was postponed. It was a masterly display of legspin variations by the diminutive Mushtaq, who, like Ijaz, extended his impressive Australian form. If he was somewhat lucky to win umpire Bucknor's approval for lbw against Thorpe, he beat the bat many times, and also had Cork dropped at silly point. Spinning a long way out of the rough of the footmarks, Mushtaq set the same kinds of seemingly insoluble problems associated with Shane Warne of Australia. England supporters could only wonder if Ian Salisbury would ever develop such teeth.   **David Frith**

The powerful Inzamam-ul-Haq pounds England legspinner Salisbury through the covers during his five-hour 148

FIRST TEST MATCH

Lord's

July 25, 26, 27, 28, 29 1996

Toss: Pakistan

PAKISTAN

		Mins	Balls	Fours		Mins	Balls	Fours
Aamir Sohail	lbw b Brown	2	13	14	0			
Saeed Anwar	c Russell b Hick	74	162	119	10	(1) c Russell b Mullally	88	198	144	8‡
Ijaz Ahmed	b Cork	1	11	8	0	lbw b Cork	76	184	126	9‡
Inzamam-ul-Haq	b Mullally	148	299	218	19‡	(5) c Ealham b Cork	70	190	148	9
Salim Malik	run out (*Salisbury/Russell*)	7	13	12	1	(6) not out	27	95	58	3
Shadab Kabir	lbw b Cork	17	77	64	1	(2) c Russell b Cork	33	203	151	5
*Wasim Akram	lbw b Ealham	10	50	34	1	(7) not out	34	61	43	6
†Rashid Latif	c Hick b Salisbury	45	139	111	4				
Mushtaq Ahmed	c Russell b Mullally	11	27	29	2	(4) c Thorpe b Brown	5	21	11	1
Waqar Younis	c Brown b Mullally	4	14	9	1				
Ata-ur-Rehman	not out	10	76	37	2				

Extras: b3 lb5 nb3 — 11

Total: 340 ‡ plus 1 six

b4 lb14 nb1 — 19

5 wkts dec. 352 ‡ plus 1 six

Fall: 7, 12, 142, 153, 209, 257, 267, 280, 290

136, 136, 161, 279, 308

Bowling:

Cork	28–6–100–2 4nb		Cork	24–4–86–3 1nb
Brown	17–2–78–1		Brown	16–2–60–1
Mullally	24–8–44–3 1nb		Salisbury	20–4–63–0
Salisbury	12.2–1–42–1		Mullally	30.2–9–70–1
Ealham	21–4–42–1 1nb		Hick	7–2–16–0
Hick	6–0–26–1		Ealham	16–4–39–0

ENGLAND

		Mins	Balls	Fours		Mins	Balls	Fours
N.V. Knight	lbw b Younis	51	139	107	7	lbw b Younis	1	27	19	0
*M.A. Atherton	lbw b Akram	12	21	8	2	c sub (*Asif Mujtaba*) b Mushtaq	64	279	211	8
A.J. Stewart	lbw b Mushtaq	39	122	102	6	c sub (*Moin Khan*) b Mushtaq	89	261	189	8
G.P. Thorpe	b Ata-ur-Rehman	77	240	167	6	lbw b Mushtaq	3	62	35	0
G.A. Hick	b Younis	4	20	20	0	b Younis	4	7	6	1
M.A. Ealham	c Latif b Ata-ur-Rehman	25	81	79	3	b Mushtaq	5	11	8	1
†R.C. Russell	not out	41	172	110	5	c Latif b Younis	1	13	8	0
D.G. Cork	c Anwar b Ata-ur-Rehman	3	8	4	0	b Younis	3	9	10	0
I.D.K. Salisbury	lbw b Younis	5	5	5	1	c Latif b Akram	40	75	58	7
A.D. Mullally	b Younis	0	2	2	0	c sub (*Moin Khan*) b Mushtaq	6	26	18	1
S.J.E. Brown	b Ata-ur-Rehman	1	22	17	0	not out	10	40	27	2

Extras: b9 lb13 w1 nb4 — 27

Total: 285

b6 lb7 nb4 — 17

243

Fall: 27, 107, 107, 116, 180, 260, 264, 269, 269

14, 168, 171, 176, 181, 182, 186, 186, 208

Bowling:

Wasim Akram	22–4–49–1 1nb		Wasim Akram	21.1–5–45–1 4nb
Waqar Younis	24–6–69–4 1nb		Waqar Younis	25–3–85–4 1nb
Mushtaq Ahmed	38–5–92–1		Mushtaq Ahmed	38–15–57–5
Ata-ur-Rehman	15.4–3–50–4 3nb 1w		Ata-ur-Rehman	11–2–33–0 1nb
Aamir Sohail	3–1–3–0		Salim Malik	1–0–1–0
			Shadab Kabir	1–0–9–0

Umpires: S.A. Bucknor (WI) & P. Willey (Eng.). *Third umpire:* J.W. Holder (Eng.). *Referee:* P.L. van der Merwe (SA).
Debuts: S.J.E. Brown (Eng.); Shadab Kabir (Pak.). *Man of the Match:* Waqar Younis

Pakistan won by 164 runs

England v Pakistan
Second Test: Headingley
August 8–12 1996

Batsmen Make Up for Bowlers' Failings

Making their highest total in a Headingley Test, Pakistan dashed England's hopes and expectations of the first morning, when Atherton, winning the toss at last after four losses, put the tourists in under a gloomy sky and in damp conditions. With four seamers and no spinners, he needed to dismiss Pakistan cheaply. They amassed 448.

Crawley, for long the brightest of prospects, came in for the lamentably out-of-form Hick; Lewis returned; and Caddick was called up almost 2½ years since his previous Test (in which Lara made his 375 in Antigua). Pakistan were without Sohail (injured arm).

Ijaz Ahmed, with his third century in four Tests, steered Pakistan to a first-day score of 281 for 6, which left England supporters exasperated at their side's inability to exploit the conditions. The ball deviated little, and the lacklustre Cork was sometimes bowling off a short run-up. Wasim Akram's men batted, on the whole, with great responsibility, none more so than Ijaz and his brother-in-law, Salim Malik. They both employed attacking strokes at every opportunity, having come together soon after lunch at 103 for 3, when English hopes were still eager. Inzamam had just sliced a drive to point. But Ijaz and Malik put on 130 before the centurymaker reached out and slashed once too often. With 20 fours and two sixes, Ijaz was the first to make a century for Pakistan in a Leeds Test. He had been 'caught' when hooking Caddick, but no-ball had been called, and while the catcher, Cork, hurled the ball skywards, the alert batsmen took another run.

Three wickets later in the day restored some balance, Cork bowling the reinvigorated Malik with a dazzling ball, and Caddick's efforts were rewarded. But Lewis bowled too many long-hops.

The attendance was again disappointing on the second day, when the tenacious Mujtaba supported Moin (in for the injured Latif) in a new Pakistan seventh-wicket record against England of 112. Well as Caddick and Mullally bowled, the luck was with Pakistan. Moin (8) was dropped at long leg by Mullally from the eighth ball, and with 10 more to his name he was 'caught' by Stewart off another lofted hook, only for Mullally to have been no-balled (by a matter of perhaps half an inch). The cricket was tedious (100 stand in 198 minutes), but Pakistan knew where they were going. Cork had his right wrist strapped after having collided with a boundary wall on the first day and was clearly a reduced version of the exciting discovery of 1995. Moin lifted his slower ball for six onto the football-stand concourse.

In murky light, Moin reached his third Test hundred – the first by a Pakistan wicketkeeper against England – with a frantic single off the last ball before tea, and then became Russell's 150th dismissal. With Cork retrieving his oscillating display with a fifth wicket, and Caddick's perseverance being rewarded with a third, the innings ended after almost 11 hours. It was England's evening, however, for after Atherton had edged an inswinger, Hussain batted with the footwork of a matador and Stewart's rejuvenation continued, his positioning also near-faultless as he punished Waqar in particular. By the close it was 104 for 1.

The third day brought smiles at last to English faces, for their batsmen forged on to 373 for 5. The start was delayed by an hour, and the outfield was damp. But the Reader ball, chosen by Pakistan, swung unexceptionally, and in improved weather Stewart sealed his comeback with an attractive and patient 170, his eighth Test century, which banished bad memories of lost form linked with acute family anxieties early in the year. Crawley made 53 with pedigree strokeplay, the wristy push to leg prominent, after which Knight, whose injury had set up Stewart's return in June, moved confidently to 51 not out before the dusk closed in. For some it was a mercy, for there had been drunken violence on the Western Terrace, and clashes between English and Asian spectators.

Knight went to his maiden Test century on the Sunday, rain forcing another delayed start. Only when 122 overs had been bowled did Wasim Akram call for the new ball, but Knight took it all in his stride. The 26-year-old left-hander cut Wasim to the boundary for a 154-ball hundred, and then took England into the lead. They had already passed their previous highest against Pakistan on this ground.

Knight's was the eighth wicket to fall, Russell having edged in a lifter, Lewis all at sea against Mushtaq's wrong 'un as the little spinner toiled through 55 overs. Mullally casually hooked Wasim for six, and soon England reached 500, once again their batsmen having made up for the shortcomings of their bowlers.

Poor light and drizzle prevented a start that evening to Pakistan's second innings, but on a sunny fifth day, the ground almost deserted, Ijaz and Inzamam played well after two wickets had been lost for 34. At the start Thorpe had floored an easy catch off Kabir, and Russell's handling seemed distracted. Yet again the ball went out of shape and had to be changed, Inzamam's powerful driving being in part responsible. After he holed out to third man, Malik just had time to become the third Pakistan batsman to make 5000 Test runs before being deceived by Caddick's slower ball, the same bowler claiming Ijaz with one that failed to rise. The drawn match finished lightheartedly, with Thorpe, cap back-to-front, imitating Boycott's bowling action, and Atherton, having a rare bowl, trapping his opposite number for only his second Test wicket, thus relinquishing his claim as England's most expensive bowler (1 for 282). The 'record' reverts to John Warr, who took 1 for 281 in his two Tests in Australia in 1950–51.   ***David Frith***

Graham Chadwick/Allsport

More than the customary degree of emotion shows on Alec Stewart's face as he reaches the comeback century which erased the memory of being dropped from the England XI

SECOND TEST MATCH

Headingley, Leeds

August 8, 9, 10, 11, 12 1996
Toss: England

PAKISTAN

		Mins	Balls	Fours		Mins	Balls	Fours
Saeed Anwar	c Atherton b Mullally	1	12	11	0	c Russell b Cork	22	57	45	3
Shadab Kabir	lbw b Caddick	35	122	90	5	c & b Lewis	2	26	13	0
Ijaz Ahmed	c Russell b Cork	141	279	201	20§	c Russell b Caddick	52	242	150	2
Inzamam-ul-Haq	c Atherton b Mullally	2	11	10	0	c Stewart b Caddick	65	94	83	9
Salim Malik	b Cork	55	193	143	3	c Cork b Caddick	6	18	18	1
Asif Mujtaba	c Thorpe b Cork	51	267	220	4	run out (*Atherton/Thorpe*)	26	68	64	2
*Wasim Akram	c Russell b Caddick	7	17	12	1	lbw b Atherton	7	56	48	0
†Moin Khan	c Russell b Cork	105	282	191	10‡	not out	30	52	52	3
Mushtaq Ahmed	c Atherton b Caddick	20	83	43	2	not out	6	26	27	0
Waqar Younis	c & b Cork	7	11	11	1				
Ata-ur-Rehman	not out	0	4	1	0				

Extras:	b4 lb10 nb10	24		§ plus 2 sixes	b4 lb12 nb10	26	
Total:		448		‡ plus 1 six	7 wkts dec.	242	

Fall: 1, 98, 103, 233, 252, 266, 378, 434, 444   16, 34, 132, 142, 188, 201, 221

Bowling:

Caddick	40.2–6–113–3 *1nb*		Mullally	15–2–43–0 *7nb*
Mullally	41–10–99–2 *5nb*		Lewis	16–3–52–1 *6nb*
Lewis	32–4–100–0 *3nb*		Caddick	17–4–52–3 *1nb*
Cork	37–6–113–5 *5nb*		Cork	16–2–49–1
Thorpe	3–1–9–0		Thorpe	10–3–10–0
			Atherton	7–1–20–1

ENGLAND

		Mins	Balls	Fours
*M.A. Atherton	c Moin b Akram	12	12	13	2
A.J. Stewart	c & b Mushtaq	170	438	315	24
N. Hussain	c & b Younis	48	110	85	5
G.P. Thorpe	c Kabir b Mushtaq	16	82	54	2
J.P. Crawley	c Moin b Ata-ur-Rehman	53	134	115	5
N.V. Knight	c Mushtaq b Younis	113	258	176	16
†R.C. Russell	b Akram	9	73	49	1
C.C. Lewis	b Mushtaq	9	57	41	0
D.G. Cork	c Kabir b Akram	26	86	71	3
A.R. Caddick	b Younis	4	8	5	1
A.D. Mullally	not out	9	45	23	0‡

Extras:	b7 lb23 nb2	32		
Total:		501	‡ plus 1 six	

Fall: 14, 121, 168, 257, 365, 402, 441, 465, 471

Bowling:

Wasim Akram	39.5–10–106–3 *1nb*
Waqar Younis	33–7–127–3 *1nb*
Ata-ur-Rehman	22–1–90–1 *4nb*
Mushtaq Ahmed	55–17–142–3
Asif Mujtaba	7–5–6–0

Umpires: S.A. Bucknor (WI) & D.R. Shepherd (Eng.). *Third umpire:* R. Julian (Eng.). *Referee:* P.L. van der Merwe (SA).
Debuts: none. *Man of the Match:* A.J. Stewart

Match drawn

England v Pakistan
Third Test: The Oval
August 23–26 1996

England's Flat Finish

Pakistan's comprehensive victory at The Oval left England's dreams of revival in ruins. Having used 16 players in the three-match series (and 21 altogether in the six Tests of the summer), they were no nearer to assembling a convincing combination than at the start of the year. By contrast, Pakistan seemed to have no weaknesses in their reservoir of batting and bowling resources. The 2–0 series result was a fair reflection of comparative strengths.

England did salvage two important gains. John Crawley came of age as a Test batsman with his maiden century, and Robert Croft, the Welsh offspinner, brought control and variety to the bowling. The strategy this time was to omit Russell and charge Stewart again with the responsibility of opening the batting and keeping wicket. Less comprehensible was the omission of Caddick, who was probably England's best bowler at Leeds. Pakistan could afford to leave out offspinner Saqlain, who was having success against the counties.

After a torrid new-ball onslaught, Stewart misjudged a ball from Mushtaq in his first over, while Hussain played hesitantly at a rising ball from Waqar and edged. Atherton batted through the first session (100 for 2) for 27, but was soon bowled round his pads, and Thorpe was joined by Crawley. Their stand of 89 was full of enchanting strokes, but it was less than was needed. Pinned in front by Mohammad Akram as he played to leg, Thorpe had now registered 18 half-centuries in his 58 Test innings but only two hundreds.

Knight was bowled off his glove from one that Mushtaq managed to get to kick, and Lewis pottered about for 40 balls for his 5, while Crawley stroked confidently on past his previous Test-best of 72, finishing on 94. But from 278 for 6 overnight, England faded to 326 all out, Wasim and Waqar taking the wickets. Crawley duly moved to his maiden Test century with an all-run four, having batted for 4¼ hours, during which his driving and cutting were delights to the eye. He finally fell playing back to one which kept low. Mullally's old-fashioned slogging produced useful runs, but by tea (there had been no play before lunch because of rain) Pakistan's openers had already made 62 against an undemanding array of bowlers.

Aamir Sohail notched his 2000th Test run before becoming Croft's first Test wicket, driving a curling delivery to cover, and soon there was a distracting novelty as a no-ball was called when three fielders were seen behind square leg; the fact that Lewis's front foot was also over the popping crease remained undetected by umpire Cooray. The 200 appeared in only 192 minutes, and Saeed Anwar's third Test hundred came from only 135 balls, almost all of which he dealt with confidently and stylishly. When play ended at 7.28 pm, Pakistan were only 97 behind with nine wickets in hand.

Ijaz, 58 overnight, soon got a thin edge to Mullally, and with Croft bowling a tight line, it was 44 minutes before the first boundary. Legspinner Salisbury, in turn, bowled disastrously loosely, and the score moved to 334 after lunch, at which point Inzamam fell into the trap set for his pull shot and Anwar's admirable 176 closed with a mis-hit pull off Cork. Then came the rain, and only 10 more balls could be bowled that evening, leaving Pakistan 13 ahead with six wickets in hand. Over 80 overs had been lost on the first three days.

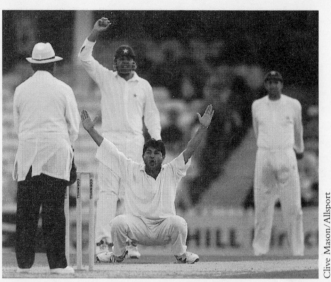

Chris Lewis, who was having a wretched match, arrived late for the fourth day, and the management censured him by omitting him from the forthcoming one-day series. And England's miseries were extended. Past 500 cruised Pakistan, Salim Malik moving methodically to his first Test hundred since the rumours of corruption had swirled around his head. Salisbury bowled Moin with a googly, but missed a high return catch from Waqar, and as Malik hooked a single for his century and carried on running to the dressing-room upon the instantaneous declaration, England were faced with a deficit of 195 and a day plus 95 minutes to survive. Atherton and Stewart made a courageous 74 that evening, the latter having kept wicket for 11 hours, and umpire Kitchen interrupted Wasim's wicked spell with a warning for intimidation.

The fifth-day situation was similar to that at Lord's, when abject collapse followed the dismissals of Atherton and Stewart. The only difference this time was that Hussain also made runs. But nobody made enough. Mushtaq Ahmed spun and dipped the ball, probing patiently, reacting feverishly to every near-miss. His reward unfolded before lunch with the wickets of both openers, caught off bat and pad, and the first three after lunch, Thorpe off an undetected 'wrong-one', Hussain rather unfortunately as he stretched well forward and padded away, and Knight with an infuriating return pat off a full-toss. Hussain looked good, his strokeplay decisive and his spirit undiminished as he dodged and parried Wasim's furious short deliveries.

England's summer of frustration continued to be a mix of poor cricket and poor luck: Crawley spliced a bouncer to silly point, the ball having been bowled when the bowler's front foot was just over the line. This was just before tea (227 for 7), leaving Wasim Akram with 298 Test wickets and three more to fall ... two after Cork had driven over a ball from Mushtaq, the leggie's sixth wicket of the innings.

Pakistan's captain was unstoppable, however, and Croft saved his facial features at the cost of his wicket, and Mullally swung across the next ball, a yorker, which flattened his wicket to elevate Wasim as the 11th in the list of those who have taken 300 Test wickets. It happened on the same ground that saw the first such instance: Hawke c Cowdrey b Trueman in 1964. The Pakistani, the first left-arm bowler to enter the list, fell to his knees in thanksgiving, and less than an hour later he was proudly taking the plaudits for a nine-wicket victory and a 2–0 series triumph.

The Oval gas-holders were flat, symbolic of England's spirits and of Ray Illingworth's. His stormy reign as 'supremo' was now ended, but there was no obvious end in view of the sorry state of England's Test performances.
                                                                                        David Frith

Mushtaq Ahmed, who spun out 17 batsmen in the three-match series, implores umpire Cooray to grant him an lbw at The Oval

THIRD TEST MATCH

The Oval

August 22, 23, 24, 25, 26 1996

Toss: England

ENGLAND

		Mins	Balls	Fours		Mins	Balls	Fours
*M.A. Atherton	b Younis	31	131	77	5	c Inzamam b Mushtaq	43	192	144	5
†A.J. Stewart	b Mushtaq	44	74	51	9	c Mujtaba b Mushtaq	54	139	100	7
N. Hussain	c Anwar b Younis	12	28	25	1	lbw b Mushtaq	51	115	96	8
G.P. Thorpe	lbw b Mohammad Akram	54	124	95	8	c Wasim b Mushtaq	9	39	24	0
J.P. Crawley	b Younis	106	257	217	12	c Sohail b Wasim	19	95	58	2
N.V. Knight	b Mushtaq	17	68	45	0‡	c & b Mushtaq	8	19	17	2
C.C. Lewis	b Wasim	5	44	40	0	lbw b Younis	4	33	22	0
I.D.K. Salisbury	c Inzamam b Wasim	5	29	21	0	(10) not out	0	5	0	0
D.G. Cork	c Moin b Younis	0	6	5	0	(8) b Mushtaq	26	40	33	6
R.D.B. Croft	not out	5	32	18	0	(9) c Ijaz b Wasim	6	23	16	1
A.D. Mullally	b Wasim	24	21	12	5	b Wasim	0	2	1	0

Extras:	lb12 w1 nb10	23			b6 lb2 w1 nb13	22	
Total:		326	‡ plus 1 six			242	

Fall: 64, 85, 116, 205, 248, 273, 283, 284, 295

96, 136, 166, 179, 187, 205, 220, 238, 242

Bowling:

Wasim Akram	29.2–9–83–3 *8nb*	Wasim Akram	15.4–1–67–3 *14nb*
Waqar Younis	25–6–95–4	Waqar Younis	18–3–55–1 *1w*
Mohammad Akram	12–1–41–1 *2nb 1w*	Mushtaq Ahmed	37–10–78–6
Mushtaq Ahmed	27–5–78–2	Aamir Sohail	2–1–4–0
Aamir Sohail	6–1–17–0	Mohammad Akram	10–3–30–0 *1nb*

PAKISTAN

		Mins	Balls	Fours		Mins	Balls	Fours
Saeed Anwar	c Croft b Cork	176	378	264	26	c Knight b Mullally	1	9	8	0
Aamir Sohail	c Cork b Croft	46	93	78	7	not out	29	32	18	5
Ijaz Ahmed	c Stewart b Mullally	61	166	136	9	not out	13	22	20	1
Inzamam-ul-Haq	c Hussain b Mullally	35	113	80	3				
Salim Malik	not out	100	290	223	10				
Asif Mujtaba	run out (*Lewis/Stewart*)	13	67	44	1				
*Wasim Akram	st Stewart b Croft	40	115	81	4‡				
†Moin Khan	b Salisbury	23	72	46	2				
Mushtaq Ahmed	c Crawley b Mullally	2	24	18	0				
Waqar Younis	not out	0	6	6	0				
Mohammad Akram	did not bat	—						

Extras:	b4 lb5 nb16	25			nb5	5	
Total:	8 wkts dec.	521	‡ plus 1 six		1 wkt	48	

Fall: 106, 239, 334, 334, 365, 440, 502, 519

7

Bowling:

Lewis	23–3–112–0 *6nb*	Cork	3–0–15–0 *4nb*
Mullally	37.1–7–97–3 *7nb*	Mullally	3–0–24–1 *2nb*
Croft	47–10–116–2	Croft	0.4–0–9–0
Cork	23–5–71–1 *8nb*		
Salisbury	29–3–116–1		

Umpires: B.C. Cooray (SL) & M.J. Kitchen (Eng.). *Third umpire:* J.C. Balderstone (Eng.). *Referee:* P.L. van der Merwe (SA).
Debut: R.D.B. Croft (Eng.). *Man of the Match:* Mushtaq Ahmed. *Man of the Series:* A.J. Stewart (Eng.); Mushtaq Ahmed (Pak.).

Pakistan won by 9 wickets

SERIES AVERAGES

ENGLAND

Batting:

	M	I	NO	R	HS	Av.	100	50	Ct/st
A.J. Stewart	3	5	0	396	170	79.20	1	2	2/1
J.P. Crawley	2	3	0	178	106	59.33	1	1	1
N.V. Knight	3	5	0	190	113	38.00	1	1	1
N. Hussain	2	3	0	111	51	37.00	0	1	1
M.A. Atherton	3	5	0	162	64	32.40	0	1	3
G.P. Thorpe	3	5	0	159	77	31.80	0	2	2
R.C. Russell	2	3	1	51	41*	25.50	0	0	9
I.D.K. Salisbury	2	4	1	50	40	16.67	0	0	0
M.A. Ealham	1	2	0	30	25	15.00	0	0	1
D.G. Cork	3	5	0	58	26	11.60	0	0	3
S.J.E. Brown	1	2	1	11	10*	11.00	0	0	1
R.D.B. Croft	1	2	1	11	6	11.00	0	0	1
A.D. Mullally	3	5	1	39	24	9.75	0	0	0
C.C. Lewis	2	3	0	18	9	6.00	0	0	1
G.A. Hick	1	2	0	8	4	4.00	0	0	1
A.R. Caddick	1	1	0	4	4	4.00	0	0	0

Bowling:

	O	M	R	W	Av.	BB	5w/i
M.A. Atherton	7	1	20	1	20.00	1–20	0
A.R. Caddick	57.2	10	165	6	27.50	3–52	0
D.G. Cork	131	23	434	12	36.17	5–113	1
A.D. Mullally	150.3	36	377	10	37.70	3–44	0
G.A. Hick	13	2	42	1	42.00	1–26	0
R.D.B. Croft	47.4	10	125	2	62.50	2–116	0
S.J.E. Brown	33	4	138	2	69.00	1–60	0
M.A. Ealham	37	8	81	1	81.00	1–42	0
I.D.K. Salisbury	61.2	8	221	2	110.50	1–42	0
C.C. Lewis	71	10	264	1	264.00	1–52	0
G.P. Thorpe	13	4	19	0	–	–	0

PAKISTAN

Batting:

	M	I	NO	R	HS	Av.	100	50	Ct/st
Moin Khan	2	3	1	158	105	79.00	1	0	3
Ijaz Ahmed	3	6	1	344	141	68.80	1	3	1
Salim Malik	3	5	2	195	100*	65.00	1	1	0
Inzamam-ul-Haq	3	5	0	320	148	64.00	1	2	2
Saeed Anwar	3	6	0	362	176	60.33	1	2	2
Rashid Latif	1	1	0	45	45	45.00	0	0	3
Aamir Sohail	2	3	1	77	46	38.50	0	0	1
Asif Mujtaba	2	3	0	90	51	30.00	0	1	1
Wasim Akram	3	5	1	98	40	24.50	0	0	1
Shadab Kabir	2	4	0	87	35	21.75	0	0	2
Mushtaq Ahmed	3	5	1	44	20	11.00	0	0	3
Waqar Younis	3	3	1	11	7	5.50	0	0	1
Ata-ur-Rehman	2	2	2	10	10*	–	0	0	0
Mohammad Akram	1	0	0	0	–	–	0	0	0

Substitute catches were held by Moin Khan (2) and Asif Mujtaba (1)

Bowling:

	O	M	R	W	Av.	BB	5w/i
Mushtaq Ahmed	195	52	447	17	26.29	6–78	2
Waqar Younis	125	25	431	16	26.94	4–69	0
Wasim Akram	128	29	350	11	31.82	3–67	0
Ata-ur-Rehman	48.4	6	173	5	34.60	4–50	0
Mohammad Akram	22	4	71	1	71.00	1–41	0
Salim Malik	1	0	1	0	–	–	0
Asif Mujtaba	7	5	6	0	–	–	0
Shadab Kabir	1	0	9	0	–	–	0
Aamir Sohail	11	3	24	0	–	–	0

Sri Lanka v Zimbabwe

First Test: Colombo

September 11–14 1996

Sri Lanka's Crushing Victory

Having held their own in the three drawn home Tests against Sri Lanka two years previously, Zimbabwe now found themselves struggling on the spin-responsive pitches of the island of Serendipity. The visitors also bore the considerable handicap of being without their best batsman Dave Houghton, who was detained by his coaching duties with Worcestershire. In the 1994–95 series against Sri Lanka, Houghton had made scores of 266 at Bulawayo and 142 at Harare.

Twelve days short of his 24th birthday, Alistair Campbell, who scored 99 the last time these two countries met, took over as captain (Andy Flower having stood down after the World Cup), while Arjuna Ranatunga remained Sri Lanka's leader despite having floated doubts about his continuation after his side's sensational World Cup triumph in March 1996.

The skipper was chiefly responsible for salvaging his side on the opening day, mounting a record Sri Lanka sixth-wicket stand of 142 with Kaluwitharana after pacemen Olonga and Streak and leg-spinner Strang had reduced Sri Lanka to 128 for 5. Gurusinha had threatened to make a telling score, but the two middle-order batsmen, with their seventies, ensured a decent total, though both were dismissed by Streak before the close of the first day. Dharmasena and Vaas put on a vital 74 for the eighth wicket (another Sri Lanka record), which frustrated the Zimbabweans acutely before Strang brought some cheer by wrapping up the innings with three wickets in four balls, a comparatively rare feat in Test cricket.

Vaas, the left-arm medium-fast bowler, then tore the top off the Zimbabwe reply, having Grant Flower caught behind in the first over, trapping Dekker and having Campbell caught. This took him past 50 Test wickets. Offcutter Dharmasena accounted for Andy Flower, and after a stand by Guy Whittall and Craig Wishart, who made a gritty maiden Test half-century, wickets toppled, three going to young slow left-armer K. J. (Jayantha) Silva, whose match figures make remarkable reading.

By the end of the third day, which was severely curtailed (26.5 overs) by poor weather, Zimbabwe, having followed on 204 in arrears, were 20 without loss, but the quality of the surface, with Sri Lanka's spin battalion in mind, did not augur well for the tourists. Sure enough, another collapse took place, the three main spinners taking all 10 wickets, half of them to Muralitharan, who put his no-balling for throwing in Australia triumphantly behind him by returning his best figures in Test cricket. Mahanama held four catches at slip, and the downcast Zimbabweans were left to contemplate a scoreboard showing 127, their lowest total in their 17 Tests to date, seven below their score when they were 'Waqared' in Karachi three years previously. Sri Lanka, on the other hand, were left to celebrate their first-ever victory by an innings. ***TMY***

FIRST TEST MATCH

Premadasa Stadium, Colombo

September 11, 12, 13, 14 1996

Toss: Sri Lanka

SRI LANKA

		Mins	Balls	Fours
R.S. Mahanama	lbw b Streak	4	4	6	1
S.T. Jayasuriya	c Evans b Olonga	0	6	1	0
A.P. Gurusinha	c Olonga b Strang	52	197	139	6
P.A. de Silva	b Strang	35	53	44	6
H.P. Tillekeratne	c A. Flower b Olonga	20	101	86	2
*A. Ranatunga	lbw b Streak	75	192	120	7
†R.S. Kaluwitharana	c & b Streak	71	155	123	10
H.D.P.K. Dharmasena	not out	42	99	78	4
W.P.U.J.C. Vaas	b Strang	34	88	46	2
M. Muralitharan	b Strang	0	5	1	0
K.J. Silva	c & b Strang	0	1	2	0

Extras: lb6 w1 nb9   16
Total: 349

Fall: 4, 4, 53, 105, 128, 270, 271, 345, 349

Bowling:
Streak   20–6–54–3 *2w*
Olonga   17–3–57–2 *5nb*
G.J. Whittall   12–1–43–0 *3nb*
Strang   34.3–3–106–5
A.R. Whittall   13–3–40–0
Evans   6–0–27–0
G.W. Flower   4–1–16–0

Shaun Botterill/Allsport

ZIMBABWE

		Mins	Balls	Fours		Mins	Balls	Fours
G.W. Flower	c Kaluwitharana b Vaas	0	1	1	0	b Muralitharan	27	112	86	1
M.H. Dekker	lbw b Vaas	10	70	49	0	c Jayasuriya b Dharmasena	20	58	60	1
*A.D.R. Campbell	c Mahanama b Vaas	12	19	15	2	(4) c Mahanama b Muralitharan	26	133	126	0
†A. Flower	c Ranatunga b Dharmasena	2	16	14	0	(5) c Mahanama b Muralitharan	0	1	1	0
G.J. Whittall	lbw b Silva	39	152	125	4	(6) c Mahanama b Silva	13	83	86	0
C.B. Wishart	c Vaas b Silva	51	205	157	2‡	(3) b Silva	3	21	20	0
H.K. Olonga	c Tillekeratne b Muralitharan	1	10	10	0	(9) c Mahanama b Silva	0	2	3	0
C.N. Evans	c Kaluwitharana b Vaas	9	20	17	1	(7) lbw b Silva	1	6	8	0
P.A. Strang	b Muralitharan	6	17	14	1	(8) c Vaas b Muralitharan	8	23	18	1
A.R. Whittall	c Dharmasena b Silva	1	40	30	0	b Muralitharan	11	30	29	1
H.H. Streak	not out	0	1	0	0	not out	3	15	9	0

Extras: b4 lb4 w2 nb4   14   b6 lb4 w1 nb4   15
Total: 145   ‡ plus 1 six   127

Fall: 0, 15, 21, 45, 103, 105, 123, 138, 145   35, 42, 65, 65, 98, 99, 102, 102, 113

Bowling:
Vaas   22–3–73–4   Vaas   12–1–34–0
Gurusinha   3–1–3–0 *2w*   Gurusinha   2–0–4–0 *1w*
Dharmasena   9–3–23–1   de Silva   2–1–1–0
Muralitharan   24–9–28–2 *4nb*   Dharmasena   14–7–19–1
Silva   14.4–9–10–3   Muralitharan   20.3–4–33–5 *3nb*
     Silva   19–12–25–4 *1nb*
     Jayasuriya   4–3–1–0

Umpires: S.A. Bucknor (WI) & B.C. Cooray (SL). *Third umpire:* K.T. Francis (SL). *Referee:* J.R. Reid (NZ).
Debuts: C.N. Evans, A.R. Whittall (Zim.). *Man of the Match:* A. Ranatunga

Sri Lanka won by an innings and 77 runs

Muralitharan, of the idiosyncratic arm action, spun out seven wickets in Sri Lanka's huge first-Test win over Zimbabwe

Sri Lanka v Zimbabwe

Second Test: Colombo

September 18–21 1996

Colombo the Spinner's Delight

Sri Lanka retained their ascendancy, winning again inside four days, their spinners once more the agents of destruction, taking 15 of Zimbabwe's wickets. The visitors collapsed dramatically on the rain-interrupted first day, having reached 119 for 2 before losing their last eight wickets for 22 runs, to Muralitharan's offspin, Silva's slow left-arm and a run-out. Captain Campbell (36) had doubled the score in a third-wicket partnership with Grant Flower, but then danced out to Silva and was stumped. That triggered the cascade of wickets. Flower, the opener, managed 52, resisting for almost three hours, but the rest of the batsmen, one by one, found their apprehension justified as they gazed at the bare surface upon which Sri Lanka's slow bowlers operated. Wishart had special cause for disappointment at his caught-behind verdict.

Zimbabwe came back into the match after the tea-break, taking three wickets for 86 before rain put a stop to proceedings when 13 overs remained to be bowled, Paul Strang claiming Jayasuriya, who had raced to 41 from 46 balls, and Aravinda de Silva, caught-and-bowled. But Gurusinha and fellow left-hander Tillekeratne seized the initiative on the second day after the early loss of Ranatunga. They added 114, Gurusinha's 88 spreading across almost five hours, and Tillekeratne's first home Test century (to add to his four overseas) spanning 5½ hours. His unbeaten 126 was the highest of his five hundreds. The lower order pushed the total to just over 200 ahead of Zimbabwe before Ranatunga declared before lunch on the third day, and by close of play they were close to victory, with Zimbabwe 162 for 6.

Ali Shah, now 37 and absent from the Test side for 3½ years, saved his team from total ignominy with a dogged 62 not out (he was out first thing next morning), occupying the middle for not far short of five hours. Entering at 9 for 1, he saw the Sri Lankan spinners weave more spells around the Zimbabweans while he himself ground out a maiden Test half-century. Paul Strang also recorded his first Test fifty, bringing some late defiance to a sad scorecard for Test cricket's newest contestants. It at least averted the innings defeat, though Sri Lanka's 10-wicket victory was not long in being sealed. The island's spinners would have tested superior opposition to this, and the two-match returns of Muralitharan (14 for 195 off 105.3 overs) and Silva (13 for 100 off 69.4 overs) were startling.

Attendances at both these Test matches were meagre, the daily gate averaging barely 2000.

Zimbabwe had lacked the services of Heath Streak, who was nursing a groin injury. His replacement, left-arm seamer Bryan Strang, strengthened the family element in the team, with brother Paul playing, as well as the Flower brothers and the Whittall cousins (Andy, the offspinner, having captained Cambridge University).　　　　　　　　　　　　　　　　　　　　　　　　　*TMY*

SECOND TEST MATCH

Sinhalese Sports Club, Colombo

September 18, 19, 20, 21 1996

Toss: Zimbabwe

ZIMBABWE

		Mins	Balls	Fours		Mins	Balls	Fours
G.W. Flower	c Mahanama b Muralitharan	52	180	117	6	lbw b Silva	13	71	45	1
M.H. Dekker	c Mahanama b Muralitharan	18	56	38	1	lbw b Vaas	4	20	14	0
A.H. Shah	c Kaluwitharana b Pushpakumara	1	23	20	0	c Vaas b Pushpakumara	62	294	261	5
*A.D.R. Campbell	st Kaluwitharana b Silva	36	92	83	3	c sub (*M.S. Atapattu*) b Silva	4	10	11	0
†A. Flower	run out (*Pushpakumara*)	3	19	15	0	c Gurusinha b Muralitharan	31	102	93	4
C.B. Wishart	c Kaluwitharana b Silva	2	23	11	0	c Kaluwitharana b Jayasuriya	25	68	58	2
G.J. Whittall	c Silva b Muralitharan	0	5	3	0	c Gurusinha b Jayasuriya	3	18	10	0
P.A. Strang	not out	2	32	22	0	(9) c & b Vaas	50	107	94	5
A.R. Whittall	c Gurusinha b Muralitharan	3	11	7	0	(8) b Muralitharan	12	89	53	1
B.C. Strang	c de Silva b Silva	3	6	3	0	b Muralitharan	2	17	16	0
H.K. Olonga	c Mahanama b Silva	3	8	7	0	not out	3	49	36	0
Extras:	b3 lb10 nb5	18				b2 lb6 w1 nb17	26		
Total:		141					235		

Fall: 44, 54, 119, 121, 123, 125, 126, 133, 136   9, 30, 34, 91, 135, 144, 167, 193, 201

Bowling:

Vaas	10–1–31–0	Vaas	26.3–11–34–2
Pushpakumara	11–3–34–1	Pushpakumara	8–0–24–1 *1nb*
Muralitharan	20–5–40–4 *4nb*	Muralitharan	41–9–94–3 *11nb 1w*
Silva	10–4–16–4	Silva	26–7–49–2 *2nb*
de Silva	2–0–7–0 *1nb*	de Silva	5–1–10–0 *3nb*
		Jayasuriya	7–3–16–2

SRI LANKA

		Mins	Balls	Fours		Mins	Balls	Fours
R.S. Mahanama	c A. Flower b B.C. Strang	3	20	11	0	(2) not out	12	28	25	1
S.T. Jayasuriya	c A.R. Whittall b P.A. Strang	41	61	46	6‡	(1) not out	18	28	15	3
A.P. Gurusinha	c Wishart b B.C. Strang	88	294	239	8‡				
P.A. de Silva	c & b P.A. Strang	16	33	25	1‡				
*A. Ranatunga	c Wishart b B.C. Strang	6	38	21	0				
H.P. Tillekeratne	not out	126	409	326	13				
†R.S. Kaluwitharana	c A. Flower b G.J. Whittall	27	86	56	2				
W.P.U.J.C. Vaas	st A. Flower b P.A. Strang	8	12	6	0				
K.R. Pushpakumara	c B.C. Strang b P.A. Strang	23	112	79	3				
M. Muralitharan	not out	1	15	6	0				
K.J. Silva	did not bat	—							
Extras:	lb4 w3 nb4	11					0		
Total:		8 wkts dec. 350			‡ plus 1 six	0 wkt 30		

Fall: 19, 58, 86, 102, 216, 267, 276, 340

Bowling:

Olonga	26–6–81–0 *1w 3nb*	Olonga	3.4–0–17–0
B.C. Strang	20–6–63–3 *1nb*	P.A. Strang	3–0–13–0
A.R. Whittall	31–7–75–0		
P.A. Strang	38–11–66–4		
G.J. Whittall	17–4–48–1 *2w*		
G.W. Flower	2–0–13–0		

Umpires: K.T. Francis (SL) & C.J. Mitchley (SA).
Third umpire: B.C. Cooray (SL).
Referee: J.R. Reid (NZ).
Man of the Match: H.P. Tillekeratne.
Man of the Series: M. Muralitharan

Sri Lanka won by 10 wickets

With his fifth Test century, Tillekeratne helped set
up another sizable home victory over Zimbabwe

Allsport

India v Australia
New Delhi
October 10–13 1996

India Cash In on the Absence of You-Know-Who

The course of the first Test to be played for the Border–Gavaskar Trophy may have been dictated well before the start. The absence of a key player from each side was to prove crucial. Australia were missing legspinner Shane Warne, who had failed a late fitness test after an operation on his sore spinning finger, and for India opener Sidhu was out on disciplinary grounds, having walked out of the tour of England. The only current batsman with a plus-40 average in both Tests and one-day internationals, Sidhu was serving a 50-day ban imposed by the Indian Board.

The Ferozeshah Kotla ground was staging its first Test in just over three years. The pitch was a typical Indian dustbowl (later described by Bishan Bedi as unsuitable for Test cricket), sure to take spin from the first day, and Australian skipper Mark Taylor was to rue the absence of his star spinner Warne. Neither Peter McIntyre nor Brad Hogg was in the same league as the Indian trio of Anil Kumble, Sunil Joshi and Aashish Kapoor. With India having bowlers better suited to the conditions, the match was over by the fourth afternoon, India securing their first victory over Australia for 15 years.

But though Kumble captured nine wickets in the match, it was wicketkeeper Nayan Mongia who made the vital difference between the two sides. Drafted in as opener in the series in England after Sidhu's withdrawal, Mongia was asked to fill that role for one more match, with the Indian selectors unable to find a specialist opener. He paid back their faith, emerging as easily the top scorer in the Test with a determined 152, over eight hours of grind and application on a pitch that troubled all the batsmen.

Once Australia were shot out for 182, the pundits were already beginning to predict an Indian victory by the third day. Taylor did not have much choice but to bat first after winning the toss. It was the first Test for both coaches, Geoff Marsh, who had taken over from Bobby Simpson, and India's Madan Lal, after the removal of Sandeep Patil. It also marked Sachin Tendulkar's first Test as captain, ending a run of 36 Tests as leader by Azharuddin. With pace bowler Javagal Srinath pulling out with a sore shoulder, India blooded his Karnataka team-mate David Johnson. Johnson is coached by Roger Binny, the only other Anglo-Indian to have played Test cricket for India. Five of the playing XI were from the southern state, who are currently both Ranji and Irani Cup champions.

Slater and Taylor made a confident 47 for the opening wicket before the skipper shouldered arms to one from Vankatesh Prasad and was adjudged leg-before. It was to be the only wicket to fall to a pace bowler in the innings. Once the spinners were introduced into the attack it seemed only a matter of time before the batting folded up in what has become a familiar sight to Indian fans fed on a steady diet of home wins and away defeats. Top-scorer Slater, the first of Kumble's four victims, hit a return catch to the legspinner, and thereafter there was nothing the hapless Aussies could do to stop the procession. India finished the day on 57 for 1 in reply as opener Vikram Rathore continued his miserable Test run which began on the England tour.

The second day was dominated by Mongia as he became the fifth Indian wicketkeeper to reach three figures in Tests. But it was the left-handed Sourav Ganguly who sparkled in their second-wicket stand of 131. Ganguly, who had scored centuries against England in each of his first two Tests, was looking to emu-late the feat of former captain Moham-mad Azharuddin, who had scored three centuries in his first three Tests against the visiting England team in 1984–85. Ganguly struck 10 fours and a six in an innings full of charming strokes. But after being softened up by a few short ones from Glenn McGrath, Ganguly gifted his wicket to debutant left-arm spinner Hogg. There was a mini-collapse as Tendulkar and Azharuddin fell cheaply, and at 199 for 4 the Aussies' hopes were briefly raised.

But Mongia was grinding his way to a maiden international century (5½ hours) at the other end, totally unflustered by everything the bowlers could conjure up.

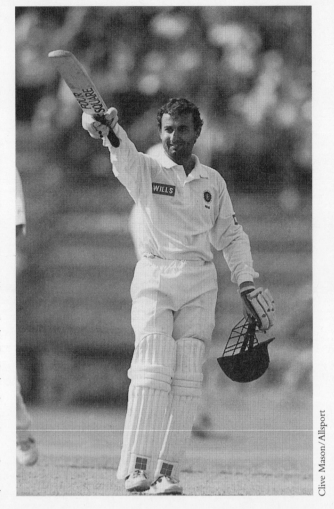

Clive Mason/Allsport

And he found an able partner in the stylish Rahul Dravid (caught brilliantly left-handed by Healy) as the pair batted their opponents out of the match. By the end of the second day, India had taken a lead of 137 with four wickets in hand and Mongia was still there on 137. One of the most popu-lar players in the Indian side, he insisted that he had an intuition that he would score a century here. Dropped briefly from the team on disciplinary grounds after a notoriously slow innings in a one-day match against West Indies in 1994, the 27-year-old from Baroda was now fully rehabilitated.

The first-innings lead was extended to 179 on the third morning, but Mongia's desire to carry his bat through the innings was not fulfilled. He was bowled by Reiffel. But he had done his job, and Australia were still 11 runs short of forcing India to bat again by the close as they limped to 168 for 6.

The visitors, with so little recent cricket behind them, reserved their fighting best for what would turn out to be the last day of a very disappointing Test for them, but it was too little, too late. Steve Waugh, the only batsman in the team with previous Test experience in India, hung on grimly for over 4½ hours for an unbeaten 67. Prasad chipped in with three wickets, though it was once again Kumble who did the major damage with five wickets, only fuelling the speculation as to what Warne might have achieved on this pitch. The Indians made heavy weather of reaching the victory target, but 56 runs was just too little to play with.   ***Gulu Ezekiel***

Nayan Mongia acknowledges the applause that greeted his century that helped seal victory over Australia at Delhi

ONLY TEST MATCH

Ferozeshah Kotla, Delhi

October 10, 11, 12, 13 1996

Toss: Australia

AUSTRALIA

		Mins	Balls	Fours			Mins	Balls	Fours
M.J. Slater	c & b Kumble	44	130	96	6	(2) c Azharuddin b Johnson	0	7	2	0
*M.A. Taylor	lbw b Prasad	27	72	51	4	(1) c Rathore b Kapoor	37	149	112	4
R.T. Ponting	b Kapoor	14	47	48	1	b Prasad	13	44	37	2
M.E. Waugh	c Dravid b Joshi	26	87	59	4	c Mongia b Kumble	23	80	56	4
S.R. Waugh	c Mongia b Kapoor	0	4	5	0	not out	67	273	221	5
M.G. Bevan	lbw b Joshi	26	63	57	3	c Azharuddin b Kumble	33	93	70	5
†I.A. Healy	b Kumble	17	58	43	3	st Mongia b Kumble	12	11	14	3
G.B. Hogg	c Rathore b Kumble	1	17	12	0	c Rathore b Kumble	4	31	29	0
P.R. Reiffel	c Dravid b Kumble	7	26	32	1	lbw b Kumble	6	37	39	0
P.E. McIntyre	not out	6	16	21	1	lbw b Prasad	16	73	62	2
G.D. McGrath	run out (*Prasad/Mongia*)	6	10	6	1	c Mongia b Prasad	0	7	8	0

Extras: b4 lb3 nb1   8

Total: 182

Extras: b9 lb6 w1 nb7   23

Total: 234

Fall: 47, 81, 93, 94, 143, 144, 147, 169, 170

4, 25, 72, 78, 145, 159, 171, 191, 232

Bowling:

Prasad	12–4–34–1	Prasad	13.3–7–18–3	
Johnson	4–1–12–0	Johnson	12–2–40–1 1w	
Joshi	23–7–36–2	Kumble	41–12–67–5 7nb	
Kumble	24–7–63–4 1nb	Joshi	20–7–52–0	
Kapoor	10–3–30–2	Kapoor	22–5–42–1 2nb	

INDIA

		Mins	Balls	Fours		Mins	Balls	Fours
V.S. Rathore	c Ponting b Reiffel	5	34	29	0	b Reiffel	14	35	28	3
†N.R. Mongia	b Reiffel	152	497	365	18‡	lbw b Reiffel	0	8	6	0
S.C. Ganguly	c M.E. Waugh b Hogg	66	190	152	10‡	not out	21	56	29	3
*S.R. Tendulkar	c M.E. Waugh b McIntyre	10	12	11	2	b McGrath	0	6	7	0
M. Azharuddin	b McGrath	17	41	41	3	not out	21	22	12	5
R.S. Dravid	c Healy b S.R. Waugh	40	65	64	5				
S.B. Joshi	c Ponting b McIntyre	23	71	42	2‡				
A.R. Kapoor	c Ponting b M.E. Waugh	22	49	44	2				
A. Kumble	lbw b Reiffel	2	37	25	0				
D. Johnson	not out	0	21	13	0				
B.K.V. Prasad	b McIntyre	3	11	7	0				

Extras: b10 lb1 nb10   21

Total: 361   ‡ plus 1 six

Extras: w1 nb1   2

Total: 3 wkts 58

Fall: 13, 144, 169, 199, 260, 303, 341, 353, 354

1, 25, 26

Bowling:

McGrath	29–10–56–1 8nb	McGrath	7–2–30–1 2nb
Reiffel	17–7–35–3	Reiffel	6–2–24–2 1nb 1w
S.R. Waugh	13–5–25–1 1nb	McIntyre	0.2–0–4–0
McIntyre	37.4–7–103–3		
Hogg	17–3–69–1 1nb		
M.E. Waugh	18–0–62–1		

Umpires: S. Venkataraghavan (Ind.) & P. Willey (Eng.). *Third umpire:* S.K. Bansal (Ind.). *Referee:* J.R. Reid (NZ).
Debuts: D. Johnson (Ind.); G.B. Hogg (Aus.). *Man of the Match:* N.R. Mongia.

India won by 7 wickets

Pakistan v Zimbabwe

First Test: Sheikhupura

October 17–21 1996

Old Records Tumble at New Ground

Test cricket's newest ground, Sheikhupura, not far from Lahore, was given a spectacular baptism. The 77th venue to host a Test, and Pakistan's 16th (only India has had more with 19), the stadium, with its grassless pitch, saw a conspicuous allround performance by a Zimbabwean and a record-breaking innings by Pakistan's captain. It mattered little in the end that there was no outright result. Both sides had played strong cricket.

Their attack lacking Mushtaq Ahmed, Pakistan still made early inroads into Zimbabwe's batting line-up, now reinforced by the return of Houghton. For once, Wasim and Waqar went wicketless, apart from the left-armer's early dismissal of Dekker, one of five lbw decisions in the innings. Wasim did have Grant Flower missed by Moin at 39, a costly error as the opener was still there at the close, on 98 not out, a reward for patience and also judgment in coolly evading Wasim's many testing bouncers.

Flower hit Sohail for six wide of long-off, and the 39-year-old Houghton helped himself to two sixes off Saqlain before misjudging a run and paying the penalty. Shahid Nazir, 19, who ran him out, took a wicket with his fourth ball in Test cricket, then two more with consecutive balls, all lbw. He swung the ball more than his seniors, for when the Grays ball went out of shape (twice) the only replacements were fairly new ones used by Zimbabwe at the nets. For once, reverse swing was no great factor.

Play was interrupted twice when spectators hurled stones onto the field in protest at the exclusion of Aaqib Javed.

From the dire scoreline of 142 for 6, Flower and Paul Strang displayed great resolution, the No.8 finishing 37 not out off 121 balls. Next morning, after six hours' batting, Flower duly completed his second Test century (the other was 201 not out against the same opponents), but fell to Saqlain when the stand was worth 131. Andy Whittall quickly followed. But the Strang brothers now resisted, frustrating Pakistan with a Zimbabwe ninth-wicket record stand of 87. When brother Bryan left him, Paul was 99 not out. Olonga held out for the remaining three balls, however, and Strang reached his maiden first-class century (290 minutes), having enjoyed let-offs at 22, 45 and 72.

Nor was his day done, for by the end he had 4 for 58, three of them key wickets, as Pakistan (missing Inzamam, who was nursing a leg injury) wobbled at 189 for 6 in reply to Zimbabwe's 375. The cracked pitch was taking spin, and the legbreak/googly bowler approached his task with relish. Pakistan had begun ebulliently against some indisciplined bowling which would have alarmed coach Houghton. Sohail actually smashed 11 fours in his 45-ball 46 before boldness was his undoing. Anwar was beaten by the googly, as was debutant Azam, while Malik, having made a serene 52, was bowled round his legs. Houghton brilliantly caught Shadab, and Henry Olonga finally broke through with a rapid delivery that had Ijaz leg-before.

The third day revealed how difficult it can be to tie Pakistan down. From the parlous position of six down and 186 behind, they now took the lead for the loss of only Moin Khan's wicket, Wasim Akram and his young partner Saqlain Mushtaq embarking on one of the most amazing lower-wicket partnerships in Test history. They batted for the rest of the day, taking the score to 395 for 7, 20 ahead, their eighth-wicket stand already worth 158, Wasim 144 not out, having reached his century with a six.

Continuing, on a day of variable light and drizzle, the pair took their historic stand to 313 (426 minutes), and Wasim Akram, dropped by Houghton at mid-off when 145, went on to 257 not out, easily his highest Test score, breaking a famous Test record as he did so: Wally Hammond's 10 sixes in an innings (England v New Zealand, Auckland, 1932–33), which had come under threat in January at Eden Park when

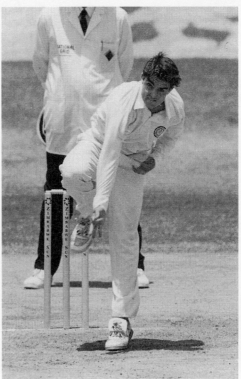

Clive Mason/Allsport

Chris Cairns blasted nine sixes in his 120, also against Zimbabwe. Wasim hoisted 12 sixes, three of them in one over by Paul Strang taking him from 195 to 213. Two other distinguished names were eclipsed as Wasim and Saqlain set a new world Test record for the eighth wicket, passing the 246 by Les Ames and Gubby Allen for England against New Zealand at Lord's in 1931. Wasim's 8¼-hour innings, full of strong drives with feet planted, was also the highest Test score by a No.8, exceeding Imtiaz Ahmed's 209 for Pakistan against New Zealand at Lahore in 1955–56.

Saqlain faced 358 balls and made his first Test half-century, seamer Guy Whittall eventually bowling him to end the marathon stand with 550 on the board. Zimbabwe's misery was soon over, leaving Paul Strang to digest figures of 5 for 212 to go with his century. He became only the 13th bowler in Test history (Vinoo Mankad featured twice) to concede 200 runs in an innings, an 'honour' offset by his having become only the 18th player to score a century and take five wickets in an innings in the same Test. The last to do so was the ubiquitous Wasim, at Adelaide in 1989–90.

Zimbabwe lost Dekker that evening and faced the final day still 140 behind, but after losing four more wickets by tea, still one run in arrears, they saw Andy Flower and Guy Whittall knuckle down to deny Pakistan's late surge. Flower's 18 occupied two hours. Earlier, Campbell was surprised to be given out lbw by umpire Khizar when bowler Waqar had not bothered to appeal. Houghton's value was again emphasised with a dedicated 65, but Pakistan's prospects were reduced from the moment Wasim hurt himself as he ran into a boundary board. This and time lost to bad light on the fourth evening and rain next morning helped Zimbabwe find an escape route. Their opener, Grant Flower, stayed 47 overs for his 46, making his 1000th Test run in the process.

To underline Wasim Akram's formidable achievement as an allrounder, he now could claim that only one player in the 1336 Tests now played had registered both a higher score and better bowling figures than his career-best 7 for 119, and that was Frank Worrell of West Indies (261 and 7 for 70). **TMY**

Legspinner Paul Strang toiled through 69 overs after his century innings, taking 5 for 212

FIRST TEST MATCH
Sheikhupura Cricket Stadium

October 17, 18, 19, 20, 21 1996
Toss: Zimbabwe

ZIMBABWE

		Mins	Balls	Fours		Mins	Balls	Fours
G.W. Flower	c sub (*Shahid Afridi*) b Saqlain	110	377	287	14	(2) c Kabir b Saqlain	46	193	147	8
M.H. Dekker	lbw b Akram	14	34	25	2	(1) c Akram b Saqlain	13	26	16	2
*A.D.R. Campbell	lbw b Nazir	8	20	17	1	lbw b Younis	15	59	49	2
D.L. Houghton	run out (*Nazir*)	43	88	60	3	b Saqlain	65	156	115	11
†A. Flower	lbw b Nazir	11	38	21	2	b Nazir	18	188	121	1
C.B. Wishart	lbw b Nazir	0	1	1	0	b Nazir	10	44	26	1
G.J. Whittall	c Kabir b Saqlain	0	4	2	0	c sub (*Shahid Afridi*) b Saqlain	32	146	97	5
P.A. Strang	not out	106	306	207	10	not out	13	45	23	1
A.R. Whittall	lbw b Nazir	0	7	3	0	not out	0	39	16	0
B.C. Strang	b Saqlain	42	92	67	5				
H.K. Olonga	b Nazir	7	18	14	1				

Extras: b9 lb16 w1 nb8   34
Total: 375

Extras: b11 lb10 nb8   29
Total: 7 wkts 241

Fall: 33, 41, 119, 141, 141, 142, 273, 274, 361

13, 40, 124, 159, 177, 221, 232

Bowling:

Wasim Akram	28–9–58–1 2nb
Waqar Younis	22–3–90–0 4nb
Saqlain Mushtaq	36.3–3–126–3
Shahid Nazir	22–3–54–5 2nb 1w
Aamir Sohail	6–0–22–0

Waqar Younis	20–3–60–1
Shahid Nazir	19–6–45–2 3nb
Saqlain Mushtaq	40–16–75–4 4nb
Wasim Akram	5–0–16–0
Aamir Sohail	11–6–12–0 1nb
Salim Malik	5–1–12–0

PAKISTAN

		Mins	Balls	Fours
Saeed Anwar	st A. Flower b P.A. Strang	51	101	87	6
Aamir Sohail	c A. Flower b P.A. Strang	46	46	45	11
Shadab Kabir	c Houghton b A.R. Whittall	2	15	14	0
Ijaz Ahmed	lbw b Olonga	9	14	13	2
Salim Malik	b P.A. Strang	52	104	106	6
Azam Khan	lbw b P.A. Strang	14	32	22	1
†Moin Khan	c A.R. Whittall b P.A. Strang	18	67	56	2
*Wasim Akram	not out	257	490	363	22§
Saqlain Mushtaq	b G.J. Whittall	79	426	359	8
Waqar Younis	b G.J. Whittall	0	1	1	0
Shahid Nazir	c Dekker b A.R. Whittall	0	13	10	0

Extras: b10 lb8 w2 nb5   25
Total: 553   § plus 12 sixes

Fall: 64, 77, 91, 142, 176, 183, 237, 550, 550

Bowling:

Olonga	19–6–60–1 1nb 1w
B.C. Strang	20–2–34–0 1nb 1w
A.R. Whittall	45.2–7–146–2 1nb
P.A. Strang	69–12–212–5 1nb
G.J. Whittall	25–5–73–2 1nb
G.W. Flower	10–4–10–0

Umpires: Khizar Hayat (Pak.) & D.L. Orchard (SA). *Third umpire:* Shakoor Rana (Pak.). *Referee:* J.L. Hendriks (WI).
Debuts: Azam Khan, Shahid Nazir (Pak.). *Man of the Match:* Wasim Akram

Match drawn

Pakistan v Zimbabwe

Second Test: Faisalabad

October 24–26 1996

Wasim the Ogre Allrounder

With Wasim Akram reverting to his fiery best as a bowler, and a grassy pitch this time, in contrast to the bare, cracked specimen in the first Test, Pakistan raced to an emphatic victory well inside three days. Choosing to bat, Zimbabwe soon began to fall apart, losing their first five wickets within 18 overs as Wasim and Waqar bowled as fearsomely as in the days when they were first paired with the new ball. Pace, testing lift and sharp movement that would have stretched better batting line-ups than this gained an ascendancy that Pakistan never let go.

Wasim seamed the ball principally in to the right-hander, at a lively pace, and bowled five batsmen in the first innings, with Dekker gloving an attempted hook. Only Andy Flower went past 19, his plucky 61, spread beyond three hours, sparing his side total embarrassment. With no real support left, he hit out and top-edged a catch. New slow left-armer Mohammad Hussain, a 20-year-old from Lahore, bowled tidily and secured his first Test wicket through a catch to slip.

Thanks to a wicket apiece to Zimbabwe's new opening pair, Everton Matambanadzo (a twin) and Mpumelelo Mbangwa, both aged 20 (Olonga, the third black fast bowler in the touring party, had been repatriated with a groin strain), Pakistan had cause to worry, and when Bryan Strang had Malik brilliantly caught behind down the leg side, a scoreline of 67 for 3, with a longish tail, suggested a competitive match. But, from a first-day score of 114 for 3, Pakistan were able to double their opponents' total.

The largest stand of the innings was 60 between the experienced Saeed Anwar, whose 81 was match top score, and Hassan Raza, a self-assured, tall, slim Karachi batsman, sporting a moustache, who was said initially to have been a mere 14 years and 227 days old, and had played for Pakistan in the recent Under-15 World Cup in England. Doubt subsequently surrounded the claim, and tests on the young man's wristbone pointed to a greater likelihood that he was 15. By chance, Pakistan's current coach, Mushtaq Mohammad, had been listed for 38 years as the youngest-ever Test player at 15 years 124 days. Raza had played in only two first-class matches before his Test selection, which, it was stated, would have been postponed had the opposition been of greater calibre.

Raza survived an lbw appeal before he had scored, but was soon displaying marked confidence by discarding his helmet after a few balls from Bryan Strang, and then walking down the pitch to urge Anwar to play more carefully in those closing overs of the day's play. The teenager was 20 not out, with four fours, having accepted his coach's advice not to pad away Paul Strang's bowling: it had been clear from the perimeter that Raza was not detecting the googly.

From his swift 69 overnight, Anwar added three more fours before Matambanadzo had him caught at the wicket, and Raza added only seven to his 20 before touching Bryan Strang to slip. Wasim and Moin, however, added precious runs, both attacking, with the wicketkeeper reaching the boundary 11 times in his timely 58. Pakistan built a lead of 134.

Zimbabwe began dreadfully: two down for 0, three for 23, Grant Flower victim of a dubious lbw decision by umpire Cowie, Wishart taken at third slip as Wasim roared in again off his shortish run-up and buzzed the ball towards the batsman's throat. At the opposite end, Waqar had recaptured his vicious inswinger, which overwhelmed Dekker.

The fourth wicket, though, was some time coming, for past captain Houghton was joined by current skipper Campbell, and they defended stoutly, finding the boundary from time to time (Houghton hooked Wasim clean over it), and adding 113 by the end of the second day, the visitors now two runs in front.

Wasim Akram had his way yet again on the third morning, removing the dangerous Houghton with an inducker first ball for 74. Nor did Campbell add to his overnight score, being given out caught at the wicket when the ball merely touched his pad. This time it was umpire Mahboob who gave the contentious decision.

Adrian Murrell/Allsport

Again, Andy Flower was left with insufficient support. The innings slid away to the fast bowlers, leaving Pakistan in need of only 67, which the left-hand openers hit off inside 19 overs, Anwar dominating and reaching his fifty with the winning boundary.

Wasim Akram had made this two-match series his own by taking 10 wickets in a Test for the fourth time. This and his hurricane double-century in the first match ensured him the Man of the Series award.   *TMY*

After his extraordinary double-century at Sheikhupura, Man of the Series and Pakistan captain Wasim Akram blew away 10 wickets in the second Test

SECOND TEST MATCH

Iqbal Stadium, Faisalabad

October 24, 25, 26 1996

Toss: Zimbabwe

ZIMBABWE		Mins	Balls	Fours		Mins	Balls	Fours
G.W. Flower	b Akram	15	29	25	2	lbw b Akram	0	2	2	0
M.H. Dekker	c Moin b Akram	19	60	43	2	lbw b Younis	0	6	1	0
C.B. Wishart	lbw b Younis	0	12	1	0	c Malik b Younis	7	39	29	1
D.L. Houghton	b Akram	1	6	3	0	lbw b Akram	74	152	102	8
*A.D.R. Campbell	c Moin b Saqlain	9	33	21	1	c Moin b Nazir	51	124	87	6
†A. Flower	c Hussain b Nazir	61	183	144	7	c Anwar b Younis	23	72	41	4
G.J. Whittall	b Akram	9	65	51	1	lbw b Nazir	0	9	6	0
P.A. Strang	c Malik b Hussain	3	34	23	0	b Younis	9	47	36	1
B.C. Strang	b Akram	1	15	14	0	not out	13	45	28	3
M. Mbangwa	b Akram	0	32	23	0	(11) lbw b Akram	2	3	3	0
E. Matambanadzo	not out	0	7	1	0	(10) b Akram	7	34	14	0

Extras: b4 lb10 nb1 — 15

Total: 133

lb8 nb6 — 14

200

Fall: 22, 33, 34, 49, 55, 102, 111, 118, 129

0, 0, 23, 136, 136, 140, 169, 174, 198

Bowling:

Wasim Akram	20–8–48–6 1nb		Wasim Akram	18.4–4–58–4 4nb
Waqar Younis	11–6–13–1		Waqar Younis	15–3–54–4 1nb
Saqlain Mushtaq	15–5–28–1 1nb		Saqlain Mushtaq	7–1–33–0
Shahid Nazir	5.5–0–23–1		Shahid Nazir	11–5–25–2
Mohammad Hussain	6–3–7–1		Mohammad Hussain	4–1–14–0
			Salim Malik	2–0–8–0

PAKISTAN		Mins	Balls	Fours		Mins	Balls	Fours
Saeed Anwar	c A. Flower b Matambanadzo	81	126	97	16	not out	50	85	66	9
Aamir Sohail	lbw b Matambanadzo	2	11	6	0	not out	18	85	47	3
Ijaz Ahmed	c A. Flower b Mbangwa	2	12	16	0				
Salim Malik	c A. Flower b B.C. Strang	18	58	33	2				
Hassan Raza	c Houghton b B.C. Strang	27	64	48	5				
*Wasim Akram	b Mbangwa	35	67	47	7				
†Moin Khan	c A. Flower b B.C. Strang	58	136	100	11				
Mohammad Hussain	run out (G.W. Flower/P.A. Strang)	0	11	7	0				
Saqlain Mushtaq	not out	15	115	88	1				
Waqar Younis	b G.W. Flower	23	36	32	5				
Shahid Nazir	lbw b P.A. Strang	1	6	3	0				

Extras: lb4 nb1 — 5

Total: 267

w1 — 1

0 wkt 69

Fall: 7, 10, 67, 127, 141, 194, 200, 235, 264

Bowling:

Matambanadzo	11–0–62–2		Matambanadzo	5–0–27–0
Mbangwa	17–1–67–2		Mbangwa	7–3–14–0
B.C. Strang	18–6–53–3 1nb		B.C. Strang	4.5–1–20–0 1w
Whittall	7–4–11–0		P.A. Strang	2–0–8–0
P.A. Strang	24.1–8–66–1			
G.W. Flower	2–0–4–1			

Umpires: D.B. Cowie (NZ) & Mahboob Shah (Pak.). *Third umpire:* Shakil Khan (Pak.). *Referee:* J.L. Hendriks (WI).
Debuts: Hassan Raza, Mohammad Hussain (Pak.); E. Matambanadzo, M. Mbangwa (Zim.). *Man of the Match:* Wasim Akram.
Man of the Series: Wasim Akram

Pakistan won by 10 wickets

India v South Africa

First Test: Ahmedabad

November 10–13 1996

Maiden Victory for India

India's brilliant home record in Test matches in the 1990s has long followed a predictable script: build up a large score, trap the opposition on a crumbling pitch, and look on smugly as the trio of spinners runs through the opposition. The sight therefore of a fast bowler slicing through the visiting team's batting line-up to fashion an amazing victory before tea on the fourth day was as welcome to the locals as it was improbable.

The fact that a fourth-innings target of 170 always looked a tough task for the South Africans was an indication not only of how underprepared this track was but also a credit to the fast bowlers on both sides. Though spinners Joshi and Kumble and Adams and Symcox bowled well in spells, it was the fiery pace of Allan Donald and Javagal Srinath that was the highlight of a low-scoring match.

Three times Srinath was on a hat-trick in the second innings as South Africa collapsed from 96 for 4 to 105 all out to lose to India for the first time. His final spell read 4.5–2–7–4, this after reducing South Africa to 0 for 2 in his opening over. India could not have asked for a better end to their 300th Test match, the first between the two teams on Indian soil. It was also the end of a mental barrier that had seen Srinath, the Karnataka speedster, claim his first five-wicket haul in his 22nd Test.

Just as in the New Delhi Test against Australia five weeks earlier, the toss once again assumed improper importance, and once again it was Tendulkar who won it. Half the match was won there and then, and three days later when asked what he felt was the turning-point of the Test, skipper Hansie Cronje replied laconically, 'The toss.'

With left-arm unorthodox spinner Paul Adams being drafted into the touring squad after recovering from injury, South Africa would have been looking to the teenager and veteran Pat Symcox to achieve the breakthroughs on the opening day. (Adams was hit by a piece of concrete thrown by a spectator, and Cronje took his players off for 10 minutes until order was restored.)

But once again Donald proved why he is considered one of the most dangerous bowlers in the world with a fiery late spell that reduced India to 215 for 8 by stumps. While Adams and Symcox accounted for three of the top-order batsmen – including Sanjay Manjrekar in the makeshift opener's role – it was the way that Donald charged in and bent his back that was an inspiration to his team-mates – and no doubt to Srinath himself, who was one of Donald's three victims on the first day.

It was the umpiring pair of George Sharp and S.K. Bansal as much as anyone else who were the talking-point after the second day's play, which saw South Africa reach 202 for 8 in reply to India's meagre 223. Recently appointed on the National Grid ICC panel ahead of the more experienced V. K. Ramaswamy, Bansal was fresh from the Sharjah three-nation tournament, where he and Sharp had stunned the New Zealanders in the final against Pakistan with a series of lbw decisions that left the TV commentators gasping with surprise. Here it was the turn of Cronje and Cullinan to suffer at Bansal's hands, while Sharp's decision against Hudson generated much comment.

South Africa lost half their side for 102, and it was left to the all-rounders Symcox and de Villiers to haul them off the ropes by close of play. Four of the eight wickets to fall were snapped up by the ever-improving left-arm spinner Sunil Joshi, whose tour of England was cut short by a finger injury which prevented him from bowling on his debut.

A lead of 21 was hardly enough on this surface, where all the batsmen struggled, and on which de Villiers's 67 not out would emerge as the unlikely top score. But with Donald picking up three of the top five Indian second-innings wickets which fell before the score had crossed three figures, the pendulum had swung once again. It was left to Vangipuram Venkata Sai Laxman, making his debut in place of the injured Ganguly, to

Adrian Murrell/Allsport

shore up the innings in the company of Anil Kumble in the only stand worth more than 50 for India in either innings. Laxman's 51 took nearly three hours, setting up the dramatics of the fourth (and final) day.

Former Test allrounder Ravi Shastri, now a television pundit, called Srinath's bowling the fastest he had seen by an Indian in many years. South Africa's batsmen were left wondering what had hit them.

Gulu Ezekiel

Javagal Srinath, the spearhead of India's bowling, returned to take eight South African wickets at Ahmedabad

FIRST TEST MATCH

Gujarat Stadium, Motera (Ahmedabad)

November 20, 21, 22, 23 1996

Toss: India

INDIA

			Mins	Balls	Fours		Mins	Balls	Fours
S.V. Manjrekar	b Adams	34	117	93	4	c Hudson b Donald	5	22	20	0
†N.R. Mongia	lbw b de Villiers	9	34	18	2	c Richardson b Donald	5	37	22	0
R.S. Dravid	lbw b Symcox	24	133	99	3	lbw b Symcox	34	150	113	5
*S.R. Tendulkar	c Rhodes b Symcox	42	79	68	7	c Rhodes b McMillan	7	44	33	1
M. Azharuddin	run out (*Rhodes*)	35	91	78	5	c McMillan b Donald	24	62	41	3
V.V.S. Laxman	lbw b Donald	11	63	63	1	lbw b Adams	51	178	126	6
S.B. Joshi	c Hudson b Donald	16	79	57	1	c McMillan b Symcox	13	58	51	1
J. Srinath	c Cullinan b Donald	14	59	51	1	lbw b de Villiers	1	6	6	0
A. Kumble	c Kirsten b Donald	17	67	56	3	not out	30	81	60	4
B.K.V. Prasad	c Donald b de Villiers	9	51	35	0	c McMillan b Adams	0	1	2	0
N.D. Hirwani	not out	0	6	4	0	c sub (*D.N. Crookes*) b Adams	9	6	4	2

Extras: lb9 nb3 — 12

Total: 223

b4 lb4 nb3 — 11

190

Fall: 22, 63, 98, 129, 159, 165, 193, 196, 221

10, 15, 38, 82, 91, 123, 124, 180, 180

Bowling:

Donald	27–14–37–4		Donald	15–3–32–3 2nb
de Villiers	18–5–55–2		de Villiers	17–4–45–1
McMillan	11–4–20–0 3nb	.	McMillan	9–4–18–1
Cronje	5–3–8–0		Symcox	22–8–47–2
Adams	17–2–46–1		Cronje	7–2–10–0
Symcox	21–5–48–2		Adams	9.2–4–30–3 1nb

SOUTH AFRICA

			Mins	Balls	Fours		Mins	Balls	Fours
A.C. Hudson	lbw b Kumble	23	93	78	3	lbw b Srinath	0	4	5	0
G. Kirsten	st Mongia b Kumble	17	63	47	2	lbw b Joshi	20	85	43	2
D.J. Cullinan	lbw b Joshi	43	85	75	4‡	c Mongia b Srinath	0	1	1	0
*W.J. Cronje	lbw b Hirwani	1	9	10	0	not out	48	173	120	6
J.N. Rhodes	c Manjrekar b Joshi	14	49	38	0	(7) lbw b Srinath	0	1	1	0
B.M. McMillan	b Joshi	8	42	25	0	(5) c Joshi b Kumble	17	28	23	2
†D.J. Richardson	b Hirwani	4	24	27	0	(6) c Mongia b Srinath	7	38	27	1
P.L. Symcox	lbw b Joshi	32	105	80	3‡	b Kumble	0	12	4	0
P.S. de Villiers	not out	67	189	134	5‡	c Azharuddin b Kumble	0	3	4	0
A.A. Donald	b Srinath	17	89	64	2	b Srinath	4	5	3	1
P.R. Adams	c Azharuddin b Srinath	1	7	7	0	b Srinath	0	1	1	0

Extras: b7 lb9 nb1 — 17

Total: 244   ‡ plus 1 six

b1 lb3 w5 — 9

105

Fall: 29, 46, 49, 95, 102, 113, 119, 182, 242

0, 0, 40, 65, 96, 96, 100, 100, 105

Bowling:

Srinath	19.1–7–47–2 1nb		Srinath	11.5–4–21–6 5w
Prasad	9–2–24–0		Prasad	7–0–18–0
Kumble	31–6–76–2		Kumble	12–2–34–3
Joshi	24–4–43–4		Joshi	8–1–28–1
Hirwani	15–3–38–2			

Umpires: S.K. Bansal (Ind.) & G. Sharp (Eng.). *Third umpire:* A. Saheba (Ind.). *Referee:* J.R. Reid (NZ). *Debut:* V.V.S. Laxman (Ind.). *Man of the Match:* J. Srinath

India won by 64 runs

India v South Africa

Second Test: Calcutta

November 27–December 1 1996

Feast of Rare Achievements

This Test match was so much one for the record books that even the statisticians struggled to keep up with the numerous records broken. There were brilliant individual performances on both sides. But the South Africans proved cricket was after all a team game as they inflicted the biggest-ever defeat on India in terms of runs, the difference between the teams being a massive 329 runs with the match ending before lunch on the last day.

Rarely can there have been such a dramatic turnaround in the performance of one player in a Test match as that of debutant South Africa fast bowler Lance Klusener. Brought in as a replacement for Fanie de Villiers – a decision hotly debated for 3½ days – the young Natalian received the hiding of his life in the first innings. Facing the brunt of Mohammad Azharuddin's onslaught as the former Indian captain raced to the joint fourth-fastest century in Test cricket, Klusener went for 75 runs in 14 overs. This included five boundaries in one over as Azharuddin set the Eden Gardens alight on the third day of this remarkable Test match.

Barely 24 hours later, how things had changed. With spearhead Allan Donald sitting it out with a severely bruised heel – he was to fly home after the match for further treatment – the onus was on Klusener and McMillan in the second innings. Set the impossible target of 467 for victory, India lost four wickets on the fourth afternoon, three to Klusener in a spell of 13 overs. The match was over and done with by then. Next morning the 25-year-old grabbed five more to become only the fifth bowler to claim eight wickets on his debut, returning the third-best bowling analysis for a South African (after Hugh Tayfield's 9 for 113 and 'Goofy' Lawrence's 8 for 53). Still, it was opener Gary Kirsten who picked up the match award as he became only the third South African (after Alan Melville and Bruce Mitchell) to hit a century in each innings of a Test. It happened at the same venue where South Africa marked their return to the international scene with a one-day international in 1991.

Indeed, it was Kirsten and fellow opener Andrew Hudson who virtually batted India out of the match on the first day itself with an opening partnership worth 236 runs, the best opening stand in a Test match at Calcutta and only 24 short of Mitchell and Siedle's South African record. But the Indians were left to rue their bad luck. Not only did Cronje finally win a vital toss, but Hudson was put down by local lad Ganguly at first slip before he had scored. Soon after, he was missed by wicketkeeper Mongia, a real sitter. Both batsmen were also 'caught' off no-balls, once strangely off the bowling of legspinner Hirwani, who was to welcome Klusener into the 'eight wickets on debut club' four days later.

South Africa ended the first day on a massive 339 for 2 with both openers out after playing on to

Shaun Botterill/Allsport

their stumps. With the other debutant, Herschelle Gibbs, and Daryll Cullinan batting confidently, it looked like the launching-pad for a massive total.

It was left to the ever-improving Venkatesh Prasad to mop up the innings as the last eight South African wickets fell for 89 runs on the second day. Prasad finished with 6 for 104, bettering his previous best of 5 for 76 at Lord's earlier this year. Still, the South African total of 428 looked an imposing one as the Indian batting once again crumbled to Allan Donald after McMillan had removed the makeshift opening pair of Mongia and Rahul Dravid. With Azharuddin retiring hurt after being struck by McMillan on the elbow, and also running a high temperature, India still needed 77 runs to avoid the follow-on at 152 for 6. They not only crossed that target the next day – they did it in style, and it was a blazing century by Azha and an impressive 88 by Kumble that did the trick.

Azha returned to the crease at the fall of the seventh wicket and then proceeded to take the bowling attack apart, playing hooks and pulls that he had long placed in cold storage. His fifty came off 35 balls and the 74-ball century was the joint-fastest by an Indian, 96 of his amazing 109 coming before lunch. The 161-run partnership with Kumble was an Indian record for the eighth wicket. Despite the heroics of Prasad and Azha, South Africa were in control for all but two sessions of this Test. Reaching 160 for 1 at stumps, they were already 259 ahead with two full days to play. And Kirsten and the elegant Cullinan now made fine hundreds, establishing a new South African second-wicket record with 212 (passing Eric Rowan and van Ryneveld's 198 at Leeds in 1951) on a pitch which still offered true bounce. It was the first instance of four centuries in a Test by South Africa. The declaration came next day, and the rest of the match belonged to the fast-medium Lance Klusener.

This memorable match was heavily attended throughout, with gates averaging 60,000.

Gulu Ezekiel

South Africa levelled at Calcutta, the major batting contribution coming from Gary Kirsten, who scored twin centuries

SECOND TEST MATCH

Eden Gardens, Calcutta

November 27, 28, 29, 30 December 1 1996
Toss: South Africa

SOUTH AFRICA

			Mins	Balls	Fours			Mins	Balls	Fours
A.C. Hudson	b Prasad	146	302	244	24	retired injured	6	43	27	1
G. Kirsten	b Srinath	102	241	171	15	run out (*Joshi/Mongia*) 133	315	197	18
H.H. Gibbs	lbw b Prasad	31	158	112	5	c Dravid b Srinath	9	24	12	2
D.J. Cullinan	lbw b Prasad	43	131	80	7	not out	153	354	261	15‡
*W.J. Cronje	c Mongia b Srinath	4	23	18	1	c & b Kumble	34	52	37	5
B.M. McMillan	lbw b Prasad	0	4	2	0	not out	17	44	35	2
†D.J. Richardson	not out	36	86	59	4					
L. Klusener	b Prasad	10	26	20	1					
P.L. Symcox	b Prasad	13	41	20	0‡					
A.A. Donald	c Laxman b Kumble	0	3	3	0					
P.R. Adams	b Kumble	4	8	8	0					

Extras: b6 lb24 nb9   39   b1 lb11 nb2 w1   15

Total: 428   ‡ plus 1 six   3 wkts dec. 367   ‡ plus 1 six

Fall: 236, 296, 346, 361, 362, 363, 379, 421, 422   39, 251, 306

Hudson retired injured at 16 for 0

Bowling:

Srinath	37–7–107–2 2nb	Srinath	24.2–2–101–1 1nb
Prasad	35–6–104–6 5nb	Prasad	15–0–63–0 1nb
Joshi	12–1–48–0 1nb	Kumble	32–4–101–1 1w
Ganguly	3–1–10–0	Hirwani	11–1–40–0
Kumble	20.1–1–78–2	Joshi	11–0–50–0
Hirwani	14–2–51–0		

INDIA

			Mins	Balls	Fours			Mins	Balls	Fours
†N.R. Mongia	run out (*Gibbs*)	35	88	68	5	c Cullinan b Klusener	8	80	57	1
R.S. Dravid	c Hudson b McMillan	31	78	48	6	b McMillan	23	192	127	4
S.C. Ganguly	b McMillan	6	25	17	1	c Richardson b Klusener	0	3	4	0
*S.R. Tendulkar	b Donald	18	91	62	3	c Kirsten b Symcox	2	29	25	0
M. Azharuddin	c & b Adams	109	126	78	18‡	(6) c McMillan b Klusener	52	85	47	9
V.V.S. Laxman	b Donald	14	55	35	2	(5) b Klusener	1	12	5	0
S.B. Joshi	run out (*Gibbs/Donald*)	4	14	9	1	c McMillan b Klusener	1	8	8	0
J. Srinath	b Donald	11	51	44	1	(9) c McMillan b Klusener	19	32	24	2
A. Kumble	run out (*Gibbs/Richardson*)	88	164	124	13	(8) b Klusener	17	50	22	2
B.K.V. Prasad	c Richardson b Adams	1	7	10	0	not out	3	9	9	0
N.D. Hirwani	not out	0	4	2	0	b Klusener	0	2	2	0

Extras: lb5 nb7   12   lb2 nb9   11

Total: 329   137

Fall: 68, 71, 77, 114, 119, 119, 161, 322, 324   ‡ plus 1 six   17, 18, 27, 28, 88, 92, 97, 132, 137

Azharuddin retired injured when 6 and returned at 161 for 7

Bowling:

Donald	21.2–4–72–3	McMillan	19–8–33–1 2nb
Klusener	14–1–75–0 8nb	Klusener	21.3–4–64–8 10nb
Adams	13–1–69–2	Cronje	7–4–10–0
McMillan	16–4–52–2	Symcox	6–1–28–1
Cronje	6–3–13–0		
Symcox	11–1–43–0		

Umpires: B.C. Cooray (SL) & V.K. Ramaswamy (Ind.). *Third umpire:* S.K. Porel (Ind.). *Referee:* J.R. Reid (NZ).
Debuts: H.H. Gibbs, L. Klusener (SA). *Man of the Match:* G. Kirsten.

South Africa won by 329 runs

India v South Africa

Third Test: Kanpur

December 8–12 1996

Azha Inspires Another Home Success

India kept intact their precious home record of not losing a Test series since being beaten 1–0 by Pakistan in 1986–87. They crushed South Africa by 280 runs in the third and final Test to take the series 2–1. It was the biggest margin of victory in terms of runs for India and followed their biggest-ever runs margin of defeat in the Calcutta Test. It also spelt South Africa's first series loss since their re-entry to Test cricket in April 1992.

South Africa had their chances, particularly after dismissing India for only 237 in the first innings. But their batting crumbled in both innings, and Man of the Match and Man of the Series Mohammad Azharuddin's century in the second innings put paid to their hopes.

If the first day's honours belonged to the visitors it was principally due to an outstanding bowling performance by young left-arm unorthodox spinner Paul Adams. After winning the toss and expectedly batting first, India lost six wickets for 204 on the opening day, with Adams picking up the wickets of Dravid, Azharuddin and Joshi. India's hopes of boosting their total rested on the shoulders of Sachin Tendulkar, and the skipper, struggling to shake off a lean patch, batted over three hours for his unbeaten 43.

Next day he added a further 18 from 22 balls. But Adams snapped up three of the last four wickets to fall to finish with a Test-best of 6 for 55. That negated India's best opening partnership in nine Tests as makeshift opener Nayan Mongia put on 76 with new partner W. V. Raman, playing in his first Test for eight years. India lost their last eight wickets for a meagre 77 runs, and it was now left to the South African batsmen to consolidate.

That they failed to do so was once again due to the bowling of legspinner Anil Kumble, who was supported by pace bowler Venkatesh Prasad. Between them they picked up seven of the nine wickets to fall to the bowlers on a helpful pitch, No.11 Adams being run out by Sunil Joshi as the ball deflected off the bowler's hand into the non-striker's stumps. Kapoor picked up two good wickets with his offspin, top-scorer Kirsten and Herschelle Gibbs, aged 22, who had just scored 200 and 171 not out against India A at Nagpur.

On a pitch that showed signs of turning in the opening session of the Test, a lead of 60 for India was worth a great deal.

It took the masterly touch of Azharuddin in the second innings to swing the advantage the bowlers had enjoyed so far back to the batsmen. The former captain, like the present incumbent, had also been going through a lean patch. His second marriage, to actress Sangeet Bijlani just days before this Test, was perhaps an omen of better things to come.

Though not quite in the vein of his blazing Calcutta hundred – it would have been
too much to expect a repeat of that amazing innings – Azha nonetheless conclusive-
ly took command of the bowling as he
struck 15 boundaries in the course of an
unbeaten 88 as India reached 270 for 5 by
the third day. Kumble showed how much
his batting had improved. Following on
from his Test-best 88 at Calcutta, he this
time scored 42 in the nightwatchman's role.
But once again it was skipper Tendulkar in
his new self-denial mode who gave an
indic-ation of how the cares of captaincy
had forced him to temper his natural incli-
nation to attack the bowling. Former and
current skippers were involved in a stand
worth 71 for the fifth wicket, with Azha
doing the bulk of the scoring.

Azharuddin duly completed his 16th century – the fifth time in his career that he had
scored two on the trot – and India's declaration at 400 for 7 effectively shut the tourists
out of the Test. Their collapse to 127 for 5
by the close in chasing a mammoth 461
meant the Test was as good as over.

Quick runs had been the need of the
hour when India had resumed on the
penultimate day, and once again it was Azha
who moved into overdrive. Seventy-five
runs came off his bat alone from only 86 balls.

Clive Mason/Allsport

The talk of the day switched to the selection of the Indian team for the tour of South Africa,
which had been announced the night before. Out of the tour party was left-arm spinner Joshi, and
he perhaps had a point to prove more than anyone else. He was to do so next morning as South
Africa folded up for 180, returning figures of 3 for 66. Now it was time for the sterner test ahead for
the Indians on the pitches of South Africa.   ***Gulu Ezekiel***

Mohammad Azharuddin: important century as a marriage 'gift'

THIRD TEST MATCH

Green Park Stadium, Kanpur

December 8, 9, 10, 11, 12 1996

Toss: India

INDIA

		Mins	Balls	Fours			Mins	Balls	Fours
†N.R. Mongia	b McMillan	41	123	96	5	(2) lbw b Klusener	18	71	56	3
W.V. Raman	c Klusener b McMillan	57	171	124	12	(1) lbw b de Villiers	2	4	6	0
S.C. Ganguly	lbw b Cronje	39	127	80	7	(4) c McMillan b Symcox	41	123	93	6
*S.R. Tendulkar	c de Villiers b Adams	61	210	173	4‡	(5) c Richardson b Klusener	36	128	98	4
R.S. Dravid	lbw b Adams	7	64	55	0	(7) c McMillan b Adams	56	181	130	8
M. Azharuddin	c & b Adams	5	8	9	0	not out	163	312	228	25‡
S.B. Joshi	c Klusener b Adams	0	6	5	0	(8) b Adams	16	24	25	3
A. Kumble	b Cronje	5	34	29	1	(3) c Gibbs b de Villiers	42	144	99	5
A.R. Kapoor	c de Villiers b Adams	11	23	24	1	not out	6	20	25	0
J. Srinath	c & b Adams	0	1	1	0					
B.K.V. Prasad	not out	1	9	6	0					

| Extras: | b3 lb6 nb1 | 10 | | | | b4 lb14 nb2 | 20 | | |
| Total: | | 237 | | ‡ plus 1 six | | 7 wkts dec. | 400 | | ‡ plus 1 six |

Fall: 76, 111, 160, 185, 193, 193, 214, 224, 224

2, 41, 91, 121, 192, 357, 385

Bowling:

de Villiers	15–7–18–0		de Villiers	24–10–58–2 2nb
Klusener	17–4–47–0 1nb		Klusener	25–7–72–2 2nb
Symcox	21–5–57–0		McMillan	16–6–36–0
McMillan	18–7–40–2		Cronje	15–5–31–0
Adams	19.1–6–55–6		Adams	20–1–84–2
Cronje	10–5–11–2		Symcox	26–2–101–1

SOUTH AFRICA

		Mins	Balls	Fours			Mins	Balls	Fours
A.C. Hudson	lbw b Kumble	15	66	45	3	c sub (*V.V.S. Laxman*) b Kumble	31	206	142	3
G. Kirsten	c Raman b Kapoor	43	166	108	5	lbw b Srinath	7	46	25	0
H.H. Gibbs	b Kapoor	17	75	67	2	b Prasad	5	18	13	1
D.J. Cullinan	c Azharuddin b Kumble	29	65	82	4	run out (*Tendulkar*)	2	15	18	0
*W.J. Cronje	c sub (*V.V.S. Laxman*) b Kumble	15	53	59	2	c Tendulkar b Joshi	50	90	94	8
B.M. McMillan	b Srinath	1	9	6	0	c sub (*V.V.S. Laxman*) b Joshi	18	65	67	2
†D.J. Richardson	b Srinath	4	9	6	0	lbw b Srinath	5	55	35	1
L. Klusener	c Dravid b Srinath	9	33	17	1	not out	34	121	100	5
P.L. Symcox	not out	23	73	40	1‡	c & b Joshi	11	50	28	1
P.S. de Villiers	lbw b Kumble	6	27	27	1	b Prasad	2	48	52	0
P.R. Adams	run out (*Joshi*)	8	20	14	1	c Azharuddin b Srinath	1	2	4	0

| Extras: | b4 lb3 | 7 | | | | lb14 | 14 | | |
| Total: | | 177 | | ‡ plus 1 six | | | 180 | | |

Fall: 34, 73, 94, 121, 126, 130, 131, 144, 163

21, 26, 29, 97, 109, 127, 138, 167, 179

Bowling:

Srinath	16–7–42–3		Srinath	19.1–6–38–3
Prasad	14–5–25–0 1nb		Prasad	11–5–25–2
Kumble	27–2–71–4		Kumble	24–11–27–1
Kapoor	8–2–19–2		Kapoor	13–8–10–0
Joshi	7.3–2–13–0		Joshi	29–9–66–3

Umpires: D.R. Shepherd (Eng.) & S. Venkataraghavan (Ind.). *Third umpire:* A.V. Jayaprakash (Ind.). *Referee:* J.R. Reid (NZ).
Man of the Match: M. Azharuddin. *Man of the Series:* M. Azharuddin

India won by 280 runs

SERIES AVERAGES

INDIA

Batting:	M	I	NO	R	HS	Av.	100	50	Ct/st
M.Azharuddin	3	6	1	388	163*	77.60	2	1	4
A. Kumble	3	6	1	199	88	39.80	0	1	1
W.V. Raman	1	2	0	59	57	29.50	0	1	1
R.S. Dravid	3	6	0	175	56	29.17	0	1	2
S.R. Tendulkar	3	6	0	166	61	27.67	0	1	1
S.C. Ganguly	2	4	0	86	41	21.50	0	0	0
S.V. Manjrekar	1	2	0	39	34	19.50	0	0	1
N.R. Mongia	3	6	0	116	41	19.33	0	0	3/1
V.V.S. Laxman	2	4	0	77	51	19.25	0	1	1
A.R. Kapoor	1	2	1	17	11	17.00	0	0	0
J. Srinath	3	5	0	45	19	9.00	0	0	0
S.B. Joshi	3	6	0	50	16	8.33	0	0	2
B.K.V. Prasad	3	5	2	14	9	4.67	0	0	0
N.D. Hirwani	2	4	2	9	9	4.50	0	0	0

Substitute catches were held by V.V.S. Laxman (3)

Bowling:	O	M	R	W	Av.	BB	5w/i
A.R. Kapoor	21	10	29	2	14.50	2–19	0
J. Srinath	127.3	33	356	17	20.94	6–21	1
A. Kumble	146.1	26	387	13	29.77	4–71	0
S.B. Joshi	91.3	17	248	8	31.00	4–43	0
B.K.V. Prasad	91	18	259	8	32.38	6–104	1
N.D. Hirwani	40	6	129	2	64.50	2–38	0
S.C. Ganguly	3	1	10	0	–	0–10	0

SOUTH AFRICA

Batting:	M	I	NO	R	HS	Av.	100	50	Ct/st
D.J. Cullinan	3	6	1	270	153*	54.00	1	0	2
G. Kirsten	3	6	0	322	133	53.67	2	0	2
A.C. Hudson	3	6	1	221	146	44.20	1	0	3
W.J. Cronje	3	6	1	152	50	30.40	0	1	0
L. Klusener	2	3	1	53	34*	26.50	0	0	2
P.S. de Villiers	2	4	1	75	67*	25.00	0	1	2
P.L. Symcox	3	5	1	79	32	19.75	0	0	0
H.H. Gibbs	2	4	0	62	31	15.50	0	0	1
D.J. Richardson	3	5	1	56	36*	14.00	0	0	4
B.M. McMillan	3	6	1	61	18	12.20	0	0	8
A.A. Donald	2	3	0	21	17	7.00	0	0	1
J.N. Rhodes	1	2	0	14	14	7.00	0	0	2
P.R. Adams	3	5	0	14	8	2.80	0	0	3

Substitute catch was held by D.N. Crookes

Bowling:	O	M	R	W	Av.	BB	5w/i
A.A. Donald	63.2	21	141	10	14.10	4–37	0
P.R. Adams	78.3	14	284	14	20.29	6–55	1
L. Klusener	77.3	16	258	10	25.80	8–64	1
B.M. McMillan	89	33	199	6	33.17	2–40	0
P.S. de Villiers	74	26	176	5	35.20	2–55	0
W.J. Cronje	50	22	83	2	41.50	2–11	0
P.L. Symcox	107	22	324	6	54.00	2–47	0

Pakistan v New Zealand

First Test: Lahore

November 21–24 1996

Kiwi Success 27 Years On

Although Mushtaq Ahmed returned and spun out 10 batsmen, the inherent value of Wasim Akram to Pakistan's cause was underlined strongly. He withdrew, on the morning of the match, with a shoulder injury, and New Zealand stole their fifth victory in the 38 Tests now played between the two countries. Simon Doull took the bowling honours for the visitors, whose conspicuous batting contributions came from Stephen Fleming (equalling his best score, on Test debut in 1994) and Chris Cairns. But even in defeat, Pakistan had some delight in the debut century by Mohammad Wasim, a 19-year-old Rawalpindi-born right-hander who batted calmly for an unbeaten 109 to go memorably with his first-innings duck.

Shakoor Rana was umpiring his first Test match for three years, and by chance there were 15 lbw decisions given by him and partner Tiffin, 10 against New Zealand batsmen and five against Pakistan. The Test record is 17 (WI v Pakistan, Port-of-Spain, 1992–93).

On a pitch lightly grassed but prone to inconsistent bounce, the somewhat rusty New Zealanders did not bat at all well on the opening day, when 15 wickets toppled as the ball moved around for the faster bowlers. As Waqar and Mushtaq bagged four wickets each, New Zealand's batsmen let themselves down with loose strokes and wavering concentration, only a third-wicket stand of 51 by Parore and Fleming preventing a complete rout. As it was, nine were out for 117 before Patel and Doull managed to add 38 for the final wicket.

Pakistan were then stunned to find themselves 52 for 5 by the close, seamer Doull claiming four of the wickets on his way to career-best figures of 5 for 46. Not for the first time in his career, Ijaz apparently suffered an injustice in his lbw dismissal. The important wicket of Inzaman, however, was gained decisively enough, when Astle at third slip clung to a fine catch off Doull. Moin Khan masterminded the rescue of the innings with a defiant 59, and worthy efforts from the later batsmen enabled Pakistan to squeeze a first-innings advantage of 36. Salim Malik was another to fall to an exceptional catch (Young, second slip), and the English-born Vaughan, like Doull, registered his best Test analysis, three of his wickets coming from lbws.

As on the first day, overs were lost at the end because of fading light, but after two days 23 wickets had already fallen. New Zealand, having wiped off the deficit before losing a wicket, then lost three to the spinners, to finish at 88 for 3, the match nervously poised. Vaughan was bowled round his legs and Young, the other opener, was taken off bat and pad for 36. Then, just before the close, Parore was lbw to Saqlain, which seemed to have shifted the odds slightly towards Pakistan.

Astle was out immediately on the third morning, and when Waqar, who was feeling a side strain, bowled Greatbatch, New Zealand were half out for 101, only 65 ahead.

Cairns then joined left-hander Fleming, and a bold stand of 141 was constructed, Cairns lacing his 89-ball 93 with 66 runs from vigorously struck boundaries. They were together for 35 overs, during which the Pakistanis could feel the match running away. But upon Cairns's dismissal, Mushtaq nipped in with more wickets, and with nine down New Zealand were no more than 226 ahead. Next, however, came a demoralising 10th-wicket stand of 49 between Fleming, who was eventually left stranded on 92, and Man of the Match Doull, who called for a runner when a hamstring began to twitch. He was finally out stumped, charging at Saqlain.

The problem in his thigh did not stop Doull from opening the bowling, and, facing a victory target of 276, Pakistan were soon in deep trouble. Replacement captain Saeed Anwar, second ball, became the 15th lbw victim; Ijaz left his leg stump unguarded, and Doull hit it; Cairns then had Inzamam held at slip; Saqlain, the nightwatchman, was caught for a duck; and debutant Elahi gave a low catch off Patel, the 38-year-old former Worcestershire off-spinner. By stumps the sorry score read 46 for the loss of five wickets, Salim Malik 15, Mohammad Wasim 0 not out, still threatened with a 'pair'.

Doull soon shifted Malik, caught behind, on the fourth morning, but Mohammad Wasim brought fresh life to Pakistan's cause with a century full of watchful defence and impressive driving. He was only the fourth Pakistani to score a hundred on Test debut. Moin stood by him in a seventh-wicket partnership of 75, after which Mushtaq helped him add 76, a stand which generated mounting anxiety among the New Zealanders. Their relief was manifest when Patel at last spun Mushtaq out. Waqar soon followed, but a dozen more runs came before the final wicket was seized by Patel, with Pakistan 45 short of an amazing turnabout victory, their likely young saviour having run out of support.

It was only the second Test win ever managed by New Zealand in Pakistan, the first having come 27 years ago, at Lahore, under Graham Dowling's captaincy, and the southernmost Test nation's first victory in 16 Tests since November 1994. **TMY**

Mohammad Wasim: century on debut

FIRST TEST MATCH

Gaddafi Stadium, Lahore

November 21, 22, 23, 24 1996
Toss: New Zealand

NEW ZEALAND			Mins	Balls	Fours			Mins	Balls	Fours
J.T.C. Vaughan	lbw b Nazir	3	27	19	0	(2) b Mushtaq	11	78	47	1
B.A. Young	lbw b Younis	8	42	26	1	(1) c Mohammad b Mushtaq	36	106	82	4
A.C. Parore	c Malik b Saqlain	37	91	68	5	lbw b Saqlain	15	55	44	1
S.P. Fleming	c Malik b Mushtaq	19	94	60	1	not out	92	279	198	13‡
N.J. Astle	lbw b Mushtaq	0	8	10	0	lbw b Mushtaq	3	5	5	0
M.J. Greatbatch	c Mohammad b Younis	18	80	37	1	b Younis	1	21	10	0
C.L. Cairns	c Inzamam b Mushtaq	4	13	12	0	lbw b Mushtaq	93	150	89	12§
C.Z. Harris	b Younis	16	33	35	2	c Malik b Mushtaq	0	11	6	0
*†L.K. Germon	lbw b Younis	0	3	2	0	lbw b Mushtaq	11	18	18	2
D.N. Patel	lbw b Mushtaq	26	64	40	3	lbw b Nazir	0	4	1	0
S.B. Doull	not out	15	44	34	2	st Moin b Saqlain	26	36	17	4‡
Extras:	b4 lb5	9				b6 lb16 nb1	23			
Total:		155					311		‡ plus 1 six	

Fall: 6, 16, 67, 70, 73, 83, 102, 102, 117   46, 59, 85, 88, 101, 242, 242, 262, 262   § plus 3 sixes

Bowling:

Waqar Younis	15–3–48–4	Waqar Younis	15–6–26–1	
Shahid Nazir	8–3–15–1	Shahid Nazir	16–1–84–1	
Mushtaq Ahmed	22.1–4–59–4	Mushtaq Ahmed	32–7–84–6	
Saqlain Mushtaq	12–3–24–1	Saqlain Mushtaq	22.2–4–95–2 1nb	

PAKISTAN			Mins	Balls	Fours			Mins	Balls	Fours
*Saeed Anwar	b Doull	8	17	11	2	lbw b Doull	0	1	2	0
Zahoor Elahi	c Fleming b Doull	22	44	26	3‡	c Young b Patel	6	81	45	1
Ijaz Ahmed	lbw b Cairns	3	11	5	0	b Doull	8	11	12	1
Inzamam-ul-Haq	c Astle b Doull	0	6	5	0	c Young b Cairns	14	30	22	2
Salim Malik	c Young b Doull	21	69	50	2	(6) c Germon b Doull	21	48	35	4
Mohammad Wasim	b Doull	0	3	4	0	(7) not out	109	215	165	17
†Moin Khan	lbw b Vaughan	59	137	96	11	(8) c Germon b Astle	38	92	75	8
Saqlain Mushtaq	lbw b Vaughan	23	125	90	1	(5) c Fleming b Vaughan	0	6	5	0
Waqar Younis	lbw b Vaughan	2	8	7	0	(10) b Patel	1	10	9	0
Mushtaq Ahmed	c Germon b Vaughan	25	50	32	4	(9) c Fleming b Patel	15	75	53	2
Shahid Nazir	not out	13	14	12	2	c Harris b Patel	1	16	7	0
Extras:	b5 lb7 nb3	15				b8 lb8 nb2	18			
Total:		191			‡ plus 1 six		231			

Fall: 21, 29, 34, 37, 37, 85, 141, 143, 164   0, 8, 25, 26, 42, 60, 135, 211, 219

Bowling:

Cairns	19–5–79–1 3nb	Doull	16–4–39–3	
Doull	16–3–46–5	Cairns	16–5–62–1 2nb	
Harris	1–0–3–0	Vaughan	14–5–48–1	
Vaughan	12.5–2–27–4	Patel	15.1–6–36–4	
Patel	7–2–24–0	Harris	6–2–20–0	
		Astle	4–1–10–1	

Umpires: Shakoor Rana (Pak.) & R.B. Tiffin (Zim.). *Third umpire:* Ikram Rabbani (Pak.). *Referee:* C.W. Smith (WI).
Debuts: Mohammad Wasim, Zahoor Elahi (Pak.). *Man of the Match:* S.B. Doull

New Zealand won by 44 runs

Pakistan v New Zealand

Second Test: Rawalpindi

November 28–December 1 1996

Mohammad Zahid's Wondrous Debut

Pakistan levelled the two-match series emphatically at Rawalpindi, almost everything going right for acting captain Saeed Anwar after he had absorbed the disappointing news that Waqar Younis had now joined Wasim Akram on the injured list. His fast attack thus relied on three young men, one of them, Mohammad Zahid, now making his Test debut. Born 20 years ago in the small market town of Gaggu Mandi, not far from Waqar's birthplace in the Punjab, Zahid now returned wonderful first-Test-match figures of 11 for 130, seventh in the list, third (behind Hirwani and Massie) since the Second World War. His innings and match figures were the best by a Pakistan bowler on Test debut.

With the only senior Pakistan bowler, Mushtaq Ahmed, taking eight further wickets, seven of them top-order batsmen, and centuries from Anwar and Ijaz and 78 from Salim Malik, the victory was achieved in 3½ days.

Anwar put New Zealand in on a blameless, bare track, and for 40 minutes the tourists had little cause for anxiety. Then Zahid broke through with two lbws, and Mushtaq's prolific form of the past year was crowned with his 100th Test wicket when he had Young leg-before (New Zealand suffered nine lbw dismissals in this Test). He teased his way through the middle order, and at 111 for 7 New Zealand were well on the way to being humbled.

The best partnership of the innings now came from the elegant Fleming and his captain, Germon going on to his maiden Test half-century (in his 10th match). The stand of 81 was followed by one of 49 between Germon and Patel before Zahid and Mushtaq completed their destructive work.

After the early loss of Elahi, Pakistan then sailed past New Zealand's 249 before the end of the second day, with Saeed Anwar and Ijaz Ahmed pairing in a 4½-hour stand of 262, a Pakistan record for the second wicket against New Zealand. During those 65 overs they batted with discretion and unleashed strokes at the wayward deliveries, which were not all that rare. The left-hander was 130 not out at stumps, the score 269 for 2, while Ijaz, whose sixth Test century had included a big six off Patel, had been given out lbw, a decision to which he reacted angrily, the gesture bringing upon him a fine of half his match fee.

With Patel unable to take the field owing to a stomach upset, the third day began ominously for New Zealand. Soon, however, wickets began to fall. Cairns, who finished with five wickets, undertook most of the work with Doull, with Harris contributing valuably with the wickets of Inzamam and the nightwatchman Mushtaq, who secured his highest Test score to go alongside his 100th wicket. It was Malik, not for the first time, who barred the opposition's progress. He and Mushtaq put on 84 for the fifth wicket, and although Malik declined to seize the initiative, and the last five wickets fell for only 55, the ultimate lead was a daunting 181.

Cairns was the second player to fall foul of the match referee, forfeiting half his match fee for theatrical behaviour either side of a not-out verdict by umpire Akhtar to an lbw appeal against Malik when he was only 27.

To the echoes of many lbw shouts, Young and Vaughan weathered the 24 overs faced on the third evening and scored 69 without being separated. But the fourth day brought collapse, newcomer Zahid being chiefly responsible. He plucked out five Kiwis before lunch and mopped up the tail to seal his memorable debut, the first Pakistan bowler to take as many as 10 wickets on Test debut. The tall, strongly-built fast-medium bowler got the ball to swing either way and deviate off the pitch. Five of his seven wickets in the innings came from lbw decisions, and Young, whose 61 spanned almost three hours, was taken at gully from a slashing cut. Germon, who had promoted himself to second-wicket-down, was yorked for a duck this time.

The luck was so much against New Zealand that when Greatbatch hit Mushtaq powerfully off the back foot, the ball curled to cover for a catch off a close fielder's boot. Fleming went in down the order because of illness, and looked out of sorts. Cairns,

Clive Mason/Allsport

averse to stonewalling, was bowled round his legs as he swept. And the match was aptly laid to rest with two leg-before decisions, taking the total to 28 out of the 70 wickets to fall in these two Test matches. The eight in Zahid's favour constituted a record.

Pakistan spirits were lifted by this innings victory, though they sustained a 10 per cent fine for a slow over rate. For their part, New Zealand, who had to absorb the loss of Larsen and Morrison (both went home injured, uncapped Wellington medium-pacer Glenn Jonas reinforcing the tour party), were grateful for their earlier rare win on the Subcontinent. *TMY*

Consistent Pakistan opener Saeed Anwar led the scoring in his country's face-saving innings victory over New Zealand at Rawalpindi

SECOND TEST MATCH

November 28, 29, 30 December 1 1996

Rawalpindi Cricket Stadium

Toss: Pakistan

NEW ZEALAND		Mins	Balls	Fours		Mins	Balls	Fours
B.A. Young	lbw b Mushtaq	39	93	67	5	c Elahi b Zahid	61	171	121	6
J.T.C. Vaughan	lbw b Zahid	12	50	32	2	lbw b Zahid	27	122	75	4
A.C. Parore	lbw b Zahid	3	10	2	0	lbw b Zahid	6	32	27	1
S.P. Fleming	c Moin b Mushtaq	67	190	109	11	(7) c Moin b Nazir	4	25	15	1
N.J. Astle	c Moin b Mushtaq	11	14	12	2	lbw b Zahid	1	26	18	0
M.J. Greatbatch	c Anwar b Mushtaq	2	9	2	0	c Anwar b Mushtaq	19	36	30	2
C.L. Cairns	c Wasim b Mushtaq	9	43	23	0	(8) b Mushtaq	11	33	18	1
C.Z. Harris	lbw b Zahid	1	3	3	0	(9) lbw b Zahid	14	38	27	3
•†L.K. Germon	c Moin b Zahid	55	154	148	9	(4) b Zahid	0	29	12	0
D.N. Patel	c Ijaz b Mushtaq	21	77	50	2	lbw b Zahid	0	19	11	0
S.B. Doull	not out	1	7	6	0	not out	4	10	6	1
Extras:	b4 lb14 nb10	28				lb7 w1 nb13	21			
Total:		249					168			

Fall: 33, 43, 69, 77, 87, 110, 111, 192, 241

82, 105, 109, 112, 119, 137, 137, 163, 163

Bowling:

Mohammad Zahid	21–5–64–4 *9nb*		Mohammad Zahid	20–3–66–7 *12nb 1w*
Shahid Nazir	9–3–23–0		Shahid Nazir	7–1–19–1
Mohammad Akram	12–1–48–0		Mohammad Akram	7–2–11–0
Mushtaq Ahmed	30–3–87–6		Mushtaq Ahmed	22–7–52–2 *1nb*
Salim Malik	2–0–9–0 *1nb*		Salim Malik	2–0–13–0

PAKISTAN		Mins	Balls	Fours
*Saeed Anwar	c Doull b Cairns	149	311	214	20
Zahoor Elahi	c Fleming b Cairns	2	8	6	0
Ijaz Ahmed	lbw b Cairns	125	273	198	19‡
Mushtaq Ahmed	lbw b Harris	42	140	101	4
Inzamam-ul-Haq	c Vaughan b Harris	1	5	4	0
Salim Malik	b Cairns	78	213	159	8
Mohammad Wasim	c Cairns b Doull	5	27	22	0
†Moin Khan	lbw b Doull	2	26	16	0
Shahid Nazir	c & b Cairns	10	42	40	1
Mohammad Zahid	lbw b Astle	0	3	1	0
Mohammad Akram	not out	0	6	1	0
Extras:	lb14 nb2	16			
Total:		430			‡ plus 1 six

Fall: 6, 268, 290, 291, 375, 394, 398, 419, 420

Bowling:

Doull	31–7–86–2
Cairns	30.4–2–137–5
Vaughan	17–1–72–0
Astle	9–1–31–1
Patel	15–4–33–0
Harris	24–7–57–2

Umpires: L.H. Barker (WI) & Javed Akhtar (Pak.).
Third umpire: Z.I. Pasha (Pak.). *Referee:* C.W. Smith (WI).
Debut: Mohammad Zahid (Pak.). *Man of the Match:* Mohammad Zahid

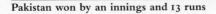

Pakistan won by an innings and 13 runs

Mohammad Zahid – 11 wickets on debut

Australia v West Indies

First Test: Brisbane

November 22–6 1996

Australia Take Up Where They Left Off in Jamaica

Australia's first victory against West Indies at the Gabba for 21 years was appropriately underwritten by a cricketer as Queensland as the Breakfast Creek Hotel. Australia's unpretentious vice-captain/keeper Ian Healy, who had been reading widely of his imminent eclipse by younger rivals in the preliminaries to the match, administered an authoritative rejoinder: 206 unbeaten runs and four catches. Healy has not been a West Indian pin-up of recent times, but the warmth with which Brian Lara shook his hand after the completion of Australia's first innings suggests that a few fences have been mended.

West Indies, meantime, were let down by their stereotyped attack on an excellent surface, which was better suited to the lesser velocities but subtler variations of Glenn McGrath and Paul Reiffel. Carl Hooper and Sherwin Campbell achieved their first centuries in the Worrell Trophy, but there was a disturbing lack of fibre in the visitors' efforts which did not augur well for a series the Australian Cricket Board hyperbolically dubbed 'The Decider'.

Australia granted new caps to the 24-year-old paceman Michael Kasprowicz, from South Brisbane via Chelmsford, and the 25-year-old Victorian left-hand opener Matthew Elliott, presenting them in a new pre-match ceremony before the biggest first-day Test crowd at the Gabba in two decades. But later that morning Elliott was rueing an uncomfortable nought, and the first session of the match was austere: only two scoring shots in front of square on the off side before lunch.

Ponting, the new Australian cornerstone at No.3, retaliated after early indignities to play a brazen selection of strokes. A lofted hook from Benjamin sailed clear of Ambrose at long leg for six, and he drove smartly straight. The direction of the day was still inconclusive, though, when he, Taylor and Mark Waugh misjudged pull shots, and Bevan uncomfortably guided to slip his first ball in Test cricket at home for 22 months.

It took Steve Waugh and Healy to put Australia back on the straight and narrow, Waugh playing with his usual pawky skill and Healy eschewing his pet hook in favour of rasping square-cuts and percussive drives. Walsh erred in not bowling himself and Ambrose until the pair were well ensconced, and their partnership of 142 in just over three hours proved a turning-point in the match. When Bishop removed Waugh from round the wicket, Healy co-opted the tail in registering what was the highest Test score by an Australian keeper and, remarkably, the first Test century at the Gabba by a born Queenslander.

West Indies lost both openers in the remaining 115 minutes that evening and Lara, from bat via pad to slip, early Sunday morning. It took Hooper, after 18 largely unproductive Worrell Trophy

Tests, and Chanderpaul, in his first, to balm the innings with a soothing four-hour alliance of 172.

Hooper manhandled Warne, pulling him hugely for six, and closed with unstinting application on a second consecutive Test century (he made 127 at The Oval in August 1995). Composure escaped him only in the later stages of his five-hour innings: he was agonisingly close to being run out in taking his 100th run – third umpire Parker rewinding the video eight times in two minutes before judging him safe – and greeted the green light with a relieved, sardonic smile.

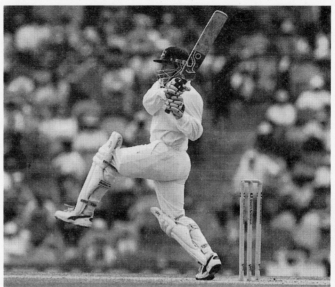

Shaun Botterill/Allsport

Much of Hooper's good work with Chanderpaul, however, was squandered in a hectic final session in which seven West Indians succumbed in the space of 74 deliveries for the addition of 28.

The instigator was Ricky Ponting. Sliding in on his elbows from forward square leg, he caught the bat-pad parabola from Hooper at 249. And, when Steve Waugh pulled up lame delivering his 49th delivery six runs later, Ponting stood in and promptly trapped Adams, lbw straddling the crease.

Reiffel's outswing and Warne's flipper so confounded the balance of the batting that, with half-an-hour remaining, Taylor was presented with a gift-wrapped opportunity to enforce the follow-on. But, as on this ground two years ago, Australia's captain elected to bat again, reasoning that Warne would flourish as the pitch deteriorated in the final day.

The West Indian bowlers kept Australia below three runs an over for much of their second innings, with only Healy (who passed 3000 Test runs) able to assert himself in an undefeated 45 from 50 deliveries. Elliott eluded his pair and shaped well but Bishop punctured his forward stroke, and the frail Bevan narrowly escaped a pair when Lara fumbled a low-flying edge at first slip. Bevan was, however, to redeem himself somewhat when Taylor set West Indies 420 in a minimum 119 overs. Shane Warne, for whom the Test was a trial gallop after a winter convalescing from a finger operation, still seemed inconvenienced and underdone, so Bevan filled the breach with three key wickets in 14 overs of wrist-spin.

Lara, on whom West Indian hopes largely rested, hit five fours in his first 29 on Monday evening, but slashed reprehensibly at Reiffel after half-an-hour next morning, reminiscent of his culpable stroke at Lord's in June 1995. Thereafter the innings was winnowed away by McGrath and Bevan, Hooper falling to a frivolous sweep, Chanderpaul playing on, and Adams lbw well forward but in line. Only the composed and meticulous Campbell threatened to thwart Australia's advance, rationing his strokes and scorning anything wide. He was ninth out after almost seven disciplined hours, having registered his second century and passed 1000 runs in only his 12th Test, and the innings ended nine minutes later when Benjamin was lbw with 52 minutes to play.

Over 50,000 saw the match, the ground unveiling the full extent of recent renovations including a sumptuous Press area. A new electronic scoreboard kept pace immaculately with the 1269 runs and, indeed, the pandemic of no-balls. Five dozen accrued in sundries, Reiffel (15), Ambrose (13) and Walsh (12) the chief transgressors.

Gideon Haigh

The first Queensland-born player to score a Test century at the Gabba, Ian Healy takes it on to the highest score by an Australian wicketkeeper

FIRST TEST MATCH

Woolloongabba, Brisbane

November 22, 23, 24, 25, 26 1996

Toss: West Indies

AUSTRALIA

			Mins	Balls	Fours			Mins	Balls	Fours
*M.A. Taylor	b Walsh	43	176	136	5	(2) c Browne b Benjamin	36	127	99	3
M.T.G. Elliott	c Browne b Ambrose	0	18	15	0	(1) b Bishop	21	98	66	2
R.T. Ponting	c Walsh b Benjamin	88	208	150	10‡	c Browne b Bishop	9	43	28	1
M.E. Waugh	c Browne b Walsh	38	112	70	5	c Browne b Bishop	57	139	95	4
S.R. Waugh	c Lara b Bishop	66	255	184	3					
M.G. Bevan	c Samuels b Walsh	0	1	1	0	(5) c sub (*A.F.G. Griffith*) b Ambrose	20	74	62	2
†I.A. Healy	not out	161	356	250	20	(6) not out	45	67	50	6
P.R. Reiffel	c & b Walsh	20	83	61	0	(7) run out (*Samuels/Browne*)	11	16	10	2
S.K. Warne	c & b Bishop	24	62	54	2‡					
M.S.Kasprowicz	c Benjamin b Bishop	6	11	10	0					
G.D. McGrath	b Benjamin	0	5	5	0					
Extras:	lb8 w3 nb22	33				b1 lb3 nb14	18			
Total:		479		‡ plus 1 six		6 wkts dec.	217			

Fall: 4, 130, 146, 196, 196, 338, 407, 468, 477

55, 74, 82, 137, 189, 217

Bowling:

Ambrose	34–4–93–1 *1w 7nb*	Ambrose	18–2–47–1 *6nb*
Walsh	35–6–112–4 *8nb*	Walsh	17–1–58–0 *4nb*
Benjamin	33–6–97–2 *2w 4nb*	Bishop	13–2–49–3 *3nb*
Bishop	30–2–105–3 *3nb*	Benjamin	15–1–52–1 *1nb*
Hooper	19–3–64–0	Hooper	2–0–7–0

WEST INDIES

		Mins	Balls	Fours			Mins	Balls	Fours
S.L. Campbell	c Warne b Reiffel	18	80	58	2	lbw b Bevan	113	407	327	9
R.G. Samuels	c Healy b McGrath	10	47	37	2	c Taylor b Warne	29	63	42	4‡
B.C. Lara	c M.E. Waugh b McGrath	26	95	69	3	c M.E. Waugh b Reiffel	44	95	75	7
C.L. Hooper	c Ponting b S.R. Waugh	102	306	228	10‡	c Healy b Bevan	23	55	41	2
S. Chanderpaul	c M.E. Waugh b Reiffel	82	284	230	4	b McGrath	14	35	30	1
J.C. Adams	lbw b Ponting	0	10	6	0	lbw b Warne	2	30	20	0
†C.O. Browne	c Healy b Reiffel	4	40	27	0	c Healy b McGrath	20	38	31	3
I.R. Bishop	lbw b Warne	0	6	6	0	c Ponting b Bevan	24	51	46	4
C.E.L. Ambrose	c sub (*J.N. Gillespie*) b Reiffel	0	11	1	0	c Warne b McGrath	7	29	30	1
K.C.G. Benjamin	lbw b Warne	9	4	7	2	lbw b McGrath	1	13	8	0
*C.A. Walsh	not out	0	1	0	0	not out	1	9	4	0
Extras:	lb8 w1 nb17	26				b8 lb3 nb7	18			
Total:		277		‡ plus 1 six			296		‡ plus 1 six	

Fall: 30, 43, 77, 249, 255, 267, 268, 268, 277

54, 118, 154, 187, 202, 241, 281, 293, 293

Bowling:

McGrath	21–7–32–2 *6nb*	McGrath	29.5–12–60–4 *1nb*
Reiffel	24.1–6–58–4 *9nb*	Kasprowicz	13–2–29–0
Kasprowicz	22–5–60–0 *1nb*	Warne	41–16–92–2
Warne	27–3–88–2 *1w 1nb*	Reiffel	9–0–58–1 *6nb*
S.R. Waugh	8.1–1–15–1	Bevan	14–3–46–3
M.E. Waugh	4–1–16–0		
Ponting	1.5–1–0–1		

Umpires: C.J. Mitchley (SA) & S.G. Randell (Aus.). *Third umpire:* P.D. Parker (Aus.). *Referee:* P.L. van der Merwe (SA). *Debuts:* M.T.G. Elliott, M.S. Kasprowicz (Aus.). *Man of the Match:* I.A. Healy

Australia won by 123 runs

Australia v West Indies

Second Test: Sydney

November 29–December 3 1996

Similar Margin at Sydney

Australia won their ninth Sydney Test in 14 starts against West Indies just before tea on the last day with an ease that had seemed predestined since a correct call at the toss. But it was a match that, at times, made for uncomfortable viewing (just under 80,000 paid to watch), suggesting once more that these are the last days of the Caribbean Empire.

While the tourists refrained from altering the ensemble that lost the first Test, three South Australians were recruited for the home XIII. Peter McIntyre was filtered out, but Greg Blewett ensured that Steve Waugh's stiffening influence was not missed by spending four hours over 69 in the first innings. And new cap Jason Gillespie – who gained his place when Paul Reiffel withdrew late, incommoded by a stiff neck – attacked the stumps with youthful zest.

After a somnolent first hour grieving the loss of the toss, West Indies applied themselves effectively on the first day. Bishop removed both openers in a speedy pre-lunch spell, and Ponting followed to the first delivery after the adjournment, chasing a loosener from Walsh. The slow pitch, militating against strokeplay, frustrated Mark Waugh into a delinquent hook and, when Bevan's inert two hours ended tamely in the over after tea, Australia had sagged to 131 for 5.

Nothing makes Healy's sap rise like adversity, however, and his street-smart strokes roused Blewett in the last session, much as they had during the youngster's head-turning Test debut almost two years ago. The slender South Australian whirled into a couple of characteristic pull shots before the close, swelling their partnership to 93 in almost even time.

Though both fell early on Saturday, Australia's tail excelled itself to such a degree that the last five of the order aggregated 200. Warne, who appears to have recovered his *savoir faire* against speed, played with composure for 28, Kasprowicz hooked Walsh for six, and McGrath and Gillespie extorted 48 in 45 minutes from a tired attack with surprisingly orthodox strokes. McGrath, exceeding 50 runs in his 22nd Test, was saluted rapturously as he passed both his best Test score (9) and his highest first-class score (18).

McGrath found little in the pitch when it was his turn with the ball, and there were few alarms for two hours as Campbell and Samuels played alert and eye-catching strokes. Head-catching, too. One Campbell pull shot was of such extravagance that it connected sharply with Healy's head; a stroke, perhaps, that Desmond Haynes would be sorry he never thought of.

McGrath, however, is now a Test bowler of great resource, and he used the old ball to great effect from round the wicket. Samuels was lbw without offering, Lara squared-up by a delivery bending the other way. Then, whistled up on a whim by captain Taylor, Blewett yorked Campbell just before the close with a curve ball that Dizzy Dean might not have scorned. With the exception of Bishop, who applied the straightest of bats and most level of heads, the remainder of the West Indian innings mistook mere occupation of the crease for ownership. Warne trapped Hooper, playing pad-first to a topspinner, and Chanderpaul, offering an indeterminate flick. McGrath, with a change-up learned from Craig McDermott, also profited when Adams turned thoughtlessly to leg, and Browne drove without due care and attention.

Shaun Botterill/Allsport

Though he didn't bowl badly, Kasprowicz because the first Australian bowler to fail to take a wicket in either of his first two Tests.

The tourists were then desperately disappointing on Monday as Australia set a last-day agenda. On a pitch inimical to their one-pace workmanship, West Indies looked like a slow-moving and obsolete machine: listless bowling complemented by faulty catching, shoddy ground-fielding and colour-by-numbers captaincy. Even Bevan, their anxious quarry for the previous fortnight, looked at home.

The left-handed Elliott, in his second Test, showed his true colours in a splendid and enterprising four-hour innings. He is tall, angular, and places a sizable chin well over the ball when he strikes it square. His pull is a dramatic red-blooded stroke that ends, occasionally, in an elegant arabesque. Elliott's 78 would have commended him to the selectors for the rest of the summer had it not been for its sorry end. Returning for a second to Walsh at long leg, both he and Waugh zigged when one should have zagged, and they ended up colliding at terminal velocity.

Typical of West Indies' outcricket on the day was that, with both players prone in mid-pitch, no run-out could be affected. Hooper's wild throw to the striker's end was too tardy to maroon Elliott, who scrambled home on one leg. But the opener, after treatment in the centre, was whisked from the arena on the drinks buggy. A tear in the lateral cartilage of the right knee was diagnosed, and at least a three-week tear in Elliott's season expected.

Needing 313 to win on the last day with a full deck, West Indies' hopes vaporised in the first half-hour. Lara, on the ground where he scored 277 almost four years previously, completed a wretched match by belatedly aborting a pull at McGrath. The edge to Healy was low and replays indeterminate, but the shot worthy of censure.

Thereafter resistance came only from Chanderpaul, who batted with thrilling abandon in a 95-minute alliance of 117 with Hooper. Light on his feet and off-driving fluently, he dished out such punishment that Taylor was compelled to replace Warne with Bevan. Ten minutes before lunch, though, Warne was reintroduced. And in the last over of the session the spinner bowled Chanderpaul with a legbreak that turned from the rough at right-angles: shades of England 1993. It was the first of six wickets to fall for 31, and McGrath fittingly took the concluding catch on patrol at deep midwicket. His seven wickets were composed exclusively of top-order batsmen, and his two-dozen runs gave rich pleasure to all but the West Indians.   ***Gideon Haigh***

Departing from the traditionally cerebral and understated behaviour of spin bowlers, Shane Warne gives Carl Hooper a send-off after having him lbw

SECOND TEST MATCH

Sydney Cricket Ground

November 29, 30 December 1, 2, 3 1996
Toss: Australia

AUSTRALIA		Mins	Balls	Fours			Mins	Balls	Fours
*M.A. Taylor	c Chanderpaul b Bishop	27	106	90	2	c Lara b Bishop	16	131	81	1
M.T.G. Elliott	c Lara b Bishop	29	78	45	5	retired injured	78	244	162	9
R.T. Ponting	c Samuels b Walsh	9	42	28	1	c Browne b Bishop	4	29	22	0
M.E. Waugh	c Lara b Walsh	19	68	43	2	c Browne b Ambrose	67	235	159	6
M.G. Bevan	c Hooper b Benjamin	16	122	92	1	c Browne b Benjamin	52	166	154	5
G.S. Blewett	c Adams b Walsh	69	239	169	8	not out	47	102	62	5
†I.A. Healy	c Lara b Walsh	44	137	107	4	not out	22	36	32	4
S.K. Warne	c Browne b Bishop	28	74	45	2				
M.S.Kasprowicz	c Campbell b Walsh	21	31	25	1‡				
J.N. Gillespie	not out	16	70	49	1				
G.D. McGrath	lbw b Adams	24	57	45	0				
Extras:	lb10 w1 nb18	29				b4 lb10 w3 nb9	26		
Total:		331			‡ plus 1 six	4 wkts dec.	312		

Elliott retired injured at 143 for 2

Fall: 54, 68, 73, 94, 131, 224, 245, 283, 288

51, 67, 209, 274

Bowling:

Ambrose	25–5–73–0 9nb		Ambrose	20–2–66–1 3nb
Walsh	30–6–98–5 3nb		Walsh	19–6–36–0 4nb
Benjamin	22–4–69–1		Bishop	20–5–54–2 1nb 3w
Bishop	23–5–55–3 3nb 1w		Benjamin	16–4–46–1 1nb
Hooper	14–6–15–0		Hooper	27–7–75–0
Adams	5.5–1–11–1		Adams	4–0–21–0

WEST INDIES		Mins	Balls	Fours			Mins	Balls	Fours
S.L. Campbell	b Blewett	77	199	155	13	lbw b McGrath	15	53	49	1
R.G. Samuels	lbw b McGrath	35	142	115	3	b Warne	16	56	46	2
B.C. Lara	c Healy b McGrath	2	20	13	0	c Healy b McGrath	1	14	10	0
C.L. Hooper	lbw b Warne	27	109	86	4	c Taylor b Bevan	57	165	124	6
S. Chanderpaul	c & b Warne	48	196	136	6	b Warne	71	95	68	10
J.C. Adams	c Bevan b McGrath	30	97	89	3	c Blewett b McGrath	5	24	20	1
†C.O. Browne	c Blewett b McGrath	0	4	4	0	not out	25	77	24	5
I.R. Bishop	c Elliott b Warne	48	95	79	6	run out (*Ponting*)	0	1	2	0
C.E.L. Ambrose	b Gillespie	9	49	17	1	b Bevan	0	6	5	0
K.C.G. Benjamin	b Gillespie	6	24	18	1	c Taylor b Warne	4	11	11	0
*C.A. Walsh	not out	2	10	5	0	c McGrath b Warne	18	19	17	2‡
Extras:	b4 lb6 nb10	20				lb2 nb1	3		
Total:		304					215			‡ plus 1 six

Fall: 92, 108, 136, 166, 229, 229, 243, 286, 298

33, 33, 35, 152, 157, 176, 176, 176, 183

Bowling:

McGrath	31–9–82–4 9nb		McGrath	17–7–36–3 1nb
Kasprowicz	13–2–37–0		Waugh	4–0–15–0
Warne	35.2–13–65–3		Gillespie	7–2–27–0
Gillespie	23–5–62–2 1nb		Warne	27.4–6–95–4
Bevan	11–0–35–0		Bevan	14–2–40–2
Blewett	4–0–13–1			

Umpires: D.B. Hair (Aus.) & D.R. Shepherd (Eng.). *Third umpire:* S. Taufel (Aus.). *Referee:* P.L. van der Merwe (SA).
Debut: J.N. Gillespie (Aus.). *Man of the Match:* G.D. McGrath

Australia won by 124 runs

Australia v West Indies

Third Test: Melbourne

December 26–28 1996

West Indies Storm Back in Three Days

On an MCG pitch offering extravagant movement vertically, if not horizontally, three days sufficed for West Indies to loosen Australia's squirrel grip on the Worrell Trophy series. Curtly Ambrose was the visitors' torch-bearer: after 97 listless overs in Brisbane and Sydney yielding just 3 for 279, he twice ruined Australia's top order, carried away the individual honours with nine wickets for 72, and sent the home Press into anguished autopsies of their side's failings.

Praised by ex-captain Allan Border for having the courage to tamper with a winning combination, Australia's selectors made four alterations to their Sydney XI. Reiffel resumed his into-the-wind role after two wicketless Tests for Kasprowicz, Steve Waugh his back-to-the-wall position after two insecure outings by Bevan. And in place of the hobbled Elliott and the humbled Ponting, they offered a second Test cap to the prolific Queenslander Matthew Hayden almost three years after his first, and a seventh to the patriotic West Australian Justin Langer almost four years after his sixth. The West Indians held their hand from wholesale changes, substituting stumper Browne for Junior Murray.

The tourists' faith seemed well vested on Boxing Day morn when Ambrose opened with a vivid 10-over spell of 3 for 8. Hayden fell first to a firm-footed drive, and before noon Taylor had played on and Mark Waugh played down the wrong line. Langer, having shaped well and once hooked coolly for six, then hesitated fatally in response to Steve Waugh's call, Adams stepping smartly from short-leg to take cover-point's return.

A penitent Waugh and a pensive Blewett aligned with great character before and after lunch, the former playing with panache off the back foot when circumstance allowed, the latter surmounting lack of fluency with deep concentration and self-denial. But after Healy had played with his customary hyperkinetic invention for an hour, his fall to Ambrose from round-the-wicket was the first of five wickets for 24 runs that terminated the home innings for 219: only the seventh completed Australian first innings in the 1990s to end shy of 250.

The reversal of fortune was borne with considerable goodwill – and perhaps a touch of nostalgia – by what became the largest home Test crowd in 21 years (and the seventh-largest in Australia's annals). Almost 73,000 had defied the seasonal reverie by the time West Indies closed the day 190 in arrears with nine wickets standing.

The visitors resumed on the second day as if awed by their good fortune, and McGrath exploited their general lack of enterprise with four further wickets in four incisive spells, including Lara, pinioned from round the wicket. The narrow man from Narromine also executed a swift run-out, when the feckless Hooper wandered off for a single to mid-on from Warne.

At times, though, the Australian dependence on McGrath seemed uncomfortably heavy. When Gillespie strained the intercostal muscle in his left side after three overs, Reiffel looked innocuous and Warne to be striving for effect (the legspinner bowled, for him, an unusual ration of full-tosses). And after Chanderpaul had spent a methodical 3½ hours over his 11th half-century in 21 Test innings, the critical cricket of the day came in 90 minutes of irreverence from Murray. With Adams a trustworthy escort, the Grenadian keeper reanimated the West Indian innings with hard hitting and purposeful running.

Though his introverted fifty took more than half a day, Adams was recovering his touch at every moment, granting not a chance. After his partner had fallen to a rash hook, Adams's studious stewardship of the tail prolonged West Indies' innings 20 minutes into Saturday morning.

With a second opening spell that wasted nary a ball, Ambrose then made his team's 36-run lead look substantial. Hayden shouldered arms to his fifth delivery and, from this statuesque pose, heard his off stump resonate; then Langer, horribly hashing a hook, became the Antiguan's 100th Australian Test victim. (Ambrose already had 117 England wickets, and so joined Lance Gibbs as only the second bowler to take 100 wickets against two countries.) Ambrose rested with 7–4–4–2 and, when Taylor completed his 12th Test innings without a half-century by edging a fine delivery from Walsh, Australia were still 10 runs in arrears.

It was first-rate fast bowling abetted by indeterminate batting, and Walsh widened the breach after lunch by pushing one into a creasebound Mark Waugh and sending one away from a nonplussed Blewett. Benjamin promptly forced Healy to play on, and trapped Reiffel with Australia only 40 runs in the black. Steve Waugh alone displayed the necessary composure but, when Ambrose returned to have Warne nimbly caught at short leg and the immobile Gillespie pinned on the back foot, he dragged on while drawing away. Without having advanced on their 87 victory target, West Indies lost Campbell to a miscued pull. McGrath from around the wicket then had Samuels lbw and Lara for the fifth time in the series pouched at gully. But Chanderpaul, the new West Indian bulwark at No.3, added 50 in less than an hour with Hooper to assuage any anxiety, and the latter straight-drove the winning runs at two minutes to six.

Heavy retrospective criticism of Tony Ware's surface tended to obscure the virtues of Ambrose, whose performance was the best by a West Indian in Melbourne since Michael Holding's 11 for 107 15 years earlier. Age seems to have cost Ambrose his yorker and a lingering hamstring strain confined him to first slip throughout the second innings, but he exploited the conditions shrewdly, maintaining a length at least a yard fuller than in the first two Tests that posed a constant threat to knuckles and forearms.

Praise was also due to McGrath, for whom Samuels was a 100th Test wicket in only his 23rd Test: a rate of progress commensurate with Warne. And it was, finally, a shame that, with the Test series now so admirably poised, spectators had a full four weeks of cricket's colourised version to wade through until the next instalment. **Gideon Haigh**

Shaun Botterill/Allsport

Mark Taylor's miserable season continues: one of Curtly Ambrose's nine wickets at the MCG

THIRD TEST MATCH
Melbourne Cricket Ground

December 26, 27, 28 1996
Toss: Australia

AUSTRALIA		Mins	Balls	Fours		Mins	Balls	Fours
*M.A. Taylor	b Ambrose	7	52	40	0	(2) c Hooper b Walsh	10	78	48	1
M.L. Hayden	c Hooper b Ambrose	5	27	19	0	(1) b Ambrose	0	3	5	0
J.L. Langer	run out (*Campbell/Adams*)	12	42	20	0‡	c Hooper b Ambrose	0	12	7	0
M.E. Waugh	lbw b Ambrose	0	1	1	0	lbw b Walsh	19	81	54	1
S.R. Waugh	c Murray b Bishop	58	163	131	4	b Benjamin	37	145	87	2
G.S. Blewett	run out (*sub: A.F.G. Griffith*)	62	223	154	4	c Murray b Walsh	7	27	17	1
†I.A. Healy	c Hooper b Ambrose	36	61	47	4	b Benjamin	0	7	5	0
P.R. Reiffel	c Samuels b Benjamin	0	8	4	0	lbw b Benjamin	8	17	11	1
S.K. Warne	c Campbell b Bishop	10	38	28	0	c Adams b Ambrose	18	36	20	4
J.N. Gillespie	not out	4	39	23	0	lbw b Ambrose	2	18	20	0
G.D. McGrath	c Hooper b Ambrose	0	5	3	0	not out	5	17	9	0
Extras:	lb8 nb17	25				lb4 w1 nb11	16		
Total:		219		‡ plus 1 six			122		

Fall: 5, 26, 26, 27, 129, 195, 200, 203, 217

0, 3, 28, 47, 64, 65, 76, 107, 113

Bowling:

Ambrose	24.5–7–55–5 9nb		Ambrose	12–4–17–4 4nb
Bishop	11–1–31–2 2nb		Bishop	10–2–26–0 3nb 1w
Benjamin	19–2–64–1 1nb		Benjamin	12.5–5–34–3
Walsh	14–0–43–0 5nb		Walsh	11–4–41–3 4nb
Adams	1–0–4–0			
Hooper	5–1–14–0			

WEST INDIES		Mins	Balls	Fours		Mins	Balls	Fours
S.L. Campbell	lbw b McGrath	7	27	31	0	c Hayden b McGrath	0	4	4	0
R.G. Samuels	c Taylor b Warne	17	141	82	2	lbw b McGrath	13	20	12	2
S. Chanderpaul	c & b McGrath	58	209	147	4	b Reiffel	40	97	82	3
B.C. Lara	c Warne b McGrath	2	26	18	0	c Hayden b McGrath	2	17	9	0
C.L. Hooper	run out (*McGrath/Warne*)	7	22	25	0	not out	27	57	36	2
J.C. Adams	not out	74	249	188	5	not out	1	4	3	0
†J.R. Murray	c Reiffel b McGrath	53	116	117	3				
I.R. Bishop	lbw b McGrath	0	8	3	0				
C.E.L. Ambrose	b Warne	8	29	19	1				
K.C.G. Benjamin	b Reiffel	11	14	13	2				
*C.A. Walsh	c M.E. Waugh b Warne	4	32	17	0				
Extras:	b4 lb7 nb3	14				nb4	4		
Total:		255				4 wkts	87		

Fall: 12, 62, 71, 86, 107, 197, 197, 215, 230

0, 25, 32, 82

Bowling:

McGrath	30–11–50–5		McGrath	9–1–41–3
Reiffel	29–8–76–1 3nb		Reiffel	9–2–16–1 4nb
Warne	28.1–3–72–3		Warne	3–0–17–0
Gillespie	3–2–5–0		Blewett	2.5–0–13–0
Blewett	9–3–19–0			
S.R. Waugh	10–5–22–0			

Umpires: P.D. Parker (Aus.) & S. Venkataraghavan (Ind.). *Third umpire:* W.P. Sheahan (Aus.). *Referee:* P.L. van der Merwe (SA). *Debuts:* none. *Man of the Match:* C.E.L. Ambrose

West Indies won by 6 wickets

Australia v West Indies

Fourth Test: Adelaide

25–8 January 1997

Bevan Inspires Crushing Comeback

Chosen contentiously for the fourth Test as an allrounder *faute de mieux*, Michael Bevan underwrote Australia's retention of the Frank Worrell Trophy with a towering contribution of 10 for 113 and 85 not out – only the fourth instance of 10 wickets and a half-century by an Australian in the same Test. But what had been billed as the most significant home Test in many a year proved anticlimactic, spanning only 20 hours' elapsed time, and proving that West Indies' Melbourne victory had been a statistical anomaly rather than a leading indicator.

The month since Melbourne had been full of anguished doubt for the Australians, especially when they failed for the first time since 1980 to qualify for the finals of their tri-cornered one-day series. And when the selectors decreed only two changes to the defeated third Test unit – the injured Gillespie and the infirm Reiffel giving way to the 26-year-old Queenslander Andrew Bichel and Bevan – they were reproached for relying on the latter's left-arm wrist-spin as a front-line weapon (although no critic could nominate a slow bowler with superior claims).

Few had noted how badly the tourists' January had been sabotaged by injuries. Benjamin and McLean had been freighted home, while Ambrose had laboured through the one-day series on ever-stiffening legs. And when he was finally invalided out of the side on match eve, the West Indians appeared gripped by mild panic. Certainly, their four inclusions in the XII were based more on speculation than substance: Cameron Cuffy, Patterson Thompson, Phil Simmons and uncapped cack-hander Adrian Griffith.

Views were hastily revised when West Indies, after winning the toss, capitulated in 3¼ hours on the first day. Campbell was undone by a fine lifter from McGrath, and Griffith – who'd opened his Test ledger with an outside edge from Bichel at catchable height between first and second slip, and an inside edge to the fine-leg fence from the same bowler – became Bichel's maiden Test wicket by playing myopically half-forward.

After a one-day run glut, much again hinged on Lara. But a vulgar slap at his first ball from Warne looped to Blewett at mid-on, and the bowler celebrated with a magnetic spell from all angles of the crease that first deceived then dismissed Chanderpaul. After Hooper had fallen to a nonchalant second-slip take and Adams to an equally casual return catch, Bevan's flat wrong 'uns were unintelligible to the tail. The solitary moment of relief was when Thompson shovelled a Warne long-hop into the pretty marquee erected near the Victor Richardson Gates.

Daggers were stared at Les Burdett's Adelaide Oval surface, but Hayden soon placed it in perspective, settling in without alarm, then pulling and driving with discretion. Betraying no anxiety about his previous Test record (25 in four innings), the burly left-hander finally resembled a batsman with a first-class average of 57 and an old head on 25-year-old shoulders.

Touch, by contrast, continued to elude Taylor. Front-foot poking indecisively, he was lbw to Bishop just after tea. Langer was also scatchy, and edged a cut after an hour. But whatever hopes these wickets raised were steadily forfeited by the tourists' error-laden outcricket, lowlighted by Hayden's life at 58: Murray's feint upset Lara at slip, and the low catch bounced out.

Hayden prospered further on the second day. Although Bishop and Cuffy confined him at 66 for 40 minutes, the former then undid all their work by overstepping as the batsman slashed to Campbell at point. Murray compounded the error 20 minutes later by diving capriciously in front of Lara, and diverting the edge wide. Hayden was then 81.

What wickets did fall on the second day accrued almost accidentally. Mark Waugh's polished 82 ended when an edge lodged luckily in Murray's pads. Brother Steve scythed the longest of hops to cover-point and was expertly caught by Hooper (the worst ball to dismiss an eminent batsman at Adelaide, perhaps, since Walter Hammond mismanaged Bradman's full-toss in 1933). And at the same score, after completing a tenacious maiden Test century with two square-cuts from Cuffy, Hayden was marooned in trying to repeat an off-driven six off Hooper.

The accidents thereafter befell the tourists. Walsh set the bungling benchmark by having Blewett (14) caught from a no-ball at slip, then dropping a gentle mishook from the same batsman (51) at forward square leg. And Bevan was twice reprieved at 8, Murray fluffing a stumping, and Bishop again transgressing as the Australian dragged on. West Indies could rage at the fates all they wished, but bowlers allowing the largesse of more than 100 no-balls in a series invite such frustrations.

Amid this travail, Blewett was competent and composed, and Bevan cussed if never convincing. Both would have coveted hundreds when Australia resumed on Monday, 304 runs ahead with five wickets in hand, but Blewett (the 16th Australian to score 99 in a Test) received a splendid inducker from Cuffy, and Bevan never achieved the momentum necessary for the milestone. He flailed a couple of boundaries when McGrath joined him, then was a bystander as the latter was yorked. Bevan will seldom have batted so long for so few: his half-century alone lasted almost as long as West Indies' first innings. Australia's 517 came in 11½ hours.

Bevan was soon in the thick of the bowling action. Chanderpaul and Campbell were skilfully taken, either side of tea, either side of Taylor. Lara belatedly played his soundest and spunkiest innings of the series, adding 96 in even time with Hooper, but watched solemnly as three wickets forfeited in the last 20 minutes scotched this spasm of resistance.

Warne then picked up Lara with a wrong 'un after 25 minutes of Tuesday, and the last three fell Bevan's way before the noonday gun. Australia's 35th Test victory against West Indies ranked as their second-largest, exceeded only by the third match between the countries at Brisbane 66 years ago. Piquantly, it came on the ground where, four years earlier, West Indies had won by the slightest of margins: just a run. Another milestone that passed unnoticed was that Healy, in an almost spotless display of glovemanship, became Australia's most successful keeper against West Indies when he caught Cuffy.   ***Gideon Haigh***

At last Queensland's Matt Hayden, so bountiful in domestic cricket, reached a century for Australia

FOURTH TEST MATCH

Adelaide Oval

January 25, 26, 27, 28 1997
Toss: West Indies

WEST INDIES

			Mins	Balls	Fours		Mins	Balls	Fours
S.L. Campbell	c Healy b McGrath	0	18	16	0	c Taylor b Bevan	24	85	76	1‡
A.F.G. Griffith	lbw b Bichel	13	34	21	3	c S.R. Waugh b McGrath	1	13	7	0
S. Chanderpaul	c Taylor b Warne	20	66	45	2	c Taylor b Bevan	8	50	38	1
B.C. Lara	c Blewett b Warne	9	40	33	2	c Healy b Warne	78	167	144	12§
C.L. Hooper	c M.E. Waugh b McGrath	17	29	23	3	lbw b Warne	45	100	85	5
J.C. Adams	c & b Warne	10	73	64	1	c M.E. Waugh b Bevan	0	14	8	0
†J.R. Murray	c Blewett b Bevan	34	56	53	6	(8) c Taylor b Bevan	25	43	42	3
I.R. Bishop	c Healy b Bevan	1	35	21	0	(7) c Bevan b Warne	0	6	5	0
*C.A. Walsh	c Healy b Bevan	0	3	4	0	c S.R. Waugh b Bevan	1	10	5	0
C.E. Cuffy	c Healy b Bevan	2	9	11	0	not out	3	16	6	0
P.I.C. Thompson	not out	10	18	15	1‡	c Hayden b Bevan	6	8	9	1

Extras: b4 lb1 nb9 — 14

Total: 130 ‡ plus 1 six

Extras (2nd): b2 lb5 nb6 — 13 ‡ plus 1 five § plus 2 sixes

Total (2nd): 204

Fall: 11, 22, 45, 58, 72, 113, 117, 117, 119

Fall (2nd): 6, 22, 42, 138, 145, 154, 181, 192, 196

Bowling:

McGrath	12–4–21–2 3nb
Bichel	10–1–31–1 6nb
Bevan	9.5–2–31–4
Warne	16–4–42–3

McGrath	17–4–31–1 5nb
Bichel	8–4–16–0
Bevan	22.4–3–82–6 1nb
Warne	20–4–68–3
Blewett	2–2–0–0

AUSTRALIA

			Mins	Balls	Fours
*M.A. Taylor	lbw b Bishop	11	52	39	1
M.L. Hayden	st Murray b Hooper	125	354	226	15‡
J.L. Langer	c Murray b Cuffy	19	60	43	2
M.E. Waugh	c Murray b Hooper	82	189	150	10‡
S.R. Waugh	c Hooper b Chanderpaul	26	56	62	3
G.S. Blewett	b Cuffy	99	215	154	9
M.G. Bevan	not out	85	324	263	6
†I.A. Healy	c Lara b Thompson	12	43	18	2
S.K. Warne	c Hooper b Bishop	9	35	23	0
A.J. Bichel	c Lara b Walsh	7	26	21	0
G.D. McGrath	b Walsh	1	7	4	0

Extras: b2 lb15 w4 nb20 — 41

Total: 517 ‡ plus 1 six

Fall: 35, 78, 242, 288, 288, 453, 475, 494, 507

Bowling:

Walsh	37.3–6–101–2 5nb
Bishop	34–6–92–2 11nb 1w
Cuffy	33–4–116–2 4nb 2w
Thompson	16–0–80–1 1w
Hooper	31–7–86–2
Adams	8–0–23–0
Chanderpaul	3–1–2–1

Umpires: S.G. Randell (Aus.) & D.R. Shepherd (Eng.). *Third umpire:* D.J. Harper (Aus.). *Referee:* R. Subba Row (Eng.).
Debuts: A.J. Bichel (Aus.); A.F.G. Griffth (WI). *Man of the Match:* M.G. Bevan

Australia won by an innings and 183 runs

Australia v West Indies

Fifth Test: Perth

February 1–3 1997

Consolation for Tourists on Gift Pitch

On a Perth pitch that no-one liked the look of and in an atmosphere that no-one liked the sound of, West Indies took only three days to secure a consolation victory that closed Australia's series margin to 3–2. In their farewell appearances on Australian soil, Curtly Ambrose and Courtney Walsh surmounted groin and hamstring strains to undermine both home innings, though their efforts could do nothing to change the resting place of the Worrell Trophy.

The WACA tarmac was the match's first talking-point. Portentous cracks on the first morning had by the third day, in airless 40-degree heat, become what looked like a host of ugly surgical scars. 'I wouldn't have liked to see it on the fifth day,' said Mark Taylor. But the local association was saved scrutiny by elongated inquests into apparent ill-feeling between the sides, touched off by Brian Lara's assertions that petulant Australians had baited opener Robert Samuels, and Mark Taylor's counter-claims that Lara was 'an antagonist'. The unedifying spectacle climaxed when Lara, acting as runner to Walsh on the third morning, collided with close fielder Matt Hayden and went down like Diego Maradona looking for a penalty: which perhaps he was, although ICC referee Peter van der Merwe levied no fines. Thankfully, the general silliness was redeemed by the firm and even-handed response of umpires Hair and Willey – who promptly called both Taylor and Walsh into a conference that ended in a perfunctory handshake – and ultimately the percolating excitement of the cricket.

The first day set a vivid tone, Ambrose bowling wonderfully on a pitch that has always seemed tailored to his talents. Hayden's loose defensive stroke from the match's third ball sent in an arc to first slip, and Taylor's wretched run was continued by a sublime snatch of in-fielding: Chanderpaul leaping left at point to arrest Blewett's square-drive, then throwing from his supine position over the striker's stumps. Blewett was skewered by Simmons' handy inducker and Steve Waugh strangled in stretching for a distant Ambrose half-volley before lunch. It wasn't until the soporific heat got the better of Walsh, Ambrose and Bishop in the afternoon that the Australians were able to settle.

With panache and pluck, Mark Waugh (who reached 4000 Test runs in his 96th innings) and Bevan added 110 between lunch and tea, both playing much their best innings of the summer. The former met the steep bounce with a succession of square-cuts, and raised their century stand by straight-driving Hooper beyond the sightscreen.

A rehydrated Ambrose, however, removed Waugh, Healy and Reiffel in 20 minutes after tea. And, though Bevan looked back to his bow-legged best, Bishop quelled the tail. The tourists' exertions had been husbanded by some thoughtful Lara leadership: Ambrose and Bishop were kept fresh by constant rotation, the former bowling his 18 overs in seven spells, the latter his 18 in nine.

The visitors began uncertainly, Campbell and Chanderpaul disappearing within half-an-hour on the second morning. But, after Warne had initiated a change of ball, troubles seemed to ease. Lara finally endowed the summer with a Test century – his eighth, and first in 17 months – and the reinstated Samuels staged a 5½-hour endurathon that made up for in mettle what it lacked in method. Their 223-minute partnership of 208 was threatened only once. Belated recourse to the third umpire after a direct hit by Blewett showed Samuels so close to the line that fully three minutes were consumed in arbitration: time for a news bulletin, or at least a long ad-break had Channel 9 been so inclined.

Tempers frayed in the enervating heat, McGrath becoming fractious with Samuels, and later Warne with Hooper, though the only censure they incurred was Lara's, who accused the Worrell Trophy winners of 'rubbing it in'. When opener Samuels was out for 76, the total was 275. Lara and Hooper both passed 1000 Test runs against Australia.

Shaun Botterill/Allsport

Lara kept his cool by scoring 90 in boundaries, culminating after tea when he hit 26 in 14 Warne deliveries. And the second new ball did not scotch West Indies' innings until an hour into the third day, by which time their lead on a pitch now playing at wildly varying altitudes was an ample 141.

Ambrose sounded the Australian retreat, squaring Taylor up with a wicked ball that seamed away, then bowling Blewett with a positively evil delivery that tunnelled beneath the batsman's defences. Walsh then rose from the treatment table to dismiss both Waughs in consecutive overs after lunch. Resistance was confined to Hayden, who played coolly until failing to offer at Hooper, and later some plucky strokes from Healy, Warne and Bichel.

But Samuels and Campbell consumed no more than three-quarters of an hour, with a dozen blazing boundaries, catching up the required 54.

Although the Test was compressed into three days, it produced enough odd phenomena to merit investigation by Agents Scully and Mulder. Walsh batted with a runner, then bowled 20 overs for five wickets – shades of Kapil Dev against Australia at Melbourne in 1981. Warne bowled a bouncer to Lara – shades of Phil Edmonds, 1983. Australia's Adelaide matchwinner, Bevan, scarcely bowled at all – shades of Allan Border, 1989 (also wicketless in the Test following his sensational Sydney bag). Ambrose was bizarrely run out on the third morning by a back-handed flick from Healy when his bat lodged in one of the pitch's crevices, while his valedictory over took a gruesome 15 deliveries – two more than Gubby Allen's ill-famed Old Trafford over in 1934 – and cost 19 runs. In all, in fact, the series was swollen by 43 overs' worth of illegitimate deliveries: West Indies 147 no-balls and 20 wides, Australia 88 no-balls and 3 wides.

It was West Indies' fifth consecutive Test victory in Perth, and also the fourth in the last 10 Worrell Trophy matches to finish inside three days: a comment on the teams' defensive frailties and one-day cricket attention spans and/or high-quality pace bowling and poor-quality pitch preparation. Take your pick. The truth is out there. ***Gideon Haigh***

After his 10 wickets at Adelaide, Michael Bevan now top-scored for Australia at Perth – though in a losing cause

FIFTH TEST MATCH

WACA Ground, Perth

February 1, 2, 3 1997

Toss: Australia

AUSTRALIA

		Mins	Balls	Fours			Mins	Balls	Fours
M.L. Hayden	c Lara b Ambrose	0	2	3	0	(2) lbw b Hooper	47	140	102	4
*M.A. Taylor	run out (*Campbell/Adams*)	2	18	5	0	(1) c Browne b Ambrose	1	14	13	0
G.S. Blewett	c Browne b Simmons	17	82	65	2	b Ambrose	0	8	1	0
M.E. Waugh	c Campbell b Ambrose	79	224	170	8‡	c Browne b Walsh	9	48	33	2
S.R. Waugh	c Browne b Ambrose	1	19	20	0	c Hooper b Walsh	0	7	6	0
M.G. Bevan	not out	87	235	164	12	c Simmons b Walsh	15	42	31	3
†I.A. Healy	b Ambrose	7	18	15	1	c Chanderpaul b Walsh	29	42	31	5
P.R. Reiffel	c Simmons b Ambrose	0	1	1	0	c Adams b Walsh	5	5	6	1
S.K. Warne	c Browne b Bishop	9	41	29	0	c Simmons b Bishop	30	77	43	4
A.J. Bichel	c Browne b Bishop	15	28	27	2	c Samuels b Bishop	18	47	31	2
G.D. McGrath	c Ambrose b Bishop	0	2	3	0	not out	2	6	6	0
Extras:	lb10 w2 nb14	26				b2 lb8 w6 nb22	38			
Total:		243		‡ plus 1 six			194			

Fall: 0, 7, 45, 49, 169, 186, 186, 216, 243

7, 17, 43, 48, 84, 105, 110, 133, 189

Bowling:

Ambrose	18–5–43–5 *8nb*		Ambrose	9–2–50–2 *15nb*
Bishop	18–5–54–3 *1nb*		Bishop	12.3–1–44–2 *3nb 6w*
Walsh	9–0–29–0 *1w*		Walsh	20–4–74–5 *1nb*
Simmons	20–5–58–1 *5nb 1w*		Simmons	3–0–9–0 *2nb*
Hooper	15–1–49–0		Hooper	3–0–7–1 *1nb*

WEST INDIES

		Mins	Balls	Fours			Mins	Balls	Fours
S.L. Campbell	b Healy b Reiffel	21	52	44	3	not out	16	44	28	4
R.G. Samuels	c M.E. Waugh b Warne	76	332	228	10§	not out	35	44	38	8
S. Chanderpaul	c Reiffel b McGrath	3	19	17	0				
B.C. Lara	c Healy b Warne	132	223	185	22‡				
C.L. Hooper	c Healy b Reiffel	57	124	83	10§				
J.C. Adams	c Healy b McGrath	18	40	31	2				
P.V. Simmons	c M.E. Waugh b Reiffel	0	3	5	0				
†C.O. Browne	c Warne b Reiffel	0	2	3	0				
I.R. Bishop	c Taylor b Reiffel	13	67	44	1				
C.E.L. Ambrose	run out (*Healy*)	15	52	44	1				
*C.A. Walsh	not out	5	26	11	0				
Extras:	b5 lb10 w1 nb28	44		§ plus 1 five		lb2 w1 nb3	6			
Total:		384		‡ plus 1 six			0 wkt 57			

Fall: 30, 43, 251, 275, 331, 332, 332, 359, 367

Bowling:

McGrath	30–5–86–2 *4nb*		McGrath	4–1–14–0 *1nb*
Bichel	18–1–79–0 *12nb*		Reiffel	5–0–24–0 *2nb*
Reiffel	26–6–73–5 *10nb 1w*		Bichel	1.2–0–17–0 *1w*
Warne	19–8–55–2 *1nb*			
Blewett	6–2–19–0			
Bevan	5–0–31–0			
S.R. Waugh	7–1–26–0 *1nb*			

Umpires: D.B Hair (Aus.) & P. Willey (Eng.). *Third umpire:* T.A. Prue (Aus.). *Referee:* R. Subba Row (Eng.). *Debuts:* none.
Man of the Match: G.D. McGrath. *Man of the Series:* G.D. McGrath

West Indies won by 10 wickets

SERIES AVERAGES

AUSTRALIA

Batting:

	M	I	NO	R	HS	Av.	100	50	Ct/st
I.A. Healy	5	9	3	356	161★	59.33	1	0	15
M.G. Bevan	4	7	2	275	87★	55.00	0	3	2
G.S. Blewett	4	7	1	301	99	50.17	0	3	4
M.T.G. Elliott	2	4	1	128	78★	42.67	0	1	1
M.E. Waugh	5	9	0	370	82	41.11	0	4	8
M.L. Hayden	3	5	0	177	125	35.40	1	0	3
S.R. Waugh	4	6	0	188	66	31.33	0	2	2
R.T. Ponting	2	4	0	110	88	27.50	0	1	2
J.N. Gillespie	2	3	2	22	16★	22.00	0	0	0
S.K. Warne	5	7	0	128	30	18.29	0	0	6
M.A. Taylor	5	9	0	153	43	17.00	0	0	9
M.S. Kasprowicz	2	2	0	27	21	13.50	0	0	0
A.J. Bichel	2	3	0	40	18	13.33	0	0	0
J.L. Langer	2	3	0	31	19	10.33	0	0	0
P.R. Reiffel	3	6	0	44	20	7.33	0	0	2
G.D. McGrath	5	7	2	32	24	6.40	0	0	2

Substitute catch was held by J.N. Gillespie

Bowling:

	O	M	R	W	Av.	BB	5w/i
R.T. Ponting	1.5	1	0	1	0.00	1–0	0
G.D. McGrath	200.5	61	453	26	17.42	5–50	1
M.G. Bevan	76.3	10	265	15	17.67	6–82	1
P.R. Reiffel	102.1	22	305	12	25.42	5–73	1
S.K. Warne	217.1	57	594	22	27.00	4–95	0
J.N. Gillespie	33	9	94	2	47.00	2–62	0
S.R. Waugh	25.1	7	63	1	63.00	1–15	0
G.S. Blewett	23.5	7	64	1	64.00	1–13	0
A.J. Bichel	37.2	6	143	1	143.00	1–31	0
M.E. Waugh	8	1	31	0	–	–	0
M.S. Kasprowicz	48	9	126	0	–	–	0

WEST INDIES

Batting:

	M	I	NO	R	HS	Av.	100	50	Ct/st
C.L. Hooper	5	9	1	362	102	45.25	1	2	9
S. Chanderpaul	5	9	0	344	82	38.22	0	3	2
J.R. Murray	2	3	0	112	53	37.33	0	1	4 /1
R.G. Samuels	4	8	1	231	76	33.00	0	1	4
B.C. Lara	5	9	0	296	132	32.89	1	1	8
S.L. Campbell	5	10	1	291	113	32.33	1	1	3
J.C. Adams	5	9	2	140	74★	20.00	0	1	3
P.I.C. Thompson	1	2	1	16	10★	16.00	0	0	0
C.O. Browne	3	5	1	49	25★	12.25	0	0	15
I.R. Bishop	5	8	0	86	48	10.75	0	0	1
C.A. Walsh	5	8	4	31	18	7.75	0	0	2
A.F.G. Griffith	1	2	0	14	13	7.00	0	0	0
C.E.L. Ambrose	4	6	0	39	15	6.50	0	0	1
K.C.G. Benjamin	3	5	0	31	11	6.20	0	0	1
C.E. Cuffy	1	2	1	5	3★	5.00	0	0	0
P.V. Simmons	1	1	0	0	0	0.00	0	0	3

Substitute catch was held by A.F.G. Griffith

Bowling:

	O	M	R	W	Av.	BB	5w/i
S. Chanderpaul	3	1	2	1	2.00	1–2	0
C.E.L. Ambrose	160.5	31	444	19	23.37	5–43	2
I.R. Bishop	171.3	29	510	20	25.50	3–49	0
C.A. Walsh	192.3	33	592	19	31.16	5–74	2
K.C.G. Benjamin	117.5	22	362	9	40.22	3–34	0
C.E. Cuffy	33	4	116	2	58.00	2–116	0
J.C. Adams	18.5	1	59	1	59.00	1–11	0
P.V. Simmons	23	5	67	1	67.00	1–58	0
P.I.C. Thompson	16	0	80	1	80.00	1–80	0
C.L. Hooper	116	25	317	3	105.67	2–86	0

Zimbabwe v England

First Test: Bulawayo

December 18–22 1996

Nearest of Misses

Half a pitch-length was all that separated Michael Atherton's men from victory in perhaps the most thrilling finish to a Test involving England since Durban in 1948. Then, Cliff Gladwin and Alec Bedser scrambled a leg-bye off the last ball to secure a breathless two-wicket win over South Africa; now, Nick Knight and Darren Gough could manage only two of the three needed from the final delivery before Andy Flower gathered Bryan Strang's throw and removed the bails to secure the first Test draw with the scores level in 119 years and 1345 matches.

The frantic finale served as the ideal start to Test relations between the two sides, and although Zimbabwe were left holding on for a share of the spoils, their ability to compete with England was the best possible response after the Test and County Cricket Board had opposed their application for Test status in 1992. That subject, along with England's poor form coming into the Test – they had lost to Mashonaland and been beaten in a low-scoring one-day international the previous weekend – were the main talking-points coming into the match. There was less cause for talk about the make-up of the visitors' side. Injuries, form, absentees (Dominic Cork, for personal reasons) and the decision to play Alec Stewart behind the stumps meant it picked itself, with a debut for Yorkshire seamer Chris Silverwood and a recall for spinner Phil Tufnell after two years in the wilderness.

Zimbabwe called up left-arm seamer Bryan Strang when pace bowler Eddo Brandes twisted an ankle in practice, while Andy Waller, the Centenary tobacco farmer, who, at 37, thought his chance of top-level cricket had gone, became their 34th Test cap.

Zimbabwe won the toss on a hot, airless day, and, as so often in the recent past – Old Trafford 1993, Brisbane 1994, Headingley 1995 – England began a series in reverse. With home captain Campbell purring along – passing 1000 Test runs when 20 – his side got away to a flyer. With three slips posted, Atherton's bowlers still conceded 57 of the 109 runs scored before lunch on the leg side.

England were revived by Robert Croft. The offspinner, in only his second Test, pegged Zimbabwe back – despite sunburnt hands – removing Campbell (slicing airily to backward point to make it nine fifties but still no Test hundred), Houghton and Waller (unluckily, it appeared, at short leg) after Silverwood gained his first Test wicket through Hussain's brilliance at third slip.

Zimbabwe remained afloat thanks to Andy Flower. The left-hander had recently resigned the captaincy, complaining it was affecting his form, and now there were no signs of any cares as he played a classic Test innings. Watchful defence stretched it past six hours, but there were fine strokes too – two thumping hooks to the pavilion off Silverwood and Mullally stood out – and his reverse sweep to reach a third Test hundred showed real nerve and talent.

Flower's innings cost England ground and any hopes they had of making it up were initially thwarted first by legspinner Paul Strang, who fizzed one through Atherton's on-side push in the over before tea, and then by rain, which forced play to be abandoned for the day.

But they did gain the ascendancy on a cooler third day thanks to Hussain and Crawley, who, like Flower, produced innings in keeping with Test match requirements. Hussain could have perished first ball, the luckless Carlisle flooring a firm push to short leg, and he took full toll of that error. The Essex man's third Test hundred, full of punchy drives, arrived just before the close to joyous celebrations, and England, 70 behind, had high hopes of a big lead.

It failed to arrive, thanks not only to Paul Strang's third five-wicket haul and a remarkable Bryan Strang catch at long leg – one-handed just inside the rope as Hussain hooked Streak – but also to timorous batting. Crawley was truly positive only when he smashed Streak over midwicket to reach his second consecutive Test hundred. It might not have arrived if Tufnell had been taken by the diving Andy Flower the previous ball.

A lead of 30 looked small, but appeared far more by the close when Zimbabwe were five down with a lead of 77. Mullally and Gough had shared the early spoils, before the spinners shared the crucial wickets of Campbell, bowled by a classic arm ball, and Houghton, miscuing to mid-on in the penultimate over.

But despite their lengthening odds, the home side came out with all guns blazing on the final morning. Waller, a real man-mountain, clobbered two sixes in a grand maiden fifty, and Whittall, calmness itself, managed to unnerve the fretting Tufnell. Paul Strang continued the resistance into the afternoon before walking for a short-leg catch off Croft, although he had been fortunate earlier to survive a similar appeal – England crying 'wolf' too often? – but a draw was looming as Whittall passed 50 in three hours, only then to drive to extra-cover; and when Olonga collected a pair in the next over, the equation was set: 205 in 37 overs.

England's intentions were quickly plain, with Knight charging to swat a Streak bouncer for four, and the tension rose. It even affected umpire Dunne: he gave an extra ball in Olonga's first over which was called wide, and the delivery which followed went for four. Would that be important?

Atherton dragged on in the fourth over, but Stewart, immediately into his stride, passed 4000 Test runs and hoisted Paul Strang for six. The rate hovered at five, but England looked comfortable.

At halfway they were 106, and 87 were needed when the last 15 overs began at 4.17 pm. Easy? Maybe, but this was no one-day slog; there was no 30-yard circle, and little restriction on where the bowlers could aim. If one wicket was lost, it would not be easy for a new man to force the pace.

And so it proved. From wanting 59 in 10 overs, England's platform suddenly crumbled. Stewart top-edged a pull to backward square leg. Hussain drove to extra-cover in the same over. And suddenly there was panic.

Knight was still there, but Whittall, with nerves of steel, came on to bowl two overs for 10, and Crawley and Thorpe perished as the equation stiffened: 33 off 5; 23 off 3; and finally 13 off the last over, from Streak to Knight.

The first ball, down the leg side, was scoreless, but Gough's brave running made two out of the next to extra-cover, with, now, all nine outfielders on the line. Eleven off four looked impossible, but Knight raised English hearts by picking up a slower ball over square leg for six: five needed off three.

Streak responded by spearing the fourth wide of off stump, and although the English fans bayed for a wide, umpire Robinson was having none of it: five off two. More brave running by Gough kept Knight on strike, but when Streak held his nerve to get the last ball full, Knight could only squeeze it out to deep cover. Gough began what would have been the third and winning run as Flower gathered Bryan Strang's throw and calmly removed the bails just before the batsmen crossed.

As at Durban in 1948, it was a truly remarkable finish, and the words of the newsreel commentator then were equally valid now: 'Phew! This *was* cricket!'

Brian Murgatroyd

FIRST TEST MATCH
Queen's Club, Bulawayo

December 18, 19, 20, 21, 22 1996
Toss: Zimbabwe

ZIMBABWE

		Mins	Balls	Fours			Mins	Balls	Fours
G.W. Flower	c Hussain b Silverwood	43	151	100	5	lbw b Gough	0	17	15	0
S.V. Carlisle	c Crawley b Gough	0	6	3	0	c Atherton b Mullally	4	14	12	1
*A.D.R. Campbell	c Silverwood b Croft	84	156	136	13	b Croft	29	68	46	4
D.L. Houghton	c Stewart b Croft	34	98	60	3‡	c Croft b Tufnell	37	158	117	5
†A. Flower	c Stewart b Tufnell	112	365	331	12	c Crawley b Tufnell	14	52	41	1
A.C. Waller	c Crawley b Croft	15	52	47	1	c Knight b Gough	50	135	109	5§
G.J. Whittall	c Atherton b Silverwood	7	37	30	1	(8) c Croft b Tufnell	56	185	184	5‡
P.A. Strang	c Tufnell b Silverwood	38	107	69	7	(9) c Crawley b Croft	19	61	40	0
H.H. Streak	b Mullally	19	71	60	2	(10) not out	8	46	24	0
B.C. Strang	not out	4	6	2	1	(7) c Mullally b Tufnell	3	10	13	0
H.K. Olonga	c Knight b Tufnell	0	2	4	0	c Stewart b Silverwood	0	6	7	0
Extras:	lb4 w3 nb13	20				b4 lb6 w2 nb2	14		‡ plus 1 six	
Total:		376					234		§ plus 2 sixes	

Fall: 3, 130, 136, 206, 235, 252, 331, 372, 376

‡ plus 1 six

6, 6, 57, 82, 103, 111, 178, 209, 233

Bowling:
Mullally	23–4–69–1 1nb 2w		Gough	12–2–44–2 1nb 1w
Gough	26–4–87–1 5nb 1w		Mullally	18–5–49–1 1w
Silverwood	18–5–63–3 6nb		Croft	33–9–62–2
Croft	44–15–77–3		Silverwood	7–3–8–1 1nb
Tufnell	26.5–4–76–2 3nb		Tufnell	31–12–61–4

ENGLAND

		Mins	Balls	Fours			Mins	Balls	Fours
N.V. Knight	lbw b Olonga	56	104	79	9	run out (B.A. Strang/A. Flower)	96	180	117	5‡
*M.A. Atherton	lbw b P.A. Strang	16	57	43	2	b Olonga	4	19	10	0
†A.J. Stewart	lbw b P.A. Strang	48	149	123	8	c Campbell b P.A. Strang	73	115	76	4§
N. Hussain	c B.C. Strang b Streak	113	357	278	14	c Carlisle b P.A. Strang	0	2	2	0
G.P. Thorpe	c Campbell b P.A. Strang	13	27	23	3	(6) c Campbell b Streak	2	5	3	0
J.P. Crawley	c A. Flower b P.A. Strang	112	374	297	9‡	(5) c Carlisle b Whittall	7	17	10	1
R.D.B. Croft	lbw b Olonga	7	30	22	1	(7) not out	3	17	7	0
D. Gough	c G.W. Flower b Olonga	2	7	6	0					
C.E.W. Silverwood	c Houghton b P.A. Strang	0	15	17	0					
A.D. Mullally	c Waller b Streak	4	45	27	1					
P.C.R. Tufnell	not out	2	44	23	0					
Extras:	b4 lb4 w1 nb24	33				b2 lb13 w3 nb1	19		‡ plus 1 six	
Total:		406				6 wkts	204		§ plus 2 sixes	

Fall: 48, 92, 160, 180, 328, 340, 344, 353, 378

‡ plus 1 six

17, 154, 156, 178, 182, 204

Bowling:
Streak	36–8–86–2 15nb		Streak	11–0–64–1 1nb 2w
B.C. Strang	17–5–54–0 2nb		Olonga	2–0–16–1 1nb 1w
P.A. Strang	58.4–14–123–5		P.A. Strang	14–0–63–2
Olonga	23–2–90–3 10nb 1w		G.W. Flower	8–0–36–0
Whittall	10–2–25–0 1nb		Whittall	2–0–10–1
G.W. Flower	7–3–20–0			

Umpires: R.S. Dunne (NZ), I.D. Robinson (Zim.).
Third umpire: R.B. Tiffin (Zim.).
Referee: Hanumant Singh (Ind.).
Debuts: A.C. Waller (Zim.); C.E.W. Silverwood (Eng.).
Man of the Match: N.V. Knight

Match drawn

England opener Nick Knight contorts himself in his vain bid to snatch victory in that memorable last over

Clive Mason/Allsport

Zimbabwe v England

Second Test: Harare

December 26–30 1996

Wooden Spoon Unclaimed

After all the excitement of the drawn first Test in Bulawayo less than a week earlier, the second encounter between Zimbabwe and England produced a damp, frustrating stalemate. Given that the seven previous Christmas holidays in Harare had all produced rain, the two inches which fell during the match to shave 150 overs off proceedings hardly helped the pursuit of a positive result, and illustrated the folly of holding the tour in Zimbabwe's rainy season. But rain was not the only factor behind this drawn Test.

More significant was what was riding on the result. With England's stock low after years of under-achievement and Zimbabwe still wet behind the ears in international terms, the losers could fairly be said to be bottom of the class in Test terms. As a result, both sides, but more particularly England, often gave the impression they were playing not to lose rather than to win. That could be seen in England's choice of allrounder Craig White, recently arrived from the A tour of Australia as a re-inforcement, as he replaced specialist seamer Chris Silverwood, who had every right to feel hard done by after a blameless debut in Bulawayo.

Zimbabwe, meanwhile, remained bullish about their chances despite their narrow escape in the first Test, and they too made changes. Out-of-form opener Stuart Carlisle made way for the left-hander Mark Dekker, while pace bowler Eddo Brandes returned following an ankle injury to replace Bryan Strang. For chicken farmer Brandes the recall meant he had two reasons to celebrate: his wife Denise had produced their second child on Christmas Eve.

But if that was a case of Christmas coming early for Brandes, it came in abundance for Zimbabwe's bowlers on the opening day of the Test, with England's batsmen in generous mood after Alistair Campbell won the toss and put the visitors in. True, the pitch started damp as rain forced the groundsman to keep it covered after he had watered it. But it quickly became clear this was no sticky dog; it was merely a slow, low seamer, with patience the order of the day, the type of pitch on which generations of English county batsmen had been reared in days gone by.

That need for patience was more acute as a woefully slow outfield made the punishing of any bad ball all the harder. Thick grass and the frequent rain put boundaries at a premium, a fact reflected in the match scoring rate of a mere 2.01 runs per over.

But patience was not a maxim employed by many England batsmen on that opening day; instead, the approach seemed more 'block-or-bash', with predictable results. Six batsmen lost their wickets in the arc between wicketkeeper and gully, with Heath Streak and medium-pacer Guy Whittall the chief beneficiaries. Whittall had managed 23 wickets at 38 apiece in 17 previous Tests; now, by bowling line and length with the odd clever change of pace, he achieved the scarcely credible figures of 16–5–18–4.

In the midst of England's débâcle, John Crawley stood out. Illustrating what was required, he batted for over 3½ hours before running out of partners on the second morning after Phil Tufnell had hung around for an hour to shame his supposed betters.

That was the prelude to perhaps the most lacklustre cricket of the series. On the one hand were Zimbabwe's batsmen, determined to build a big lead on a pitch still woefully slow; on the other, England's bowlers, desperate to get back into the Test. The match ground to a halt as 93 runs were scraped together in almost 50 overs, and it was almost a blessing when a post-tea deluge washed out play for the rest of the day.

But if the second day was turgid, the third was a classic day of Test cricket, with a stirring fightback by England, an umpiring controversy and a sting in the tail. That fightback was spearheaded by Darren Gough, who mixed vicious inswingers and slower balls in a spell of 11–4–17–3 after the previous day's rain delayed the start by 160 minutes. The end of Gough's spell was, however, shrouded in controversy. The last ball, a slower delivery, was ruled dead ball by square-leg umpire K. T. Francis. The Sri Lankan ruled that by moving forward after a signal by the bowler, wicket-keeper Alec Stewart and the slips were infringing Law 42:6, 'Incommoding the striker', as their actions were taking place behind the batsman's back.

Francis justified his actions at tea by saying he and colleague Russell Tiffin had noticed the practice the previous day, but it opened up a whole can of worms and left England's players bewildered and angry. What, they argued, was the difference between the wicketkeeper walking in and, say, third man doing the same? And why had Francis decided to act now if he had said he had noticed the practice the day before? To many, it brought back memories of the clash between Shakoor Rana and Mike Gatting in Faisalabad nine years earlier, but thankfully, this time, things remained amicable, although it needs to be said the umpiring in the series was poor.

Zimbabwe gained a lead of 59 thanks to the diligence of Man of the Match Grant Flower, whose innings of 73 spanned six hours, and Paul Strang, who showed that positive batting was not impossible. Strang drove and carved the tiring bowlers to distraction, and his unbeaten 47 looked crucial, first as Robert Croft gained some sharp turn to take the last three wickets, and then when Streak removed Atherton just before the close to complete a miserable series haul of 34 runs in four innings for the England captain. Zimbabwe hopes were high on an overcast fourth morning, but although Brandes bowled superbly without luck and Strang removed Knight and Hussain by the time the lead had reached 30, they were ultimately frustrated by Stewart and his Surrey team-mate Thorpe, who ended a barren run of form with only his second fifty of the tour.

Stewart's Test career looked, at best, on hold in May after a disastrous two-year spell of injury and poor form. But after returning to the side in June following an injury to Knight, he had reached fifty in every Test, and he continued that run with his first hundred as wicketkeeper and his ninth in all. Stewart's innings was not pretty but it staved off defeat, and critics of England's reckless first-innings display could not have things both ways. And for Stewart, whose hundred took 368 minutes, there was also the personal satisfaction of becoming the leading Test run-scorer in the calendar year.

And that was it. Overnight rain which got under the covers to saturate parts of the square put paid to any hopes of a positive result on the final day, and instead the action took place in the post-match Press conferences. After the first Test, England coach David Lloyd had been censured for inflammatory remarks, and now a war of words erupted between the two captains: Atherton claimed his side would have won given five clear days, while Campbell lamented what he called England's 'superiority complex'.

So, the wooden-spoon battle remained unresolved; but on the evidence of the series, neither side deserved to be wholly free of that tag.

Brian Murgatroyd

SECOND TEST MATCH

Harare Sports Club

December 26, 27, 28, 29, 30 (*no play*) 1996
Toss: Zimbabwe

ENGLAND

		Mins	Balls	Fours		Mins	Balls	Fours
N.V. Knight	c A. Flower b Olonga	15	33	20	1	c Campbell b Strang	30	134	83	3
*M.A. Atherton	c Campbell b Whittall	13	89	49	0‡	c Campbell b Streak	1	9	3	0
†A.J. Stewart	c G.W. Flower b Streak	19	61	44	1	not out	101	380	267	8
N. Hussain	c A. Flower b Streak	11	71	53	1	c Houghton b Strang	6	34	37	0
G.P. Thorpe	c Dekker b Streak	5	36	20	0	not out	50	220	169	6
J.P. Crawley	not out	47	218	169	3				
C. White	c Campbell b Whittall	9	59	47	0				
R.D.B. Croft	c G.W. Flower b Whittall	14	79	55	2				
D. Gough	b Strang	2	9	8	0				
A.D. Mullally	c & b Whittall	0	3	2	0				
P.C.R. Tufnell	b Streak	9	57	37	1				

Extras: b1 lb5 w1 nb5 — 12

Total: 156 ‡ plus 1 six

lb5 w1 nb1 — 7

3 wkts 195

Fall: 24, 50, 50, 65, 73, 94, 128, 133, 134

7, 75, 89

Bowling:

Streak	24.1–7–43–4 *2nb 1w*
Brandes	16–6–35–0
Olonga	9–1–23–1 *3nb*
Whittall	16–5–18–4
Strang	18–7–31–1

Streak	18–5–47–1
Brandes	21–6–45–0 *1w*
Olonga	7–0–31–0 *1nb*
Whittall	14–6–16–0
Strang	26–6–42–2
G.W. Flower	7–2–9–0

ZIMBABWE

		Mins	Balls	Fours
G.W. Flower	c Crawley b Gough	73	353	255	5‡
M.H. Dekker	c Stewart b Mullally	2	18	16	0
*A.D.R. Campbell	c Thorpe b White	22	71	53	2
D.L. Houghton	c Stewart b Gough	29	152	124	1
†A. Flower	lbw b Gough	6	49	24	0
A.C. Waller	lbw b Tufnell	4	18	18	0
G.J. Whittall	b Gough	1	6	9	0
P.A. Strang	not out	47	105	82	4
H.H. Streak	c Crawley b Croft	7	44	34	0
E.A. Brandes	c Gough b Croft	9	16	16	0‡
H.K. Olonga	c Hussain b Croft	0	9	6	0

Extras: lb8 w1 nb6 — 15

Total: 215 ‡ plus 1 six

Fall: 5, 46, 110, 131, 136, 138, 159, 197, 211

Bowling:

Mullally	23–7–32–1 *1w*
Gough	26–10–40–4 *3nb*
Croft	15–2–39–3
White	16–4–41–1
Tufnell	25–3–55–1 *4nb*

Umpires: K.T. Francis (SL) & R.B. Tiffin (Zim.).
Third umpire: I.D. Robinson (Zim.). Referee: Hanumant Singh (Ind.).
Debuts: none. Man of the Match: G.W. Flower

Match drawn

Heath Streak jubilant after the important dismissal of England captain Mike Atherton

Clive Mason/Allsport

South Africa v India

First Test: Durban

December 26–28 1996

Demolition at Durban

The transformation from the dustbowl at Kanpur to the hard, grassy pitch at Kingsmead was complete. A fortnight after South Africa had been soundly beaten by 280 runs in the third Test in India, they hurtled to an astonishing 328-run win in less than three days at the start of their home three-match rubber in Durban. The turnabout was remarkable. The South Africans, happy to be home, had expected to bounce back in familiar conditions, but no-one thought victory would come so quickly and comprehensively. The pitch at Kingsmead was hard and bouncy, tailor-made for the South African attack, and South Africa predictably opted for an all-pace quartet of Allan Donald, Shaun Pollock, who had returned to full fitness after missing the Indian tour, Lance Klusener and Brian McMillan, while omitting unorthodox spinner Paul Adams. India, seeking to bolster their pace attack and their top order, drafted in the inexperienced David Johnson and opening bat Vikram Rathore.

Sachin Tendulkar was delighted to win an important toss on a pitch which promised early-morning life and prodigious lateral movement. The United Cricket Board, practising their own form of daylight-saving to beat off the threat of evening gloom, had opted for a 9 am start and the early-morning moisture added to the batsmen's problems each day. But the UCB could not get the Indians to agree to making another piece of cricket history – by playing Test cricket under floodlights. The Kingsmead lights had been used during the four-day domestic provincial competition and the ICC's chief executive David Richards had supported the proposal if both teams were in favour. India were not. It mattered not. The Test, played under clear skies and in intense heat throughout, ended just after tea on the third day.

India made a promising start when Gary Kirsten was bowled through the gate by an excellent Venkatesh Prasad delivery. Hudson, with admirable discipline and some good fortune, survived while Adam Bacher, making his debut and, like Uncle Ali, batting at No.3 for his country, could not have asked for a more testing baptism. Showing remarkable composure and astute shot selection in the steamy conditions, he helped carry South Africa through to lunch at 70 for 1. Bacher perished immediately after the break, leg-before to a Srinath delivery which cut back, but both captain Hansie Cronje and coach Bob Woolmer said later that the 62-run partnership had been crucial to South Africa's ultimate success. 'We could easily have been 50 for 4 at lunch if Hudson and Bacher had not played so well,' said Woolmer.

The second session belonged to India as four wickets fell for 72, Daryll Cullinan and Cronje edging deliveries from Prasad which left them while Gibbs, playing loosely outside off stump to Johnson, provided Mongia with his fourth catch of the innings (113 for 5).

Tendulkar had left the field in the middle of his third over after straining a chest muscle trying to bounce Hudson – a revealing comment on the state of the pitch – and his replacement Laxman, at third slip, dropped Hudson on 39. Hudson was caught off a no-ball by the same fielder shortly afterwards but, as he admitted later, 'You never feel in on this type of pitch and you need a bit of luck.' Hudson's good fortune ended when the gentle awayswing of Ganguly found the outside edge, but his 80 in just under five hours had laid the foundation for victory. There were valuable contributions in the lower order from McMillan, Pollock and Richardson, but the total of 235 was about 30 runs short of what Woolmer thought would have been 'average' in the circumstances. Prasad's variation and movement brought him 5 for 60, but Srinath posed as many problems. India survived the 12 deliveries before the close, but Donald did enough in the opening over to suggest that 235 would prove a most testing target.

The match, as a contest, ended in the first session of the second day. Left-hander Raman was bowled by Pollock's first delivery of the morning, swinging and of full length, and Rathore was well taken by Hudson at third slip off Donald. Ganguly, uncharacteristically, aimed to pull Pollock and skyed a catch to Klusener at long leg, but it was Donald who struck the blow of the match. Tendulkar, after a slow start, struck successive Donald deliveries to the off-side boundary, but the third, an exceptionally fast offcutter, beat his defensive bat to send the off stump spinning out of the ground. Donald admitted the wicket had given him more pleasure than any other during his Test career.

Azharuddin, in compelling form while South Africa were in India, appeared to have little stomach for the fight. Careless rather than carefree, he swung lustily at McMillan and was taken by Bacher, who had been placed on the leg boundary moments before. India were soon eight down as three wickets fell on 74 immediately after the break. Dravid fell leg-before to McMillan; Mongia wafted and edged the next delivery – from Donald – and Srinath received the nastiest of first-ballers, a short lifter which flew over the close cordon, from which first slip Cullinan, turning, sprinting and diving, brought off a spectacular catch. Srinath was unhappy with the decision but did not match the verbal dissent of Johnson, who also rubbed his shoulder after being taken at short leg by Bacher from a similar Donald delivery. He was later reprimanded by match referee Barry Jarman, who said that Johnson's inexperience at Test level had 'saved him from a heavy fine'. The innings closed on 100 and Donald's devastating mix of pace, control, bounce and movement had brought him 5 for 40.

The lead of 135 on a responsive pitch was critical, and South Africa had stretched it to 299 by the close of the second day. Hudson, far more fluent, and Bacher went to stylish half-centuries in adding 111 for the second wicket after Kirsten had failed for a second time. Both fell to the spin of Kumble, and Cullinan also did not linger, but South Africa, with six wickets in hand and three days remaining, were in total command at 164 for 4 at the close of the second day.

The end came at an almost indecent rush as 16 wickets fell in just over two sessions on the third day. Indian heads lifted briefly as South Africa lost five wickets for 21 during the first hour, but McMillan, after a shaky start, and Donald, surviving two chances in an innings of 26, added 74 in a rollicking 10th-wicket stand. It was the second-highest partnership of the match and Dravid, with an undefeated 27 in the second innings, was the only Indian batsman to score more than Donald in the match. McMillan, pulling three sixes off Srinath, ended on 51 not out off only 54 deliveries and India faced an impossible target of 395. The Indian second innings was a disaster, lasting just 34.1 overs, and their total of 66 was the fourth-lowest in their Test history. The South African pace attack was irresistible, but they were brilliantly supported in the field as Kirsten pulled off a sensational diving catch at gully to remove Tendulkar, Hudson took two sharp chances at third slip, while short-leg Bacher's reflex stop and throw ran out Srinath. Only Dravid, with an undefeated 27 in two hours, showed any application and technique as Donald finished with 4 for 14.

The 328-run defeat (the 100th in India's 303 Tests) obscured Prasad's first Test haul of 10 wickets and Mongia's Indian record of eight catches. Hudson's two half-centuries, in a Test dominated by bowlers, earned him the match award, but it was the impact of Donald, with a match haul of 9 for 54, which will linger longest with the Indians. Tendulkar, gracious in defeat, said the Indians had batted badly and had no excuses 'on a fair pitch', while Cronje thought that South Africa's top-quality fast-bowling support for Donald and Pollock, and India's excessive reliance on Srinath and Prasad, had been the major difference. And, in this Test anyway, it was major.   *John Bishop*

FIRST TEST MATCH
Kingsmead, Durban

December 26, 27, 28 1996
Toss: India

SOUTH AFRICA

		Mins	Balls	Fours		Mins	Balls	Fours
A.C. Hudson	c Mongia b Ganguly	80	288	191	12	c Tendulkar b Kumble	52	165	97	8
G. Kirsten	b Prasad	2	18	12	0	c Dravid b Prasad	2	16	17	0
A.M. Bacher	lbw b Srinath	25	109	73	3‡	c Tendulkar b Kumble	55	129	101	9
D.J. Cullinan	c Mongia b Prasad	1	6	5	0	c Mongia b Prasad	3	13	8	0
*W.J. Cronje	c Mongia b Prasad	15	45	41	3	c Mongia b Prasad	17	71	46	1
H.H. Gibbs	c Mongia b Johnson	0	17	10	0	lbw b Srinath	25	69	47	3
B.M. McMillan	lbw b Johnson	34	127	99	3	not out	51	96	54	4‡
S.M. Pollock	not out	23	96	47	3	c Rathore b Prasad	2	15	14	0
†D.J. Richardson	b Prasad	24	40	31	4	b Srinath	4	12	4	0
L. Klusener	c Mongia b Srinath	1	4	4	0	c Mongia b Srinath	4	3	4	1
A.A. Donald	c Rathore b Prasad	5	8	11	1	c Rathore b Prasad	26	57	35	3
Extras:	b4 lb10 nb11	25				b7 lb6 nb5	18		
Total:		235		‡ plus 1 six			259		‡ plus 3 sixes

Fall: 8, 70, 71, 99, 113, 162, 190, 229, 230

4, 115, 120, 120, 164, 164, 171, 181, 185

Bowling:

Srinath	20–7–36–2	Srinath	23–5–80–3 1nb
Prasad	19–6–60–5 2nb	Prasad	25–4–93–5 2nb
Johnson	15–2–52–2 9nb	Johnson	9–1–39–0 2nb
Tendulkar	2.4–2–0–0	Kumble	11–3–26–2
Kumble	20.2–3–61–0	Ganguly	2–0–8–0
Ganguly	9–4–12–1		

INDIA

		Mins	Balls	Fours		Mins	Balls	Fours
V.S. Rathore	c Hudson b Donald	7	49	41	0	c Richardson b Donald	2	2	2	0
W.V. Raman	b Pollock	0	13	3	0	b Donald	1	21	8	0
S.C. Ganguly	c Klusener b Pollock	16	81	45	1	b Donald	0	1	1	0
*S.R. Tendulkar	b Donald	15	57	45	2	c Kirsten b Pollock	4	31	25	1
M. Azharuddin	c Bacher b McMillan	15	29	15	1‡	c Klusener b Pollock	8	27	14	1
R.S. Dravid	lbw b McMillan	7	32	22	0	not out	27	121	73	5
†N.R. Mongia	c Richardson b Donald	4	17	13	1	c Cronje b Klusener	4	34	28	0
A. Kumble	not out	13	46	27	0‡	c Hudson b Klusener	2	21	17	0
J. Srinath	c Cullinan b Donald	0	1	1	0	run out (*Bacher*)	7	13	17	0
D. Johnson	c Bacher b Donald	3	19	10	0	c Klusener b Pollock	5	13	12	1
B.K.V. Prasad	c Richardson b Klusener	4	21	16	0	c Hudson b Donald	1	20	10	0
Extras:	b4 lb3 w2 nb7	16				lb2 nb3	5		
Total:		100		‡ plus 1 six			66		

Fall: 2, 22, 36, 52, 68, 74, 74, 74, 89

2, 2, 7, 15, 20, 25, 40, 51, 59

Bowling:

Donald	16–5–40–5 1w	Donald	11.1–4–14–4
Pollock	8–2–18–2 5nb	Pollock	12–4–25–3 1nb
Klusener	7.1–2–8–1 2nb	Klusener	9–2–16–2 2nb
McMillan	8–2–27–2 1w	McMillan	2–0–9–0

Umpires: R.S. Dunne (NZ) & D.L.Orchard (SA). *Third umpire:* R.E. Koertzen (SA).
Referee: B.N. Jarman (Aus.). *Debut:* A.M. Bacher (SA). *Man of the Match:* A.C. Hudson

South Africa won by 328 runs

Allan Donald, one of the world's most destructive bowlers, took nine wickets in India's disastrous Durban Test match

Clive Mason/Allsport

South Africa v India

Second Test: Cape Town

January 2–6 1997

Three Astonishing Centuries

The smile returned to the batsmen's faces on the shaved pitch at Cape Town, but the result was the same as at Kingsmead – an emphatic victory in the second Test as South Africa took a 2–0 lead in the three-match rubber.

Newlands, with large, enthusiastic crowds under clear skies, provided the perfect stage for a remarkably entertaining, if ultimately one-sided, contest. In contrast to Kingsmead, where the highest individual score was Andrew Hudson's 80, Newlands produced five first-innings centuries, with almost 1300 runs in the match coming off fewer than 400 overs at a lively clip of well over three to the over.

The South African camp, surprised by the amount of grass taken off before play started, opted for five frontline bowlers and replaced specialist batsman Gibbs with frog-in-a-blender spinner Paul Adams in the only change from Kingsmead. India, with obvious limitations at the top of the order and seeking accurate seam support for the admirable Javagal Srinath and Venkatesh Prasad, included young batsman V. V. S. Laxman and debutant medium-pacer Dodda Ganesh for Rathore and Johnson.

Hansie Cronje was delighted at winning a rare toss and India immediately added to South Africa's good fortune by twice dropping Gary Kirsten – before he had scored (at slip, Azharuddin) and on 10 (at gully, Kumble) – off Prasad. The Western Province left-hander took full advantage, batting positively and scoring all round the wicket in making his third Test century of the summer against the Indians and his first in front of his home Cape Town crowd.

Kirsten lost Hudson, edging Prasad as the ball bounced on him, and Adam Bacher, who was baited into an attempted pull by Srinath and gloved a catch (89 for 2). But Cullinan, stylish and positive, helped Kirsten build the foundation with a third-wicket partnership of 114 in 140 minutes. Cullinan briefly turned villain when he called Kirsten for a run and then retreated to the safety of his crease as Azharuddin fielded superbly at square leg, threw to wicketkeeper Mongia, who in turn off-loaded to bowler Ganguly as Kirsten narrowly failed to complete two lengths of the pitch. Kirsten, who had batted for almost five hours and struck 15 boundaries in making 103, left muttering darkly.

Cullinan (77) also fell to a leg-side catch but Cronje, on 35, and Brian McMillan (13) took South Africa through to a comfortable 280 for 4 at stumps. Coach Bob Woolmer said later that South Africa would be looking for 400 the next day, with the tail 'coming to the party'. They did, and hogged the limelight.

Cronje, bothered by Srinath's bounce and gloving down the leg side, and Pollock left early next morning, but India lacked the bowling back-up and McMillan and the sensible Dave Richardson settled South Africa with a seventh-wicket stand of 83.

What followed changed the mood and direction of the Test. Klusener, down at No.9, arrived bristling with aggression, and took 15 off his first six balls from Srinath. Later he became more circumspect as he helped pilot McMillan to his third Test century and indeed came perilously close to running himself out to give his partner his 100th run.

But, after reaching his first Test half-century, Klusener started to blaze away again and his second 50 came off 36 deliveries. While McMillan had tiptoed agonisingly through the nineties, Klusener went from 90 to 102 with three successive boundaries off Ganesh and reached his maiden hundred off 100 deliveries (13 fours, two sixes). He immediately turned for the pavilion as Cronje declared on 529 for 7.

McMillan had set out to play the anchor role and did so to perfection, staying for almost six hours for his undefeated 103. The unbroken eighth-wicket stand of 147 broke one of South Africa's oldest records, set in 1903 by Dave Nourse and Ernest Halliwell against England, and Klusener's hundred was the fastest ever for South Africa in terms of balls faced. (J.H. Sinclair's 80-minute century against Australia in 1902–03, also at Newlands, is the fastest by the clock.)

India returned to face 16 overs on the second evening and found Klusener still on a high. The South African allrounder first ran out Raman with a hard, flat throw and then he bowled Dravid – opening in place of Mongia, who had taken a ball in the eye while keeping – off a bottom edge with his sixth delivery as India ended the day 29 for 3.

There is nothing subtle about the 25-year-old Klusener whether batting or bowling. At the crease he stands, bat raised and ready to club anything too wide, too full or too short; as a bowler, he charges to the wicket and bangs it in, producing awkward bounce and often at genuine pace. His brief Test career has been spectacular, touching dizzy heights in between a couple of lows. After just four Tests he twice had his name in the South African history books – for his eight wickets in an innings on debut and the fastest Test century.

The third day belonged to India or, to be precise, Tendulkar and Azharuddin, even if South Africa remained in control of the contest. The early overs saw the departure of Ganguly and Laxman, and India were facing disaster when former captain Azharuddin joined his successor Tendulkar a 58 for 5.

While Azharuddin admitted he had batted 'crap' in Durban, Tendulkar had been criticised for being too inhibited in his strokeplay since taking over as captain. While Azharuddin was less reckless at the start of his innings, Tendulkar

Clive Mason/Allsport

Lance Klusener, in his fourth Test, rattled up South Africa's fastest century (in terms of balls faced)

looked to play more positively. India ended the session on 145 for 5, and a lunch meeting with President Nelson Mandela appeared to inspire the visitors, and Azharuddin, rather than the South Africans. Klusener was promptly smashed for four boundaries in his first over after the break and went for 60 in six overs. In the ferocity of the onslaught, South Africa's catching suffered, with Azha dropped on 55 by Hudson and 88 by Cronje, while Tendulkar was also given a chance on 80, again by Hudson. Their errors provided the huge crowd with a memorable afternoon of dashing stroke-play, controlled and classical batsmanship from Tendulkar, wristy improvisation and savage hitting from Azharuddin.

In 175 minutes, 222 runs were added in thrilling fashion as the total was lifted to 280 before Azha was run out by a snappy Hudson throw from backward point. He had batted for a shade under three hours, providing rich entertainment in racing to 115 off 109 deliveries, with 19 fours and a six.

The Indian tail offered little, but the follow-on mark of 330 was reached as Tendulkar sped on to 169. Fittingly, it took a piece of magic to end the innings with Bacher, deep on the square-leg fence, somehow plucking an astonishing catch, one-handed and diving backwards, as Tendulkar pulled a McMillan bouncer.

Tendulkar's superb timing, his straight-driving and placement, had brought him 26 boundaries in a stay of 331 minutes, and India's total of 359 had come in only 92.2 overs, turning a day of gloom for India into one of pride.

South Africa lost further ground on the evening of the third day as Kirsten and Bacher both fell leg-before without scoring, but, at 24 for 2, South Africa still led by 194 at the close.

Elegant half-centuries by Hudson and Cullinan, followed by an unbroken seventh-wicket partnership of 101 by the solid McMillan and Pollock, further tightened South Africa's grip as they advanced to 256 for 6 in 72 overs. The rapid progress enabled Cronje to declare immediately after the tea break on the fourth day with a lead of 426 and India, with 28 awkward overs to negotiate, lost three wickets to Donald, Pollock and Adams by the close.

India were backed hard against the wall and were again looking for miracles from Tendulkar and Azharuddin in their battle for survival on the final day. South Africa's worst moment came when Donald sank to the ground in a faint after his eighth delivery, but he finally stood up and set up South Africa for the kill by having Azharuddin taken at third slip by Hudson. Tendulkar again fell pulling at McMillan, and only Ganguly and Laxman, with an undefeated 35 in two hours, provided any resistance as India were bundled out for 144 in early afternoon. The wickets were again shared by the well-balanced South African attack, but Adams did provide veteran wicketkeeper Richardson, who is almost twice his age, with his first stumping in 33 Tests and 114 dismissals to end the match.

The margin was a massive 282 runs and, for the ill-equipped Indians, the gloomy prospect of the third Test and the bouncy Wanderers pitch still lay ahead.

John Bishop

Sachin Tendulkar reinforced his reputation as probably the world's best batsman with a fine 169 at Newlands

SECOND TEST MATCH

Newlands, Cape Town

January 2, 3, 4, 5, 6 1997
Toss: South Africa

SOUTH AFRICA

		Mins	Balls	Fours		Mins	Balls	Fours
A.C. Hudson	c Mongia b Prasad	16	71	52	1	b Srinath	55	196	134	7
G. Kirsten	run out (*Azharuddin/*								
	Mongia/Ganguly)	103	290	204	15	lbw b Ganesh	0	15	10	0
A.M. Bacher	c Mongia b Srinath	25	78	60	4	lbw b Srinath	0	4	3	0
D.J. Cullinan	c Mongia b Prasad	77	201	143	6‡	(5) b Kumble	55	116	74	7
*W.J. Cronje	c Mongia b Srinath	41	116	79	3‡	(6) c Dravid b Kumble	18	34	30	2
B.M. McMillan	not out	103	348	235	9	(7) not out	59	109	76	6
S.M. Pollock	c Tendulkar b Prasad	1	22	13	0	(8) not out	40	87	76	3
†D.J. Richardson	c Dravid b Srinath	39	124	106	5				
L. Klusener	not out	102	143	100	13§	(4) c Dravid b Srinath	12	43	30	1
A.A. Donald	did not bat								
P.R. Adams	did not bat								

Extras: b5 lb9 nb8   22   ‡ plus 1 six   b4 lb12 w1   17
Total: 7 wkts dec. 529   § plus 2 sixes   6 wkts dec. 256

Fall: 37, 89, 203, 251, 291, 299, 382   6, 7, 33, 127, 133, 155

Bowling:

Srinath	38–8–130–3 2nb	Srinath	18–5–78–3
Prasad	36–1–114–3 5nb	Ganesh	10–3–38–1
Ganesh	23.5–6–93–0	Prasad	7–1–16–0
Kumble	51–7–136–0	Kumble	25–4–58–2
Ganguly	9–1–24–0 1nb	Ganguly	2–0–5–0
Raman	5–1–18–0	Raman	10–0–45–0 1w

INDIA

		Mins	Balls	Fours		Mins	Balls	Fours
W.V. Raman	run out (*Klusener/Richardson*)	5	11	11	1	c Richardson b Pollock	16	74	48	1
R.S. Dravid	b Klusener	2	54	42	0	(3) c Richardson b Adams	12	69	48	1
S.C. Ganguly	c McMillan b Donald	23	58	38	2	(4) c McMillan b Pollock	30	113	82	5
B.K.V. Prasad	b Adams	0	1	2	0	(10) st Richardson b Adams	15	20	16	2
*S.R. Tendulkar	c Bacher b McMillan	169	331	253	26	c Klusener b McMillan	9	39	28	1
V.V.S. Laxman	c Richardson b Pollock	5	32	23	0	(7) not out	35	116	108	4
M. Azharuddin	run out (*Hudson/Richardson*)	115	175	109	19‡	(6) c Hudson b Donald	2	6	4	0
†N.R. Mongia	lbw b Adams	5	28	31	1	(2) b Donald	2	22	17	0
A. Kumble	c Richardson b Donald	2	23	18	0	(8) c Richardson b Adams	14	59	45	1
J. Srinath	b Pollock	11	37	27	1	absent ill	—	—	—	—
D.Ganesh	not out	2	20	11	0	(9) b Donald	1	10	7	0

Extras: lb9 nb11   20   lb1 w2 nb5   8
Total: 359   ‡ plus 1 six   144

Fall: 7, 24, 25, 33, 58, 280, 298, 315, 340   7, 26, 44, 59, 61, 87, 115, 121, 144

Bowling:

Donald	24–3–99–2	Donald	18–5–40–3
Pollock	23–2–76–2 7nb	Pollock	12–2–29–2 4nb
Adams	18–5–49–2	Klusener	9–3–13–0
Klusener	12–1–88–1 4nb	McMillan	11–4–16–1 1w
McMillan	6.2–0–22–1	Adams	16.2–4–45–3 1w 1nb
Cronje	9–5–16–0		

Umpires: D.B. Hair (Aus.) & R.E. Koertzen (SA). *Third umpire:* C.J. Mitchley (SA). *Referee:* B.N. Jarman (Aus.).
Debut: D. Ganesh (Ind.). *Man of the Match:* B.M. McMillan

South Africa won by 282 runs

South Africa v India

Third Test: Johannesburg

January 16–20 1997

India's Slide Firmly Arrested

There was a late, ironic twist to what had been a richly entertaining and largely good-humoured series when the third and final Test between South Africa and India at the Wanderers, pockmarked by the weather, ended in a tense draw and an unexpected rash of disciplinary hearings. South Africa took the series 2–0 but they were surprised by the fresh resolve of the Indians, who bounced back from two heavy defeats to come within two wickets of victory. They were eventually denied as first a noon thunderstorm chopped 152 minutes out of the final day's play and then an admirable, unde-feated century by Daryll Cullinan, with stern support from the tail, carried South Africa to safety.

Match referee Barry Jarman, at the tail-end of a generally relaxed series, also suddenly found him-self taking out the big stick. Mohammad Azharuddin was 'severely reprimanded' for showing dis-sent after being given out leg-before by Peter Willey to a fired-up Pollock in the second innings, his excellent disciplinary record over 12 years saving him from further penalty, while Ganguly and substitute fielder Dharmani were fined 25 per cent of their match fee for bringing the game into dis-repute and attempting to intimidate the English umpire on the final day.

The United Cricket Board's disciplinary committee also had their share of late problems with all-rounder Brian McMillan handed a one-match suspension or R3000 fine for jostling a spectator in an off-field incident. McMillan had 'pushed the highly intoxicated spectator after being continu-ously subjected to abuse', according to UCB managing director Ali Bacher. 'Though there was severe provocation, McMillan accepted he was in breach of the code of conduct,' he added.

But there were also moments of marvellous cricket. Tendulkar won the toss and India's new deter-mination was immediately apparent on a Wanderers pitch that lacked its customary pace and bounce. India were helped by some wayward bowling in the critical first session, when the conditions were at their most responsive to seam and swing. Their batsmen played along the straight and narrow, and the result was a pedestrian if solid start as India advanced to only 41 in the 30 overs before lunch, losing Rathore to Adams's first delivery in the Test. Donald, slanting in from wide of the crease, beat Mongia for pace almost immediately after the break, while Tendulkar was just starting to take charge when he drove loosely at a full, wide, swinging Cronje delivery to edge to McMillan at second slip.

The rest of the day belonged to the disciplined Rahul Dravid and left-hander Ganguly, and the two young batsmen took India through to the close at 233 for 3. The 24-year-old Dravid, sound in temperament and technique, refused to budge, batting for 276 minutes in reaching 81 at stumps, while Ganguly was a perfect and elegant foil, stroking 10 fours and a six in his fifty. They added 116 in the final session and this allowed coach Madan Lal, for almost the first time on tour, to des-cribe the day as 'a good one for India'. Bob Woolmer, meanwhile, expressed disappointment at the sluggish nature of the pitch and some of South Africa's bowling.

Heavy overnight rain delayed the start of the second day until after lunch – only 61 overs were bowled on the second day – but Dravid remained undisturbed, soldiering on to his maiden Test century after Klusener had made early inroads into the batting, running one across Ganguly and finding the edge, bouncing one at Azharuddin, who mis-hit the pull to mid-on, and then breaking Laxman's finger as he defended against his fourth ball.

India were, in effect, six down for 266, but this time Dravid found solid support from the tail, with Kumble and Srinath chipping in invaluably in half-century partnerships. Dravid stuttered nervously through the nineties for 40 minutes – 'my mind did flash back to Lord's, when I reached 95' – surviving a couple of confident appeals before reaching his century, and he was finally last out for 148, remorselessly fashioned in nine hours of intense concentration and astute shot selection.

India's 410 had come off 150.3 overs, and with a further 13 overs lost at the end of the day because of bad light South Africa faced only two deliveries before play was abandoned. Too little had been achieved by the morning of the third day to suggest that anything but a high-scoring draw was in prospect. Instead, with the series secured, the South Africans set about reviving the Test with a positive response, scoring at close to four runs an over in spite of the fairly regular loss of wickets and a splendid and protracted spell of fast bowling from Srinath throughout the morning session.

The door was also opened for India, with Hudson, Kirsten, Bacher, Cullinan and Cronje all quickly playing themselves in – and then getting out, to leave South Africa at 147 for 5 in the 34th over. But, again, their allrounders rescued the situation, with Pollock and the unflappable McMillan adding 112 in 131 minutes for the sixth wicket. Pollock, always looking to play his strokes, hitting 12 fours, had a special wave to Dad after passing 75. 'It's always nice to have one up on the old man,' he explained later. Peter Pollock, mainstay of the South African attack in the 1960s and current national selection convenor, had a Test best of 75. The hard-working Srinath finished with 5 for 104 as South Africa fell 89 runs short of India just minutes before the close on the third day. Even coach Woolmer, who had been looking for a positive approach, was surprised at the batsmen's willingness to carry the attack to the Indians.

India were quick to regain the initiative, reaching 266 for 8 in 83 overs, before declaring to leave South Africa with a victory target of 357 in 95 overs, a rate of almost four to the over. They were given a solid start of 90 by Rathore and Mongia, but again lost Tendulkar – Cronje picked him off for the second time in the match – and Azharuddin cheaply before Dravid, far more fluent, and Ganguly repeated their first-innings heroics with a partnership of 108 in two hours. India had wanted a lead of 370–380 but the early loss of their quicker run-scorers pegged them back. Still, they did declare before the close, to leave South Africa with five overs to negotiate, and they had their reward when Kumble bowled Hudson, half-forward, with a perfect delivery.

South Africa started the final day with hopes of an unlikely victory, but they had a disast-rous morning as five wickets went down for 76. A relieved cheer from the crowd greeted the clap of thunder at noon, and there was a three-hour delay before the players returned. Pollock immediately departed (78 for 6), and Richardson left on 95, before Cullinan and Klusener, refusing to remain shackled, added 127 in two hours for the eighth wicket to take South Africa close to safety. Klusener, who has the habit of consistently producing the unexpected, made 49 off 77 balls, but his departure left a tense Donald with 16 deliveries to face before the umpires abandoned play in the gloom with four overs remaining and South Africa on 228 for 8. Cullinan was the real hero of the day, and Cronje compared his 262-minute effort to Atherton's marathon rearguard action of the previous summer. Cullinan, a delightful strokemaker, faced 194 deliveries in making his undefeated 122, a most timely apology to his captain, whom he had run out for 6 earlier in the day. Cronje praised the bold response of the Indians after two heavy defeats, while conceding that South Africa had not only been lucky with the weather but had also been too relaxed going into the Test. Tendulkar was clearly disappointed at being denied by a combination of the weather, Cullinan and the lack of pace support for Srinath and Prasad, but added that the draw had boosted the confidence of his young side.   **John Bishop**

THIRD TEST MATCH

Wanderers, Johannesburg

January 16, 17, 18, 19, 20 1997

Toss: India

INDIA

		Mins	Balls	Fours		Mins	Balls	Fours
V.S. Rathore	c Richardson b Adams	13	93	69	1	lbw b Donald	44	149	111	5
†N.R. Mongia	b Donald	21	142	104	3	c McMillan b Donald	50	132	89	6
R.S. Dravid	c Pollock b Cronje	148	540	362	21	c Cullinan b Adams	81	208	146	11
*S.R. Tendulkar	c McMillan b Cronje	35	72	55	7	c Richardson b Cronje	9	13	11	2
S.C. Ganguly	c McMillan b Klusener	73	174	138	13‡	b Adams	60	124	93	11‡
M. Azharuddin	c Hudson b Klusener	18	19	20	4	lbw b Pollock	2	6	6	0
V.V.S. Laxman	retired injured	0	5	4	0				
A. Kumble	c Richardson b Klusener	29	103	80	3	(7) b Adams	6	29	17	0
J. Srinath	c Hudson b Donald	41	83	65	4	(8) lbw b Donald	4	9	11	0
D.Ganesh	c Cullinan b Donald	1	19	13	0	(9) not out	0	15	10	0
B.K.V. Prasad	not out	2	5	3	0	(10) not out	1	9	10	0

Extras:	lb15 w5 nb9	29			lb3 w4 nb2	9	
Total:		410	‡ plus 1 six		8 wkts dec. 266		‡ plus 1 six

Fall: 25, 46, 100, 245, 266, 327, 403, 408, 410

90, 109, 124, 232, 235, 256, 265, 265

Bowling:

Donald	32.1–9–88–3 *3w*	Donald	18–6–38–3 *4w*
Pollock	30–11–55–0 *6nb*	Klusener	13–1–41–0
McMillan	20.5–4–50–0	Pollock	11–0–28–1 *1nb*
Klusener	27–6–75–3 *3nb 2w*	McMillan	11–0–48–0 *1nb*
Adams	24–6–88–1	Adams	21–1–80–3
Cronje	16.3–5–39–2	Bacher	1–0–4–0
		Cronje	8–3–24–1

SOUTH AFRICA

		Mins	Balls	Fours		Mins	Balls	Fours
A.C. Hudson	c Azharuddin b Kumble	18	40	27	1‡	b Kumble	3	19	22	0
G. Kirsten	b Prasad	29	74	48	5	c Rathore b Prasad	1	22	10	0
A.M. Bacher	lbw b Srinath	13	23	25	3	b Prasad	23	50	33	4
D.J. Cullinan	c sub (*P. Dharmani*) b Srinath	33	70	46	6	not out	122	262	194	15‡
*W.J. Cronje	c Mongia b Srinath	43	77	57	7	run out (*Kumble/Mongia*)	6	30	21	1
B.M. McMillan	lbw b Ganguly	47	136	83	4	c sub (*P. Dharmani*) b Srinath	2	6	5	0
S.M. Pollock	c Mongia b Srinath	79	205	158	12	b Srinath	0	7	4	0
†D.J. Richardson	c Azharuddin b Ganguly	13	52	46	1	c Azharuddin b Kumble	7	23	28	1
L. Klusener	not out	22	62	38	1‡	c Dravid b Kumble	49	119	77	5‡
A.A. Donald	b Prasad	4	21	14	0	not out	0	25	16	0
P.R. Adams	c Dravid b Srinath	2	12	8	0				

Extras:	b2 lb7 w1 nb8	18			b1 lb13 nb1	15	
Total:		321	‡ plus 1 six		8 wkts 228		‡ plus 1 six

Fall: 36, 64, 73, 139, 147, 259, 285, 303, 318

4, 4, 49, 71, 76, 78, 95, 222

Bowling:

Srinath	25.1–3–104–5 *6nb*	Srinath	24–6–89–2 *1nb*
Prasad	20–2–83–2	Prasad	15–1–59–2
Kumble	25–5–63–1	Kumble	23–7–40–3
Ganesh	7–1–26–0 *2nb 1w*	Ganesh	2–0–8–0
Ganguly	12–2–36–2	Tendulkar	2–0–18–0
		Ganguly	2–2–0–0

Umpires: C.J. Mitchley (SA) & P. Willey (Eng.).
Third umpire: D.L. Orchard (SA).
Referee: B.N. Jarman (Aus.). *Debuts:* none.
Man of the Match: R.S. Dravid.
Man of the Series: A.A. Donald

Match drawn

*Daryll Cullinan, one of the more elegant international batsmen,
kept India at bay with his second-innings century at the Wanderers*

Ben Radford/Allsport

SERIES AVERAGES

SOUTH AFRICA

Batting:

	M	I	NO	R	HS	Av.	100	50	Ct/st
B.M. McMillan	3	6	3	296	103*	98.67	1	2	5
D.J. Cullinan	3	6	1	291	122*	58.20	1	2	3
L. Klusener	3	6	2	190	102*	47.50	1	0	4
A.C. Hudson	3	6	0	224	80	37.33	0	3	6
S.M. Pollock	3	6	2	145	79	36.25	0	1	1
A.M. Bacher	3	6	0	141	55	23.50	0	1	3
W.J. Cronje	3	6	0	140	43	23.33	0	0	1
G. Kirsten	3	6	0	137	103	22.83	1	0	1
D.J. Richardson	3	5	0	87	39	17.40	0	0	11/1
H.H. Gibbs	1	2	0	25	25	12.50	0	0	0
A.A. Donald	3	4	1	35	26	11.67	0	0	0
P.R. Adams	2	1	0	2	2	2.00	0	0	0

Bowling:

	O	M	R	W	Av.	BB	5w/i
A.A. Donald	119.2	33	319	20	15.95	5–40	1
S.M. Pollock	96	21	231	10	23.10	3–25	0
W.J. Cronje	33.3	13	79	3	26.33	2–39	0
P.R. Adams	79.2	16	262	9	29.11	3–45	0
L. Klusener	77.1	15	241	7	34.43	3–75	0
B.M. McMillan	59.1	10	172	4	43.00	2–27	0
A.M. Bacher	1	0	4	0	—	—	0

INDIA

Batting:

	M	I	NO	R	HS	Av.	100	50	Ct/st
R.S. Dravid	3	6	1	277	148	55.40	1	1	6
S.R. Tendulkar	3	6	0	241	169	40.17	1	0	3
V.V.S. Laxman	2	3	2	40	35*	40.00	0	0	0
S.C. Ganguly	3	6	0	202	73	33.67	0	2	0
M. Azharuddin	3	6	0	160	115	26.67	1	0	3
V.S. Rathore	2	4	0	66	44	16.50	0	0	4
N.R. Mongia	3	6	0	86	50	14.33	0	1	14
A. Kumble	3	6	1	66	29	13.20	0	0	0
J. Srinath	3	5	0	63	41	12.60	0	0	0
B.K.V. Prasad	3	6	2	23	15	5.75	0	0	0
W.V. Raman	2	4	0	22	16	5.50	0	0	0
D. Johnson	1	2	0	8	5	4.00	0	0	0
D. Ganesh	2	4	2	4	2*	2.00	0	0	0

2 substitute catches were held by P. Dharmani

Bowling:

	O	M	R	W	Av.	BB	5w/i
B.K.V. Prasad	122	15	425	17	25.00	5–60	2
S.C. Ganguly	36	9	85	3	28.33	2–36	0
J. Srinath	148.1	34	517	18	28.72	5–104	1
D. Johnson	24	3	91	2	45.50	2–52	0
A. Kumble	155.2	29	384	8	48.00	3–40	0
D. Ganesh	42.5	10	165	1	165.00	1–38	0
S.R. Tendulkar	4.4	2	18	0	—	—	0
W.V. Raman	15	1	63	0	—	—	0

New Zealand v England

First Test: Auckland

January 24–28 1997

The Great Rearguard

At the Press conference after the first day's play, New Zealand coach Steve Rixon, his team inserted by Mike Atherton, said: 'I don't think you'll get 500s in this series . . . I wouldn't want to be batting last on that.' His England counterpart, David Lloyd, responded: 'He might easily be batting last.' Lloyd won the prediction contest, but at the climax he didn't want to: it was precisely because the Kiwis batted last that England didn't clinch what looked like a sure victory by lunch on the fifth day.

By that point Dipak Patel, whose batting now is negligible under any pressure, had just completed a pair and the home team, eight down for 105, were still 26 runs away from an innings loss. But after the break Simon Doull hit four boundaries in a quick 26, and Danny Morrison was making his world Test ducks record the running joke of this benefit season. His car advertised it was Danny Duck's; his benefit tie featured only ducks; NZC made 100,000 duck-callers in his honour; the benefit match involved sides captained by the man with most Test runs (Allan Border) and the one with 24 ducks. Now Morrison destroyed his own credibility by saving the Test by scoring 14 not out in 165 minutes. His batting doesn't look as bad as his record suggests. His forward defensive is serviceable, he shoulders arms as well as most, and he wasn't required to do a lot more by a plain attack on a pitch that lasted.

Cometh the hour – 4 hours 39 minutes this time – few better men cometh than Nathan Astle. He doesn't flap. To January 28, Astle endured a long bout of secondseasonitis, after five international centuries in 1995–96, including his first two in successive Caribbean Tests. Returning to form on the right day for his country, he played more attacking strokes and looked even more secure. Phil Tufnell made a few kick awkwardly from footmarks outside the right-handers' leg stump, but the lead grew. The unbroken stand became 106 (easily a record for England–New Zealand Tests), the time diminished, and the attack caused remarkably few problems. Atherton never tried quarter-hour-before-tea bowlers like Thorpe and himself. Astle crashed White for a characteristic boundary through extra cover for his third and most important century in seven Tests, and Atherton abandoned the chase for a win which had earlier appeared his without much chasing.

The dramatic last afternoon should not obliterate the fact that over five days England played better. Several locals batted well early before England dominated the middle days. England's bowlers wasted the opportunity by early inaccuracy. Stewart's subsequent achievements should be seen in the light of his dislocating a finger in the course of diving repeatedly to gather in the first session. No wide, surprisingly, was signalled till the 36th over, when Mullally spilled away for two. The fast trio were all bad, Mullally the worst. Young and Pocock could leave a lot and looked comparatively at ease at 72 without loss at lunch.

Given the platform his country had badly lacked since before he entered the team in March 1994, Stephen Fleming constructed on it his long-awaited first Test century, 129 in six hours. While one would never mistake one for the other – Fleming is tall and as dark as David Gower is fair – there are similarities in their graceful batting styles and manner. Compare their square- and cover-drives, and their propensity, despite high talent levels, to be dismissed without fully having capitalized. Cairns, dropped at 6 and 20, let loose on the second morning, without Fleming's smoothness but with more power – two sixes came off Tufnell in a five-over spell costing 34. The innings reached 390 by Saturday mid-afternoon. Gough took the last three in 12 balls.

Stewart, not the unhappily inactive Russell, was wicketkeeper throughout the series, to allow an extra bowler. After needing to throw himself windward and leeward after wild deliveries, he had four catches. And he had to be back in action before tea when Doull swung one in too abruptly for Knight. Establishing himself as the best batsman of the series, Stewart stayed four minutes over a full day's play, without signs of exhaustion, to reach 173, highest by any England Test wicketkeeper (previous record: Les Ames, 149, Kingston, 1930). He batted with the verve of someone fresh after several days' rest, as if he were 10 years younger. Concentrating primarily on back-foot shots, he cut efficiently and repeatedly played remarkable pull shots, completed with front foot nearly as high as at the climax of a goosestep.

Atherton, till then out of touch and a constant lbw candidate, made steady steps towards better form while reaching 83. Stewart's Surrey team-mate, Thorpe, was the solid, unspectacular, almost error-free left-hand middle-order player New Zealand seriously lacked – the nearest approach is another experienced county pro, Roger Twose, and he made himself unavailable for New Zealand for the whole season. You don't remember a stroke, but five hours later you see a century on the board.

Cork started adventurously late on the third afternoon, but subsided into surprising quiescence next day, as did the whole innings. Lead established, 177 minutes elapsed going from 400 to 500. Cork eventually fell to the best catch of its type in New Zealand since Verdun Scott held Don Tallon in the world's first post-war Test, at Wellington in March 1946. Young raced full-tilt back towards deep mid-wicket, and threw himself towards the boundary. His sunglasses went flying but he held the ball. This was one of the last three wickets with whose capture Morrison, at below full steam, gained the best bowling figures, 3 for 104. Doull was the most dangerous against good batsmen, Vaughan the steadiest.

New Zealand had several times in recent seasons batted in can't-win-can-draw situations late in Tests. They had saved none of them, and did not look likely this time. Hussain, who perhaps shaded Young as the best allround fieldsman of the series, started by catching him. Next morning, he threw out Germon brilliantly from just in front of point after a bad call by Parore, who improved his shining hour by stranding himself in charging Tufnell. Vaughan received a bad Bucknor lbw decision after Tufnell beat him and would have beaten leg stump after turning sharply from the rough. Astle survived without distinction till the advent of Doull, then Morrison, for the surprise ending. **Terry Power**

Graham Thorpe on his way to his third Test century, something for which his England supporters had had to wait patiently. It was quickly followed by another at Wellington

FIRST TEST MATCH

Eden Park, Auckland

January 24, 25, 26, 27, 28 1997

Toss: England

NEW ZEALAND

			Mins	Balls	Fours			Mins	Balls	Fours
B.A. Young	lbw b Mullally	44	141	119	5	(2) c Hussain b Cork	3	35	24	0
B.A. Pocock	lbw b Gough	70	286	197	8	(1) lbw b Gough	20	74	62	2
A.C. Parore	c Stewart b Cork	6	48	28	1	st Stewart b Tufnell	33	139	108	4
S.P. Fleming	c & b Cork	129	368	254	18‡	c Crawley b Tufnell	9	36	30	0
N.J. Astle	c Stewart b White	10	27	25	2	(6) not out	102	279	214	13
J.T.C. Vaughan	lbw b Cork	3	24	21	0	(7) lbw b Tufnell	2	16	10	0
C.L. Cairns	c Stewart b White	67	140	113	7§	(8) b Mullally	7	25	23	1
*†L.K. Germon	c Stewart b Gough	14	40	26	1‡	(5) run out (*Hussain*)	13	53	36	3
D.N. Patel	lbw b Gough	0	2	1	0	lbw b Mullally	0	22	15	0
S.B. Doull	c Knight b Gough	5	16	10	1	b Gough	26	37	40	4
D.K. Morrison	not out	6	17	15	0	not out	14	165	133	0
Extras:	b5 lb12 w2 nb17	36		‡ plus 1 six		lb11 nb8	19			
Total:		390		§ plus 2 sixes		9 wkts dec.	248			

Fall: 85, 114, 193, 210, 215, 333, 362, 362, 380

17, 28, 47, 88, 90, 92, 101, 105, 142

Bowling:

Cork	32.5–8–96–3 *4nb*		Cork	16–3–45–1 *1nb*
Mullally	27–11–55–1 *4nb 2w*		Mullally	26–11–47–2 *4nb*
Gough	32–5–91–4 *6nb*		White	10–2–26–0
Tufnell	25–5–80–0		Gough	22–3–66–2 *4nb*
White	15–3–51–2 *3nb*		Tufnell	40–18–53–3 *3nb*

ENGLAND

		Mins	Balls	Fours
N.V. Knight	lbw b Doull	5	32	28	1
*M.A. Atherton	c & b Patel	83	273	213	11
†A.J. Stewart	c & b Doull	173	364	277	23‡
N. Hussain	c Fleming b Patel	8	26	22	1
G.P. Thorpe	hit wkt b Cairns	119	340	245	17
J.P. Crawley	run out (*Doull/Germon*)	14	62	43	1
C. White	lbw b Vaughan	0	1	1	0
D.G. Cork	c Young b Morrison	59	237	192	6‡
D. Gough	c Germon b Morrison	2	30	19	0
A.D. Mullally	c Germon b Morrison	21	84	40	2
P.C.R. Tufnell	not out	19	55	49	2
Extras:	b2 lb12 w2 nb2	18		‡ plus 1 six
Total:		521		

Fall: 18, 200, 222, 304, 339, 339, 453, 471, 478

Bowling:

Morrison	24.4–4–104–3 *3nb*
Doull	39–10–118–2 *1w*
Cairns	30–3–103–1 *1w*
Astle	14–3–33–0
Vaughan	36–10–57–1
Patel	44–10–92–2

Umpires: S.A. Bucknor (WI) & R.S. Dunne (NZ). *Third umpire:* D.B. Cowie (NZ). *Referee:* P.J.P. Burge (Aus.).
Debuts: none. *Man of the Match:* N.J. Astle & A.J. Stewart (joint)

Match drawn

New Zealand v England

Second Test: Wellington

February 6–10 1997

England Come Good at Last

As a Christchurch youngster in the late 1980s, Andy Caddick was a fringe player in the New Zealand Youth side, competing with Chris Cairns, Shane Thomson, Chris Pringle and Aaron Gale for a pace-bowling spot. He left seeking English first-class fame if not fortune, feeling aggrieved and underused – just one outing, for instance, in the 1988 World Youth Cup in Australia. Having forced his way into the second Test team ahead of Craig White, Caddick began as if justifying those omissions. His early overs wasted the new ball, but he settled down to have three wickets before stumps and four in the innings. And on the fifth day it was Caddick who finished off a thoroughly convincing victory with the last two wickets, matters being made even sweeter for him in that his final victim, taken low at second slip after one lifted more than the batsman expected, was Cairns.

New Zealand dropped Morrison and an unlucky Vaughan, the most economical first-Test bowler and recipient of a rough lbw decision. Canterbury's left-armer Geoff Allott, after both Tests against Zimbabwe a year before, replaced Morrison, but the big news was the introduction of Daniel Vettori, a left-arm spinner who left St Paul's Collegiate School, Hamilton, earlier in the season to make his first-class debut, still 17, in the Northern Districts–England match. Sensible and intelligent, junior but not juvenile, and with remarkable control for his age, Vettori was proclaimed 'special' by convener Ross Dykes. For the inaugural tour of England in 1927, Bill Merritt was picked as an inexperienced Canterbury 19-year-old leggie to become the top wicket-taker. Selectors since had tried numerous untested spinning hunches – including Freeman, Bell, Vivian, Alabaster, Haslam, and last year Loveridge – but Vettori (at 18 years 10 days replacing Doug Freeman as New Zealand's youngest Test player) was the first in 70 years to succeed promptly.

Only a minority of Tests have decisive events at the outset and proceed, with few important turns of fortune, to an easily anticipated conclusion – as in this big English victory. Rain restricted Thursday to one late-afternoon 30-over spell. New Zealand chose both spinners, which presumably helped influence Germon to bat first in conditions encouraging to England's pacemen. That put into the firing-line Young and Pocock, whose immediate match preparation, as determined by the NZC season programme, was a 10-overs-an-innings cricket slog the previous Sunday. 'I don't think an enormous amount of thought went into the programme,' said Rixon.

Pocock tapped to Cork a ball so far outside off that he had no business being near it. That set Gough and Caddick off to take the first five wickets within nine runs and seven overs. The New Zealand batting, which throughout the series looked insecure compared to England's top six, fell with the ball swinging and in mediocre but playable light, all to catches, to English bowling that was

businesslike but not as deadly as
it was made to look.

Gough bowled an excellent
seamer to Parore, who packed
up behind it as best he could
but still could not avoid an outside edge; the others all were
seriously at fault. Astle creamed
several through the covers and
Patel pulled well in making a
rare, worthwhile batting contribution of 45 next morning,
but removing the opposition
for 124 gave England an early,
winning advantage. All 10 fell
to catches, four to Stewart.

Knight, who throughout the
series looked too loose for a
successful Test opener, again

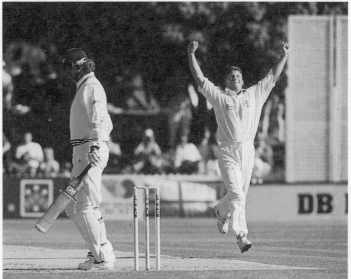

fell early to Doull. But England spent the rest of Friday building to 204 for 3. Stewart, a living argument for the view that batsmen reach their peak in their thirties, again looked very strong off the
back foot, till taken left-handed at full dive by first slip Fleming. The health of the innings became
more robust after he left. Hussain, mostly a fieldsman before and after, made his most significant
batting contribution of the tour. He had been Vettori's first first-class wicket, and early on the third
morning became his first Test scalp the same way – a slip catch taken by Young.

Thorpe produced one memorable on-drive, but the chief impression of his second successive century, 108 from 249 balls, was of solidity, not flair. Crawley, whom he had badly run out in Auckland,
this time stayed with him for the biggest stand of the innings, 118 for the fifth wicket. Allott caused
bleeding when he hit Crawley hard on the helmet, at which Germon ostentatiously applauded, hands
above head. Caddick introduced vigour, missing at Auckland, to the tail, and England's lead was 259.
Doull (Gough was his 50th wicket) was dangerous, but Cairns's ankle injury, suffered in Gavin
Larsen's benefit match, limited him to four overs.

Pocock and Young reached stumps unscathed, and next day did not need to resume until 3.14 pm
because of rain. At 125 for 1 after 6 pm – with the delay having extended nominal stumps time to 6.30
pm – a modern New Zealand first looked to be in the offing: a long, rearguard action to save a Test.
Pocock and Parore were both showing the necessary dedication, without looking entirely comfortable. Then the offspinner Croft had the most important and dubious of his numerous successes in
New Zealand. He spun one back further from outside the off stump than any other in the match.
Padding up, Parore was taken by surprise, and hit in front. But balls that beat batsmen all ends up
often also beat the stumps. The altitude of this delivery made the decision as doubtful as it was vital.

Fleming played a foolish shot against the spin and lollied one back off a leading edge to Croft.
Sending Patel in was a poor move given his fragility under pressure: he padded up second ball to one
that was unquestionably out. Germon, characteristically if belatedly, took it on his own shoulders to
be second nightwatchman, and survived with Pocock, but the three wickets at the same score had
greatly shortened the odds on an England win.

Back near his strong, self-confident Australian tour form, Gough bowled Germon after 50
minutes next morning, and when next over he also ended Pocock's worthy resistance – 64 in 336
minutes – the result was in no further doubt. **Terry Power**

Darren Gough found his old sparkle during the New Zealand series: here rejoicing at the capture of Chris Cairns's wicket

SECOND TEST MATCH

Basin Reserve, Wellington

February 6, 7, 8, 9, 10 1997

Toss: New Zealand

NEW ZEALAND

		Mins	Balls	Fours			Mins	Balls	Fours
B.A. Young	c Stewart b Gough	8	40	29	0	(2) c Stewart b Tufnell	56	133	103	6
B.A. Pocock	c Cork b Caddick	6	34	22	0	(1) c Knight b Gough	64	336	271	5
A.C. Parore	c Stewart b Gough	4	15	5	1	lbw b Croft	15	116	94	0
S.P. Fleming	c & b Caddick	1	26	19	0	c & b Croft	0	10	11	0
N.J. Astle	c Croft b Gough	36	117	90	3	(7) c Stewart b Gough	4	26	13	0
C.L. Cairns	c Hussain b Gough	3	5	6	0	(8) c Knight b Caddick	22	62	59	3
*†L.K. Germon	c Stewart b Caddick	10	46	27	0	(6) b Gough	11	60	49	0
D.N. Patel	c Cork b Caddick	45	97	66	5	(5) lbw b Croft	0	4	2	0
S.B. Doull	c Stewart b Gough	0	2	2	0	c Knight b Gough	0	2	3	0
G.I. Allott	c Knight b Cork	1	31	18	0	b Caddick	2	26	15	0
D.L. Vettori	not out	3	14	10	0	not out	2	14	7	0

Extras: lb5 nb2 — 7

Total: 124

b5 lb4 nb6 — 15

191

Fall: 14, 18, 19, 19, 23, 48, 85, 85, 106

89, 125, 125, 125, 161, 164, 175, 175, 182

Bowling:

Cork	14–4–34–1 2nb
Caddick	18.3–5–45–4
Gough	16–6–40–5 1nb

Cork	10–1–42–0 2nb
Caddick	27.2–11–40–2
Croft	20–9–19–3 1nb
Gough	23–9–52–4
Tufnell	23–9–29–1 4nb

ENGLAND

		Mins	Balls	Fours
N.V. Knight	c Patel b Doull	8	11	10	1
*M.A. Atherton	lbw b Doull	30	94	70	3
†A.J. Stewart	c Fleming b Allott	52	122	86	6
N. Hussain	c Young b Vettori	64	190	158	6‡
G.P. Thorpe	st Germon b Patel	108	331	249	12
J.P. Crawley	c Germon b Doull	56	187	141	4‡
D.G. Cork	lbw b Astle	7	60	45	0
R.D.B. Croft	c Fleming b Doull	0	7	4	0
D. Gough	c Fleming b Doull	18	49	34	3
A.R. Caddick	c Allott b Vettori	20	25	17	2
P.C.R. Tufnell	not out	6	21	14	0

Extras: b3 lb9 nb2 — 14

Total: 383

‡ plus 1 six

Fall: 10, 80, 106, 213, 331, 331, 331, 357, 357

Bowling:

Doull	28–10–75–5
Allott	31–6–91–1 2nb
Vettori	34.3–10–98–2
Cairns	4–2–8–0
Astle	14–5–30–1 1nb
Patel	24–6–59–1
Pocock	2–0–10–0

Umpires: S.A. Bucknor (WI) & D.B. Cowie (NZ). *Third umpire:* E.A. Watkin (NZ). *Referee:* P.J.P. Burge (Aus.).
Debut: D.L. Vettori (NZ). *Man of the Match:* G.P. Thorpe

England won by an innings and 68 runs

New Zealand v England

Third Test: Christchurch

February 14–18 1997

Atherton Steers the Lions Home

Dominic Cork's arrival at the crisis of the series on the fifth afternoon was not the reassuring sign that it would have been in his 1995 Test-hero days. Having stayed home, attending to marital problems, during the Zimbabwe tour leg, after England's failures there his arrival looked likely to boost prospects in New Zealand. But Cork had had a disappointing visit. He limped off against Northern Districts, whereupon Lloyd said deflatingly he 'needed a bit of a cuddle'. The Derbyshire man's voluble mouthing while bowling was a discordant feature in a generally civilized series; length and direction were often ill-controlled; and in Wellington he tuned out because of a run-up problem. In England's first innings here at Christchurch, Cork arrived to play a toddler-level swipe across a straight one (survived evidently through the ball's altitude), then first over next morning was caught behind off a version of the hook deserving a place in a coaching video's Vulgar Errors section.

But with that unpromising background, when it mattered most Cork batted responsibly and, with John Crawley, won the match. Crawley's previous visit to New Zealand was as captain and chief redeeming feature of the otherwise disappointing 1990–91 Young England team, who lost both their 'Test' and one-day series 0–2. Now Crawley played the bigger part in ensuring that this time the 2–0 count was England's way. Against a team who were on top when Cork and Crawley joined forces, and remained keen, they added with few alarms the final 74 runs. The pace increased towards the end and victory was completed inside the final hour, with 12.2 more overs available.

While the final nails were Cork's and Crawley's, the win's construction was mostly Michael Atherton's. Carrying his bat for 94 through England's first innings, England's captain was on the field for the first 26½ hours of the match – all except part of the final afternoon – before he left to a tired prod outside off, having made 118 very responsible runs, characterised more by intense concentration than the occasional flourishing offside drives.

The best contest of the series, this match was decided by England's steadier, less risky second-innings batting. That was a fair overall indication of the biggest difference between the countries in 1996–97. Atherton, attacked in English tabloids though better treated in New Zealand and respected throughout by his team, had diligently worked his way back to form.

New Zealand dropped Parore for Otago batsman Matt Horne. Then Parore, left without first-class prospects after Auckland suspended him, was reinstated as keeper/batsman on Test eve when Germon exacerbated a groin strain at training. Wellington fast bowler Heath Davis was added, and Vettori was preferred as sole spinner to Patel, after 43 Tests during which his bowling average varied from above 300 to above 40. The better-performed but persistently ignored left-armer

Mark Priest, having won Canterbury a Shell Trophy match over champions Auckland with 5 for 31, said on TV that if selectors said they were choosing on form – as they had indeed repeatedly stated – they were lying.

Stephen Fleming was suggested by Ken Rutherford as preferred successor in 1994, not expecting his own reign to end so soon. Fleming, graceful batsman from a background as sole child from a solo parent home in a working-class Christchurch suburb, now became New Zealand's 24th and youngest skipper at 23 years 319 days, succeeding John Parker (25/252 at Karachi, 1976).

By contrast, though Silverwood was fit again, England made no change for the first time in 33 Tests (nigh on three years). They chose two spinners, New Zealand one. Inserted, New Zealand took 522 minutes over 346. At 53 for 1 Horne, who early on drove everything available, had a hand-bone broken by Gough, continued with deflections to 42 and bravely batted with Cairns late in the second innings. Fleming looked great against everyone but Croft, who deservedly got him for 62. His aren't what are called in New Zealand 'Pommy offies' (pushed flat, little turn), but demonstrate expert flight and real spin. Once allowed to participate, Croft was the best spinner in the series. Parore, not at his peak but working hard and never flinching, and Cairns, with bold strokes but more inclined to move away from anything quick and/or lifting (he reached 1000 Test runs in this match), had four fours and a six each in an overnight sixth-wicket stand leading to half-centuries. Tufnell, clumsiest fielder on either side by miles, startled everyone by removing striker's middle stump from mid-on to despatch Doull.

Apart from Atherton and, again, Croft, England's reply was mediocre minus and produced a deficit of 118. Allott's angle across the left-handers brought him three of the first five, and in both innings Fleming used his Christchurch flatmate Astle unerringly as partnership-breaker: 'He cooked the meal last night. That's worth 20 overs.'

Cork bowled Pocock immediately, and Young, the only confident batsman, had lost four partners for 76 before, at 49, umpire Hair made the most important decision of the series. The ball did hit bat as well as pad. The issue was whether Knight, diving forward from silly point, secured it on the full. He could have done if it landed on Knight's little and/or ring fingers and stayed off the ground. Replays were inconclusive. Young, best placed to see, was sure it didn't, said so to Knight, and stayed put. Hair gestured 'out' briefly, belatedly consulted umpire Dunne, and gestured out again. Young left the second time, saying afterwards he'd not seen the first signal, and was let off by referee Burge because of his 'exemplary record'.

Calls arose for third umpires to decide some catches: louder when, two days later, Caddick had one from Vettori lodge briefly between him and the back of his bat. It fell onto his boot, and Fleming dived to take it. Unlike the Young case, replays made it clear the ball had not hit the ground. It was not in law a dead ball. This would have been hard to decide for the bowler's umpire at one look.

Knight's three catches also included judging well a skimmer from Cairns on the long-off boundary. That ended the best stand, 71 with Vettori, who had 54 for once out, albeit with bat often distant from body for offside shots. Only at Melbourne, in January 1929, had England previously exceeded 300 to win – 332 for 7 on the seventh day, Herbert Sutcliffe 135 – but by removing New Zealand for 186 by the fourth lunchtime they gave themselves an attainable target of 305.

And they attained it, in 555 enthralling minutes. Stewart was uncharacteristically marooned on 1 from 43 balls before reaching 17 from 108 and going to a short-leg lob catch. Vettori had footmarks outside leg to bowl at, but no mate. Alone against the Lions, Daniel slew four of them for 97 in 57 overs, attacking yet economical, steady and awkward, maybe somewhat short of variety. Caddick, his not-out catch thrown in, was a good nightwatchman; then in the first half of the fifth day captain and vice-captain increasingly looked like seeing the team home with dedicated, unadventurous batting. The final Kiwi peck removed both, and took three wickets for five in 2.3 overs, before the memorable Crawley/Cork stand. **Terry Power**

THIRD TEST MATCH

Lancaster Park, Christchurch

February 14, 15, 16, 17, 18 1997

Toss: England

NEW ZEALAND

			Mins	Balls	Fours			Mins	Balls	Fours
B.A. Young	b Cork	11	10	11	2	(2) c Knight b Tufnell	49	165	135	5
B.A. Pocock	c Atherton b Croft	22	97	65	1	(1) b Cork	0	2	4	0
M.J. Horne	c Thorpe b Gough	42	154	124	4	(8) c Stewart b Caddick	13	29	32	1
*S.P. Fleming	st Stewart b Croft	62	217	167	6	c Knight b Tufnell	11	30	34	1
N.J. Astle	c Hussain b Croft	15	36	23	1	c Hussain b Croft	5	37	36	1
†A.C. Parore	c Hussain b Croft	59	216	167	4‡	(3) c Stewart b Gough	8	84	55	0
C.L. Cairns	c Stewart b Caddick	57	158	126	4‡	(6) c Knight b Tufnell	52	133	106	4‡
S.B. Doull	run out (Tufnell)	1	13	5	0	(7) c Knight b Croft	5	22	19	1
D.L. Vettori	run out (Thorpe/Stewart)	25	74	59	2	not out	29	103	78	5
H.T. Davis	c Hussain b Croft	8	47	31	0	b Gough	1	23	25	0
G.I. Allott	not out	8	13	18	1	c Stewart b Gough	1	8	12	0
Extras:	b1 lb16 nb19	36				lb8 nb4	12			
Total:		346			‡ plus 1 six		186			‡ plus 1 six

Fall: 14, 78, 106, 137, 201, 283, 288, 310, 337

0, 42, 61, 76, 80, 89, 107, 178, 184

Bowling:

Cork	20–3–78–1 14nb
Caddick	32–8–64–1 2nb
Gough	21–3–70–1 4nb
Croft	39.1–5–95–5 1nb
Tufnell	16–6–22–0
Thorpe	1–1–0–0

Cork	6–2–5–1
Caddick	10–1–25–1 2nb
Croft	31–13–48–2
Gough	13.3–5–42–3
Tufnell	28–9–58–3 3nb

ENGLAND

			Mins	Balls	Fours			Mins	Balls	Fours
N.V. Knight	c Fleming b Allott	14	25	22	2	c Davis b Vettori	29	107	80	2
*M.A. Atherton	not out	94	345	235	10	c Parore b Astle	118	399	311	11
†A.J. Stewart	c sub (C.Z. Harris) b Allott	15	14	10	3	c Pocock b Vettori	17	115	108	1
N. Hussain	c Parore b Cairns	12	46	34	1	(5) c Fleming b Vettori	33	113	88	3
G.P. Thorpe	b Astle	18	54	49	3	(6) c & b Vettori	2	10	8	0
J.P. Crawley	c Parore b Allott	1	5	6	0	(7) not out	40	152	113	5
D.G. Cork	c Parore b Davis	16	57	44	2	(8) not out	39	144	123	5
R.D.B. Croft	c Davis b Astle	31	84	67	5					
D. Gough	b Vettori	0	9	9	0					
A.R. Caddick	c sub (C.Z. Harris) b Allott	4	26	23	0	(4) c Fleming b Doull	15	64	52	0‡
P.C.R. Tufnell	c Young b Doull	13	16	15	2					
Extras:	lb4 w1 nb5	10				b2 lb8 w1 nb3	14			‡ plus 1 six
Total:		228				6 wkts 307				

Fall: 20, 40, 70, 103, 104, 145, 198, 199, 210

64, 116, 146, 226, 226, 231

Bowling:

Allott	18–3–74–4 2nb 1w
Doull	17.4–3–49–1
Davis	18–2–50–1 3nb
Vettori	12–4–13–1
Cairns	8–5–12–1
Astle	11–2–26–2

Allott	12.4–2–32–0 1w
Davis	18–6–43–0 2nb
Doull	21–8–57–1
Vettori	57–18–97–4
Cairns	10–1–23–0 1nb
Astle	28–10–45–1

Umpires: R.S. Dunne (NZ) & D.B. Hair (Aus.).
Third umpire: D.M. Quested (NZ). *Referee:* P.J.P. Burge (Aus.).
Debut: M.J. Horne (NZ). *Man of the Match:* M.A. Atherton

England won by 4 wickets

Mike Atherton returns to his best at Lancaster Park, recording two remarkable innings that set up a revivifying England victory

SERIES AVERAGES

NEW ZEALAND

Batting:

	M	I	NO	R	HS	Av.	100	50	Ct /st
D.L. Vettori	2	4	3	59	29*	59.00	0	0	1
S.P. Fleming	3	6	0	212	129	35.33	1	1	7
C.L. Cairns	3	6	0	208	67	34.67	0	3	5
N.J. Astle	3	6	1	172	102*	34.40	1	0	0
B.A. Pocock	3	6	0	182	70	30.33	0	2	1
B.A. Young	3	6	0	171	56	28.50	0	1	3
M.J. Horne	1	2	0	55	42	27.50	0	0	0
A.C. Parore	3	6	0	125	59	20.83	0	1	4
L.K. Germon	2	4	0	48	14	12.00	0	0	3 / 1
D.N. Patel	2	4	0	45	45	11.25	0	0	2
S.B. Doull	3	6	0	37	26	6.17	0	0	1
H.T. Davis	1	2	0	9	8	4.50	0	0	2
G.I. Allott	2	4	1	12	8*	4.00	0	0	1
J.T.C. Vaughan	1	2	0	5	3	2.50	0	0	0
D.K. Morrison	1	2	2	20	14*	—	0	0	0

2 substitute catches were held by C.Z. Harris

Bowling:

	O	M	R	W	Av.	BB	5w/i
D.L. Vettori	103.3	32	208	7	29.71	4–97	0
S.B. Doull	105.4	31	299	9	33.22	5–75	1
N.J. Astle	67	20	134	4	33.50	2–26	0
D.K. Morrison	24.4	4	104	3	34.67	3–104	0
G.I. Allott	61.4	11	197	5	39.40	4–74	0
D.N. Patel	68	16	151	3	50.33	2–92	0
J.T.C. Vaughan	36	10	57	1	57.00	1–57	0
C.L. Cairns	52	11	146	2	73.00	1–12	0
H.T. Davis	36	8	93	1	93.00	1–50	0
B.A. Pocock	2	0	10	0	—	—	0

ENGLAND

Batting:

	M	I	NO	R	HS	Av.	100	50	Ct /st
M.A. Atherton	3	4	1	325	118	108.33	1	2	1
A.J. Stewart	3	4	0	257	173	64.25	1	1	14/2
G.P. Thorpe	3	4	0	247	119	61.75	2	0	1
D.G. Cork	3	4	1	121	59	40.33	0	1	3
P.C.R. Tufnell	3	3	2	38	19*	38.00	0	0	0
J.P. Crawley	3	4	1	111	56	37.00	0	1	1
N. Hussain	3	4	0	117	64	29.25	0	1	6
A.D. Mullally	1	1	0	21	21	21.00	0	0	0
R.D.B. Croft	2	2	0	31	31	15.50	0	0	2
N.V. Knight	3	4	0	56	29	14.00	0	0	9
A.R. Caddick	2	3	0	39	20	13.00	0	0	1
D. Gough	3	3	0	20	18	6.67	0	0	0
C. White	1	1	0	0	0	0.00	0	0	0

Bowling:

	O	M	R	W	Av.	BB	5w/i
R.D.B. Croft	90.1	27	162	10	16.20	5–95	1
D. Gough	127.3	31	361	19	19.00	5–40	1
A.R. Caddick	87.5	25	174	8	21.75	4–45	0
A.D. Mullally	53	22	102	3	34.00	2–47	0
P.C.R. Tufnell	132	47	242	7	34.57	3–53	0
C. White	25	5	77	2	38.50	2–51	0
D.G. Cork	98.5	21	300	7	42.86	3–96	0
G.P. Thorpe	1	1	0	0	—	—	0

South Africa v Australia

First Test: Johannesburg

February 28–March 4 1997

A Crushing Recordbreaker

It was enthusiastically billed as the world championship Test decider, but it ended in a tame mismatch as the South Africans rolled over in the face of the remorseless, professional Australians in the three-Test series opener.

Australia, back at their venue of shame where Shane Warne and Merv Hughes had been disciplined in 1994 during their decisive defeat in the first Test, were determined to make amends. They could hardly have done so more emphatically, rushing to victory by an innings and 196 runs.

It was the manner of the home side's defeat, their tame surrender, which stunned South Africans. After the Australians had threatened, but failed, to take control in the face of South African obstinacy on the first two days, middle-order batsmen Greg Blewett and Steve Waugh grabbed the Test by the scruff of the neck with a fifth-wicket partnership of 385, and the Test became an Australian victory parade.

Rhodes for injured allrounder McMillan and Kallis for Bacher were the changes to the South Africa team, while Australia, beaten in Perth by West Indies, brought in top-order batsman Matthew Elliott and new-ball bowler Jason Gillespie for Reiffel (nursing a hamstring strain) and Bichel.

South Africa had hoped to catch the Australians on the hop with their superior pace attack on a bouncy Wanderers pitch. But heavy top-dressing over previous summers had left a benign pitch lacking in pace. Groundsman Andy Atkinson, looking to compensate for the lack of bounce, had left a fair spread of grass, and Hansie Cronje, winning the toss, had a choice of contending with the early movement or taking on the prospect of batting last against wrist-spinners Warne and Bevan. In the end, ironically, he got both.

South Africa were quickly in trouble as the Australian pacemen exploited the conditions underfoot and overhead. McGrath, in a devastating unbroken spell of 10 overs for 10 runs, dismissed Hudson with the fourth ball of the series, Kallis, roughed up and then caught in the slips, and Kirsten, bottom-edging a pull from outside off stump.

Cullinan and Rhodes started promisingly but both fell to edged catches and only Cronje of the top order soldiered on, unorthodox in his foot movement against the fast bowlers but handling the spinners easily. He stayed for three hours in making 76 before blasting Warne straight at short cover. As the pitch eased under the drying sun, an assured Pollock sparked South Africa's tail-end revival with a carefree cameo of 35, but Klusener did not linger and South Africa, 195 for 8, were in danger of being rushed out of the contest.

But South African hearts were lifted in the closing 100 minutes of play as Richardson, enjoying the even bounce and driving and pulling with freedom, raced to an undefeated 72 in less than two hours, hitting a six off Warne. He received, in contrasting fashion, telling support from first Donald and then Adams. Flaying wildly, winking and even poking his tongue at McGrath when his antics at the crease brought angry response, Adams stayed while 49 were added for the last wicket. Twice McGrath had to be calmed by the umpires, but it was easy to understand his frustration.

Eventually Adams aimed an outrageous reverse sweep at Warne – the audacity of the stroke left Healy convulsed with laughter – but then fell, predictably, leg-before to the flipper which followed. Australia, after dominating the first two sessions in spite of four dropped catches, had lost some of their initiative in the third.

The trend continued as Australia spent most of the second day building a solid platform, but then allowed South Africa to wriggle free during the last 10 overs of a rain-shortened day.

Taylor's lean spell continued as he chopped on to Pollock but Hayden and Elliott, helped by an over-eager Donald who struggled with his rhythm and line, carried Australia to 128. Elliott, in only his third Test, was the more fluent of the two left-handers, playing positively from the start.

Hayden fell to a good Cullinan catch at slip but Elliott steamed on with Mark Waugh and Australia were again in command. (The Waugh twins were playing together for the 44th time, beating Ian and Greg Chappell's Test record.)

But once again South Africa clawed back, with Donald, pitching short, having first Waugh bottom-edging a pull and Elliott mistiming a similar stroke to mid-on as Australia were reduced to 174 for 4. Rain and bad light reduced the final session and with Australia 191 for 4, South Africa were back, only just, in contention.

The first session of the third day proved the turning-point, a period when Australia took charge of the contest – and this time did not allow South Africa to recover. With the second new ball due after a further 20 overs, it was vital for Australia that overnight batsmen Steve Waugh and Blewett stood firm.

They played their hand to perfection, steering Australia to lunch (284 for 4), then on to the tea interval (378 for 4) and then through to stumps, matching each other run for run.

By the close, and after well over six hours at the crease, Blewett was 156, Waugh 137 . . . and the South Africans were on their knees. It was Blewett's third hundred – following the two he made in his first two Tests against England in 1995 Tests – and Waugh's 12th. The South Africans, to their credit, never flagged and they did well to restrict the Australians to 288 runs on the day.

Blewett was the more extravagant in his strokeplay, while Waugh, who plays every delivery on its merits and is clinical in his approach, seldom offered the bowlers any encouragement, only leg cramp threatening to end his long stay. He is surely the most difficult batsman in world cricket to dislodge once set.

It was only the 12th time in Test history that a full day's play had failed to produce a wicket. The last of the previous nine pairs to bat through a day were the current Australian captain Taylor and coach Geoff Marsh, at Trent Bridge in 1989.

Australia continued on their record-breaking path with the bat, declaring their first innings at 628 for 8, a lead of 326, and then quickly reducing South Africa to 99 for 4 at the close as Warne returned to haunt them.

It was another day of scrambling through the record books. Australia's total (the biggest in a first-class match at the Wanderers) was the highest in the history of Test cricket between the two countries, overtaking South Africa's 622 for 9 at Durban in 1969–70 (and Australia's 578 at Melbourne back in 1910–11). Blewett's marathon 214 was the highest by an Australian in South Africa – and only Don Bradman, twice, has made larger scores against South Africa – while the Waugh–Blewett partnership of 385 was the highest for any wicket between the two countries and also bettered the best stand against South Africa, a record previously held by Compton and Edrich (Lord's, 1947).

The Blewett–Waugh roadshow continued, undisturbed by the third new ball, and it was a surprise when Waugh did finally depart, driving and edging Kallis 15 minutes before the lunch break. The stamina and concentration of Waugh and Blewett had stretched over eight hours. Australia went to lunch at 574 for 5, in sight of their planned declaration.

Blewett finally fell attempting to lift the tempo. His clean hitting on both sides of the wicket had brought him 34 boundaries from the 421 balls he faced.

South Africa, facing a deficit of 326, were looking to survive for nine hours on a pitch which was still playing well, but not only were three quick wickets lost, but the clouds blew away to the east and South Africa's slim hopes of survival went with them. Kirsten dragged a Warne delivery into his stumps, Hudson progressed fluently until a late call from Kallis and superb pick-up, swivel and direct hit by Steve Waugh ran him out – and subsequently cost him his Test place – and Cullinan (0) edged Warne to Healy. The departure of Cronje, flicking at a wide leg-side delivery, completed a miserable day for South Africa.

Wrist-spinners Warne and Bevan spun Australia to victory on the final day, but what was surprising was how meekly South Africa surrendered. England, in a similar position the previous summer, had played out a stirring draw at the Wanderers. But South Africa had no Atherton and Russell – and Australia had Warne at close to his most effective.

South Africa were bundled out in 75 minutes for 130. Warne, bowling into the rough outside leg stump, made the initial breakthrough, to finish with 235 wickets after 50 Tests. But it was Bevan who brought the innings down in an untidy heap with four wickets in 12 deliveries for only two runs.

Cronje took defeat on the chin: 'I don't want to make any excuses. We were well below par. We have to improve in all areas and by about 200 per cent by the second Test. We bowled both sides of the wicket and our batting lacked discipline. We have to find more consistency in Test cricket.'

Taylor said the win was one of the most satisfying of his career. He said he was slightly surprised South Africa had gone down so tamely on the final morning. 'But facing Warne on the last day and still over 200 runs behind is a prospect no-one would fancy.'

John Bishop

Mike Hewitt/Allsport

Having batted all day long, Greg Blewett and Steve Waugh return to a contented dressing-room. Their stand ended after 385 runs had been added

FIRST TEST MATCH

Wanderers, Johannesburg

February 28, March 1, 2, 3, 4 1997
Toss: South Africa

SOUTH AFRICA

		Mins	Balls	Fours		Mins	Balls	Fours
A.C. Hudson	c Healy b McGrath	0	3	4	0	run out (S.R. Waugh)	31	80	62	5
G. Kirsten	c Healy b McGrath	9	62	36	1	b Warne	8	63	47	0
J.H. Kallis	c M.E. Waugh b McGrath	6	25	36	1	b Warne	39	172	155	5
D.J. Cullinan	c Healy b McGrath	27	101	73	5	c Healy b Warne	0	14	10	0
*W.J. Cronje	c M.E. Waugh b Warne	76	187	144	10‡	c Healy b S.R. Waugh	22	61	49	4
J.N. Rhodes	c Healy b Gillespie	22	35	37	3	lbw b Warne	8	56	44	1
S.M. Pollock	c S.R. Waugh b Bevan	35	44	42	8	not out	14	43	33	2
L. Klusener	c Taylor b Bevan	9	21	22	2	c Hayden b Bevan	0	9	4	0
†D.J. Richardson	not out	72	112	87	10‡	c Hayden b Bevan	2	3	5	0
A.A. Donald	c Healy b Gillespie	21	57	45	4	b Bevan	0	5	4	0
P.R. Adams	lbw b Warne	15	44	33	2	b Bevan	0	2	2	0

Extras: b1 lb3 w3 nb3 10

Total: 302 ‡ plus 1 six

b4 lb2 6

130

Fall: 0, 15, 25, 78, 115, 165, 183, 195, 253

36, 41, 46, 90, 108, 127, 128, 130, 130

Bowling:

McGrath	26–8–77–4 1nb
Gillespie	17–6–66–2 2w
Warne	27.4–9–68–2 2nb
Bevan	17–1–64–2 1w
Blewett	4–0–23–0

McGrath	10–5–17–0
Gillespie	11–4–24–0
Warne	28–15–43–4
Bevan	15–3–32–4
S.R. Waugh	4–1–4–1
M.E. Waugh	1–0–4–0

AUSTRALIA

		Mins	Balls	Fours
*M.A. Taylor	b Pollock	16	48	35	2
M.L. Hayden	c Cullinan b Pollock	40	157	115	5
M.T.G. Elliott	c Adams b Donald	85	162	113	12‡
M.E. Waugh	c Richardson b Donald	26	46	34	4
S.R. Waugh	c Richardson b Kallis	160	502	366	22
G.S. Blewett	c Adams b Klusener	214	519	421	34
M.G. Bevan	not out	37	72	58	6
†I.A. Healy	c Kirsten b Adams	11	35	22	1
S.K. Warne	b Cronje	9	11	9	0‡
J.N. Gillespie	did not bat	–			
G.D. McGrath	did not bat	–			

Extras: b1 lb15 w4 nb10 30

Total: 8 wkts dec. 628 ‡ plus 1 six

Fall: 33, 128, 169, 174, 559, 577, 613, 628

Bowling:

Donald	35–7–136–2 2w 1nb
Pollock	32–3–105–2 8nb
Klusener	37–10–122–1 1nb
Kallis	21–4–54–1 2w
Adams	52–7–163–1
Cronje	16.4–5–32–1

Umpires: C.J. Mitchley (SA) & S. Venkataraghavan (Ind.). *Third umpire:* R.E. Koertzen (SA). *Referee:* R. Subba Row (Eng.).
Debuts: none. *Man of the Match:* G.S. Blewett & S.R. Waugh (joint)

Australia won by an innings and 196 runs

South Africa v Australia
Second Test: Port Elizabeth
March 14–17 1997

A Classic Nailbiter

Mark Waugh, in his 100th Test innings, reckoned it was the highpoint of his batting career. And all Australia, heaving a sigh of relief, agreed as South Africa were beaten by two wickets at Port Elizabeth.

The victory, tense and hard-earned, gave the Australians their first Test series win over South Africa in 39 years. It was also just reward for Waugh's elegant, matchwinning century on a demanding surface, and sealed Australia's remarkable comeback from a seemingly hopeless position.

This was a Test of dramatically changing moods and fortunes (and the occasional seven-ball over) but, finally, it was Waugh's 11th Test hundred (all made at different venues) – 'the most valuable and best I have made in any grade of cricket' – which proved the difference.

South Africa made three changes. McMillan returned for Rhodes, adding resolve to the South Africans' brittle mental state and their middle order, while Hudson again found himself the scapegoat for the batting failures, making way for Adam Bacher, and batsman Herschelle Gibbs was preferred to paceman Lance Klusener.

The grassy St George's strip almost persuaded Australia to play a third seamer (Reiffel). It did persuade Taylor to send in South Africa. Kingsmead groundsman Phil Russell had been flown in to help in transforming the traditionally low, slow Port Elizabeth pitch into one which would be more responsive to bounce and seam, a questionable tactic aimed largely at assisting South Africa's pace attack and reducing Australia's batting strength. The irony, of course, is that South Africa lost the toss, and had the worst of the conditions, and then pace bowler Pollock departed with a hamstring tear after six overs with the new ball. Locals could not remember seeing more grass – Taylor labelled it 'under-prepared' – and there was bounce and lateral movement for most of this low-scoring dogfight.

South Africa floundered, losing four wickets in the first hour to the excellent line of McGrath and the sharp lift of Gillespie. Kirsten and Kallis, taken on the gloves before they had scored, were undone by steep bounce while McGrath had Bacher steering into the gully and Cronje (o) playing on. Cullinan and Gibbs, under intense pressure but looking to play their strokes, added 48 for the fifth wicket.

The return of an inspired Gillespie, who ended with a career-best 5 for 54, brought another flurry of wickets as he dismissed Cullinan and then Gibbs and Pollock with successive balls. The old firm of McMillan and Dave Richardson then set about the familiar task of salvaging a tottering innings.

Australia were a paceman light in the ideal seaming conditions and McMillan, unflappable and strong on the pull, and the sensible Richardson took advantage of a tiring attack to add 85. Warne brought the revival to an end as both Richardson and McMillan were caught in the deep and Donald was caught-and-bowled. South Africa had struggled through to 209 in 74.4 overs, and Australia lost Hayden (o), edging Pollock to slip, and reached 10 for 1 in the 13 overs before stumps.

The second day belonged to South Africa, and their resilience and determination should have laid the foundation for victory. Pollock, in obvious discomfort, had Taylor taken behind in his second over and then hobbled from the field and did not return. Australia were 13 for 2 and Donald, aggressive and accurate, was at his most potent, bothering all the batsmen but gaining scant reward.

South Africa turned elsewhere for their wickets as the runs dried up and Cronje, press-ganged into a lengthy spell by Pollock's departure, trapped Mark Waugh in front. The South African captain also made the stop and throw from cover to run out Elliott, who, though pummelled by Donald, had lingered bravely for almost three hours in making 23. The innings then became a procession as McMillan chipped in, having Steve Waugh splendidly caught by a diving Richardson and Bevan (0) edging down the leg side. Healy top-edged a pull and Donald gained his only success when he beat Blewett for pace and bowled him. Only a couple of blows by Warne enabled Australia to reach 100 before Adams and Kallis ended the innings. Australia's 108 was their second-lowest total in Tests against South Africa – they made 75 at Kingsmead in 1949–50.

Kirsten (41) and Bacher (38) played with freedom and good fortune to reach 83 without loss in the two hours before the close as the Australians wilted for the first time on tour. The Test had been turned on its head in six hours and South Africa, 184 ahead at stumps with 10 wickets in hand, could not have been better placed. Most thought another 120 for a 300-run lead would be sufficient.

Instead, a mixture of poor stroke-selection by the batsmen and high-quality bowling by Gillespie and wrist-spinners Warne and Bevan brought the innings tumbling down, only 85 runs being added for the loss of 10 wickets on the third day.

Gillespie broke through, bowling Kirsten, but it was Bacher's advance to 49 which may well have turned the innings. First, he called for a run to midwicket, Blewett, who promptly ran out Kallis; and then the young opener pulled ambitiously at Gillespie and top-edged to long leg: South Africa 99 for 3. Cullinan did not linger, falling lbw, and Gibbs, driving, was held at slip.

Bevan had McMillan (pulling) lbw in the over before lunch and South Africa were 137 for 6, only 238 ahead. Cronje misread the wrist-spin of Bevan and edged the left-hander's googly, and Pollock, with a runner, made a quick 17 before he was lbw to Warne, and Donald skyed Bevan into the covers. The innings closed when Adams aimed a reverse sweep at Warne and gloved to slip. Richardson, standing helplessly at the non-striker's end, was clearly disgusted.

Australia's target of 270 was still a testing one. They lost Taylor to McMillan and were 30 for 2 when Hayden was run out after a dreadful mix-up with Elliott, who promptly aimed to pull the next delivery, which he top-edged to long leg, where Adams lost the ball against the crowd.

Elliott settled Australian nerves with a composed 44 before hitting a low full-toss back to Adams. He and Mark Waugh added 83 in almost even time to set the mood of the Australian run-chase and they were 145 for 3 at the close of the third day. The Waugh twins took the total to 167 before Steve was caught at cover by a diving Cronje off Kallis. Mark, obviously the key to the Test, and indeed the series, played with elegance and composure in the atmosphere of high tension, remaining positive in his strokeplay even to the threatening Donald. There was another stutter at 192 as Adams yorked Blewett (who reached 1000 Test runs in his 25th innings), but, unperturbed, Waugh advanced to the most deserving and classical of Test centuries in 284 minutes, off 198 balls.

He and Bevan appeared to be taking Australia to a comfortable victory when they reached 258, 12 runs short. Waugh had been given a life on 105 by Cullinan in the slips – Donald was the long-suffering bowler – but he was finally bowled by a Kallis inswinger for 116.

Suddenly South Africa were back in the game. Kallis immediately trapped Warne in front, Cronje had Bevan edging to slip, and Australia had slumped to 265 for 8, only five short; but three wickets had fallen in 11 deliveries and South Africa were deep into the tail.

Gillespie survived an over from Kallis but Healy was bent on a romantic finish, swinging Cronje high over backward square leg for a six to settle an extraordinary Test and the series.   *John Bishop*

SECOND TEST MATCH

St George's Park, Port Elizabeth

March 14, 15, 16, 17 1997

Toss: Australia

SOUTH AFRICA

		Mins	Balls	Fours		Mins	Balls	Fours
G. Kirsten	c Hayden b Gillespie	0	26	19	0	b Gillespie	43	138	106	7
A.M. Bacher	c Elliott b McGrath	11	50	34	2	c McGrath b Gillespie	49	174	129	7
J.H. Kallis	c Blewett b Gillespie	0	19	12	0	run out (*Blewett*)	2	32	26	0
D.J. Cullinan	c Warne b Gillespie	34	79	59	4	lbw b Gillespie	2	15	11	0
*W.J. Cronje	b McGrath	0	11	7	0	c Healy b Bevan	27	89	66	5
H.H. Gibbs	b Gillespie	31	93	64	5	c M.E. Waugh b McGrath	7	32	21	0
B.M. McMillan	c S.R. Waugh b Warne	55	185	105	7	lbw b Bevan	2	20	15	0
S.M. Pollock	lbw b Gillespie	0	1	1	0	lbw b Warne	17	27	22	4
†D.J. Richardson	c McGrath b Warne	47	115	106	4‡	not out	3	32	21	0
A.A. Donald	c & b Warne	9	46	30	1	c Warne b Bevan	7	22	19	1
P.R. Adams	not out	5	8	8	1	c Taylor b Warne	1	5	8	0

Extras: b8 lb8 w1 — 17

Total: — 209 ‡ plus 1 six

Extras: b1 lb5 nb2 — 8

Total: — 168

Fall: 13, 17, 21, 22, 70, 95, 95, 180, 204

87, 98, 99, 100, 122, 137, 152, 156, 167

Bowling:

McGrath	22–7–66–2
Gillespie	23–10–54–5 1w
Warne	24.4–5–62–3
Blewett	4–2–3–0
Bevan	2–0–8–0

McGrath	13–3–43–1 1nb
Gillespie	18–4–49–3
S.R. Waugh	4.3–0–16–0
Blewett	7.3–3–16–0
Warne	17.4–7–20–2 1nb
Bevan	13–3–18–3

AUSTRALIA

		Mins	Balls	Fours		Mins	Balls	Fours
M.L. Hayden	c Cullinan b Pollock	0	15	14	0	(2) run out (*Bacher/Cronje*)	14	64	37	2
*M.A. Taylor	c Richardson b Pollock	8	66	44	0	(1) lbw b McMillan	13	43	31	4
M.T.G. Elliott	run out (*Cronje/Bacher*)	23	167	120	4	c & b Adams	44	115	91	8
M.E. Waugh	lbw b Cronje	20	66	36	3	b Kallis	116	328	228	17§
S.R. Waugh	c Richardson b McMillan	8	55	49	1	c Cronje b Kallis	18	90	55	1
G.S. Blewett	b Donald	13	81	46	0	b Adams	7	46	42	1
M.G. Bevan	c Richardson b McMillan	0	17	13	0	c Cullinan b Cronje	24	100	62	3
†I.A. Healy	c Bacher b Cronje	5	47	33	0	not out	10	19	9	1‡
S.K. Warne	lbw b Adams	18	48	27	2	lbw b Kallis	3	7	3	0
J.N. Gillespie	not out	1	45	37	0	not out	0	7	5	0
G.D. McGrath	c Richardson b Kallis	0	5	7	0				

Extras: b1 lb7 w2 nb2 — 12

Total: — 108

Extras: b11 lb8 w3 — 22

8 wkts 271

§ plus 1 six and 1 five (helmet)

‡ plus 1 six

Fall: 1, 13, 48, 64, 66, 70, 85, 86, 106

23, 30, 113, 167, 192, 258, 258, 265

Bowling:

Donald	23–13–18–1 1nb
Pollock	6–3–6–2 1nb
Adams	4–0–5–1
McMillan	14–2–32–2
Cronje	14–7–21–2
Kallis	9.4–2–18–1 2w

Donald	26–6–75–0 1w
McMillan	21–5–46–1
Cronje	9.3–1–36–1 1w
Kallis	16–7–29–3
Adams	21–4–66–2 1w

Umpires: R.E. Koertzen (SA) & S. Venkataraghavan (Ind.).
Third umpire: D.L. Orchard & B.G. Jerling (4th day) (SA).
Referee: R. Subba Row (Eng.). *Debuts:* none.
Man of the Match: M.E. Waugh

Australia won by 2 wickets

*Jason Gillespie's eight wickets did much to set up Australia's thrilling Port Elizabeth victory.
Here he traps Cullinan lbw, and the South African second-innings collapse continues*

Mike Hewitt/Allsport

South Africa v Australia

Third Test: Centurion Park

March 21–24 1997

Consolation at Centurion

The South African batsmen finally found the grit and application which had been missing at the Wanderers and, even more critically, in Port Elizabeth to gain a satisfying eight-wicket win in the third Test, at Centurion Park. It was important for the South Africans if only because it deservedly rewarded the fresh mood of resolve in the side and the devastating fast bowling of Allan Donald.

Australia were unchanged for the third successive Test, though this time they were to pay a heavy price for the lack of a third seamer to support the admirable efforts of McGrath and Gillespie. South Africa made three changes, with left-arm paceman Brett Schultz – after a break from Test cricket of 15 months – taking over from the injured Shaun Pollock, offspinner Pat Symcox replacing Paul Adams, and Lance Klusener returning for middle-order batsman Herschelle Gibbs. The irascible Symcox was selected as much for his ability to turn the ball away from Australia's cluster of left-handers as for his combative, uninhibited approach out in the middle. Brian McMillan, a heel injury debarring him from bowling, was selected as a specialist batsman to fill the troublesome No.3 spot.

The contest saw a return to old-fashioned, tough Test cricket, a hard grind to victory tinged with the odd umpiring controversy. Ian Healy was just one of those left to ponder on the highs and lows of Test cricket. In Port Elizabeth, he had dramatically swung Hansie Cronje away for six to settle the series; a week later he was on the carpet at Centurion Park, suspended for the first two one-day internationals by referee Raman Subba Row for showing dissent. Cronje, winning the toss on a pitch which had some grass but was expected to turn in the latter stages, gambled by sending in Australia. At 110 for 4, the decision appeared to be the right one; at 190 for 4 and with Steve Waugh and Greg Blewett threatening to repeat their Wanderers heroics, Cronje's critics were sharpening their knives.

But Symcox and Schultz, assisted by Dave Richardson and English umpire Merv Kitchen, made the vital breakthrough and Australia were dismissed for 227 in the final over of the day to vindicate Cronje's decision. Symcox turned one back at Blewett, who edged as he aimed to force off the back foot, and Waugh was given out caught down the leg side off Schultz though television replays indicated the ball had clipped pad and not bat.

Schultz continued to test Kitchen and the Australian batsmen. He appeared to have Healy straight in front to the first ball he faced, and a series of lusty appeals followed before Bevan and Warne both fell leg-before in the space of four deliveries (212 for 8). Donald and Klusener ended the Australian innings, but Schultz, bristling and vocal, had made the biggest impact.

Donald's 3 for 60, in his 33rd Test, took him to 150 wickets, the second South African to reach the mark after Hugh Tayfield's record of 170.

South Africa tightened their control on the second day as they reached 240 for 3, a lead of 13 by the close. Adam Bacher batted all day for an undefeated 94, later acknowledging that his dark Port Elizabeth experiences of less than a week before – he ran out Kallis and then lost his wicket on 49 – had helped. He lost Kirsten to McGrath, edging outside off stump, and Healy became only the second wicketkeeper after Rodney Marsh to claim 300 Test dismissals. But the reassuring figure of McMillan inspired confidence in Bacher and they carefully constructed South Africa's first century partnership of the series.

The Australians were convinced McMillan was caught behind on 23 but Kitchen turned down the appeal and the South African batted for almost three hours all told, helping lay the foundation for a winning total.

Bacher and Cullinan produced a second century stand in two hours as Australia's lack of pace support became obvious for the first time on the tour. South Africa were in the lead when Cullinan played on to McGrath shortly before the close. Bacher, who cited Steve Waugh's epic Wanderers innings as his inspiration, was in sight of his maiden Test century, but became agonisingly becalmed on the third morning, adding just two more runs in 83 minutes before McGrath had him leg-before, and the mood spread down the wobbly South African order. Nightwatchman Symcox, Kallis and Richardson also departed cheaply and a repeat of Port Elizabeth's Bloody Sunday was threatening.

At 262 for 7 South Africa were only 35 in front with three wickets in hand and Australia were back in the match. This time Cronje and Klusener decided to take the fight to the Australians. An hour of aggressive strokeplay brought 68 for the eighth wicket and, with Donald and Schultz later propping up one end as an innovative Cronje blazed away, 122 runs were added for the last three wickets. Cronje's undefeated 79 contained one remarkable slash over cover point for six off McGrath, and it took South Africa into a lead of 157. An overworked McGrath bowled unchanged through the morning session, but Warne, without any luck, had his worst figures (0–89) since his third Test and it was the first time in 15 innings against South Africa that he had failed to take a wicket.

With Donald at his most menacing, South Africa quickly tightened their grip on the third afternoon as Australia were reduced to 28 for 3. The Waughs then steadied the innings, Mark playing his strokes elegantly while Steve took the body blows from Donald. Had they stayed together to the close, Australia might still have set South Africa a testing target on the fourth day. But, minutes before stumps, an over-eager Mark Waugh aimed an extravagant drive at a wide Symcox delivery, dragged on and Australia ended on 96 for 4, still 61 behind.

Australia, Steve Waugh apart, did not provide the expected fight on the fourth day. While Waugh battled on to the end, Donald quickly broke through at the other end, producing a swinging yorker to bowl Blewett with his first delivery of the day. Bevan was bowled behind his legs, sweeping at Symcox, and Healy was controversially caught behind off Schultz. The Australian vice-captain glowered angrily at South African umpire Cyril Mitchley, stomped from the field and, with the television cameras faithfully recording his every movement, threw his bat at the top of the steps to bring Subba Row into play. The end came quickly as Donald scattered the tail to complete his first five-wicket haul against Australia. Waugh was left stranded, and bruised, after a typically brave stay of 266 minutes, though his second half-century of the Test sealed the Man-of-the-Series award.

South Africa lost both openers in reaching the 29 required for victory but they won emphatically with a day-and-a-half remaining. Donald, with 8 for 96, took the match award and said that he had never bowled better and more consistently than this season. Cronje said South Africa had taken some 'mighty lessons from the Australians'. 'You need guys with strong minds to play the Aussies,' he added. 'We could all kick ourselves for what happened at St George's Park,' he said.

Mark Taylor, candid and never one to look for excuses, said that he did not think his players lacked motivation in the Centurion Test. 'We didn't play that badly and I was happy with the commitment. I think that South Africa simply played better than we did.'   **John Bishop**

THIRD TEST MATCH

Centurion Park

March 21, 22, 23, 24 1997

Toss: South Africa

AUSTRALIA

			Mins	Balls	Fours		Mins	Balls	Fours
*M.A. Taylor	c Richardson b Klusener	38	197	138	5	c Richardson b Donald	5	25	19	1
M.L. Hayden	b Schultz	10	34	22	2	lbw b Schultz	0	9	6	0
M.T.G. Elliott	c Schultz b Donald	18	69	52	2	b Donald	12	50	35	1
M.E. Waugh	b Donald	5	26	15	1	b Symcox	42	138	100	7
S.R. Waugh	c Richardson b Schultz	67	173	132	9	not out	60	266	179	8
G.S. Blewett	c Richardson b Symcox	37	95	90	5	b Donald	0	12	10	0
M.G. Bevan	lbw b Schultz	6	39	22	1	b Symcox	5	31	20	1
†I.A. Healy	c Richardson b Donald	19	67	47	1	c Richardson b Schultz	12	32	24	1
S.K. Warne	lbw b Schultz	0	3	3	0	lbw b Donald	12	56	43	2
J.N. Gillespie	not out	6	49	24	0	b Donald	0	2	0	0
G.D. McGrath	b Klusener	0	9	7	0	b Klusener	11	19	17	2
Extras:	b1 lb4 w7 nb9	21				b2 lb6 w4 nb14	26		
Total:		227					185		

Fall: 23, 60, 72, 110, 190, 197, 212, 212, 226   5, 10, 28, 94, 99, 108, 131, 164, 164

Bowling:

Donald	20–5–60–3 4nb 3w	Donald	18–5–36–5 3w
Schultz	20–4–52–4 8nb 3w	Schultz	17–4–39–2 9nb 1w
Cronje	5–3–5–0	Klusener	14.4–1–40–1 3nb
Klusener	14.5–4–23–2 1w	Kallis	5–1–13–0 1nb
Symcox	23–4–62–1	Symcox	19–5–49–2
Kallis	7–2–20–0 1nb		

SOUTH AFRICA

			Mins	Balls	Fours		Mins	Balls	Fours
G. Kirsten	c Healy b McGrath	16	58	42	2	c Taylor b Blewett	6	18	16	1
A.M. Bacher	lbw b McGrath	96	448	324	10‡	c Elliott b Gillespie	5	11	6	1
B.M. McMillan	c Hayden b M.E. Waugh	55	164	119	8	not out	7	19	10	0
D.J. Cullinan	b McGrath	47	124	103	8	not out	12	11	9	3
P.L. Symcox	c Blewett b Gillespie	16	43	30	3				
J.H. Kallis	c S.R. Waugh b McGrath	2	21	15	0				
*W.J. Cronje	not out	79	148	111	9§				
†D.J. Richardson	b McGrath	0	2	2	0				
L. Klusener	b Gillespie	30	59	46	3‡				
A.A. Donald	c Healy b Gillespie	8	31	15	2				
B.N. Schultz	c Healy b McGrath	2	17	9	0				
Extras:	b11 lb16 w1 nb5	33		‡ plus 1 six		w1 nb1	2		
Total:		384		§ plus 2 sixes		2 wkts	32		

Fall: 26, 128, 229, 252, 255, 262, 262, 330, 367   11, 15

Bowling:

McGrath	40.4–15–86–6	Gillespie	3.4–0–19–1 1w
Gillespie	31–13–75–3 1w 1nb	Blewett	3–0–13–1 1nb
Blewett	5–0–19–0 1nb		
Warne	36–11–89–0 4nb		
Bevan	15–3–54–0		
M.E. Waugh	7–1–34–1		

Umpires: M.J. Kitchen (Eng.) & C.J. Mitchley (SA). *Third umpire:* R.E. Koertzen (SA).
Referee: R. Subba Row (Eng.). *Debuts:* none. *Man of the Match:* A.A. Donald.
Man of the Series: S.R. Waugh.

South Africa won by 8 wickets

Adam Bacher batted watchfully for 7½ hours against
Australia at Centurion Park, but just missed his century

SERIES AVERAGES

SOUTH AFRICA

Batting:

	M	I	NO	R	HS	Av.	100	50	Ct/st
W.J. Cronje	3	5	1	204	79★	51.00	0	2	1
D.J. Richardson	3	5	2	124	72★	41.33	0	1	12
A.M. Bacher	2	4	0	161	96	40.25	0	1	1
B.M. McMillan	2	4	1	119	55	39.67	0	2	0
D.J. Cullinan	3	6	1	122	47	24.40	0	0	3
S.M. Pollock	2	4	1	66	35	22.00	0	0	0
H.H. Gibbs	1	2	0	38	31	19.00	0	0	0
P.L. Symcox	1	1	0	16	16	16.00	0	0	0
A.C. Hudson	1	2	0	31	31	15.50	0	0	0
J.N. Rhodes	1	2	0	30	22	15.00	0	0	0
G. Kirsten	3	6	0	82	43	13.67	0	0	1
L. Klusener	2	3	0	39	30	13.00	0	0	0
J.H. Kallis	3	5	0	49	39	9.80	0	0	0
A.A. Donald	3	5	0	45	21	9.00	0	0	0
P.R. Adams	2	4	1	21	15	7.00	0	0	3
B.N. Schultz	1	1	0	2	2	2.00	0	0	1

Bowling:

	O	M	R	W	Av.	BB	5w/i
B.N. Schultz	37	8	91	6	15.17	4–52	0
W.J. Cronje	45.1	16	94	4	23.50	2–21	0
B.M. McMillan	35	7	78	3	26.00	2–32	0
J.H. Kallis	58.4	16	134	5	26.80	3–29	0
S.M. Pollock	38	6	111	4	27.75	2–6	0
A.A. Donald	122	36	325	11	29.55	5–36	1
P.L. Symcox	42	9	111	3	37.00	2–49	0
L. Klusener	66.3	15	185	4	46.25	2–23	0
P.R. Adams	77	11	234	4	58.50	2–66	0

AUSTRALIA

Batting:

	M	I	NO	R	HS	Av.	100	50	Ct/st
S.R. Waugh	3	5	1	313	160	78.25	1	2	3
G.S. Blewett	3	5	0	271	214	54.20	1	0	2
M.E. Waugh	3	5	0	209	116	41.80	1	0	3
M.T.G. Elliott	3	5	0	182	85	36.40	0	1	2
M.G. Bevan	3	5	1	72	37★	18.00	0	0	0
M.A. Taylor	3	5	0	80	38	16.00	0	0	3
I.A. Healy	3	5	1	57	19	14.25	0	0	11
M.L. Hayden	3	5	0	64	40	12.80	0	0	4
S.K. Warne	3	5	0	42	18	8.40	0	0	3
J.N. Gillespie	3	4	3	7	6★	7.00	0	0	0
G.D. McGrath	3	3	0	11	11	3.67	0	0	2

Bowling:

	O	M	R	W	Av.	BB	5w/i
M.G. Bevan	62	10	176	9	19.56	4–32	0
S.R. Waugh	8.3	1	20	1	20.00	1–4	0
J.N. Gillespie	103.4	37	287	14	20.50	5–54	1
G.D. McGrath	111.4	38	289	13	22.23	6–86	1
S.K. Warne	134	47	282	11	25.64	4–43	0
M.E. Waugh	8	1	38	1	38.00	1–34	0
G.S. Blewett	23.3	5	74	1	74.00	1–13	0

West Indies v India

First Test: Kingston

March 6–10 1997

West Indies Seek Early Initiative

For over 50 years West Indies have had a tradition of recovering from an unsuccessful or unsatisfactory tour of Australia by beating an Indian touring team. It was time to try again. The selection of the home side for the first Test at Sabina Park was not without surprises, especially for two local players. Opening batsman Robert Samuels made way for Stuart Williams, who had been scoring highly in the Red Stripe Cup, and Jimmy Adams, who until recently was statistically the leading batsman in the world, was dropped in favour of Roland Holder, a Barbadian with several overseas tours for the region behind him without quite catching the eye of the selectors. Jamaican pride was soothed by the inclusion of Franklyn Rose, a tall fast bowler of whom much had been heard a few seasons earlier: he, too, after a temporary retirement from the game, had impressed in the Red Stripe Cup. Interest in the Indian XI centred on the return of opening batsman Navjot Singh Sidhu, absent since he walked out on the tour of England, and the loss of leading strike bowler Javagal Srinath, injured and sent home even before the series began, in whose place 6ft 6in debutant Abey Kuruvilla, aged 28, was chosen.

With Courtney Walsh electing to bat, West Indies struggled initially against the probing Indian attack. Yet in spite of scoring slowly they saw off the opening bowlers for the loss of only Williams, who was deceived by Kuruvilla's slower ball. Even from this early session the play was marked by a number of unanswered appeals for lbw, a feature which would magnify in later matches. (Umpire Kitchen failed to refer a perilously close run-out call against Hooper in the second innings.) Campbell and Chanderpaul struggled for survival, and when the third wicket went down at 143 neither side could claim the advantage.

That was when Brian Lara and Carl Hooper, two of the most exciting strokeplayers in contemporary cricket, took charge in a fourth-wicket partnership of 147 runs in 142 minutes. Hooper was in his Dr Jekyll mood as he caned all bowlers with superlative driving, at no time more effectively than when he took aesthetic and sadistic liking to the new ball. Such a cavalier approach gave some hope to the fieldsmen as Hooper repeatedly lifted the ball into the outfield, but this time his placing and timing ensured his safety. In contrast, Lara, favouring the drive, kept the ball on the turf until Mongia caught him down the leg side.

Although he reached 3000 Test runs and his seventh hundred next morning, Hooper was not as dominant as on the first day, when he made 77 in the final session, and he, too, was beaten by Kuruvilla's change of pace. The lower order afforded little opposition to legspinner Anil Kumble as he wrapped up the innings for 427.

At the start of the second day the teams, management and match officials stood for a minute's silence in respect for Michael Manley, the former Prime Minister of Jamaica, whose passing had followed so closely that of Dr Cheddi Jagan, the President of Guyana, in whose memory they had stood similarly on the preceding morning. Both politicians, whose careers had much in common, were passionate followers of cricket.

The Indian batsmen were put under immediate pressure by the home fast bowlers, even though they were not helped by missed chances in the field. Junior Murray, who had an undistinguished match with the gloves, dropped Sidhu before he had scored. Bishop was the luckless bowler, and his partner Ambrose saw Laxman loft the ball within inches of Williams and also dropped by Lara, both in the slips. When the initial attack had been staunched Laxman proved himself to be as effective as he was elegant, and with the more phlegmatic Dravid took the total to 108 for 1 by the close.

The batsmen survived the opening spell of Ambrose and Walsh only to fall in a pre-lunch blitz by Rose. The 25-year-old Jamaican's performance – the best by any West Indies fast bowler on debut – recalled memories of the similar debut by his compatriot Lester King against India on the same ground in 1962. Bowling to a consistent line on a pitch which was too slow for real pace, he dismissed Laxman, Dravid and Tendulkar while the score advanced by only 13 runs – in the same spell Murray missed Ganguly – and finished with 6 for 100. Unlike some of their predecessors, these Indians did not buckle in adversity, and inspired by Nayan Mongia came within 81 runs of their opponents' total. West Indies held the initiative but the prolongation of the innings through spilled chances – and the intervention, and further threat, of rain – gave them little time to force victory.

That prospect changed dramatically when Lara joined Chanderpaul after the openers had proceeded hesitantly to 81. From the moment of his arrival the Trinidadian was majestic and magnificent. It is not possible even to précis the repertoire of his strokeplaying genius. In contrast to the first innings, Lara was as prepared to hit the ball into the open spaces, being particularly severe on left-arm spinner Joshi, as he was to drive along the ground. Inevitably Chanderpaul was overshadowed in spite of some exquisite batting of his own. Their 122-runs partnership from 22 overs lasted only 93 minutes, and they were out within a ball of each other at 203. West Indies closed the fourth day at 241 for 4 – 322 runs ahead – and it remained to be seen whether they would declare overnight or continue batting into the morning.

The decision was taken from them when rain made further inroads into the available time. Play could not begin until after lunch. In spite of uneven bounce and Sidhu's dismissal by Walsh before he had scored, India were never in serious danger of being bowled out. Dravid took the tourists to 99 for 2 with only nine overs remaining, at which point the rain returned for good. Though frustrated by the weather West Indies had greater cause for satisfaction in holding the balance of advantage and in finding a new potentially matchwinning fast bowler.   ***Clayton Goodwin***

Shaun Botterill/Allsport

West Indies' solid first-innings total was built principally on Carl Hooper's century, his seventh in Tests

FIRST TEST MATCH

Sabina Park, Kingston, Jamaica

March 6, 7, 8, 9, 10 1997
Toss: West Indies

WEST INDIES

			Mins	Balls	Fours			Mins	Balls	Fours
S.L. Campbell	c Mongia b Joshi	40	160	123	4	b Kumble	43	200	111	4
S.C. Williams	b Kuruvilla	23	45	25	3	b Kumble	26	158	67	3
S. Chanderpaul	c Mongia b Prasad	52	164	117	4	c Tendulkar b Kuruvilla	48	135	89	5
B.C. Lara	c Mongia b Kuruvilla	83	187	141	10	c Mongia b Kumble	78	92	83	8‡
C.L. Hooper	c Prasad b Kuruvilla	129	274	212	17	not out	12	44	18	0
I.R. Bishop	c Joshi b Kumble	24	104	71	2					
R.I.C. Holder	b Azharuddin b Kumble	17	98	73	2	(6) not out	21	41	29	2
†J.R. Murray	lbw b Kumble	1	6	4	0					
C.E.L. Ambrose	c Ganguly b Kumble	23	46	40	3					
F.A. Rose	not out	14	26	21	2					
*C.A. Walsh	b Kumble	4	10	11	0					

Extras:	lb9 nb8	17				b4 lb9	13	
Total:		427					4 wkts dec. 241	‡ plus 1 six

Fall: 41, 96, 143, 290, 357, 368, 370, 408, 423

68, 81, 203, 203

Bowling:

Prasad	28–5–104–1 5nb		Prasad	15–2–46–0
Kuruvilla	30–6–82–3 4nb		Kuruvilla	17–2–56–1 1nb
Kumble	42.4–5–120–5 3nb		Kumble	23–6–76–3
Joshi	27–6–81–1		Joshi	6–1–27–0
Ganguly	7–1–17–0		Laxman	3–0–14–0
Laxman	3–0–14–0		Tendulkar	2–0–9–0

INDIA

			Mins	Balls	Fours			Mins	Balls	Fours
V.V.S. Laxman	b Rose	64	224	169	7	c Holder b Rose	27	130	111	1
N.S. Sidhu	lbw b Bishop	10	49	32	1	c Holder b Walsh	0	13	7	0
R.S. Dravid	c Murray b Rose	43	202	149	5	not out	51	160	141	5
*S.R. Tendulkar	b Rose	7	41	30	1	not out	15	42	36	1
S.C. Ganguly	c Lara b Rose	42	162	111	5					
M. Azharuddin	c Lara b Rose	5	10	3	0					
†N.R. Mongia	c Holder b Walsh	78	300	205	6					
A. Kumble	b Bishop	7	26	23	0					
S.B. Joshi	b Bishop	43	194	148	3					
A. Kuruvilla	b Rose	0	13	9	0					
B.K.V. Prasad	not out	10	44	32	0					

Extras:	b5 lb9 nb23	37				lb1 nb5	6
Total:		346					2 wkts 99

Fall: 32, 127, 140, 145, 153, 234, 248, 315, 320

6, 68

Bowling:

Ambrose	24–9–35–0 8nb		Ambrose	6–3–7–0
Bishop	24.5–4–62–3 11nb		Walsh	8–3–7–1 2nb
Rose	33–7–100–6 6nb		Rose	9–1–23–1 3nb
Walsh	32–6–73–1 3nb		Hooper	16–6–27–0
Hooper	21–9–40–0		Chanderpaul	6–0–18–0
Chanderpaul	11–4–22–0 1nb		Lara	3–0–16–0

Umpires: S.A. Bucknor (WI) & M.J. Kitchen (Eng.). *Third umpire:* J. Gill (WI). *Referee:* P.L. van der Merwe (SA).
Debuts: R.I.C. Holder, F.A. Rose (WI); A Kuruvilla (Ind.). *Man of the Match:* F.A. Rose

Match drawn

West Indies v India

Second Test: Port-of-Spain

March 14–18 1997

Stubborn Sidhu Stays 11 Hours

India were content to move on to their 'home' ground at the Queen's Park Oval with the honours still even. Their two previous victories in the Caribbean had been achieved here, and the substantial Asian community in Trinidad could be expected to support the land of their (grand)fathers. The one team change was the introduction of local fast bowler Mervyn Dillon, 22, in place of his injured compatriot Ian Bishop. With an exclusively pace attack – legspinner Rawle Lewis was left out again – Courtney Walsh must have been tempted to give the visitors first innings on winning the toss, but after consulting his colleagues he decided to bat.

The early exchanges went the way of the Indians. Although Williams started confidently against wayward bowling by Prasad, the two openers were out to Anil Kumble by the time the total reached 29. Lara could have gone as well. Before scoring he survived a confident lbw appeal by Kuruvilla, and shortly afterwards the same player just missed catching him at short leg off Kumble. However, Lara did not last long. Coming up to lunch, the Trinidadian attempted to drive Joshi and Azharuddin held the first of his two spectacular catches at slip.

The West Indians struggled to get the ball away on a slow pitch, and, although both batsmen hit sixes early in the afternoon, the proceedings were remarkable less for anything the players did than for umpire Randell's 'deferred digit': appeal as they might, bowlers of neither side could persuade him to raise his finger right throughout the match. Prasad bowled more effectively in the second session, having Chanderpaul caught at the wicket, and with the dismissal after tea of Hooper (who showed his customary mix of versatility and vulnerability) and Murray, India held the advantage.

Unheralded hero Roland Holder, 29, the regular bridesmaid but never the bride on his five overseas tours, rallied the region with pugnacity and common-sense in partnership with first Ambrose and then Rose, who clumped Kumble for a huge six just before the close of the first day at 239 for 7. The Barbadian continued to press the next morning until, after punishing the left-armer's flighted deliveries, he was deceived when Joshi bowled one flatter. Rose's competent rather than eye-catching batting may well provide the stability which the West Indian middle order needs. Debutant Dillon was fortunate to survive an appeal by the wicketkeeper, as his foot seemed to be on, not behind, the line; but the innings soon ended at 296 by lunch.

With the second ball of India's innings Laxman was lbw to Ambrose before a run had been scored. Sidhu and Dravid then batted tenaciously through an afternoon of tight fast bowling. Dillon had a memorable opening spell: his first delivery beat Sidhu; in the same over the ball fell onto the stumps from the batsman's thigh-pad without disturbing the bails; and not long afterwards he had him missed by Hooper in the slips. When Williams dropped Sidhu on 47 at third slip in spite of two attempts, it was apparent where the luck was residing.

Sidhu batted for the rest of that day, and all of the next. Dravid, who kept him company in a second-wicket stand of 171 by the end of the second day, was bowled by Ambrose, the ball keeping low, in the first over of the third morning. Two deliveries later Tendulkar, padding up, survived a close shout for lbw. After that Sidhu and his captain ground on remorselessly. The former, who had reached his century (200 balls, 258 minutes) just before the close, passed his own previous highest Test score at 125; Tendulkar (in his 50th Test) brought up the hundred partnership and his own fifty with the same edged shot; and Sidhu clipped Hooper to leg to reach his 150 (477 minutes, 361 balls).

India went ahead in the third over after tea. Their highest third-wicket stand in any Test in the region ended at 174 when Walsh, whose weakened throwing arm had been tested by both batsmen, ran out Tendulkar, running round to pick up the ball driven between the bowler and the stumps to throw down the wicket. The main interest thereafter was whether Sidhu would reach his double-century that evening: he didn't, being 196 when the teams came off. On the fourth morning he saw two partners depart early – Azharuddin bowled spectacularly on the back foot by Ambrose – before he hit the Antiguan to leg to reach his 200 in 671 minutes and 488 balls. It was the second-slowest double-century in Test history. He didn't score another run. A ball from Ambrose straying outside leg stump struck his pads and bounced back onto the stumps at 382. The end came quickly after that. In a lively few minutes Dillon obtained his first Test wicket by bowling Mongia, brought one back to hit Kumble below the belt and cause him to retire for a while, and took two wickets with consecutive deliveries on the stroke of lunch.

Trailing by 140, West Indies began shakily in losing Campbell before tea, but Stuart Williams grew in confidence as the day progressed. Chanderpaul, without being entirely comfortable, stayed with him until the close at 118 for 1 and this partnership effectively made the match safe in the first session of the fifth day. Williams began by hitting Laxman straight for six and even the introduction of Kumble after three overs by the offspinner did not trouble the batsmen – any more than the sequence of rejected, but seemingly reasonable, appeals troubled anyone. Williams's shot off Joshi dropped Dravid at silly-point (almost rebounding to the wicketkeeper), forcing him to leave the field, and the batsman reached his maiden Test hundred (355 minutes, 241 balls) off the penultimate ball before lunch.

Afterwards Azharuddin ended the 176-run stand by catching Chanderpaul, and then Lara at the second attempt, as, frustrated by his own slow scoring on the sluggish pitch, he started to go for his strokes. With Williams's dismissal the match tottered towards the inevitable draw, which was hastened by rain in the last hour. The Indians had won on points – just as their opponents held the advantage in Jamaica – but cricket isn't boxing, and perhaps West Indies had just as much satisfaction in surviving on the pitch which the tourists considered gave them their best chance of success.   ***Clayton Goodwin***

Adrian Murrell/Allsport

Navjot Singh Sidhu worked at the crease for over 11 hours to construct a double-century that lifted Indian spirits in Trinidad

SECOND TEST MATCH

Queen's Park Oval, Port-of-Spain

March 14, 15, 16, 17, 18 1997

Toss: West Indies

WEST INDIES

		Mins	Balls	Fours		Mins	Balls	Fours
S.L. Campbell	c Prasad b Kumble	8	48	36	1	lbw b Kuruvilla	4	70	55	1
S.C. Williams	b Dravid b Kumble	18	37	27	4	c Kumble b Joshi	128	452	299	11‡
S. Chanderpaul	c Mongia b Prasad	42	125	82	2‡	c Azharuddin b Joshi	79	295	241	9
B.C. Lara	c Azharuddin b Joshi	14	65	51	1	c Azharuddin b Kumble	19	68	57	1
C.L. Hooper	c Azharuddin b Kumble	40	115	85	1‡	c Laxman b Kumble	14	47	49	1
R.I.C. Holder	b Joshi	91	293	238	7	c Laxman b Joshi	9	36	28	0
†J.R. Murray	c & b Kumble	11	29	24	2	not out	12	34	25	0
C.E.L. Ambrose	c Dravid b Kumble	16	66	55	2	not out	10	29	35	1‡
F.A. Rose	c Dravid b Joshi	34	139	85	2§				
★C.A. Walsh	c Mongia b Ganguly	0	4	3	0				
M.V. Dillon	not out	0	5	3	0				

Extras:	lb20 nb2	22		‡ plus 1 six	b8 lb13 nb3		24	
Total:		296		§ plus 2 sixes		6 wkts	299	‡ plus 1 six

Fall: 26, 29, 59, 99, 149, 169, 220, 289, 290

25, 201, 244, 252, 271, 273

Bowling:

Prasad	26–9–54–1 1nb		Prasad	20–7–38–0 1nb
Kuruvilla	22–9–36–0		Kuruvilla	23–6–47–1 1nb
Kumble	39–8–104–5		Kumble	40–9–109–2 1nb
Joshi	22.3–2–79–3		Joshi	36–11–57–3
Ganguly	5–3–3–1 1nb		Ganguly	3–0–6–0
			Laxman	9–3–21–0

INDIA

		Mins	Balls	Fours
V.V.S. Laxman	lbw b Ambrose	0	1	2	0
N.S. Sidhu	b Ambrose	201	673	491	19‡
R.S. Dravid	b Ambrose	57	267	182	4
★S.R. Tendulkar	run out (*Walsh*)	88	306	233	9
S.C. Ganguly	c Chanderpaul b Rose	6	65	55	0
M. Azharuddin	b Ambrose	1	4	6	0
†N.R. Mongia	b Dillon	17	62	39	2
A. Kumble	not out	12	65	46	1
S.B. Joshi	c Walsh b Ambrose	24	63	41	1
A. Kuruvilla	c Murray b Dillon	2	21	18	0
B.K.V. Prasad	c Lara b Dillon	0	1	1	0

Extras:	b9 lb11 nb8	28	
Total:		436	‡ plus 1 six

Fall: 0, 171, 345, 370, 371, 382, 401, 420, 420

Kumble retired injured for 8 at 406 for 7; returned at fall of 9th wicket

Bowling:

Ambrose	41.4–10–87–5 3nb
Walsh	36–11–71–0 2nb
Rose	35–6–93–1 5nb
Dillon	35–6–92–3 2nb
Hooper	28–9–53–0
Chanderpaul	8–1–20–0

Umpires: L.H. Barker (WI) & S.G. Randell (Aus.). *Third umpire:* R. Gosein (WI). *Referee:* P.L. van der Merwe (SA). *Debut:* M.V. Dillon (WI). *Man of the Match:* N.S. Sidhu

Match drawn

West Indies v India

Third Test: Bridgetown

March 27–31 1997

India Blasted to Oblivion

Courtney Walsh's failure to pass a fitness test saved West Indies from the awkward decision – now that Bishop was fit again – of which in-form fast bowler to leave out on a lively pitch at Kensington Oval which promised to be the most likely to produce a definite result. With the unusually wet weather in the region and the fact that the concluding Test was to be played in Georgetown, which has become associated all too often with rain, whichever team won here was almost certain to take the series.

In Walsh's absence Brian Lara had his first opportunity of leading the region. Wicketkeeper Courtney Browne returned on his home ground at the expense of Junior Murray. The Indians, too, shifted their balance in favour of pace by bringing in Dodda Ganesh for Sunil Joshi.

Tendulkar's decision to bowl first seemed to indicate a fear of what the home fast bowlers might do to his batting on the opening morning. The Indian fast bowlers made good use of the conditions, but several potential catches went only close to hand or failed to stick, and Chanderpaul settled into the obdurate role once associated with Larry Gomes. Shuffling across his stumps, he worked the ball frequently to leg, a dangerous practice against bowling which, in spite of Ganesh's propensity to bowl no-balls and his unusual habit of knocking off the bails in delivery, was tight.

The batsmen survived because the umpires – and this time it was usually Lloyd Barker – appeared to consider it rude to stick up their fingers in public during Holy Week. Kuruvilla's appeal for lbw against Chanderpaul with the total at 96 for 3 seemed to be particularly justified. Yet Azharuddin escaped from a similarly close call later in the match without having the West Indian left-hander's tenacity to profit from his good fortune.

Kumble did not come into the attack properly until half-an-hour after tea. By then Chanderpaul, supported by Ambrose, was approaching his first Test century (he had made 13 half-centuries in his previous 18 Tests), which amid much tension he reached by driving Ganesh for three just before the close at 240 for 7. Next morning he took his score to 137 out of 298 as, running out of partners – and possibly running out a partner, Franklyn Rose (both batsmen found themselves at the same end) – he showed greater aggression.

Sidhu feasted on some loose deliveries from Dillon immediately before lunch but Rose, who dismissed him spectacularly with a ball which left him late, and Ambrose tested the batsmen thoroughly with hostile bowling and a somewhat intimidating field-placing which resembled the Carmody field of the late 1940s. Dillon improved his control after yielding 29 runs in his first two overs. Yet as the afternoon wore on the bowlers tended to pitch too short and Tendulkar, particularly, and Dravid were able to punish the bad balls.

The slow over rate and proliferation of no-balls indicated indiscipline. While commentators have criticised West Indies for their slow over rate and short-pitched bowling as being unfair to their opponents, it could be construed that such laxity erodes a sense of purpose and has contributed substantially to the team's failure to play up to its potential in recent years. The abundance of no-balls can lead to unfairness if the umpires should become blasé and permit some deliveries as legitimate which they should have 'called'. Video-replay suggested that Barker erred in allowing Bishop to overstep the line when he had Tendulkar caught two-handed by Campbell springing superbly at gully when the Indian was eight runs short of his hundred. (On the last day Sidhu may have had similar cause to complain, the bowler being Rose.)

The West Indian bowlers applied themselves more effectively on the third day, which India started at 249 for 3, apparently assured of a substantial lead. Once Bishop, who had beaten Dravid several times, had forced him to play on, nobody could really resist the whittling-down of the innings. The 21-run lead did not seem enough, even allowing for the deterioration of the pitch. West Indies would have to falter badly to put India back into the game with any realistic chance, and that is just what happened.

Prasad ripped a ball back from outside off stump to bowl Williams before he had scored, and Chanderpaul was so palpably in front playing back to Kuruvilla that even umpire Randell was moved to concur. The Indian bowlers stole the advantage over their opponents' earlier performance by pitching the ball up, though, if the lesson were learned, it would sow the seed of their own defeat. Only Lara prevented a complete collapse as he hit repeatedly through the off-side field in the manner of Tendulkar. When he was out for 45 of the then 86 for 5 total his side's hopes seemed to have perished with him.

Dillon joined Ambrose at 107 for 9 and immediately hit two boundaries, one off each bowler, through mid-off. Both batsmen took the attack to bowlers who may have become tired. Kuruvilla missed a hard caught-and-bowled chance from Ambrose not long before Dillon, showing the irrelevance of Tendulkar's spreading the field, hit the same bowler for a massive six over square leg, and next ball was dropped by the normally secure Azharuddin at slip. The 33-run partnership, the highest of the innings, renewed West Indies' fighting spirit.

That spirit was renewed with vigour next morning (India starting at 2 without loss). Rose gave a preview of things to come by beating Laxman with an outswinger in the opening over and having Sidhu caught from a seemingly unplayable delivery which kicked from a near-perfect length. He hit a tentative Laxman on the chest with a no-ball which jumped from a pitch whose nature was becoming nastier and more unpredictable by the minute, especially at the end to which Rose was operating. Earlier speculation that India would achieve the 140-run target without undue difficulty had to be revised when Rose – who had already dismissed Dravid – broke through Laxman's defence, and two runs later Lara dived forward at slip to grasp at grass-level the catch which ended any further danger from Tendulkar. Now the talk turned to memories of West Indies' similar return from the 'dead' to snatch victory from South Africa on the same ground five years earlier. When Ambrose scuppered Azharuddin with a vicious ball which kept low, after previous deliveries had gone through at head height, it was obvious that the Indians could no longer console themselves that, in a parody of Hirst and Rhodes, they would 'get them in no-balls'. Nothing seemed to go right for the tourists. Mongia padded up to Bishop only to see the ball nip back and clip his off bail, and Kuruvilla was taken on his forearm by a short ball from the same bowler which raised a bruise.

In achieving victory by what was eventually the comfortable margin of 38 runs all three fast bowlers – Dillon's services were not required – had made splendid use of a spiteful pitch. This contrast to conditions in the drawn matches at Kingston and Port-of-Spain had led to India's dismissal for 81, their lowest in a Test in West Indies, and still 16 short of the controversial confrontation at Sabina Park in 1976 when through injured body or injured morale five of their batsmen did not come to the crease.

Clayton Goodwin

THIRD TEST MATCH

Kensington Oval, Bridgetown, Barbados

March 27, 29, 30, 31 1997
Toss: India

WEST INDIES

		Runs	Mins	Balls	Fours		Mins	Balls	Fours
S.L. Campbell	c Azharuddin b Prasad	6	12	11	1	c Mongia b Ganesh	18	77	58	4
S.C. Williams	b Laxman b Ganesh	24	60	41	5	b Prasad	0	12	7	0
S. Chanderpaul	not out	137	442	284	12	lbw b Kuruvilla	3	18	13	0
*B.C. Lara	c Tendulkar b Prasad	19	85	57	3	c Azharuddin b Prasad	45	104	67	6
C.L. Hooper	c Mongia b Ganesh	19	44	30	3	lbw b Ganesh	4	25	14	0
R.I.C. Holder	c Azharuddin b Prasad	5	21	16	1	c Mongia b Prasad	13	50	30	2
†C.O. Browne	c Tendulkar b Kumble	24	94	74	4	c Mongia b Kuruvilla	1	3	4	0
I.R. Bishop	b Prasad	4	12	7	0	lbw b Kuruvilla	6	22	12	1
C.E.L. Ambrose	c Tendulkar b Kuruvilla	37	87	61	6‡	not out	18	60	30	2
F.A. Rose	run out (*Prasad/Mongia/Kumble*)	11	29	16	2	c Ganguly b Kuruvilla	4	27	20	0
M.V. Dillon	lbw b Prasad	0	16	4	0	b Kuruvilla	21	24	17	3‡
Extras:	lb5 nb7	12				lb5 nb2	7		
Total:		298		‡ plus 1 five			140		‡ plus 1 six

Fall: 10, 40, 88, 118, 131, 187, 193, 258, 290

9, 18, 37, 65, 86, 87, 91, 95, 107

Bowling:

Prasad	31.4–9–82–5 2nb		Prasad	18–6–39–3
Kuruvilla	28–4–88–1		Kuruvilla	21–5–68–5 2nb
Ganesh	21–2–70–2 6nb		Ganesh	6–1–28–2
Kumble	16–1–44–1 1nb			
Ganguly	2–1–9–0			

INDIA

		Runs	Mins	Balls	Fours		Mins	Balls	Fours
V.V.S. Laxman	b Ambrose	6	40	34	0	b Rose	19	77	61	2
N.S. Sidhu	c Browne b Rose	26	56	31	6	c Williams b Rose	3	21	10	0
R.S. Dravid	b Bishop	78	372	243	8	c Browne b Rose	2	36	21	0
*S.R. Tendulkar	c Campbell b Bishop	92	223	147	14‡	c Lara b Bishop	4	25	14	0
S.C. Ganguly	c Browne b Dillon	22	75	53	3	b Ambrose	8	25	18	2
M. Azharuddin	c Browne b Rose	17	118	70	1	b Ambrose	9	26	14	2
†N.R. Mongia	c Williams b Bishop	1	21	14	0	b Bishop	5	39	24	0
A. Kumble	not out	23	81	53	1	c Holder b Bishop	1	8	6	0
A. Kuruvilla	b Ambrose	0	6	7	0	(10) c Holder b Ambrose	9	24	21	0
D. Ganesh	c Browne b Rose	8	30	24	1	(9) not out	7	60	30	0
B.K.V. Prasad	c Holder b Rose	0	2	2	0	b Bishop	0	12	10	0
Extras:	b2 lb12 w2 nb30	46				b2 lb1 nb11	14		
Total:		319		‡ plus 1 six			81		

Fall: 23, 42, 212, 253, 273, 275, 295, 296, 319

3, 16, 32, 32, 45, 51, 57, 66, 80

Bowling:

Ambrose	29–8–74–2 21nb		Ambrose	15–3–37–3 8nb
Bishop	28–6–70–3 9nb		Bishop	11.5–4–22–4
Dillon	19–5–56–1 1w 4nb		Rose	9–2–19–3 6nb
Rose	22–4–77–4 8nb 1w			
Hooper	8–1–28–0			

Umpires: L.H. Barker (WI) & S.G. Randell (Aus.). *Third umpire:* H. Moore (WI).
Referee: P.L. van der Merwe (SA). *Debuts:* none. *Man of the Match:* S. Chanderpaul

West Indies won by 38 runs

*After a steady stream of Test half-centuries, Shivnarine Chanderpaul
finally made it to three figures in the Barbados Test*

Mike Hewitt/Allsport

West Indies v India

Fourth Test: Antigua

April 4–8 1997

Going Through the Motions

So to the Antigua Recreation Ground, where the teams had plenty of time for recreation as rain washed out play on the first two days and the effect of rain prevented a start on the third. There was some speculation that as a two-day Test match had no realistic chance of reaching a decision it might be replaced by two *ad hoc* one-day games or that the scheduled duration should be extended over a further three days. Nobody recommended a change of venue, though the Indians may have mused wistfully on April 1976 when, owing to adverse weather conditions, the third Test match was moved from Georgetown to Port-of-Spain, and they had responded by hitting a record winning fourth-innings score of 406 for 4.

No, a Test match is a Test match, and the calendar days over which it is played were preordained.

Although the match could hardly be lost, individual reputations could be impaired. Walsh, whose expected return for Dillon was the region's only change, had no hesitation in batting when he won the toss. But the confidence of the West Indian opening batsmen was soon as washed-away as the match itself. Williams, who had made his first Test century just two matches earlier, collected his second duck in successive innings, while Campbell erred in running against the speed and accuracy of Jadeja at mid-off as he picked up one-handed magnificently and threw down the stumps.

Brian Lara started with unwonted circumspection, taking 36 minutes over his first run, but after losing Hooper to another smart slip catch by Azharuddin, shortly after hitting a six out of the ground, he took the attack to the bowlers. In spite of some alert Indian fielding, Lara and Holder found the boundary regularly. The latter drove Joshi for six and then tucked into an over by Kumble with 12 runs. Lara lashed the same bowler for another six to bring up his century, his first against India and ninth in all, but almost at once he was caught behind from a delivery by Prasad which moved away. When Holder followed shortly afterwards the scoring dried up.

Wicketkeeper Courtney Browne, whose inclusion at the expense of local hero Ridley Jacobs had been much criticised here, made only four runs in 85 minutes that evening, before opening up in partnership with Ambrose (who reached 1000 Test runs in his 99th innings) and Walsh next morning.

Neither Indian opener was specialist to the position. Aday Jadeja was making his first appearance in the series, but Laxman, who, like his partner, was more at home in the middle order, had been retained in the team only after Sidhu's withdrawal through illness. In the absence of the flu-stricken Rose, who neither batted nor bowled, Ambrose and Bishop maintained a lively attack. The ball found the edge regularly but did not go to hand. When it did the catch was from a no-ball.

Laxman, reaching his half-century out off 77 runs scored, set the pace until he snicked Walsh to

FOURTH TEST MATCH

St John's Recreation Ground, Antigua

April 4, 5, 6, 7, 8 1997 (no play first 3 days)
Toss: West Indies

WEST INDIES		Mins	Balls	Fours
S.L. Campbell	run out (*Jadeja*)	10	59	47	1
S.C. Williams	c Tendulkar b Kuruvilla	0	7	3	0
S. Chanderpaul	c Laxman b Kumble	24	81	53	1
B.C. Lara	c Mongia b Prasad	103	217	178	11‡
C.L. Hooper	c Azharuddin b Joshi	26	50	41	2‡
R.I.C. Holder	c Mongia b Kumble	56	156	103	4‡
†C.O. Browne	not out	39	181	113	5‡
I.R. Bishop	c Dravid b Joshi	17	65	63	3
C.E.L. Ambrose	c Mongia b Kuruvilla	22	50	45	3
*C.A. Walsh	c Dravid b Joshi	21	42	29	2
F.A. Rose	absent ill	–	–	–	–
Extras:	b1 lb5 nb9	15		
Total:		333		‡ plus 1 six

Fall: 0, 32, 40, 82, 224, 230, 252, 295, 333

Bowling:
Prasad   24–4–65–1 *6nb*
Kuruvilla   24–1–69–2 *2nb*
Kumble   36–14–93–2
Joshi   23.4–7–76–3 *4nb*
Ganguly   3–0–24–0

INDIA		Mins	Balls	Fours
A.D. Jadeja	run out (*Williams/Browne*)	96	250	212	7§
V.V.S. Laxman	c Browne b Walsh	56	137	93	5
R.S. Dravid	not out	37	133	105	3
S.B. Joshi	not out	10	20	17	1‡
*S.R. Tendulkar				
S.C. Ganguly				
M. Azharuddin				
†N.R. Mongia				
A. Kumble				
A. Kuruvilla				
B.K.V. Prasad				
Extras:	lb3 nb10	13		‡ plus 1 six
Total:	2 wkts	212		§ plus 2 sixes

Fall: 97, 198

Bowling:
Ambrose   9–1–26–0 *4nb*
Bishop   16–3–47–0 *8nb*
Walsh   15–3–37–1 *1nb*
Hooper   15–4–40–0
Chanderpaul   11–0–40–0
Williams   3–0–19–0

Umpires: S.A. Bucknor (WI) & B.C. Cooray (SL).
Third umpire: C. Mack (WI).
Referee: P.L. van der Merwe (SA). *Debuts:* none.
Man of the Match: B.C. Lara

Match drawn

> the keeper in the first over after tea. Thereafter Jadeja, encouraged by already having hit Hooper for six, raced past his previous Test-best of 73 towards his hundred; he failed because he chanced an unnecessary second run as Williams at third man threw the ball straight into Browne's gloves. The match had long since lost all point.

Clayton Goodwin

Brian Lara returned to his vintage best in the Antigua Test, making his second century of the Test match year

Allsport

West Indies v India

Fifth Test: Georgetown

April 17–21 1997

Jupiter Pluvius the Winner

Whereas West Indies remained unchanged from what they considered their best XI, the Indians recalled Sidhu, now recovered from malarial flu, in place of Laxman and gave themselves a perceived option of forcing the victory which they needed by including an extra bowler, Dodda Ganesh, at the expense of Ganguly. It would be as incorrect as it is inelegant to suggest that nobody gave a toss about the result on a dead pitch with the endemic rain threatening, but the toss, after all, proved to be just about the only thing of competitive interest. Once Tendulkar called correctly and elected to bat, the match settled soon into stalemate.

In the opening session neither side made the progress required. The tourists crawled to 38 for 1 by lunch, hardly the urgency necessary to build a sufficient total against which they could dismiss their hosts twice, and the West Indians dropped both batsmen with the score 17 – Williams in the slips and Bishop at gully were the offending fieldsmen then, though the catching was generally below standard throughout. Even so, Walsh probed the line of the off stump effectively and Bishop gained intelligent movement off the pitch.

The spirit went out of the game early in the afternoon. Drizzle dampened enthusiasm, Rose was absent from the field either side of the interval, and with the score at 80 for 2 Ambrose spilt a caught-and-bowled chance from Tendulkar at hip-height which, if taken, could have broken through the depleted Indian batting. Thereafter, as the West Indians showed their frustration with the lacklustre pitch and the circumstances, it appeared from ringside that the participants were merely going through the motions of a contest they knew was predestined to be drawn. Occasional legspinner Chanderpaul, whom Dravid had hit earlier for six, tied up one end by bowling outside leg stump with monotone consistency.

Although Dravid reached his 1000th run in his 14th Test and the batsmen attained their century partnership off 254 balls in 163 minutes, the first day's total of 194 for 2 did little to suggest that a positive result would be achieved. Pedants were distracted by such trivial pursuits as noting that 12th man Rawl Lewis had been on the field all day because Roland Holder had cut his mouth in practice and that Chanderpaul was no-balled for having three fielders behind square leg. If only they had known what was to come they would have been thankful for even those small mercies.

It rained throughout the second day, throughout much of the third, and for sufficiently long into the fourth as to restrict play to just under two hours in the evening. In whiling away the wasted hours the Indians could have found out from back-numbers of the local newspaper that the first three of this season's Red Stripe Cup matches scheduled to be played in Guyana had been abandoned without a ball bowled, and, if they had bothered to ask, that the name 'Guyana' itself means 'Land of Waters'. In the short time available Tendulkar failed again to reach three figures as he hit a catch back to Bishop, and even closer to his hundred Dravid reached far from his body to hit a wide delivery from Rose to Hooper at point. One ball later the teams came off for poor light.

Adrian Murrell/Allsport

West Indies had bowled and fielded more positively after the rains, and, irrespective of the circumstance, the exchanges on the last day had Test match character. Mohammad Azharuddin, who passed 5000 runs in his 83rd Test, got a thin edge on an unplayable ball from Rose: unplayable, but film replay suggested that a no-ball should have been called. Much attention had been given to the potential batting and bowling records which the downpours had ruined in the last two Tests, but over the first three encounters Azharuddin had approached a series record for catches, only to have the chance washed away.

There was some excitement immediately after lunch as Walsh took a lightning left-handed catch low down at slip to dismiss Kumble. Mongia then appeared to have the benefit of a close appeal for run-out, umpire Sharp declining to refer to the third umpire. And Joshi hit Chanderpaul high to midwicket where Lewis, perhaps fearing that the ball would clear the ropes, stayed back on the boundary instead of taking a step forward and spilled a catch he attempted to hold too low. Thereafter, apart from the interest in Ganesh being caught and then stumped in one action by Browne, the innings unwound to its conclusion and it remained only for West Indies to bat out time patiently.

That was not how it happened. Stuart Williams, who could have been expected to play carefully for his place in the side, struck a string of boundaries while local hero Chanderpaul, opening in place of Campbell, who was suffering from sinusitis, provided more sedate support. It seemed that in emergency West Indies had found their most effective opening partnership. Williams's lbw dismissal in Kumble's first over when the stand had made 72 runs in 65 minutes/balls did not staunch the flow of runs. Brian Lara rewarded the patience and loyalty of the crowd with a display of strokeplay which was majestic by even his standards. His first six scoring strokes were fours to the boundary, and then he struck Joshi over the top for six. In trying to repeat the stroke next ball he was caught by Sidhu. Chanderpaul, who was batting with increased maturity, found the rope regularly, one straight-drive off Ganesh shaving the bowler's stumps before going on to the boundary.

While they were together neither captain dared to close the game. With Lara out and Hooper hesitant, the momentum was lost, and play ended in farce with both batsmen almost at the same end. As the fieldsmen fumbled the ball Hooper might well have made his ground on being sent back, had he tried. Instead he ambled off. That was the point it seemed that for the first time since play had resumed nobody really cared ... and the curtains were drawn on a series which contained much individual initiative that was commendable and encouraging, a friendly ambience between the teams, and Jupiter Pluvius triumphant.   ***Clayton Goodwin***

Rahul Dravid finished a prolific first year in Test cricket with a patient 92 at Bourda, passing 1000 runs in only his 14th Test

FIFTH TEST MATCH

Bourda, Georgetown, Guyana

April 17, 18, 19, 20, 21 1997 (no play 2nd and 3rd days)

Toss: India

INDIA

			Mins	*Balls*	*Fours*
A.D. Jadeja	c Browne b Bishop	8	*98*	*68*	*1*
N.S. Sidhu	c Hooper b Walsh	36	*164*	*104*	*6*
§R.S. Dravid	c Hooper b Rose	92	*380*	*295*	*8‡*
★S.R. Tendulkar	c & b Bishop	83	*287*	*221*	*9*
M. Azharuddin	c Browne b Rose	31	*103*	*68*	*3*
†N.R. Mongia	c Hooper b Rose	39	*217*	*154*	*2*
A. Kumble	c Walsh b Hooper	15	*49*	*48*	*1*
S.B. Joshi	c Browne b Chanderpaul	7	*21*	*19*	*1*
D. Ganesh	c Browne b Hooper	7	*29*	*27*	*0*
A. Kuruvilla	c Bishop b Hooper	5	*32*	*26*	*0*
B.K.V. Prasad	not out	0	*5*	*3*	*0*
Extras:	b8 lb8 w3 nb13	32			
Total:		355		‡plus 1 six	

Fall: 32, 68, 231, 241, 280, 303, 320, 343, 355

§kept wicket throughout WI innings after Mongia sustained injured foot while batting

Bowling:

Ambrose	29–14–36–0 *4nb 1w*
Bishop	31–9–61–2 *5nb*
Rose	33.1–7–90–3 *5nb*
Walsh	28.2–9–62–1 *1nb*
Hooper	18–7–34–3 *1nb*
Chanderpaul	29–8–56–1 *1nb 2w*

WEST INDIES

			Mins	*Balls*	*Fours*
S.C. Williams	lbw b Kumble	44	*65*	*46*	*5‡*
S. Chanderpaul	not out	58	*131*	*100*	*7*
B.C. Lara	c Sidhu b Joshi	30	*31*	*16*	*6‡*
C.L. Hooper	run out (*Jadeja*)	1	*34*	*16*	*0*
†C.O. Browne	not out	0	*4*	*6*	*0*
Extras:	b7 lb2 w1 nb2	12			
Total:		3 wkts 145		‡plus 1 six	

Did not bat: S.L. Campbell, R.I.C. Holder, I.R. Bishop, F.A. Rose, C.E.L. Ambrose, ★C.A. Walsh

Fall: 72, 127, 144

Bowling:

Prasad	7–0–37–0
Kuruvilla	7–1–34–0 *4nb*
Ganesh	7–2–24–0 *1w*
Kumble	4–1–30–1
Joshi	5–1–11–1

Umpires: E. Nicholls (WI) & G. Sharp (Eng.). *Third umpire:* C.R. Duncan (WI). *Referee:* P.L. van der Merwe (SA).
Debuts: none. *Man of the Match:* S. Chanderpaul & R.S. Dravid (joint)

Match drawn

SERIES AVERAGES

WEST INDIES

Batting:

	M	I	NO	R	HS	Av.	100	50	Ct/st
S. Chanderpaul	5	8	2	443	137*	73.83	1	3	1
B.C. Lara	5	8	0	391	103	48.88	1	2	4
R.I.C. Holder	5	7	1	212	91	35.33	0	2	6
C.L. Hooper	5	8	1	245	129	35.00	1	0	3
S.C. Williams	5	8	0	263	128	32.88	1	0	2
C.O. Browne	3	4	2	64	39*	32.00	0	0	10
C.E.L. Ambrose	5	6	2	126	37	31.50	0	0	0
F.A. Rose	5	4	1	63	34	21.00	0	0	0
S.L. Campbell	5	7	0	129	43	18.43	0	0	1
I.R. Bishop	4	4	0	51	24	12.75	0	0	2
J.R. Murray	2	3	1	24	12*	12.00	0	0	2
M.V. Dillon	2	3	1	21	21	10.50	0	0	0
C.A. Walsh	4	3	0	25	21	8.33	0	0	2

Bowling:

	O	M	R	W	Av.	BB	5w/i
I.R. Bishop	111.4	26	262	12	21.83	4–22	0
F.A. Rose	141.1	27	402	18	22.33	6–100	1
C.E.L. Ambrose	153.4	48	302	10	30.20	5–87	1
M.V. Dillon	54	11	148	4	37.00	3–92	0
C.A. Walsh	119.2	32	250	4	62.50	1–7	0
C.L. Hooper	106	36	222	3	74.00	3–34	0
S. Chanderpaul	65	13	156	1	156.00	1–56	0
B.C. Lara	3	0	16	0	–	–	0
S.C. Williams	3	0	19	0	–	–	0

INDIA

Batting:

	M	I	NO	R	HS	Av.	100	50	Ct/st
R.S. Dravid	5	7	2	360	92	72.00	0	4	5
S.R. Tendulkar	5	6	1	289	92	57.80	0	3	5
A.D. Jadeja	2	2	0	104	96	52.00	0	1	0
N.S. Sidhu	4	6	0	276	201	46.00	1	0	1
V.V.S. Laxman	4	6	0	172	64	28.67	0	2	4
N.R. Mongia	5	5	0	140	78	28.00	0	1	13
S.B. Joshi	4	4	1	84	43	28.00	0	0	1
S.C. Ganguly	4	4	0	78	42	19.50	0	0	2
A. Kumble	5	5	2	58	23*	19.33	0	0	2
M. Azharuddin	5	5	0	63	31	12.60	0	0	9
D. Ganesh	2	3	1	22	8	11.00	0	0	0
B.K.V. Prasad	5	5	2	10	10*	3.33	0	0	2
A. Kuruvilla	5	5	0	16	9	3.20	0	0	0

Bowling:

	O	M	R	W	Av.	BB	5w/i
S.B. Joshi	120.1	28	331	11	30.09	3–57	0
A. Kumble	200.4	44	576	19	30.32	5–104	2
D. Ganesh	34	5	122	4	30.50	2–28	0
A. Kuruvilla	172	34	480	13	36.92	5–68	1
B.K.V. Prasad	169.4	42	465	11	42.27	5–82	1
S.C. Ganguly	20	5	59	1	59.00	1–3	0
S.R. Tendulkar	2	0	9	0	–	–	0
V.V.S. Laxman	15	3	49	0	–	–	0

New Zealand v Sri Lanka

First Test: Dunedin
March 7–10 1997

Declaration Thwarts Young's Approach to Record

New Zealand began better prepared than Sri Lanka, whose sole scheduled first-class lead-up match at Gisborne was abandoned through rain and inadequate covering. The home team had been boosted since England's Test series win by a tie then two victories in their last three one-dayers to square the series. Their selectors plunged by dropping from captaincy and team Lee Germon. He had a creditably strong sense of jutting-jaw duty towards a big load as skipper, keeper and often No.3 batsman of a mostly unsuccessful team, without often looking a convincing international player. Having been given confidence by his showing at Christchurch, they installed Stephen Fleming, an articulate, naturally gracious 23-year-old, who said: 'It would be great if I could have it for 10 years. That's got to be my goal and ambition.' Germon was officially stated to have been dropped because of form, but Sir Richard Hadlee, as ambassador of the sponsor, Bank of New Zealand, told a meeting of bank customers in Hamilton before the second Test that he had been privy to discussions and there was more to Germon's sacking than was made public.

Allott suffered a leg injury at Test-eve practice and, with the Cairns ankle allowing him only to bat, New Zealand went in with just Doull and Davis as pace bowlers, bringing back Patel. Sri Lanka included the tall, lean, fast Nuwan Zoysa, so both teams had an 18-year-old left-armer. Both sides intended to insert the other. Ranatunga won the toss. That turned out to be Sri Lanka's high point.

Dashers can be productive batsmen; others dash themselves on the rocks. This time, New Zealand took the first role and Sri Lanka the second. Bryan Young's innings of his life, after early struggles against Zoysa, conquered a long-lasting concentration problem. The 32-year-old's back-foot strength fed by short bowling, he hit only 15 in the V, with 173 runs on the off side, and 37 fours. The shots bringing his century – a back-foot forced four from his ribs through cover after having been given no width – and double-century – a tennis overhead single backwards to third man – were memorably unusual.

New Zealand gained permanent ascendancy, largely through boldly attacking the previously troublesome Muralitharan, in Young's 140-run stand with Horne, a second-wicket record against Sri Lanka. The fielding was ragged, the first-day cold, as difficult for the visitors as equatorial heat is for tourists in Sri Lanka, providing some excuse. Mahanama dropped Young on 155 early on the second morning – the only chance he offered, though he was lucky to survive a Zoysa lbw appeal to the final delivery the previous evening – but the four Mahanama did take at second slip equalled the Sri Lankan Test record. Fleming, with one gorgeous square-drive, and Cairns made very different but impressive half-centuries, the batsmen topping four runs an over without looking reckless.

The declaration at 586 for 7 at tea on Saturday, after Young was told of it at the previous drinks break, provoked much discussion. It prevented Young, while scoring freely, from attacking Martin Crowe's New Zealand Test record of 299.

As it turned out his team had more than a day to spare. Jayasuriya chopped Doull on for 0 and much of the criticism was silenced when Sri Lanka lost four for 78 before stumps. One casualty was Atapattu, but before Doull trapped him he had multiplied his Test batting average 21-fold in 82 minutes. It was previously 0.17 from five ducks and a single against India and Australia. His 25 lifted that to 3.71. Sri Lanka at no point put their heads down to work for an attainable draw on Peter Domigan's admirably true, medium-paced pitch. Doull, whose nine wickets against England were inadequate reward, this time had figures to match his skill and persistence, with his third five-wicket bag against New Zealand's three Test opponents of the season.

Mike Cooper/Allsport

There were numerous injudicious out-shots. The worst came from the two senior batsmen: de Silva cut Davis from the fourth ball he faced and Patel had a smart, low gully catch. Next morning, first delivery he faced, Ranatunga tried driving a Doull warmer-upper starting well outside off and going further, for Young to take him face-high. A record sixth-wicket stand, just 56, was broken unluckily by Kaluwitharana's freezing. A ball from Patel lodged not in his clothing, where law 23(1)(d) declares it dead, but between glove and leg. Silly point Fleming swooped to pluck the ball out, and umpire Robinson raised his finger, which seemed correct. Referee Burge undertook to recommend a law-change. Next over, this rare situation recurred. Vettori had one lodge similarly with Vaas, but he emptied it out to boot, then pitch, just before Fleming arrived.

Sri Lanka, following on 364 behind, were reprieved at 37 for 0 by a deluge at 4.25 pm. A bad lbw verdict from umpire King accounted for de Silva when the ball from Astle was clearly passing outside off stump, and the batting reached its nadir when Ranatunga was fifth out at 115. He played a cow shot from outside off stump, though this became a dismissal only through a spectacular, leaping one-hander from mid-on Horne, whose work boosted an already strong fielding team. Kaluwitharana, expressive face shining with determination and increasing pleasure, had 103 from 103 balls, an admirably defiant and well-judged hand, though, from No.7, it was too late to save the side. He added a record 137 in 109 minutes with Vaas on the final afternoon.

More primitive hitting by Murilatharan, batting middle and umpire throughout, produced 20 off an over, including six over point, to Davis's vocal exasperation. Doull, swinging both ways with control and aggression in his first-ever full Test season, was the match's best bowler, by a bigger margin than indicated in figures influenced by third man's absence. A year ago, selectors persistently believed Robert Kennedy superior, and Doull, complaining of being 'told blatant [selectorial] lies', was omitted from the home Tests and Caribbean tour. Fleming justifiably set attacking fields throughout.

NZC marketed the first three days for senior citizens, children and families, and attendance over four days jumped to over 11,000 in a city of 108,000, each weekend day topping 4000. An equivalent proportion of Londoners descending on Lord's would mean over 1,000,000 bums on seats.

New Zealand's 35th Test win, their seventh by an innings, was the first at home since February 1994. David Lloyd faxed Steve Rixon from Lord's: 'You'll be a national hero now.'   *Terry Power*

Bryan Young came within 33 runs of a triple-century at Carisbrook that would have brought him the New Zealand Test record

FIRST TEST MATCH

Carisbrook, Dunedin

March 7, 8, 9, 10 1997
Toss: Sri Lanka

NEW ZEALAND			*Mins*	*Balls*	*Fours*
B.A. Young	not out	267	*605*	*422*	*37*
B.A. Pocock	c Mahanama b Vaas	18	*85*	*64*	*0*
M.J. Horne	c Mahanama b Ranatunga	66	*173*	*108*	*8‡*
*S.P. Fleming	c Zoysa b Wickremasinghe	51	*69*	*59*	*8*
N.J. Astle	b Vaas	27	*54*	*48*	*5*
D.L. Vettori	c Mahanama b Vaas	1	*14*	*13*	*0*
C.L. Cairns	c Mahanama b Zoysa	70	*141*	*123*	*9‡*
†A.C. Parore	c Wickremasinghe b Vaas	19	*45*	*28*	*3*
D.N. Patel	not out	30	*47*	*42*	*1‡*
H.T. Davis	did not bat	—			
S.B. Doull	did not bat	—			

Extras: b14 nb21 w2   37   ‡ plus 1 six
Total: 7 wkts dec. 586

Fall: 55, 195, 271, 337, 343, 466, 512

....

Bowling:
Vaas   35–6–144–4 *7nb 2w*
Zoysa   40–6–112–1 *14nb*
Wickremasinghe   25–4–117–1 *9nb*
Muralitharan   33–6–136–0
Ranatunga   5–0–29–1
Jayasuriya   8–0–34–0

SRI LANKA			*Mins*	*Balls*	*Fours*			*Mins*	*Balls*	*Fours*
S.T. Jayasuriya	b Doull	0	*12*	*7*	*0*	c Parore b Doull	50	*111*	*68*	*6*
R.S. Mahanama	lbw b Doull	26	*107*	*75*	*2*	b Doull	21	*65*	*46*	*3*
M.S. Atapattu	lbw b Doull	25	*82*	*66*	*3*	b Patel	22	*88*	*57*	*2*
P.A. de Silva	c Patel b Davis	3	*4*	*4*	*0*	lbw b Astle	0	*20*	*14*	*0*
*A. Ranatunga	c Young b Doull	14	*48*	*40*	*1*	c Horne b Vettori	13	*58*	*45*	*1*
H.P. Tillekeratne	not out	55	*246*	*160*	*8*	run out (*sub: C.Z. Harris*)	8	*61*	*55*	*0*
†R.S. Kaluwitharana	c Fleming b Patel	43	*81*	*50*	*5*	c & b Vettori	103	*134*	*103*	*13§*
W.P.U.J.C. Vaas	c Horne b Patel	2	*18*	*17*	*0*	c & b Davis	57	*130*	*97*	*0*
G.P. Wickremasinghe	c Parore b Davis	43	*77*	*75*	*6*	c Doull b Astle	0	*5*	*8*	*0*
D.N.T. Zoysa	c Young b Davis	0	*11*	*7*	*0*	not out	16	*33*	*16*	*3*
M. Muralitharan	c Cairns b Doull	0	*13*	*10*	*0*	c & b Doull	26	*18*	*14*	*4‡*

Extras: lb10 w1   11   lb9 nb3   12   ‡ plus 1 six
Total: 222   328   § plus 2 sixes

Fall: 4, 55, 58, 58, 79, 135, 141, 214, 215   49, 82, 85, 99, 115, 133, 270, 271, 285

....

Bowling:

Doull	21.2–5–58–5 *1w*		Doull	20.3–5–82–3
Davis	19–6–34–3		Davis	22–2–79–1 *2nb*
Horne	6–5–4–0		Horne	4–2–18–0
Astle	3–0–11–0		Astle	15–3–51–2 *1nb*
Patel	22–4–67–2		Patel	10–3–36–1
Vettori	14–5–38–0		Vettori	15–3–53–2

Umpires: C.E. King (NZ) & I.D. Robinson (Zim.). *Third umpire:* R.S. Dunne (NZ). *Referee:* P.J.P. Burge (Aus.).
Debut: D.N.T. Zoysa (SL). *Man of the Match:* B.A. Young

New Zealand won by an innings and 36 runs

New Zealand v Sri Lanka
Second Test: Hamilton
March 14–17 1997

Vettori's Promise Grows

Test season's end, 20 minutes after tea on the fourth day, with New Zealand's first win in five attempts at Trust Bank Park, illustrated the series well. Muralitharan's swipe was more excusable from a No.11 than numerous comparable aggressive suicides were from his predecessors. The only department in the series consistently of top international standard was the New Zealand fielding, and Cairns did nothing to lower that in moving to extra cover to take a semi-skyer. This was the ninth wicket on his home ground for Vettori, Man of the Match and New Zealand's best spinning discovery since offie John Bracewell, picked as a batsman, emerged for Otago when his first 10 first-class wickets came for 64, also at Hamilton, New Year 1979.

Nuwan Zoysa, the other 18-year-old left-armer in the match, shone earlier. Unlucky at Dunedin, he helped himself by putting the ball up further and looked dangerous throughout. The delivery which zoomed back in at Astle before he had scored, giving him no time to contemplate what to do next, and hitting front foot to have him lbw, remained the best wicket-taking delivery of the match. Sri Lanka dropped pace bowler Wickremasinghe and Atapattu for Sajeewa de Silva and Dharmasena to have four left-arm bowlers for the first time in their history. Before lunch, all were used – Vaas, Zoysa, de Silva, then Jayasuriya, off whom Horne hit the best shot of the session, a flick-sweep fine for four.

The second delivery of the match, Vaas to Pocock, removed a divot, short of a length at the pavilion end. Murilatharan, who cost under two an over through improved accuracy and in the second innings became the first Sri Lankan to reach 100 Test wickets, gained more turn on the first day than anyone did later. These events precipitated many comments, mostly unfavourable, with Bruce Yardley, Sri Lanka's new coach, the most heavily and persistently critical. Ian McKendry's first Test pitch, since coming from being assistant at Lancaster Park, was easier during later days, developed some bounce but remained too slow for full satisfaction. The block will be relaid over the 1997 winter.

New Zealand lost Young and later Parore to run-outs. Both featured attempted singles which were always bad ideas, ball-watching by the strikers; absence of the immediate consultations between batsmen required by the situations; prompt Sri Lanka tosses to appropriately manned bowlers' stumps; and Pocock at the other end. It was just as well he survived. The tall Northern Districts captain had just five fours in 268 minutes; he is New Zealand's only real grafter. Pocock's 85, his best Test score, with a straight-drive his sole memorable stroke, was essential to his team's reaching bare respectability at 222, eight minutes from scheduled stumps.

Next day, Mahanama batted with the dedication Sri Lanka badly needed till Vettori deceived him with a non-turner. Dharmasena and Vaas provided for the seventh wicket their country's only grafting stand of the series, 51 in 105 minutes, but bogging down near the end. The middle-order batting was negligible – the first six batsmen fell within 54 runs by soon after lunch. Vettori had Aravinda de Silva lobbing up a bat-to-body nick second ball, and, after some drifted down leg early in seeking more turn than was available, proceeded with admirable control of line to four wickets at under two an over. Doull lacked zing, and unusually operated as container more than attacker. Bowling courageously despite knee and ankle niggles, with more control if a little less pace than when he left vast trails of no-balls and wides in his wake, Heath Davis deserved his first Test five-wicket bag.

Zoysa's first over when New Zealand recommenced 52 ahead produced an unhappy incident in a mostly pleasant series. Young offered an obvious edge to second slip Mahanama and remained after the unsuccessful concerted appeal. Replays showed he was right to stay put. Mahanama, diving, had dropped the ball. He must have known; probably nearby team-mates did, too. Young continued till nearly noon Monday for a top-score 62, more than usual off the front foot. Fleming had a stylish half-century and Astle a lucky one, with more playing and missing than he ever recalled before. Parore was run out again, this time all his own work. Doull, with no noticeable defence, hits briefly and effectively with increasing frequency in internationals, and led a 30-run last-wicket stand.

Doull intervened again when Sri Lanka aimed from 5.03 on the third evening for 326 to win. At fine leg after his first over, he raced right. An immaculate low throw had Jayasuriya just short, trying for two. Vettori bowled Tillekeratne, swinging across the line, not around his legs but straight past them. Sri Lanka 20 for 2 at stumps.

This became 50 for 4 when Aravinda de Silva fell to Doull to leave with his series aggregate 9 in four innings. Failures from Sri Lanka's best batsman surprised Kiwis after his Shell Cup successes for Auckland over Christmas and New Year. Two injuries had stopped him playing much since. 'He is sad in his eyes,' noted Yardley. 'He thinks he's let the team down.' This dismissal was plumb, with Doull back to his swinging, pacy best. But his two other important lbws later in the day from umpire Cowie, against Mahanama and Kaluwitharana, while coming from excellent deliveries, looked likely candidates to hit the stumps, not certainties.

Mahanama (who passed 2000 Test runs) and Ranatunga had a 79-run fifth-wicket stand either side of lunch, with Mahanama looking solid and the captain's aggression more selective than earlier; Fleming later admitted worry. The series was effectively settled at 1.56 pm. Ranatunga got underneath Vettori in swinging him to long leg. Doull thought it would be easy. The ball dipped faster than expected, to his right, but though he finished awkwardly, he completed the lowest reverse-cup catch of the season.

Vettori should have had his first Test 'fivefer' before instead of after tea. He nicked the outside of Dharmasena's off stump and dislodged a bail. Parore complicated the issue by whipping the other off within a second; the umpires were not sure and could not ask for TV assistance. (Referee Burge will recommend to ICC that umpires can in future refer such situations.) Keeper and close fieldsmen talked. Dharmasena objected, saying he could not concentrate. Vettori, his appeal refused, characteristically was the calmest on the scene, just seeking the ball to get on with it. Barring serious injury, he can bowl for 20 Test years if he wants to – for how many hundred wickets is anyone's guess.

Official attendance in a city of 106,000 was 12,077, excluding corporate boxes.

A fortnight after this match, Sri Lanka sacked their chief selector, Duleep Mendis, who was manager when his country won the 1996 limited-overs World Cup.   ***Terry Power***

Clive Mason/Allsport

A refreshing addition to Test ranks in 1996–97 was Daniel Vettori. Only 18, he secured his first five-wicket haul in his fourth Test match

SECOND TEST MATCH

Trust Bank Park, Hamilton

March 14, 15, 16, 17 1997
Toss: New Zealand

NEW ZEALAND		Mins	Balls	Fours		Mins	Balls	Fours
B.A. Pocock	c Tillekeratne b Muralitharan	85	268	239	5	(2) c Mahanama b Zoysa 7	22	11	1
B.A. Young	run out					(1) c Ranatunga b Dharmasena 62	167	127	8‡
	(P.A. de Silva/S.C. de Silva)	4	44	26	0	st Kaluwitharana			
M.J. Horne	b Zoysa	21	102	82	2	b Muralitharan 16	83	64	2
★S.P. Fleming	c Mahanama b Zoysa	2	15	14	0	b Muralitharan 59	177	117	8‡
N.J. Astle	lbw b Zoysa	0	10	12	0	c Mahanama b Vaas 52	191	151	5§
C.L. Cairns	c Ranatunga b Dharmasena	10	62	53	0	c sub (U.U. Chandana)			
						b Muralitharan 4	21	17	1
†A.C. Parore	run out					run out			
	(Mahanama/Muralitharan)	25	47	35	4	(Tillekeratne/Kaluwitharana) 2	5	4	0
D.N. Patel	c Dharmasena b Muralitharan	13	36	21	2	c P.A. de Silva b Dharmasena 4	14	15	0
D.L. Vettori	b Muralitharan	4	17	12	1	b Zoysa 6	36	36	0
S.B. Doull	c P.A. de Silva b Vaas	20	47	30	2	c Mahanama b Zoysa 25	41	30	3
H.T. Davis	not out	8	31	34	1	not out 2	36	19	0
Extras:	b11 lb9 nb10	30				b9 lb11 w7 nb7 34			‡ plus 1 six
Total:		222				273			§ plus 2 sixes

Fall: 19, 88, 96, 100, 126, 172, 172, 178, 203

14, 64, 108, 183, 198, 201, 211, 239, 243

Bowling:

Vaas	12.4–1–32–1 3nb	Vaas	15–3–34–1
Zoysa	18–3–47–3 9nb	Zoysa	22.4–7–53–3 4nb 7w
S.C. de Silva	15–4–36–0	Dharmasena	24–5–75–2
Dharmasena	22–7–39–1	S.C. de Silva	10–2–29–0
Muralitharan	22–4–43–3 3nb	Muralitharan	26–7–62–3 5nb
Jayasuriya	1–0–5–0		

SRI LANKA		Mins	Balls	Fours		Mins	Balls	Fours
S.T. Jayasuriya	c Astle b Davis	20	46	36	2	run out (Doull/Parore) 3	7	4	0
R.S. Mahanama	lbw b Vettori	45	136	84	4	lbw b Doull 65	252	188	6
H.P. Tillekeratne	c Young b Doull	2	41	28	0	b Vettori 10	35	26	1
P.A. de Silva	c Parore b Vettori	1	3	2	0	(5) lbw b Doull 5	24	16	0
★A. Ranatunga	lbw b Davis	4	30	23	0	(6) c Doull b Vettori 33	99	70	3‡
†R.S. Kaluwitharana	c Parore b Davis	11	26	24	2	(7) lbw b Doull 13	23	12	2
H.D.P.K. Dharmasena	c Fleming b Davis	27	119	86	2‡	(8) not out 38	69	57	4‡
W.P.U.J.C. Vaas	c Pocock b Vettori	28	120	98	4	(4) c Patel b Vettori 8	51	36	1
D.N.T. Zoysa	c Doull b Vettori	14	28	16	1‡	c Parore b Vettori 13	31	30	1
S.C. de Silva	not out	0	19	12	0	c Young b Davis 0	12	8	0
M. Muralitharan	c Parore b Davis	5	5	4	1	c Cairns b Vettori 7	16	11	1
Extras:	lb9 w1 nb3	13			‡ plus 1 six	b4 lb5 w1 10			‡ plus 1 six
Total:		170				205			

Fall: 39, 57, 58, 76, 87, 93, 144, 154, 165

5, 16, 40, 50, 129, 147, 152, 185, 186

Bowling:

Doull	13–4–19–1 2nb	Doull	15–4–34–3
Davis	20.2–3–63–5 1nb 1w	Davis	17–4–35–1 1w
Astle	3–1–8–0	Vettori	29.2–8–84–5
Vettori	24–8–46–4	Patel	12–5–34–0
Patel	8–2–25–0	Astle	3–1–9–0

Umpires: D.B. Cowie (NZ) & Mahboob Shah (Pak.). *Third umpire:* B.F. Bowden (NZ). *Referee:* P.J.P. Burge (Aus.).
Debut: S.C. de Silva (SL). *Man of the Match:* D.L. Vettori

New Zealand won by 120 runs

Sri Lanka v Pakistan
First Test: Colombo
April 19–23 1997

Justice Through the Magic Eye

The 18th Test encounter between these two countries was a showcase for some fine batting, stoic slow bowling, and controversial umpiring, but when five days of intense competition at the Premadasa Stadium were over and done, the sides were a long way from a positive result. Had it been a timeless Test, Pakistan's quest for victory through a 400-plus target might have had some chance of success, though the spin-bowling strength of the home side was little behind that of the visitors.

Pakistan seemed set for a big first-innings lead after two days, having bowled Sri Lanka out for 330 and advanced to 200 for 2, with Ijaz Ahmed on 90 and Salim Malik 47. Hashan Tillekeratne had saved Sri Lanka with his sixth Test hundred, a patient effort of almost six hours (Mushtaq Ahmed missed him at 85 at mid-off) during which he found his best touch elusive. His tenacity paid off, and his stands of 89 for both the fifth and sixth wickets, with skipper Ranatunga and then the audacious little Kaluwitharana, assured his side of a decent total after all. They had been 90 for 4, with de Silva gone.

Umpire Wickremasinghe caused a stir by refusing appeals for lbw first ball against Ranatunga and what seemed a certain caught-behind against Tillekeratne. It was suggested in some quarters that the official had been dismayed at criticism after giving a lot of lbws during the recent Sharjah tournament. Television replay at least verified de Silva's dismissal, stumped.

On a slow surface and in debilitating heat and humidity, the bowlers were made to toil, and in the end spin did the job, offspinner Saqlain securing his first five-wicket haul. Wasim Akram and Waqar Younis were understandably missed.

On the third day, Ijaz and Malik were soon parted, but in a most unusual way. Refusing a call from his brother-in-law, Malik stayed put while Ijaz ran to the bowler's end. The throw went to the keeper, and Ijaz was adjudged out. It was only when he was back in the dressing-room that the third umpire, having established that the batsmen crossed, relayed a reconsidered verdict to umpire Shepherd, and Ijaz, then on 98, was recalled and Malik had to go. It was a unique occurrence in the 120 years of Test match history. At Christchurch in 1951, Cyril Washbrook was still on his way back to the pavilion when Walter Hadlee persuaded the umpire to revoke his decision, the lbw appeal being withdrawn by New Zealand when it was realised that the batsman had edged the ball.

There were to be no more big stands in the innings, which had started with Elahi's first-ball dismissal, playing no stroke. Captain Ramiz and Ijaz then put on a crucial 102, followed by the Ijaz/Malik partnership of 117. Then all became caution. In a day's play of 95 overs, Pakistan eked out a mere 170 runs in the six hours, the tourists' fears mounting when three wickets fell for one run to Muralitharan in 14 balls. Ijaz's seventh Test century, consecutive to his 125 against New

Zealand at Rawalpindi five months previously, ended after 5½ hours of judicious batting, with some fierce shots along the way, one of which badly cut Muralitharan's right hand. The offspinner gamely bowled on to his best Test figures, helped by substitute Kalpage's brilliant short midwicket catch to dismiss Inzamam and Moin Khan's rashness either side of Ijaz's downfall. 'Murali's' wickets spared Sri Lanka potentially extensive hardship because Zoysa was unable to bowl after damaging a muscle in his left leg, and Jayasuriya was in confinement all day with tonsillitis.

Sri Lanka lost debutant left-hander Russel Arnold before the arrears of 48 had been accounted for (the 23-year-old beat de Silva's domestic run record in the 1995–96 season). He was caught at cover, and Atapattu holed out at long-on, both off Saqlain as he settled into a marathon spell which would take his match tally to nine wickets and bring him the match award, his long and important innings of 58 from the No.8 spot clinching it.

Any thoughts Pakistan might have had about running through the home side were gradually snuffed out, however, as Aravinda de Silva and his captain joined in a century stand lasting over three hours during which the bowlers' sting was drawn. Ranatunga's 25th half-century was resolute and measured, and after his departure, top-edging a sweep off Mushtaq Ahmed, his partner went on his occasionally explosive way, emphatically placing 18 months of disappointment behind him. No bowler felt the heat of his bat more than Mohammad Zahid, who was hit for six over midwicket and went for 16 off one over. De Silva's last Test fifty came as long ago as September 1995, at Faisalabad, since when he had played 14 innings.

Here, had he been given out lbw at 10 to Mushtaq Ahmed no-one would have been surprised. But umpire Wickremasinghe decided against. The nuggety little batsman reached his fifty off 98 balls and, 79 overnight, had been in for almost 5½ hours when his century came next day. It was his ninth, and fifth against Pakistan. Tillekeratne added a fifty to his first-innings century, and Jayasuriya, feeling more himself, contributed a lively 62 from the No.7 position.

Ranatunga allowed his men to bat right through since the injuries among his bowlers ruled out a challenge to Pakistan through a declaration. The new ball was seen off, and Sri Lanka's batting, centring on de Silva's important rehabilitation, seemed to have regained its assurance.   ***TMY***

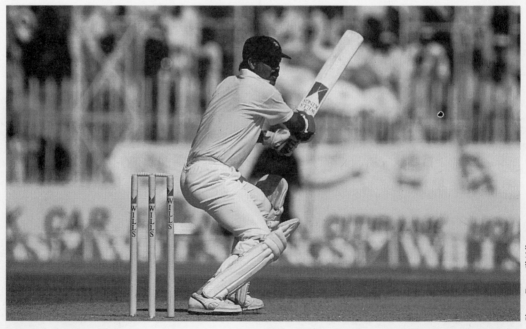

Shaun Botterill/Allsport

Making his third century, Ijaz Ahmed took his average for the Test match year to a satisfying 50

FIRST TEST MATCH

Premadasa Stadium, Colombo

April 19, 20, 21, 22, 23 1997

Toss: Sri Lanka

SRI LANKA

			Mins	Balls	Fours			Mins	Balls	Fours
S.T. Jayasuriya	b Ahmed	31	112	65	4	(7) c Elahi b Saqlain	62	126	84	7‡
R.P. Arnold	b Ahmed	24	118	82	0‡	c Nazir b Saqlain	15	64	36	1
M.S. Atapattu	c Inzamam b Saqlain	0	6	8	0	(1) c Nazir b Saqlain	25	99	69	3
P.A. de Silva	st Moin b Ahmed	23	46	31	4	(3) c Saqlain b Ahmed	168	508	383	14‡
*A. Ranatunga	c Elahi b Mujtaba	49	168	131	5	(4) c Ramiz b Ahmed	58	206	165	5
H.P. Tillekeratne	c Mujtaba b Saqlain	103	349	228	10	(5) c Ramiz b Saqlain	54	105	95	5
†R.S. Kaluwitharana	b Saqlain	57	106	89	8	(6) c Moin b Nazir	17	78	54	0
H.P.D.K. Dharmasena	b Saqlain	1	27	22	0	not out	11	54	52	1
W.P.U.J.C. Vaas	c Moin b Zahid	17	90	59	1	c sub (*Mohammad Hussain*) b Ahmed	1	14	7	0
D.N.T. Zoysa	lbw b Saqlain	0	12	6	0					
M. Muralitharan	not out	8	6	5	1					

Extras:	b3 lb9 w1 nb4	17			b3 lb4 nb5	12	
Total:		330		‡plus 1 six	8 wkts	423	‡plus 1 six

Fall: 61, 62, 64, 90, 179, 268, 280, 322, 322

38, 53, 182, 265, 315, 390, 420, 423

Bowling:

Mohammad Zahid	17–2–44–1 1w 3nb
Shahid Nazir	18–6–37–0 1nb
Saqlain Mushtaq	44.2–10–89–5
Mushtaq Ahmed	34–2–123–3
Asif Mujtaba	9–2–25–1

Mohammad Zahid	11–1–60–0 4nb
Shahid Nazir	12–0–61–1 1nb
Saqlain Mushtaq	63–13–137–4
Mushtaq Ahmed	39.1–9–94–3
Asif Mujtaba	30–5–64–0

PAKISTAN

		Mins	Balls	Fours
Salim Elahi	lbw b Vaas	0	1	1	0
*Ramiz Raja	c Ranatunga b Dharmasena	50	121	85	3
Ijaz Ahmed	c Dharmasena b Muralitharan	113	324	245	11
Salim Malik	run out (*Ranatunga/Kaluwitharana*)	58	144	115	3
Inzamam-Ul-Haq	c sub (*R.S. Kalpage*) b Muralitharan	12	50	41	1
Asif Mujtaba	c & b Muralitharan	21	118	97	2
†Moin Khan	b Muralitharan	0	2	2	0
Saqlain Mushtaq	run out (*Arnold*)	58	301	248	5
Mushtaq Ahmed	b Muralitharan	26	58	54	2
Shahid Nazir	c Ranatunga b Muralitharan	2	37	26	0
Mohammad Zahid	not out	6	97	64	1

Extras:	b11 lb7 nb14	32
Total:		378

Fall: 0, 102, 219, 247, 248, 248, 298, 336, 349

Bowling:

Vaas	32–6–75–1
Zoysa	10–0–55–0 7nb
Dharmasena	52.5–19–93–1
Muralitharan	53–19–98–6 7nb
Jayasuriya	3–0–15–0
de Silva	4–0–16–0
Ranatunga	3–1–5–0
Arnold	2–1–3–0

Umpires: D.R. Shepherd (Eng.) & U. Wickremasinghe (SL). *Third umpire:* K.T. Francis (SL). *Referee:* J.R. Reid (NZ).
Debut: R.P. Arnold (SL). *Man of the Match:* Saqlain Mushtaq

Match Drawn

Sri Lanka v Pakistan

Second Test: Colombo

April 26–30 1997

Two Not-Out Centuries by de Silva

Through 1366 Test matches over 120 years no batsman had registered two not-out centuries in a match. On 43 occasions batsmen had scored twin Test centuries, sometimes coupling a double-century with a single century and in Graham Gooch's case, against India at Lord's in 1990, a *triple-century* with a century in the second innings. Now, in Colombo, viewed by some as a unique glory and others as a mere statistical oddity, Aravinda de Silva followed his 168 in the previous Test with unbeaten innings of 138 and 103 as Sri Lanka's second Test in the mini-series against Pakistan ground to a draw.

Statisticians searched for a parallel when de Silva raised his bat having reached a third Test century within seven days of each other. It was a resounding return to form after his 83 runs at 11.86 in the earlier part of the Test match year. It was also in striking contrast to the shuddering starts to both Pakistan innings: a wicket lost before a run had been made, and two down for under 20.

Such is the strength of Pakistan's batting that they recovered adequately both times, though life might have been less easy had Sri Lanka's leading wicket-taker, Muralitharan, not been forced to miss the match through injury (as was Zoysa).

Jayasuriya gave Sri Lanka a characteristic burst of positive batting at the start, seeing 95 on the board with Arnold. Pakistan's spinners then struck, and it was left to de Silva to hold the innings together. By the close, Sri Lanka were 281 for 7 from 90 overs, and de Silva had his 10th Test century, and sixth against Pakistan. He had raced to a 72-ball fifty and an even swifter century (119 balls).

Pakistan's spinners finished the job next morning, though fieldsman Ijaz Ahmed was left to rue a 20 per cent fine plus five-month probation after the match referee had found him guilty of uttering abuse at Sri Lanka captain Arjuna Ranatunga. Ijaz was one of four batsmen dispatched by the left-arm pacemen Vaas and Sajeeva de Silva for only 83 before tea.

The recovery by the middle order featured an aggressive 98 off only 109 balls by Moin Khan, who reached 1000 Test runs but narrowly missed a fourth Test century, and the eventual deficit was no worse than 39. However, Sri Lanka went all out for a win, their chances enhanced by the absence of Pakistan's new-ball bowlers, Mohammad Zahid and Shahid Nazir, who were both injured, as was wicketkeeper Moin (heel), his place being taken by Salim Elahi.

By the close of the third day, Sri Lanka, 102 without loss, were already 141 ahead. Arnold made his maiden Test fifty, while Jayasuriya exceeded his previous century (112) by one, passing 1000 runs in his 23rd Test before falling to the persevering Saqlain. The Pakistan first innings had been wrapped up by S. C. de Silva, who, in his second Test match, took five wickets for the first time. The steady

Vaas took another four, while slow left-armer Jayantha Silva found wicket-taking less straightforward than during his two Tests early in the season against Zimbabwe, when he took 13 wickets at 7.69.

Sri Lanka's second-innings charge was taken up by skipper Ranatunga in company with Aravinda de Silva following the first-wicket stand of 157, and the climax of de Silva's second century of the match signalled a declaration that challenged Pakistan to score 426. When Vaas removed both openers on the fourth evening, reducing Pakistan to 28 for 2 at the close, the visitors faced a demanding final day.

Salim Malik was their lifeline. In his 96th Test, the 34-year-old former captain batted for 5½ hours for 155, his 15th Test century, and one of the more crucial. He and broth-er-in-law Ijaz Ahmed (who passed 2000 runs in his 36th Test) made only 55 incidental runs in the 29 overs before lunch, but the stand extended to 127, and when Ijaz fell to Silva, Inzamam joined with Malik in anoth-er century stand, this one of 121 coming fast (100 minutes). When Malik was finally caught behind off spinner Silva, Sri Lanka were left to regret missed chances: a return catch to Kalpage at 44, by Silva at cover at 58,

Mark Thompson/Allsport

and by Ranatunga off Vaas with the new ball at 135. Ijaz too had been missed by Vaas in the deep when 46.

When poor light ended proceedings, Sri Lanka had long since been resigned to having to wait for a second Test victory over Pakistan. Instead, they felt a glow at Aravinda de Silva's conspicuous achievement.　　　　　　　　　　　　　　　　　　　　　　　　　　　　　　　　　　　**TMY**

The return to his explosive best found Aravinda de Silva reeling off three centuries in the last two Tests of the twelvemonth

SECOND TEST MATCH
Sinhalese Sports Club, Colombo

April 26, 27, 28, 29, 30 1997
Toss: Sri Lanka

SRI LANKA

		Mins	Balls	Fours		Mins	Balls	Fours
S.T. Jayasuriya	c Ahmed b Saqlain	72	129	96	3§	c sub (*Abdul Razzaq*) b Saqlain 113	290	212	9‡
R.P. Arnold	run out (*Moin*)	37	183	129	4	b Ahmed 50	233	168	5
M.S. Atapattu	c Elahi b Saqlain	14	47	40	2	run out (*Ijaz/Elahi*) 4	19	13	0
P.A. de Silva	not out	138	273	208	19	not out 103	169	99	11‡
*A. Ranatunga	c Elahi b Saqlain	4	6	3	1	st Elahi b Ahmed 66	81	62	9§
H.P. Tillekeratne	b Zahid	10	13	9	2	not out 24	50	26	2
†R.S. Kaluwitharana	b Mujtaba	22	67	41	3				
R.S. Kalpage	c Elahi b Saqlain	5	37	31	1				
W.P.U.J.C. Vaas	c Elahi b Saqlain	17	94	81	2				
S.C. de Silva	st Moin b Ahmed	0	36	18	0				
K.J. Silva	run out (*Ahmed*)	0	20	8	0				

Extras:	b6 lb3 nb3	12	b12 lb6 w1 nb7 26 ‡plus 1 six
Total:		331 §plus 1 five	4 wkts dec. 386 §plus 3 sixes

Fall: 95, 124, 124, 129, 144, 204, 224, 300, 321

157, 171, 203, 308

Bowling:

Mohammad Zahid	12–1–44–1 *1nb*		Salim Malik	9–2–33–0 *2nb*
Shahid Nazir	8–1–50–0		Ijaz Ahmed	5–0–18–0 *3nb*
Mushtaq Ahmed	32–6–90–2		Saqlain Mushtaq	42.5–4–171–1 *2nb 1w*
Saqlain Mushtaq	45–12–115–4 *2nb*		Mushtaq Ahmed	33–4–113–2
Asif Mujtaba	15–3–23–1		Asif Mujtaba	6–0–33–0

PAKISTAN

		Mins	Balls	Fours		Mins	Balls	Fours
¶Salim Elahi	c Tillekeratne b Vaas	0	5	4	0	(2) c Arnold b Vaas 14	32	29	2
*Ramiz Raja	c Arnold b S.C. de Silva	36	62	33	6	(1) c Kaluwitharana b Vaas 0	3	4	0
Ijaz Ahmed	c Arnold b Vaas	4	12	5	1	c Vaas b Silva 47	265	180	7‡
Salim Malik	c Ranatunga b S.C. de Silva	24	93	56	4	c Kaluwitharana b Silva 155	338	240	26
Inzamam-Ul-Haq	c Kaluwitharana b Vaas	43	187	134	3	not out 54	133	85	7
Asif Mujtaba	c P.A. de Silva b Vaas	49	274	233	7	c Ranatunga b Atapattu 6	16	19	1
†Moin Khan	c Atapattu b Silva	98	175	109	9§				
Saqlain Mushtaq	b S.C. de Silva	23	91	50	3	(7) not out 5	15	14	1
Mushtaq Ahmed	c Atapattu b S.C. de Silva	1	17	16	0				
Mohammad Zahid	c Kaluwitharana b S.C. de Silva	0	8	4	0				
Shahid Nazir	not out	0	20	14	0				

Extras:	lb4 w4 nb6	14	lb3 nb1 4
Total:		292 §plus 3 sixes	5 wkts 285 ‡plus 1 six

Fall: 0, 13, 59, 83, 147, 238, 276, 283, 283

0, 19, 146, 267, 279

¶kept wicket during part of SL 2nd innings after Moin Khan injured heel

Bowling:

Vaas	27–7–60–4		Vaas	16–7–40–2
S.C. de Silva	24.2–5–85–5 *6nb 4w*		S.C. de Silva	19–2–73–0
Silva	25–5–91–1		Silva	28–10–71–2
Kalpage	23–8–42–0		Kalpage	20–6–60–0
Ranatunga	4.1–1–8–0		Atapattu	4–0–9–1
Arnold	5–3–2–0		Arnold	6–0–26–0 *1nb*
			Tillekeratne	2–1–3–0

Umpires: P. Manuel (SL) & I.D. Robinson (Zim.). *Third umpire:* I. Anandappa (SL). *Referee:* J.R. Reid (NZ). *Debuts:* none.
Man of the Match: P.A. de Silva. *Man of the Series:* P.A. de Silva.

Match drawn

Test Match Records

TEST MATCH RESULTS Country v Country

Complete to June 1 1997

	v England	v Australia	v South Africa	v West Indies
ENGLAND P734 W249 L207 D278 Tosses won: 361 First Test: March 1877, v Australia, Melbourne No. of players: 583	–	285/90/111/84	110/47/20/43	115/27/48/40
AUSTRALIA P566 W237 L160 D167 T2 Tosses won: 282 First Test: March 1877, v England, Melbourne No. of players: 371	285/111/90/84	–	62/33/14/15	86/35/29/21/1
SOUTH AFRICA P209 W53 L86 D70 Tosses won: 100 First Test: March 1889, v England, Port Elizabeth No. of players: 266	110/20/47/43	62/14/33/15	–	1/0/1/0
WEST INDIES P332 W128 L80 D123 T1 Tosses won: 173 First Test: June 1928, v England, Lord's No. of players: 216	115/48/27/40	86/29/35/21/1	1/1/0/0	–
NEW ZEALAND P252 W36 L104 D112 Tosses won: 129 First Test: January 1930, v England, Christchurch No. of players: 201	78/4/36/38	32/7/13/12	21/3/12/6	28/4/10/14
INDIA P310 W57 L102 D150 T1 Tosses won: 157 First Test: June 1932, v England, Lord's No. of players: 211	84/14/32/38	51/9/24/17/1	10/2/4/4	70/7/28/35
PAKISTAN P237 W66 L54 D117 Tosses won: 116 First Test: October 1952, v India, Delhi No. of players: 144	55/9/14/32	40/11/14/15	1/0/1/0	31/7/12/12
SRI LANKA P72 W9 L33 D30 Tosses won: 37 First Test: February 1982, v England, Colombo (PSS) No. of players: 68	5/1/3/1	10/0/7/3	3/0/1/2	1/0/0/1
ZIMBABWE P22 W1 L10 D11 Tosses won: 13 First Test: October 1992, v India, Harare No. of players: 34	2/0/0/2	–	1/0/1/0	–

v New Zealand	v India	v Pakistan	v Sri Lanka	v Zimbabwe
78/36/4/38	84/32/14/38	55/14/9/32	5/3/1/1	2/0/0/2

v New Zealand	v India	v Pakistan	v Sri Lanka	v Zimbabwe
32/13/7/12	51/24/9/17/1	40/14/11/15	10/7/0/3	–

v New Zealand	v India	v Pakistan	v Sri Lanka	v Zimbabwe
21/12/3/6	10/4/2/4	1/1/0/0	3/1/0/2	1/1/0/0

v New Zealand	v India	v Pakistan	v Sri Lanka	v Zimbabwe
28/10/4/14	70/28/7/35	31/12/7/12	1/0/0/1	–

	v India	v Pakistan	v Sri Lanka	v Zimbabwe
–	35/6/13/16	39/5/18/16	15/6/2/7	4/1/0/3

v New Zealand		v Pakistan	v Sri Lanka	v Zimbabwe
35/13/6/16	–	44/4/7/33	14/7/1/6	2/1/0/1

v New Zealand	v India		v Sri Lanka	v Zimbabwe
39/18/5/16	44/7/4/33	–	19/9/3/7	8/5/1/2

v New Zealand	v India	v Pakistan		v Zimbabwe
15/2/6/7	14/1/7/6	19/3/9/7	–	5/2/0/3

v New Zealand	v India	v Pakistan	v Sri Lanka	
4/0/1/3	2/0/1/1	8/1/5/2	5/0/2/3	–

HIGHEST TOTALS

903	for 7 dec.	Eng. v Aus., Oval	1938
849		Eng. v WI, Kingston	1929–30
790	for 3 dec.	WI v Pak., Kingston	1957–58
758	for 8 dec.	Aus. v WI, Kingston	1954–55
729	for 6 dec.	Aus. v Eng., Lord's	1930
708		Pak. v Eng., Oval	1987
701		Aus. v Eng., Oval	1934
699	for 5	Pak. v Ind., Lahore	1989–90
695		Aus. v Eng., Oval	1930
692	for 8 dec.	WI v Eng., Oval	1995
687	for 8 dec.	WI v Eng., Oval	1976
681	for 8 dec.	WI v Eng., Port-of-Spain	1953–54
676	for 7	Ind. v SL, Kanpur	1986–87
674	for 6	Pak. v Ind., Faisalabad	1984–85
674		Aus. v Ind., Adelaide	1947–48
671	for 4	NZ v SL, Wellington	1990–91
668		Aus. v WI, Bridgetown	1954–55
660	for 5 dec.	WI v NZ, Wellington	1994–95
659	for 8 dec.	Aus. v Eng., Sydney	1946–47
658	for 8 dec.	Eng. v Aus., Trent Bridge	1938
657	for 8 dec.	Pak. v WI, Bridgetown	1957–58
656	for 8 dec.	Aus. v Eng., Old Trafford	1964
654	for 5	Eng. v SA, Durban	1938–39
653	for 4 dec.	Eng. v Ind., Lord's	1990
653	for 4 dec.	Aus. v Eng., Headingley	1993
652	for 7 dec.	Eng. v Ind., Madras	1984–85
652	for 8 dec.	WI v Eng., Lord's	1973
652		Pak. v Ind., Faisalabad	1982–83
650	for 6 dec.	Aus. v WI, Bridgetown	1964–65

Highest innings for the other three countries are:

622	for 9 dec.	SA v Aus., Durban	1969–70
547	for 8 dec.	SL v Aus., Colombo (SSC)	1992–93
544	for 4 dec.	Zim. v Pak., Harare	1994–95

LOWEST TOTALS

26	NZ v Eng., Auckland	1954–55	42*	Ind. v Eng., Lord's	1974
30	SA v Eng., Port Elizabeth	1895–96	43	SA v Eng., Cape Town	1888–89
30	SA v Eng., Edgbaston	1924	44	Aus. v Eng., Oval	1896
35	SA v Eng., Cape Town	1898–99	45	Eng. v Aus., Sydney	1886–87
36	Aus. v Eng., Edgbaston	1902	45	SA v Aus., Melbourne	1931–32
36	SA v Aus., Melbourne	1931–32	46	Eng. v WI, Port-of-Spain	1993–94
42	Aus. v Eng., Sydney	1887–88	47	SA v Eng., Cape Town	1888–89
42	NZ v Aus., Wellington	1945–46	47	NZ v Eng., Lord's	1958

* one batsman short

Lowest innings for the other four countries are:

53	WI v Pak., Faisalabad	1986–87	62	Pak. v Aus., Perth	1981–82
71	SL v Pak., Kandy	1994–95	127	Zim. v SL, Colombo (Premadasa)	1996–97

HIGHEST MATCH AGGREGATES OF RUNS

1981	(35 wkts) SA v Eng., Durban	1938–39	
1815	(34 wkts) WI v Eng., Kingston	1929–30	
1764	(39 wkts) Aus. v WI, Adelaide	1968–69	
1753	(40 wkts) Aus. v Eng., Adelaide	1920–21	
1723	(31 wkts) Eng. v Aus., Headingley	1948	
1661	(36 wkts) WI v Aus., Bridgetown	1954–55	

HIGHEST FOURTH-INNINGS TOTALS

654	for 5	Eng. v SA, Durban	1938–39
445		Ind. v Aus., Adelaide	1977–78
440		NZ v Eng., Trent Bridge	1973
429	for 8	Ind. v Eng., Oval	1979
423	for 7	SA v Eng., Oval	1947
417		Eng. v Aus., Melbourne	1976–77
411		Eng. v Aus., Sydney	1924–25
408	for 5	WI v Eng., Kingston	1929–30
★406	for 4	Ind. v WI, Port-of-Spain	1975–76
★404	for 3	Aus. v Eng., Headingley	1948

★ To win the match

Next-highest scores to win Tests have been:

362	for 7	Aus. v WI, Georgetown	1977–78
348	for 5	WI v NZ, Auckland	1968–69
344	for 1	WI v Eng., Lord's	1984

MOST RUNS IN A DAY

ALTOGETHER

588	Eng. (398 for 6); Ind. (190 for 0)	Old Trafford (2nd day)	1936
522	Eng. (503 for 2); SA (19 for 0)	Lord's (2nd day)	1924
508	Eng. (221 for 2); SA (287 for 6)	Oval (3rd day)	1935

BY ONE SIDE

503	Eng. (503 for 2) v SA, Lord's (2nd day)	1924	
494	Aus. (494 for 6) v SA, Sydney (1st day)	1910–11	
475	Aus. (475 for 2) v Eng., Oval (1st day)	1934	
471	Eng. (471 for 8) v Ind., Oval (1st day)	1936	
458	Aus. (458 for 3) v Eng., Headingley (1st day)	1930	
455	Aus. (455 for 1) v Eng., Headingley (2nd day)	1934	

LOWEST MATCH AGGREGATES OF RUNS (completed Tests)

234	for 29 wkts	Aus. v SA, Melbourne (Aus. by inns and 72)	1931–32
291	for 40 wkts	Eng. v Aus., Lord's (Aus. by 61 runs)	1888
295	for 28 wkts	NZ v Aus., Wellington (Aus. by inns and 103)	1945–46
309	for 29 wkts	WI v Eng., Bridgetown (Eng. by 4 wkts)	1934–35
323	for 30 wkts	Eng. v Aus., Old Trafford (Eng. by inns and 21)	1888

FEWEST RUNS IN FULL DAY'S PLAY

95	Aus. (80); Pak. (15 for 2)	Karachi (1st day)	1956–57
104	Pak. (104 for 5) v Aus.	Karachi (4th day)	1959–60
106	Eng. (92 for 2 to 198) v Aus.	Brisbane (4th day)	1958–59
112	Aus. (138 for 6 to 187); Pak. (63 for 1)	Karachi (4th day)	1956–57
115	Aus. (116 for 7 to 165; 66 for 5 following on) v Pak.	Karachi (4th day)	1988–89

MOST WICKETS IN A DAY

27	Eng. (18 for 3 to 53; and 62); Aus. (60)	Lord's (2nd day)	1888
25	Aus. (112; and 48 for 5); Eng. (61)	Melbourne (1st day)	1901–02

MOST TEST APPEARANCES

156	A.R. Border (Aus.)			
131	Kapil Dev (Ind.)	116	D.B. Vengsarkar (Ind.)	
125	S.M. Gavaskar (Ind.)	114	M.C. Cowdrey (Eng.)	
124	Javed Miandad (Pak.)	110	C.H. Lloyd (WI)	
121	I.V.A. Richards (WI)	108	G. Boycott (Eng.)	
118	G.A. Gooch (Eng.)	108	C.G. Greenidge (WI)	
117	D.I. Gower (Eng.)	107	D.C. Boon (Aus.)	
116	D.L. Haynes (WI)	102	I.T. Botham (Eng.)	

Record number of appearances for the other four countries are:

86	R.J. Hadlee (NZ)	50	J.H.B. Waite (SA)
67	A. Ranatunga (SL)	22	A.D.R. Campbell, A. Flower, G.W. Flower (Zim. jointly)

MOST CONSECUTIVE TEST APPEARANCES

153	A.R. Border (Aus.)	1978–79 to 1993–94
106	S.M. Gavaskar (Ind.)	1974–75 to 1986–87

MOST TESTS AS CAPTAIN

		W	L	D
93★	A.R. Border (Aus.)	32	22	38†
74	C.H. Lloyd (WI)	36	12	26
50	I.V.A. Richards (WI)	27	8	15
48	G.S. Chappell (Aus.)	21	13	14
48	Imran Khan (Pak.)	14	8	26
47	S.M. Gavaskar (Ind.)	9	8	30
41	P.B.H. May (Eng.)	20	10	11
40	Nawab of Pataudi jnr (Ind.)	9	19	12
40	M.A. Atherton (Eng.)	10	13	17
40	A. Ranatunga (SL)	7	15	18
39	R.B. Simpson (Aus.)	12	12	15
39	G.S. Sobers (WI)	9	10	20
37	M. Azharuddin (Ind.)	11	9	17

  ★ consecutively

  † plus 1 tied match

Record number of Tests as captain for the other three countries are:

21	W.J. Cronje (SA)	10	6	5
34	J.R. Reid (NZ)	3	18	13
12	A. Flower (Zim.)	1	5	6

HIGHEST PARTNERSHIPS FOR EACH WICKET

1st:	413 M.H. Mankad (231) and Pankaj Roy (173)	Ind. v NZ, Madras	1955–56
2nd:	451 W.H. Ponsford (266) and D.G. Bradman (244)	Aus. v Eng., Oval	1934
3rd:	467 A.H. Jones (186) and M.D. Crowe (299)	NZ v SL, Wellington	1990–91
4th:	411 P.B.H. May (285★) and M.C. Cowdrey (154)	Eng. v WI, Edgbaston	1957
5th:	405 S.G. Barnes (234) and D.G. Bradman (234)	Aus. v Eng., Sydney	1946–47
6th:	346 J.H.W. Fingleton (136) and D.G. Bradman (270)	Aus. v Eng., Melbourne	1936–37
7th:	347 D.S. Atkinson (219) and C.C. Depeiaza (122)	WI v Aus., Bridgetown	1954–55
8th:	313 Wasim Akram (257★) and Saqlain Mushtaq (79)	Pak. v Zim., Sheikhupura	1996–97
9th:	190 Asif Iqbal (146) and Intikhab Alam (51)	Pak. v Eng., Oval	1967
10th:	151 B.F. Hastings (110) and R.O. Collinge (68★)	NZ v Pak., Auckland	1972–73

OTHER PARTNERSHIPS OF 350 OR MORE

451	for 3rd	Mudassar Nazar (231) and Javed Miandad (280★)	Pak. v Ind., Hyderabad	1982–83
446	for 2nd	C.C. Hunte (260) and G.S. Sobers (365★)	WI v Pak., Kingston	1957–58
399	for 4th	G.S. Sobers (226) and F.M.M. Worrell (197★)	WI v Eng., Bridgetown	1959–60
397	for 3rd	Qasim Omar (206) and Javed Miandad (203★)	Pak. v SL, Faisalabad	1985–86
388	for 4th	W.H. Ponsford (181) and D.G. Bradman (304)	Aus. v Eng., Headingley	1934
387	for 1st	G.M. Turner (259) and T.W. Jarvis (182)	NZ v WI, Georgetown	1971–72
385	for 5th	S.R. Waugh (160) and G.S. Blewett (214)	Aus. v SA, Johannesburg	1996–97
382	for 2nd	L. Hutton (364) and M. Leyland (187)	Eng. v Aus., Oval	1938
382	for 1st	W.M. Lawry (210) and R.B. Simpson (201)	Aus. v WI, Bridgetown	1964–65
370	for 3rd	W.J. Edrich (189) and D.C.S. Compton (208)	Eng. v SA, Lord's	1947
369	for 2nd	J.H. Edrich (310★) and K.F. Barrington (163)	Eng. v NZ, Headingley	1965
359	for 1st	L. Hutton (158) and C. Washbrook (195)	Eng. v SA, Johannesburg†	1948–49
351	for 2nd	G.A. Gooch (196) and D.I. Gower (157)	Eng. v Aus., Oval	1985
350	for 4th	Mushtaq Mohammad (201) and Asif Iqbal (175)	Pak. v NZ, Dunedin	1972–73

† Ellis Park

415 runs were scored for India's 3rd wicket against England at Madras, 1981–82. D.B. Vengsarkar and G.R. Viswanath (222) put on 99 before the former retired injured for 71, whereupon Yashpal Sharma (140) and Viswanath added a further 316

HIGHEST INDIVIDUAL SCORES

375	B.C. Lara	WI v Eng., St John's	1993–94
365★	G.S. Sobers	WI v Pak., Kingston	1957–58
364	L. Hutton	Eng. v Aus., Oval	1938
337	Hanif Mohammad	Pak. v WI, Bridgetown	1957–58
336★	W.R. Hammond	Eng. v NZ, Auckland	1932–33
334	D.G. Bradman	Aus. v Eng., Headingley	1930
333	G.A. Gooch	Eng. v Ind., Lord's	1990
325	A. Sandham	Eng. v WI, Kingston	1929–30
311	R.B. Simpson	Aus. v Eng., Old Trafford	1964
310★	J.H. Edrich	Eng. v NZ, Headingley	1965
307	R.M. Cowper	Aus. v Eng., Melbourne	1965–66
304	D.G. Bradman	Aus. v Eng., Headingley	1934
302	L.G. Rowe	WI v Eng., Bridgetown	1973–74
299★	D.G. Bradman	Aus. v SA, Adelaide	1931–32
299	M.D. Crowe	NZ v SL, Wellington	1990–91
291	I.V.A. Richards	WI v Eng., Oval	1976
287	R.E. Foster	Eng. v Aus., Sydney	1903–04
285★	P.B.H. May	Eng. v WI, Edgbaston	1957
280★	Javed Miandad	Pak. v Ind., Hyderabad	1982–83
278	D.C.S. Compton	Eng. v Pak., Trent Bridge	1954
277	B.C. Lara	WI v Aus., Sydney	1992–93
274	R.G. Pollock	SA v Aus., Durban	1969–70
274	Zaheer Abbas	Pak. v Eng., Edgbaston	1971
271	Javed Miandad	Pak. v NZ, Auckland	1988–89
270★	G.A. Headley	WI v Eng., Kingston	1934–35
270	D.G. Bradman	Aus. v Eng., Melbourne	1936–37

268	G.N. Yallop	Aus. v Pak., Melbourne	1983–84
267★	B.A. Young	NZ v SL, Dunedin	1996–97
267	P.A. de Silva	SL v NZ, Wellington	1990–91
266	W.H. Ponsford	Aus. v Eng., Oval	1934
266	D.L. Houghton	Zim. v SL, Bulawayo	1994–95
262★	D.L. Amiss	Eng. v WI, Kingston	1973–74
261	F.M.M. Worrell	WI v Eng., Trent Bridge	1950
260	C.C. Hunte	WI v Pak., Kingston	1957–58
260	Javed Miandad	Pak. v Eng., Oval	1987
259	G.M. Turner	NZ v WI, Georgetown	1971–72
258	T.W. Graveney	Eng. v WI, Trent Bridge	1957
258	S.M. Nurse	WI v NZ, Christchurch	1968–69
257★	Wasim Akram	Pak. v Zim., Sheikhupura	1996–97
256	R.B. Kanhai	WI v Ind., Calcutta	1958–59
256	K.F. Barrington	Eng. v Aus., Old Trafford	1964
255★	D.J. McGlew	SA v NZ, Wellington	1952–53
254	D.G. Bradman	Aus. v Eng., Lord's	1930
251	W.R. Hammond	Eng. v Aus., Sydney	1928–29
250	K.D. Walters	Aus. v NZ, Christchurch	1976–77
250	S.F.A. Bacchus	WI v Ind., Kanpur	1978–79

The highest score for India is 236★ by S.M. Gavaskar v WI, Madras, 1983–84

HIGHEST SCORES ON TEST DEBUT

287	R.E. Foster	Eng. v Aus., Sydney	1903–04
214	L.G. Rowe‡	WI v NZ, Kingston	1971–72
201★	D.S.B.P. Kuruppu	SL v NZ, Colombo (CCC)	1986–87
176	G.A. Headley†	WI v Eng., Bridgetown	1929–30
166	Khalid Ibadulla	Pak. v Aus., Karachi	1964–65
165★	C. Bannerman	Aus. v Eng., Melbourne	1876–77
164	A.A. Jackson	Aus. v Eng., Adelaide	1928–29
163	Javed Miandad	Pak. v NZ, Lahore	1976–77
163	A.C. Hudson	SA v WI, Bridgetown	1991–92
162	K.C. Wessels	Aus. v Eng., Brisbane	1982–83
159	W.B. Phillips	Aus. v Pak., Perth	1983–84
155	K.D. Walters	Aus. v Eng., Brisbane	1965–66
154★	K.S. Ranjitsinhji†	Eng. v Aus., Old Trafford	1896
152	W.G. Grace	Eng. v Aus., Oval	1880

Highest debut scores made for the other three countries are:

117	J.E. Mills	NZ v Eng., Wellington	1929–30
137	†G.R. Viswanath	Ind. v Aus., Kanpur	1969–70
121	D.L. Houghton	Zim. v Ind., Harare	1992–93

† in second innings of match

‡ Rowe scored 100★ in the second innings, the only instance of twin hundreds on debut. His aggregate of 314 on debut is also a record

HUNDREDS IN BOTH INNINGS

In 1996–97, G. Kirsten (SA v Ind., Calcutta) and P.A. de Silva (SL v Pak., SSC, Colombo) became the 36th and 37th batsmen to score twin centuries in a Test match. S.M. Gavaskar (Ind.) did so three times, and the feat was performed twice each by C.L. Walcott (WI, in same series), H. Sutcliffe (Eng.), G.A. Headley (WI), G.S. Chappell (Aus.) and A.R. Border (Aus.).

Five batsmen have coupled a multiple-century with a century: G.A. Gooch (333 and 123, Eng. v Ind., Lord's, 1990); K.D. Walters (242 and 103, Aus. v WI, Sydney, 1968–69); S.M. Gavaskar (124 and 220, Ind. v WI, Port-of-Spain, 1970–71); L.G. Rowe (as above); G.S. Chappell (247★ and 133, Aus. v NZ, Wellington, 1973–74).

MOST RUNS IN A TEST

456	G.A. Gooch	(333 and 123, as above)

MOST RUNS IN A SERIES

974	in 7 inns	D.G. Bradman (av. 139.14)	Aus. v Eng.	1930
905	in 9 inns	W.R. Hammond (av. 113.13)	Eng. v Aus.	1928–29
839	in 11 inns	M.A. Taylor (av. 83.90)	Aus. v Eng.	1989
834	in 9 inns	R.N. Harvey (av. 92.67)	Aus. v SA	1952–53
829	in 7 inns	I.V.A. Richards (av. 118.43)	WI v Eng.	1976
827	in 10 inns	C.L. Walcott (av. 82.70)	WI v Aus.	1954–55
824	in 8 inns	G.S. Sobers (av. 137.33)	WI v Pak.	1957–58
810	in 9 inns	D.G. Bradman (av. 90.00)	Aus. v Eng.	1936–37
806	in 5 inns	D.G. Bradman (av. 201.50)	Aus. v SA	1931–32
798	in 8 inns	B.C. Lara (av. 99.75)	WI v Eng.	1993–94
779	in 7 inns	E.D. Weekes (av. 111.29)	WI v Ind.	1948–49
774	in 8 inns	S.M. Gavaskar (av. 154.80)	Ind. v WI	1970–71
765	in 10 inns	B.C. Lara (av. 85.00)	WI v Eng.	1995
761	in 8 inns	Mudassar Nazar (av. 126.83)	Pak. v Ind.	1982–83
758	in 8 inns	D.G. Bradman (av. 94.75)	Aus. v Eng.	1934
753	in 8 inns	D.C.S. Compton (av. 94.13)	Eng. v SA	1947
752	in 6 inns	G.A. Gooch (av. 125.33)	Eng. v Ind.	1990

SCORERS OF 5000 TEST RUNS

	T	I	NO	R	HS	Av.	100
A.R. Border (Aus.)	156	265	44	11,174	205	50.56	27
S.M. Gavaskar (Ind.)	125	214	16	10,122	236*	51.12	34
G.A. Gooch (Eng.)	118	215	6	8900	333	42.58	20
Javed Miandad (Pak.)	124	189	21	8832	280*	52.57	23
I.V.A. Richards (WI)	121	182	12	8540	291	50.24	24
D.I. Gower (Eng.)	117	204	18	8231	215	44.25	18
G. Boycott (Eng.)	108	193	23	8114	246*	47.73	22
G.S. Sobers (WI)	93	160	21	8032	365*	57.78	26
M.C. Cowdrey (Eng.)	114	188	15	7624	182	44.07	22
C.G. Greenidge (WI)	108	185	16	7558	226	44.72	19
C.H. Lloyd (WI)	110	175	14	7515	242*	46.68	19
D.L. Haynes (WI)	116	202	25	7487	184	42.30	18
D.C. Boon (Aus.)	107	190	20	7422	200	43.66	21
W.R. Hammond (Eng.)	85	140	16	7249	336*	58.46	22
G.S. Chappell (Aus.)	87	151	19	7110	247*	53.86	24
D.G. Bradman (Aus.)	52	80	10	6996	334	99.94	29
L. Hutton (Eng.)	79	138	15	6971	364	56.67	19
D.B. Vengsarkar (Ind.)	116	185	22	6868	166	42.13	17
K.F. Barrington (Eng.)	82	131	15	6806	256	58.67	20
R.B. Kanhai (WI)	79	137	6	6227	256	47.53	15
R.N. Harvey (Aus.)	79	137	10	6149	205	48.42	21
G.R. Viswanath (Ind.)	91	155	10	6080	222	41.93	14
R.B. Richardson (WI)	86	146	12	5949	194	44.40	16
D.C.S. Compton (Eng.)	78	131	15	5807	278	50.06	17
M.A. Taylor (Aus.)	81	145	9	5799	219	42.64	14
S.R. Waugh (Aus.)	89	138	28	5570	200	50.64	12
Salim Malik (Pak.)	96	142	21	5528	237	45.69	15
M.D. Crowe (NZ)	77	131	11	5444	299	45.37	17
J.B. Hobbs (Eng.)	61	102	7	5410	211	56.95	15
K.D. Walters (Aus.)	74	125	14	5357	250	48.26	15
I.M. Chappell (Aus.)	75	136	10	5345	196	42.42	14
J.G. Wright (NZ)	82	148	7	5334	185	37.83	12
Kapil Dev (Ind.)	131	184	15	5248	163	31.05	8
W.M. Lawry (Aus.)	67	123	12	5234	210	47.15	13

I.T. Botham (Eng.)	102	161	6	5200	208	33.55	14
J.H. Edrich (Eng.)	77	127	9	5138	310*	43.54	12
Zaheer Abbas (Pak.)	78	124	11	5062	274	44.80	12
M. Azharuddin (Ind.)	83	120	6	5011	199	43.96	17

The highest runscorers for the other three countries are:

B. Mitchell (SA)	42	80	9	3471	189*	48.89	8
A. Ranatunga (SL)	67	114	6	3793	135*	35.12	4
D.L. Houghton (Zim.)	20	32	2	1396	266	46.53	4

The only batsmen who have scored 15 or more Test centuries but do not qualify for the above list are:

H. Sutcliffe (Eng.)	54	84	9	4555	194	60.73	16
E.D. Weekes (WI)	48	81	5	4455	207	58.62	15
C.L. Walcott (WI)	44	74	7	3798	220	56.69	15

TEST AVERAGE OF 50 OR MORE Qualification 20 innings

Av.		T	I	NO	R	HS	100
99.94	D.G. Bradman (Aus.)	52	80	10	6996	334	29
60.97	R.G. Pollock (SA)	23	41	4	2256	274	7
60.83	G.A. Headley (WI)	22	40	4	2190	270*	10
60.73	H. Sutcliffe (Eng.)	54	84	9	4555	194	16
59.23	E. Paynter (Eng.)	20	31	5	1540	243	4
58.67	K.F. Barrington (Eng.)	82	131	15	6806	256	20
58.62	E.D. Weekes (WI)	48	81	5	4455	207	15
58.46	W.R. Hammond (Eng.)	85	140	16	7249	336*	22
57.78	G.S. Sobers (WI)	93	160	21	8032	365*	26
56.95	J.B. Hobbs (Eng.)	61	102	7	5410	211	15
56.89	J.C. Adams (WI)	29	46	11	1991	208*	5
56.69	C.L. Walcott (WI)	44	74	7	3798	220	15
56.67	L. Hutton (Eng.)	79	138	15	6971	364	19
55.49	B.C. Lara (WI)	43	72	2	3884	375	9
55.00	G.E. Tyldesley (Eng.)	14	20	2	990	122	3
54.21	C.A. Davis (WI)	15	29	5	1301	183	4
54.20	V.G. Kambli (Ind.)	17	21	1	1084	227	4
53.86	G.S. Chappell (Aus.)	87	151	19	7110	247*	24
53.85	S. Chanderpaul (WI)	21	33	6	1454	137*	1
53.82	A.D. Nourse (SA)	34	62	7	2960	231	9
52.57	Javed Miandad (Pak.)	124	189	21	8832	280*	23
51.95	R.S. Dravid (Ind.)	14	23	3	1039	148	1
51.63	J. Ryder (Aus.)	20	32	5	1394	201*	3
51.12	S.M. Gavaskar (Ind.)	125	214	16	10,122	236*	34
50.64	S.R. Waugh (Aus.)	89	138	28	5570	200	12
50.56	A.R. Border (Aus.)	156	265	44	11.174	205	27
50.24	I.V.A. Richards (WI)	121	182	12	8540	291	24
50.24	S.R. Tendulkar (Ind.)	53	80	8	3617	179	11
50.06	D.C.S. Compton (Eng.)	78	131	15	5807	278	17

CARRIED BAT THROUGH TEST INNINGS

A.B. Tancred	26*	(47)	SA v Eng., Cape Town	1888–89
J.E. Barrett	67*	(176)	Aus. v Eng., Lord's	1890
R. Abel	132*	(307)	Eng. v Aus., Sydney	1891–92
P.F. Warner	132*	(237)	Eng. v SA, Johannesburg†	1898–99
W.W. Armstrong	159*	(309)	Aus. v SA, Johannesburg†	1902–03
J.W. Zulch	43*	(103)	SA v Eng., Cape Town	1909–10
W. Bardsley	193*	(383)	Aus. v Eng., Lord's	1926
W.M. Woodfull	30*	(66)‡	Aus. v Eng., Brisbane§	1928–29
W.M. Woodfull	73*	(193)†	Aus. v Eng., Adelaide	1932–33
W.A. Brown	206*	(422)	Aus. v Eng., Lord's	1938
L. Hutton	202*	(344)	Eng. v WI, Oval	1950
L. Hutton	156*	(272)	Eng. v Aus., Adelaide	1950–51
Nazar Mohammad	124*	(331)	Pak. v Ind., Lucknow	1952–53

F.M.M. Worrell	191★	(372)	WI v Eng., Trent Bridge	1957
T.L. Goddard	56★	(99)	SA v Aus., Cape Town	1957–58
D.J. McGlew	127★	(292)	SA v NZ, Durban	1961–62
C.C. Hunte	60★	(131)	WI v Aus., Port-of-Spain	1964–65
G.M. Turner	43★	(131)	NZ v Eng., Lord's	1969
W.M. Lawry	49★	(107)	Aus. v Ind., Delhi	1969–70
W.M. Lawry	60★	(116)†	Aus. v Eng., Sydney	1970–71
G.M. Turner	223★	(386)	NZ v WI, Kingston	1971–72
I.R. Redpath	159★	(346)	Aus. v NZ, Auckland	1973–74
G. Boycott	99★	(215)	Eng. v Aus., Perth	1979–80
S.M. Gavaskar	127★	(286)	Ind. v Pak., Faisalabad	1982–83
Mudassar Nazar	152★	(323)	Pak. v Ind., Lahore	1982–83
S. Wettimuny	63★	(144)	SL v NZ, Christchurch	1982–83
D.C. Boon	58★	(103)	Aus. v NZ, Auckland	1985–86
D.L. Haynes	88★	(211)	WI v Pak., Karachi	1986–87
G.A. Gooch	154★	(252)	Eng. v WI, Headingley	1991
D.L. Haynes	75★	(176)	WI v Eng., Oval	1991
A.J. Stewart	69★	(175)	Eng. v Pak., Lord's	1992
D.L. Haynes	143★	(382)	WI v Pak., Port-of-Spain	1992–93
M.H. Dekker	68★	(187)	Zim. v Pak., Rawalpindi	1993–94
M.A. Atherton	94★	(228)	Eng. v NZ, Christchurch	1996–97

‡ Two batsmen absent   † Old Wanderers ground
† One batsman absent   § Exhibition Ground

FASTEST INNINGS

FIFTY

Mins

28	J.T. Brown (140)	Eng. v Aus., Melbourne	1894–95
29	S.A. Durani (61★)	Ind. v Eng., Kanpur	1963–64
30	E.A.V. Williams (72)	WI v Eng., Bridgetown	1947–48
30	B.R. Taylor (124)	NZ v WI, Auckland	1968–69
33	C.A. Roach (56)	WI v Eng., Oval	1933
34	C.R. Browne (70★)	WI v Eng., Georgetown	1929–30

Balls (most innings pre-Second World War were measured only in minutes)

30	Kapil Dev (73)	Ind. v Pak., Karachi	1982–83
32	I.V.A. Richards (61)	WI v Ind., Kingston	1982–83
32	I.T. Botham (59★)	Eng. v NZ, Oval	1986
33	R.C. Fredericks (169)	WI v Aus., Perth	1975–76
33	Kapil Dev (59)	Ind. v Pak., Karachi	1978–79
33	Kapil Dev (65)	Ind. v Eng., Old Trafford	1982
33	A.J. Lamb (60)	Eng. v NZ, Auckland	1991–92

HUNDRED

Mins

70	J.M. Gregory (119)	Aus. v SA, Johannesburg†	1921–22
75	G.L. Jessop (104)	Eng. v Aus., Oval	1902
78	R. Benaud (121)	Aus. v WI, Kingston	1954–55
80	J.H. Sinclair (104)	SA v Aus., Cape Town	1902–03
81	I.V.A. Richards (110★)	WI v Eng., St John's	1985–86
86	B.R. Taylor (124)	NZ v WI, Auckland	1968–69

† Old Wanderers ground

Balls

56	I.V.A. Richards (110★)	WI v Eng., St John's	1985–86
67	J.M. Gregory (119)	Aus. v SA, Johannesburg†	1921–22
71	R.C. Fredericks (169)	WI v Aus., Perth	1975–76
74	Majid Khan (112)	Pak. v NZ, Karachi	1976–77
74	Kapil Dev (163)	Ind. v SL, Kanpur	1986–87
74	M. Azharuddin (109)	Ind. v SA, Calcutta	1996–97
76	G.L. Jessop (104)	Eng. v Aus., Oval	1902

† Old Wanderers ground

DOUBLE-CENTURY
Mins

214	D.G. Bradman (334)	Aus. v Eng., Headingley	1930
223	S.J. McCabe (232)	Aus. v Eng., Trent Bridge	1938
226	V.T. Trumper (214*)	Aus. v SA, Adelaide	1910–11
234	D.G. Bradman (254)	Aus. v Eng., Lord's	1930
240	W.R. Hammond (336*)	Eng. v NZ, Auckland	1932–33
241	S.E. Gregory (201)	Aus. v Eng., Sydney	1894–95
245	D.C.S. Compton (278)	Eng. v Pak., Trent Bridge	1954

Balls

220	I.T. Botham (208)	Eng. v Ind., Oval	1982
232	C.G. Greenidge (214*)	WI v Eng., Lord's	1984
240	C.H. Lloyd (242*)	WI v Ind., Bombay	1974–75
241	Zaheer Abbas (215)	Pak. v Ind., Lahore	1982–83
242	D.G. Bradman (244)	Aus. v Eng., Oval	1934
242	I.V.A. Richards (208)	WI v Aus., Melbourne	1984–85

TRIPLE-CENTURY
Mins

288	W.R. Hammond (336*)	Eng. v NZ, Auckland	1932–33
336	D.G. Bradman (334)	Aus. v Eng., Headingley	1930

MOST RUNS IN A DAY

309	D.G. Bradman (334)	Aus. v Eng., Headingley	1930
295	W.R. Hammond (336*)	Eng. v NZ, Auckland	1932–33
273	D.C.S. Compton (278)	Eng. v Pak., Trent Bridge	1954
271	D.G. Bradman (304)	Aus. v Eng., Headingley	1934

HUNDRED BEFORE LUNCH ON FIRST DAY

	Place in order	*Score at lunch*		
V.T. Trumper (104)	No. 1	103*	Aus. v Eng., Old Trafford	1902
C.G. Macartney (151)	No. 3	112	Aus. v Eng., Headingley	1926
D.G. Bradman (334)	No. 3	105*	Aus. v Eng., Headingley	1930
Majid Khan (112)	No. 2	108*	Pak. v NZ, Karachi	1976–77

MOST SIXES IN AN INNINGS

12	Wasim Akram (257*)	Pak. v Zim., Sheikhupura	1996–97
10	W.R. Hammond (336*)	Eng. v NZ, Auckland	1932–33
9	C.L. Cairns (120)	NZ v Zim., Auckland	1995–96
7	B. Sutcliffe (80*)	NZ v SA, Johannesburg†	1953–54
7	I.V.A. Richards (110*)	WI v Eng., St John's	1985–86
7	C.G. Greenidge (213)	WI v NZ, Auckland	1986–87

† Ellis Park

MOST RUNS OFF AN OVER

EIGHT-BALL

25	(66061600)	B. Sutcliffe and R.W. Blair (off H.J. Tayfield)	NZ v SA, Johannesburg†	1953–54

SIX-BALL

25	(46266 L–B)	A.M.E. Roberts (off I.T. Botham)	WI v Eng., Port-of-Spain	1980–81
24	(4440444) (3rd ball was a no-ball)	S.M. Patil (off R.G.D. Willis)	Ind. v Eng., Old Trafford	1982
24	(464604)	I.T. Botham (off D.A. Stirling)	Eng. v NZ, Oval	1986
24	(006666)	Kapil Dev (off E.E. Hemmings)	Ind. v Eng., Lord's	1990
24	(244266)	I.D.S. Smith (off A.S. Wassan)	NZ v Ind., Auckland	1989–90

† Ellis Park

MOST RUNS FROM FOURS AND SIXES

	6s	5s	4s			
238	5	0	52	J.H. Edrich (310★)	Eng. v NZ, Headingley	1965
196	10	0	34	W.R. Hammond (336★)	Eng. v NZ, Auckland	1932–33
190	3	0	43	G.A. Gooch (333)	Eng. v Ind., Lord's	1990
184	0	0	46	D.G. Bradman (334)	Aus. v Eng., Headingley	1930
184	2	0	43	D.G. Bradman (304)	Aus. v Eng., Headingley	1934
180	0	0	45	B.C. Lara (375)	WI v Eng., St John's	1993–94
177	0	1	43	R.G. Pollock (274)	SA v Aus., Durban	1969–70
168	0	0	42	R.B. Kanhai (256)	WI v Ind., Calcutta	1958–59
166	1	0	40	D.L. Amiss (262★)	Eng. v WI, Kingston	1973–74
160	0	0	40	P.A. de Silva (267)	SL v NZ, Wellington	1990–91
160	12	0	22	Wasim Akram (257★)	Pak. v Zim., Sheikhupura	1996–97
158	3	0	35	D.L. Houghton (266)	Zim. v SL, Bulawayo	1994–95
157	0	1	38	G.S. Sobers (365★)	WI v Pak., Kingston	1957–58
152	2	0	35	F.M.M. Worrell (261)	WI v Eng., Trent Bridge	1950
152	0	0	38	Zaheer Abbas (274)	Pak. v Eng., Edgbaston	1971
152	0	0	38	I.V.A Richards (291)	WI v Eng., Oval	1976
152	0	0	38	B.C. Lara (277)	WI v Aus., Sydney	1992–93
150	1	0	36	L.G. Rowe (302)	WI v Eng., Bridgetown	1973–74

SLOWEST INNINGS

FIFTY
Mins

357	T.E. Bailey (68)	Eng. v Aus., Brisbane	1958–59
350	C.J. Tavaré (82)	Eng. v Pak., Lord's	1982
333	B.A. Young (51)	NZ v SA, Durban	1994–95
326	S.M. Gavaskar (51)	Ind. v SL, Colombo (SSC)	1985–86

HUNDRED
Mins

557	Mudassar Nazar (114)	Pak. v Eng., Lahore	1977–78
545	D.J. McGlew (105)	SA v Aus., Durban	1957–58
535	A.P. Gurusinha (128)	SL v Zim., Harare	1994–95
515	J.J. Crowe (120★)	NZ v SL, Colombo (CCC)	1986–87
500	S.V. Manjrekar (104)	Ind. v Zim., Harare	1992–93
488	P.E. Richardson (117)	Eng. v SA, Johannesburg	1956–57
487	C.T. Radley (158)	Eng. v NZ, Auckland	1977–78

DOUBLE-CENTURY
Mins

778	D.S.B.P. Kuruppu (201★)	SL v NZ, Colombo (CCC)	1986–87
671	N.S. Sidhu (201)	Ind. v WI, Port-of-Spain	1996–97
656	Shoaib Mohammad (203★)	Pak. v NZ, Karachi	1990–91
652	A.D. Gaekwad (201)	Ind. v Pak., Jullundur	1983–84
608	R.B. Simpson (311)	Aus. v Eng., Old Trafford	1964
596	A.R. Border (205)	Aus. v NZ, Adelaide	1987–88
595	G.S. Sobers (226)	WI v Eng., Bridgetown	1959–60

LONGEST INNINGS

England	797 mins	L. Hutton (364) v Aus., Oval	1938
Australia	762 mins	R.B. Simpson (311) v Eng., Old Trafford	1964
South Africa	575 mins	D.J. McGlew (105) v Aus., Durban	1957–58
West Indies	768 mins	B.C. Lara (375) v Eng., St John's	1993–94
New Zealand	704 mins	G.M. Turner (259) v WI, Georgetown	1971–72
India	708 mins	S.M. Gavaskar (172) v Eng., Bangalore	1981–82
Pakistan	970 mins	Hanif Mohammad (337) v WI, Bridgetown	1957–58
Sri Lanka	778 mins	D.S.B.P. Kuruppu (201★) v NZ, Colombo (CCC)	1986–87
Zimbabwe	675 mins	D.L. Houghton (266) v SL, Bulawayo	1994–95

NINE OR MORE WICKETS IN AN INNINGS

10 for 53	J.C. Laker	Eng. v Aus., Old Trafford	1956
9 for 28	G.A. Lohmann	Eng. v SA, Johannesburg†	1895–96
9 for 37	J.C. Laker	Eng. v Aus., Old Trafford	1956
9 for 52	R.J. Hadlee	NZ v Aus., Brisbane	1985–86
9 for 56	Abdul Qadir	Pak. v Eng., Lahore	1987–88
9 for 57	D.E. Malcolm	Eng. v SA, Oval	1994
9 for 69	J.M. Patel	Ind. v Aus., Kanpur	1959–60
9 for 83	Kapil Dev	Ind. v WI, Ahmedabad	1983–84
9 for 86	Sarfraz Nawaz	Pak. v Aus., Melbourne	1978–79
9 for 95	J.M. Noreiga	WI v Ind., Port-of-Spain	1970–71
9 for 102	S.P. Gupte	Ind. v WI, Kanpur	1958–59
9 for 103	S.F. Barnes	Eng. v SA, Johannesburg†	1913–14
9 for 113	H.J. Tayfield	SA v Eng., Johannesburg	1956–57
9 for 121	A.A. Mailey	Aus. v Eng., Melbourne	1920–21

† Old Wanderers ground

   There have been 57 instances of 8 wickets in an innings, Lohmann having achieved the feat 3 times (in addition to his 9 for 28 above). S.F. Barnes (Eng.), I.T. Botham (Eng.), N.D. Hirwani (Ind.), Imran Khan (Pak.), Kapil Dev (Ind.), M.H. Mankad (Ind.), R.A.L. Massie (Aus.), C.J. McDermott (Aus.) all did it twice, Massie and Hirwani each twice in his debut Test. The others who took 8 wickets in an innings on debut were: A.E. Trott (8 for 43, Aus. v Eng., Adelaide 1894–95), A.L. Valentine (8 for 104, WI v Eng., Old Trafford 1950), and L. Klusener (8 for 64, SA v Ind., Calcutta 1996–97).

FOURTEEN OR MORE WICKETS IN A MATCH

19:	9 for 37 & 10 for 53	J.C. Laker	Eng. v Aus., Old Trafford	1956
17:	8 for 56 & 9 for 103	S.F. Barnes	Eng. v SA, Johannesburg†	1913–14
16:	8 for 61 & 8 for 65	N.D. Hirwani	Ind. v WI, Madras	1987–88
	8 for 84 & 8 for 53	R.A.L. Massie	Aus. v Eng., Lord's	1972
15:	7 for 17 & 8 for 11	J. Briggs	Eng. v SA, Cape Town	1888–89
	7 for 38 & 8 for 7	G.A. Lohmann	Eng. v SA, Port Elizabeth	1895–96
	8 for 59 & 7 for 40	C. Blythe	Eng. v SA, Headingley	1907
	7 for 61 & 8 for 43	H. Verity	Eng. v Aus., Lord's	1934
	9 for 52 & 6 for 71	R.J. Hadlee	NZ v Aus., Brisbane	1985–86
	7 for 56 & 8 for 68	W. Rhodes	Eng. v Aus., Melbourne	1903–04
14:	7 for 46 & 7 for 44	F.R. Spofforth	Aus. v Eng., Oval	1882
	7 for 55 & 7 for 44	A.V. Bedser	Eng. v Aus., Trent Bridge	1953
	7 for 28 & 7 for 74	W. Bates	Eng. v Aus., Melbourne	1882–83
	8 for 58 & 6 for 58	Imran Khan	Pak. v SL, Lahore	1981–82
	9 for 69 & 5 for 55	J.M. Patel	Ind. v Aus., Kanpur	1959–60
	7 for 56 & 7 for 88	S.F. Barnes	Eng. v SA, Durban‡	1913–14
	8 for 92 & 6 for 57	M.A. Holding	WI v Eng., Oval	1976
	7 for 116 & 7 for 83	C.V. Grimmett	Aus. v SA, Adelaide	1931–32

† Old Wanderers ground
‡ first Test ground (known as 'Lord's')

MOST WICKETS IN A SERIES

49 (av. 10.94)	S.F. Barnes (4 Tests)	Eng. v SA	1913–14
46 (av. 9.61)	J.C. Laker (5 Tests)	Eng. v Aus.	1956
44 (av. 14.59)	C.V. Grimmett (5 Tests)	Aus. v SA	1935–36
42 (av. 21.26)	T.M. Alderman (6 Tests)	Aus. v Eng.	1981
41 (av. 12.85)	R.M. Hogg (6 Tests)	Aus. v Eng.	1978–79
41 (av. 17.37)	T.M. Alderman (6 Tests)	Aus. v Eng.	1989
40 (av. 13.95)	Imran Khan (6 Tests)	Pak. v Ind.	1982–83
39 (av. 17.49)	A.V. Bedser (5 Tests)	Eng. v Aus.	1953
39 (av. 22.31)	D.K. Lillee (6 Tests)	Aus. v Eng.	1981
38 (av. 23.18)	M.W. Tate (5 Tests)	Eng. v Aus.	1924–25
37 (av. 17.08)	W.J. Whitty (5 Tests)	Aus. v SA	1910–11
37 (av. 17.19)	H.J. Tayfield (5 Tests)	SA v Eng.	1956–57
36 (av. 21.75)	A.E.E. Vogler (5 Tests)	SA v Eng.	1909–10
36 (av. 26.28)	A.A. Mailey (5 Tests★)	Aus. v Eng.	1920–21

35 (av. 5.80)	G.A. Lohmann (3 Tests)	Eng. v SA	1895–96
35 (av. 18.91)	B.S. Chandrasekhar (5 Tests)	Ind. v Eng.	1972–73
35 (av. 12.66)	M.D. Marshall (5 Tests)	WI v Eng.	1988

★ Bowled in only 4 Tests

200 OR MORE TEST WICKETS

	W	Av.	T	Balls bowled	5w/i	10w/m	Balls per wkt
Kapil Dev (Ind.)	434	29.65	131	27,740	23	2	63.92
R.J. Hadlee (NZ)	431	22.30	86	21,918	36	9	50.85
I.T. Botham (Eng.)	383	28.40	102	21,815	27	4	56.96
M.D. Marshall (WI)	376	20.95	81	17,584	22	4	46.77
Imran Khan (Pak.)	362	22.81	88	19,458	23	6	53.75
D.K. Lillee (Aus.)	355	23.92	70	18,467	23	7	52.02
C.A. Walsh (WI)	332	25.84	91	19,449	13	2	58.58
R.G.D. Willis (Eng.)	325	25.20	90	17,357	16	0	53.41
Wasim Akram (Pak.)	311	22.68	72	16,464	21	4	52.94
L.R. Gibbs (WI)	309	29.09	79	27,115	18	2	87.75
F.S. Trueman (Eng.)	307	21.58	67	15,178	17	3	49.44
D.L. Underwood (Eng.)	297	25.84	86	21,862	17	6	73.61
C.E.L. Ambrose (WI)	295	21.71	70	16,203	17	3	54.93
C.J. McDermott (Aus.)	291	28.63	71	16,586	14	2	57.00
B.S. Bedi (Ind.)	266	28.71	67	21,364	14	1	80.32
J. Garner (WI)	259	20.98	58	13,169	7	0	50.85
J.B. Statham (Eng.)	252	24.85	70	16,056	9	1	63.71
M.A. Holding (WI)	249	23.69	60	12,680	13	2	50.92
R. Benaud (Aus.)	248	27.03	63	19,108	16	1	77.05
G.D. McKenzie (Aus.)	246	29.79	60	17,681	16	3	71.87
B.S. Chandrasekhar (Ind.)	242	29.75	58	15,963	16	2	65.96
S.K. Warne (Aus.)	240	23.94	52	15,225	10	3	63.44
A.V. Bedser (Eng.)	236	24.90	51	15,918	15	5	67.45
Abdul Qadir (Pak.)	236	32.81	67	17,126	15	5	72.57
G.S. Sobers (WI)	235	34.04	93	21,599	6	0	91.91
R.R. Lindwall (Aus.)	228	23.03	61	13,650	12	0	59.87
Waqar Younis (Pak.)	227	21.34	44	9071	19	4	39.96
C.V. Grimmett (Aus.)	216	24.22	37	14,513	21	7	67.19
M.G. Hughes (Aus.)	212	28.38	53	12,285	7	1	57.95
A.M.E. Roberts (WI)	202	25.61	47	11,136	11	2	55.13
J.A. Snow (Eng.)	202	26.67	49	12,021	8	1	59.51
J.R. Thomson (Aus.)	200	28.01	51	10,535	8	0	52.68

Leading wicket-takers for the other three countries are:

	W	Av.	T	Balls bowled	5w/i	10w/m	Balls per wkt
H.J. Tayfield (SA)	170	25.91	37	13,568	14	2	79.81
M. Muralitharan (SL)	107	30.64	28	7536	7	0	70.43
H.H. Streak (Zim.)	69	22.48	15	3641	3	0	52.77

WICKET WITH FIRST BALL IN TEST CRICKET

			Batsman dismissed
A. Coningham	Aus. v Eng., Melbourne	1894–95	A.C. MacLaren
W.M. Bradley	Eng. v Aus., Old Trafford	1899	F.J. Laver
E.G. Arnold	Eng. v Aus., Sydney	1903–04	V.T. Trumper
G.G. Macaulay	Eng. v SA, Cape Town	1922–23	G.A.L. Hearne
M.W. Tate	Eng. v SA, Edgbaston	1924	M.J. Susskind
M. Henderson	NZ v Eng., Christchurch	1929–30	E.W. Dawson
H.D. Smith	NZ v Eng., Christchurch	1932–33	E. Paynter
T.F. Johnson	WI v Eng., Oval	1939	W.W. Keeton
R. Howorth	Eng. v SA, Oval	1947	D.V. Dyer
Intikhab Alam	Pak. v Aus., Karachi	1959–60	C.C. McDonald
R.K. Illingworth	Eng. v WI, Trent Bridge	1991	P.V. Simmons

HAT-TRICKS

F.R. Spofforth	Aus. v Eng., Melbourne	1878–79
W. Bates	Eng. v Aus., Melbourne	1882–83
J. Briggs	Eng. v Aus., Sydney	1891–92
G.A. Lohmann	Eng. v SA, Port Elizabeth	1895–96
J.T. Hearne	Eng. v Aus., Headingley	1899
H. Trumble	Aus. v Eng., Melbourne	1901–02
H. Trumble	Aus. v Eng., Melbourne	1903–04
T.J. Matthews (2)	Aus. v SA, Old Trafford	1912
M.J.C. Allom★	Eng. v NZ, Christchurch	1929–30
T.W.J. Goddard	Eng. v SA, Johannesburg†	1938–39
P.J. Loader	Eng. v WI, Headingley	1957
L.F. Kline	Aus. v SA, Cape Town	1957–58
W.W. Hall	WI v Pak., Lahore	1958–59
G.M. Griffin	SA v Eng., Lord's	1960
L.R. Gibbs	WI v Aus., Adelaide	1960–61
P.J. Petherick★	NZ v Pak., Lahore	1976–77
C.A. Walsh‡	WI v Aus., Brisbane	1988–89
M.G. Hughes‡	Aus. v WI, Perth	1988–89
D.W. Fleming★	Aus. v Pak., Rawalpindi	1994–95
S.K. Warne	Aus. v Eng., Melbourne	1994–95
D.G. Cork	Eng. v WI, Old Trafford	1995

Matthews performed the feat in each innings of the match, which was part of the 1912 Triangular Tournament

★ on debut

† Old Wanderers ground

‡ Spread over the 2 innings

FOUR WICKETS IN FIVE BALLS

M.J.C. Allom (w.www)	Eng. v NZ, Christchurch	1929–30
C.M. Old (wwn-bww)	Eng. v Pak., Edgbaston	1978
Wasim Akram (ww.ww)	Pak. v WI, Lahore	1990–91

Allom was on debut

MOST BALLS BOWLED IN A TEST

S. Ramadhin	774 balls	WI v Eng., Edgbaston	1957
H. Verity	766 balls	Eng. v SA, Durban	1938–39
J.C. White	749 balls	Eng. v Aus., Adelaide	1928–29

MOST BALLS BOWLED IN A TEST INNINGS

S. Ramadhin	588 balls	WI v Eng., Edgbaston	1957
T.R. Veivers	571 balls	Aus. v Eng., Old Trafford	1964
A.L. Valentine	552 balls	WI v Eng., Trent Bridge	1950

OVER 200 RUNS CONCEDED IN AN INNINGS

			O	M	R	W
L.O. Fleetwood-Smith	Aus. v Eng., Oval	1938	87	11	298	1
O.C. Scott	WI v Eng., Kingston	1929–30	80.2	13	266	5
Khan Mohammad	Pak. v WI, Kingston	1957–58	54	5	259	0
Fazal Mahmood	Pak. v WI, Kingston	1957–58	85.2	20	247	2
S.L. Boock	NZ v Pak., Auckland	1988–89	70	10	229	1
M.H. Mankad	Ind. v WI, Kingston	1952–53	82	17	228	5

B.S. Bedi	Ind. v Eng., Lord's	1974	64.2	8	226	6
M. Muralitharan	SL v Aus., Perth	1995–96	54	3	224	2
Kapil Dev	Ind. v Pak., Faisalabad	1982–83	38.4	3	220	7
I.T. Botham	Eng. v Pak., Oval	1987	52	7	217	3
P.A. Strang	Zim. v Pak., Sheikhupura	1996–97	69	12	212	5
I.A.R. Peebles	Eng. v Aus., Oval	1930	71	8	204	6
M.H. Mankad	Ind. v WI, Bombay★	1948–49	75	16	202	3
Haseeb Ahsan	Pak. v Ind., Madras†	1960–61	84	19	202	6

★ Brabourne Stadium
† Corporation (Nehru) Stadium

CENTURY AND FIVE WICKETS IN AN INNINGS

ENGLAND

A.W. Greig	v WI, Bridgetown	1973–74
I.T. Botham	v NZ, Christchurch	1977–78
I.T. Botham	v Pak., Lord's	1978
I.T. Botham★	v Ind., Bombay	1979–80
I.T. Botham	v Aus., Headingley	1981
I.T. Botham	v NZ, Wellington	1983–84

★ 6 wickets in lst innings and 7 in the 2nd

AUSTRALIA

C. Kelleway	v SA, Old Trafford	1912
J.M. Gregory	v Eng., Melbourne	1920–21
K.R. Miller	v WI, Kingston	1954–55
R. Benaud	v SA, Johannesburg	1957–58

SOUTH AFRICA

J.H. Sinclair	v Eng., Cape Town	1898–99
G.A. Faulkner	v Eng., Johannesburg†	1909–10

† Old Wanderers ground

WEST INDIES

D.S. Atkinson	v Aus., Bridgetown	1954–55
O.G. Smith	v Ind., Delhi	1958–59
G.S. Sobers	v Ind., Kingston	1961–62
G.S. Sobers	v Eng., Headingley	1966

NEW ZEALAND

B.R. Taylor	v Ind., Calcutta	1964–65
(on debut)		

INDIA

M.H. Mankad	v Eng., Lord's	1952
P.R. Umrigar	v WI, Port-of-Spain	1961–62

PAKISTAN

Mushtaq Mohammad	v NZ, Dunedin	1972–73
Mushtaq Mohammad	v WI, Port-of-Spain	1976–77
Imran Khan★	v Ind., Faisalabad	1982–83
Wasim Akram	v Aus., Adelaide	1989–90

★ 6 wickets in 1st innings and 5 in the 2nd

ZIMBABWE

P.A. Strang	v Pak., Sheikhupura	1996–97

CAREER DOUBLE OF 1000 RUNS AND 100 WICKETS

ENGLAND	T	R	W	*Test in which double achieved*
T.E. Bailey	61	2290	132	47th
I.T. Botham	102	5200	383	21st
J.E. Emburey	64	1713	147	46th
A.W. Greig	58	3599	141	37th
R. Illingworth	61	1836	122	47th
W. Rhodes	58	2325	127	44th
M.W. Tate	39	1198	155	33rd
F.J. Titmus	53	1449	153	40th
AUSTRALIA				
R. Benaud	63	2201	248	32nd
A.K. Davidson	44	1328	186	34th
G. Giffen	31	1238	103	30th
M.G. Hughes	53	1032	212	52nd
I.W. Johnson	45	1000	109	45th
R.R. Lindwall	61	1502	228	38th
K.R. Miller	55	2958	170	33rd
M.A. Noble	42	1997	121	27th
SOUTH AFRICA				
T.L. Goddard	41	2516	123	36th
WEST INDIES				
C.E.L. Ambrose	70	1015	295	69th
M.D. Marshall	81	1810	376	49th
G.S. Sobers	93	8032	235	48th
NEW ZEALAND				
J.G. Bracewell	41	1001	102	41st
R.J. Hadlee	86	3124	431	28th
INDIA				
Kapil Dev	131	5248	434	25th
M.H. Mankad	44	2109	162	23rd
R.J. Shastri	80	3830	151	44th
PAKISTAN				
Abdul Qadir	67	1029	236	62nd
Imran Khan	88	3807	362	30th
Intikhab Alam	47	1493	125	41st
Sarfraz Nawaz	55	1045	177	55th
Wasim Akram	72	1944	311	45th

Of the above, only Botham (120) and Sobers (109) have also held 100 catches

MOST DISMISSALS BY WICKETKEEPERS

IN AN INNINGS

7ct	Wasim Bari	Pak. v NZ, Auckland	1978–79
	R.W. Taylor	Eng. v Ind., Bombay	1979–80
	I.D.S. Smith	NZ v SL, Hamilton	1990–91
6ct	A.T.W. Grout*	Aus. v SA, Johannesburg	1957–58
	D.T. Lindsay	SA v Aus., Johannesburg	1966–67
	J.T. Murray	Eng. v Ind., Lord's	1967
	R.W. Marsh	Aus. v Eng., Brisbane	1982–83
	S.A.R. Silva	SL v Ind., Colombo (SSC)	1985–86
	R.C. Russell	Eng. v Aus., Melbourne	1990–91
	R.C. Russell	Eng. v SA, Johannesburg	1995–96
5ct/1st	S.M.H. Kirmani	Ind. v NZ, Christchurch	1975–76
5st	K.S. More	Ind. v WI, Madras	1987–88

* on debut

IN A TEST

11ct	R.C. Russell	Eng. v SA, Johannesburg	1995–96
10ct	R.W. Taylor	Eng. v Ind., Bombay	1979–80
9ct	D.A. Murray	WI v Aus., Melbourne	1981–82
	R.W. Marsh	Aus. v Eng., Brisbane	1982–83
	S.A.R. Silva	SL v Ind., Colombo (SSC)	1985–86
	D.J. Richardson	SA v Ind., Port Elizabeth	1992–93
	Rashid Latif	Pak. v NZ, Auckland	1993–94
	I.A. Healy	Aus. v Eng., Brisbane	1994–95
	C.O. Browne	WI v Eng., Trent Bridge	1995
8ct/1st	G.R.A. Langley	Aus. v Eng., Lord's	1956
	S.A.R. Silva	SL v Ind., Colombo (PSS)	1985–86
7ct/2st	R.C. Russell	Eng. v SA, Port Elizabeth	1995–96

Only J.J. Kelly (8ct Aus. v Eng., Sydney 1901–02) and L.E.G. Ames (6ct 2st Eng. v WI, Oval 1933) made as many as 8 wicketkeeping dismissals in a Test in the first 78 years of Test cricket; G.R.A. Langley (8ct Aus. v WI, Kingston 1954–55) became the third to do so. It was the 407th Test

IN A SERIES

28(ct)	R.W. Marsh (5 Tests)	Aus. v Eng.	1982–83
27(25ct/2st)	R.C. Russell (5)	Eng. v SA	1995–96
26(23/3)	J.H.B. Waite (5)	SA v NZ	1961–62
26(ct)	R.W. Marsh (6)	Aus. v WI	1975–76
26(21/5)	I.A. Healy (6)	Aus. v Eng.	1993
25(23/2)	I.A. Healy (5)	Aus. v Eng.	1994–95
24(22/2)	D.L. Murray (5)	WI v Eng.	1963
24(ct)	D.T. Lindsay (5)	SA v Aus.	1966–67
24(21/3)	A.P.E. Knott (6)	Eng. v Aus.	1970–71
24(ct)	I.A. Healy (5)	Aus. v Eng.	1990–91
23(16/7)	J.H.B. Waite (5)	SA v NZ	1953–54
23(22/1)	F.C.M. Alexander (5)	WI v Eng.	1959–60
23(20/3)	A.T.W. Grout (5)	Aus. v WI	1960–61
23(21/2)	A.E. Dick (5)	NZ v SA	1961–62
23(21/2)	R.W. Marsh (5)	Aus. v Eng.	1972
23(22/1)	A.P.E. Knott (6)	Eng. v Aus.	1974–75
23(ct)	R.W. Marsh (6)	Aus. v Eng.	1981
23(ct)	P.J.L. Dujon (5)	WI v Aus.	1990–91
23(19/4)	I.A. Healy (5)	Aus. v WI	1992–93
22(ct)	S.J. Rixon (5)	Aus. v Ind.	1977–78
22(21/1)	S.A.R. Silva (3)	SL v Ind.	1985–86

Prior to the 1946–47 series (Aus. v Eng.), when D. Tallon effected 20 dismissals (16ct 4st), only one wicketkeeper had made as many in a series. This was H. Strudwick, who completed 15 catches and 6 stumpings for Eng. v SA, 1913–14

WICKETKEEPERS WITH 100 TEST DISMISSALS

	Tests in which kept wicket	Ct	St	Total
R.W. Marsh (Aus.)	96	343	12	355
I.A. Healy (Aus.)	88	282	20	302
P.J.L. Dujon (WI)★	79	265	5	270
A.P.E. Knott (Eng.)	95	250	19	269
Wasim Bari (Pak.)	81	201	27	228
T.G. Evans (Eng.)	91	173	46	219
S.M.H. Kirmani (Ind.)	88	160	38	198
D.L. Murray (WI)	62	181	8	189
A.T.W. Grout (Aus.)	51	163	24	187
I.D.S. Smith (NZ)	63	168	8	176
R.W. Taylor (Eng.)	57	167	7	174
R.C. Russell (Eng.)	49	141	11	152
J.H.B. Waite (SA)	50	124	17	141
D.J. Richardson (SA)	37	134	1	135
W.A.S. Oldfield (Aus.)	54	78	52	130
K.S. More (Ind.)	49	110	20	130
J.M. Parks (Eng.)†	43	101	11	112
Salim Yousuf (Pak.)	32	91	13	104

★ Dujon played in 2 other Tests and held 2 further catches in the field
† Parks played in 3 other Tests and held 2 further catches in the field

Most dismissals for the other two countries are:

S.A.R. Silva (SL)	9	33	1	34
A. Flower (Zim.)	22	50	4	54

MOST CATCHES BY FIELDSMEN

IN AN INNINGS

5	V.Y. Richardson	Aus. v SA, Durban	1935–36
	Yajurvindra Singh	Ind. v Eng., Bangalore	1976–77
	M. Azharuddin	Ind. v Pak., Karachi	1989–90
	K. Srikkanth	Ind. v Aus., Perth	1991–92

IN A TEST

7	G.S. Chappell	Aus. v Eng., Perth	1974–75
	Yajurvindra Singh	Ind. v Eng., Bangalore	1976–77
	H.P. Tillekeratne	SL v NZ, Colombo (SSC)	1992–93

IN A SERIES

15	J.M. Gregory	Aus. v Eng. (5 Tests)	1920–21
14	G.S. Chappell	Aus. v Eng. (6 Tests)	1974–75
13	R.B. Simpson	Aus. v SA (5 Tests)	1957–58
	R.B. Simpson	Aus. v WI (5 Tests)	1960–61

IN CAREER

156	A.R. Border (Aus. 156 Tests)
122	G.S. Chappell (Aus. 87 Tests)
122	I.V.A. Richards (WI 122 Tests)
120	M.C. Cowdrey (Eng. 114 Tests)
120	I.T. Botham (Eng. 102 Tests)
117	M.A. Taylor (Aus. 81 Tests)
110	W.R. Hammond (Eng. 85 Tests)
110	R.B. Simpson (Aus. 62 Tests)
109	G.S. Sobers (WI 93 Tests)
108	S.M. Gavaskar (Ind. 125 Tests)
105	I.M. Chappell (Aus. 75 Tests)
103	G.A. Gooch (Eng. 118 Tests)

CATCHES BY SUBSTITUTE FIELDSMEN

IN AN INNINGS

3	H. Strudwick	Eng. v Aus., Melbourne	1903–04
	Haroon Rashid	Pak. v Eng., Headingley	1982
	Gursharan Singh	Ind. v WI, Ahmedabad	1983–84

IN A TEST

4	Gursharan Singh	Ind. v WI, Ahmedabad	1983–84

YOUNGEST TEST PLAYERS

Years	Days			
15	124	Mushtaq Mohammad	Pak. v WI, Lahore	1958–59
16	189	Aqib Javed	Pak. v NZ, Wellington	1988–89
16	205	S.R. Tendulkar	Ind. v Pak., Karachi	1989–90
16	221	Aftab Baloch	Pak. v NZ, Dacca	1969–70
16	248	Nasim-ul-Ghani	Pak. v WI, Bridgetown	1957–58
16	352	Khalid Hassan	Pak. v Eng., Trent Bridge	1954

Hassan Raza played for Pak. v Zim. in October 1996 when allegedly aged only 14 yrs 227 days, but the Pakistan Cricket Board refused to accept this claim following medical examination

Youngest players for the other seven countries are:

18	149	D.B. Close	Eng. v NZ, Old Trafford	1949
17	239	I.D. Craig	Aus. v SA, Melbourne	1952–53
18	340	P.R. Adams	SA v Eng., Port Elizabeth	1995–96
17	122	J.E.D. Sealy	WI v Eng., Bridgetown	1929–30
18	10	D.L. Vettori	NZ v Eng., Wellington	1996–97
17	189	C.D.U.S. Weerasinghe	SL v Ind., Colombo (PSS)	1985–86
18	212	H.K. Olonga	Zim. v Pak., Harare	1994–95

YOUNGEST CENTURYMAKERS

Years	Days			
17	82	Mushtaq Mohammad (101)	Pak. v Ind., Delhi	1960–61
17	112	S.R. Tendulkar (119*)	Ind. v Eng., Old Trafford	1990
18	328	Salim Malik (100*)	Pak. v SL, Karachi	1981–82

YOUNGEST DOUBLE-CENTURIONS

19	141	Javed Miandad (206)	Pak. v NZ, Karachi	1976–77
20	315	G.A. Headley (223)	WI v Eng., Kingston	1929–30

OLDEST TEST PLAYERS

ON DEBUT

Years	Days			
49	119	J. Southerton	Eng. v Aus., Melbourne	1876–77
47	284	Miran Bux	Pak. v Ind., Lahore	1954–55
46	253	D.D. Blackie	Aus. v Eng., Sydney	1928–29
46	237	H. Ironmonger	Aus. v Eng., Brisbane†	1928–29
42	242	N. Betancourt	WI v Eng., Port-of-Spain	1929–30
41	337	E.R. Wilson	Eng. v Aus., Sydney	1920–21
41	27	R.J.D. Jamshedji	Ind. v Eng., Bombay‡	1933–34

† Exhibition Ground   ‡ Gymkhana Ground

For the other four countries:

40	295	O. Henry	SA v Ind., Durban	1992–93
38	101	H.M. McGirr	NZ v Eng., Auckland	1929–30
39	251	D.S. de Silva	SL v Eng., Colombo (PSS)	1981–82
37	84	A.C. Waller	Zim. v Eng., Bulawayo	1996–97

OLDEST ON LAST DAY OF CAREER

Years	Days			
52	165	W. Rhodes	Eng. v WI, Kingston	1929–30
50	327	H. Ironmonger	Aus. v Eng., Sydney	1932–33
50	320	W.G. Grace	Eng. v Aus., Trent Bridge	1899
50	303	G. Gunn	Eng. v WI, Kingston	1929–30
49	139	J. Southerton	Eng. v Aus., Melbourne	1876–77
47	302	Miran Bux	Pak. v Ind., Peshawar	1954–55
47	249	J.B. Hobbs	Eng. v Aus., Oval	1930
47	87	F.E. Woolley	Eng. v Aus., Oval	1934

OLDEST CENTURYMAKERS

Years	Days			
42	294	A.W. Nourse (111)	SA v Aus., Johannesburg†	1921–22
39	256	E.H. Bowley (109)	Eng. v NZ, Auckland	1929–30
39	191	A. Sandham (152)	Eng. v WI, Bridgetown	1929–30
39	173	J.W.H. Makepeace (117)	Eng. v Aus., Melbourne	1920–21
39	163	E.A.B. Rowan (156★)	SA v Eng., Johannesburg‡	1948–49
39	84	P.N. Kirsten (104)	SA v Eng., Headingley	1994

† Old Wanderers ground
‡ Ellis Park

UMPIRES: MOST TEST MATCHES

66	H.D. Bird (Eng.)	1973 to 1996
48	F. Chester (Eng.)	1924 to 1955
42	C.S. Elliott (Eng.)	1957 to 1974
36	D.J. Constant (Eng.)	1971 to 1988
34	Khizar Hayat (Pak.)	1979–80 to 1996–97
34	D.R. Shepherd (Eng.)	1985 to 1996–97
33	J.S. Buller (Eng.)	1956 to 1969
33	A.R. Crafter (Aus.)	1978–79 to 1991–92
32	R.W. Crockett (Aus.)	1901–02 to 1924–25
31	D. Sang Hue (WI)	1961–62 to 1980–81

LARGE ATTENDANCES

SERIES

943,000	Aus. v Eng. (5 Tests)	1936–37

(in England: 549,650 Eng. v Aus., 5 Tests, 1953)

TEST MATCH

350,534	Aus. v Eng., Melbourne, 3rd Test	1936–37
325,000 at least	Ind. v Eng., Calcutta	1972–73

(in England: 158,000 Eng. v Aus., Headingley, 1948)
(Perhaps as many as 394,000 spectators attended the Ind. v Eng. Test at Calcutta in 1981–82, but no official figure was given.)

FOR ONE DAY

90,800	Aus. v WI, Melbourne (5th Test, 2nd day)	1960–61

Book Reviews

by David Frith

The downturn in cricket book publishing is perceptible, but there remains scope for the big name (and his agent) to make print, with one eye on lucrative serialisation prospects, while the need for standard works of reference will always be requited.

In the twelvemonth under review, the most remarkable cricketer of all, Don Bradman, was the subject of two biographies. **Bradman: An Australian Hero** (Little, Brown £20) by (Lord) Charles Williams is the better written and sets the subject against a broad cultural and historical canvas, crafted wisely from the research resources of friends in the wide brown land. The author has managed to restrain himself in the matter of statistics within the text. Not so Roland Perry in **The Don** (Sidgwick £25), a book which weighs more but is riddled with tabloidese. Nonetheless, this is recommended for younger readers who want a first taster of this legend, including the insight into the religious divide and the jealousies that shadowed Bradman.

Ray Illingworth was the victim not so much of jealousy but of his own no-nonsense nature. Stubbornness and what was seen as a fatal generation gap rendered his years as boss of the England XI distractingly painful. At least in **One-Man Committee** (Headline £17.99) he has the chance to explain his viewpoint clearly and without interruption, supported by co-writer Jack Bannister. It is an eye-opener.

The worst thing to have happened to David Boon was that he came close to losing a testicle after being hit by a ball from Allan Donald. In **Under the Southern Cross** (HarperCollins) the 'Keg on Legs' writes touchingly of his Dad and amusingly of others, including the steward at Lord's who refused him entry to the pavilion with his 15-month-old daughter ('Women aren't allowed to enter here'). He made 21 centuries for Australia, and may yet prove irreplaceable. Critical of the ICC's handling of the Salim Malik affair, elsewhere he provides almost a laugh a page.

In **Allan Lamb: My Autobiography** (CollinsWillow £15.99) the brazen little (dare one mention it?) South African-born batsman sets out also to create a giggle a line, and often succeeds. The main theme is: What a naughty boy am I. But the disturbing item, without which the book would not have any outstanding purpose, is Lamb's inside observations on the ball-tampering cover-up and a court case or two. Not least interesting is a frank chapter by his longsuffering wife.

In **Wally Hammond: The Reasons Why** (Robson £17.95) the subject is long dead, so it now seems safe to enquire into the murkier side of his life with no inhibitions (and less than comprehensive evidence). The venereal-disease theory has been around for a long time, and it is well-known that this greatest of England cricketers was hard to live with. David Foot now endeavours to explain the moodiness and the problem with human relations (though only

as far as males were concerned), and has researched impressively. Hammond was so damned good that a book *ought* to be written about him every few years.

On the other hand, how many more books must there need to be about the popular Dickie Bird, umpire emeritus? **Free As a Bird** (Robson £14.95) is David Hopps's regurgitation of a thousand features and interviews with this music-hall character in a white coat, who has replaced 'Johnners' as the focus of dewy-eyed affection.

Uncorked! Diary of a Cricket Year (Cohen £15.99) was unwittingly timed to mark the cork's firm return to the neck of the bottle. That first spectacular year as an England player was followed by marital strife and serious loss of form. Dominic Cork (with David Norrie's help) sprays the pages with nicknames and emotional outpourings as his exciting first few Tests unfurl, to the heartbreak in South Africa and the World Cup. He concludes with a pledge not to be a one-year wonder.

Another feisty cricketer, Dermot Reeve, takes the stand in **Winning Ways** (Boxtree £15.99), firing off with a cluster of asterisks that marked his exchange with Brian Lara in a 1994 Warwickshire match. His enduring confidence and aggression were rewarded with three Test caps and unique success as captain of Warwickshire, but he rubbed so many people the wrong way that an appendix listing those he had never offended would have been helpful.

As for Simon Hughes, no Test player himself, **A Lot of Hard Yakka** (Headline £16.99) reveals many of the things Test cricketers (mostly Middlesex) get up to after dark. Those who have regarded Hughes as an irritating little nerd may begin to warm to him, to some degree at any rate, after reading this uninhibited offering. Almost subtly, he builds himself up and puts himself down as he describes the agonies of playing cricket for a living.

And as for the good old days, Barry Phillips' memoir of a Somerset hero, **Arthur Wellard: No Mere Slogger** (Leisuresolve £15.99), serves as a reminder that there were 'characters' years ago. Wellard was the Botham of his day, though nothing like as extrovert. His 561 sixes are probably unrivalled, and he regularly made hits over 100 yards. One struck the Old Trafford clocktower, and he helped Compton save the 1938 Lord's Test with a bold 38, which included a hit into the Grandstand. Even at 48 he was capable of bowling 44 overs of brisk medium-pace in a day. Wellard was lazy, liked pubs, card sessions and snooker-halls. And universally did people like him.

To a yet gentler age, and **Wheelwrights to Wickets** (Boundary £13.95) is J. W. Hearne jnr's plural biography of his ancestors, the cricketing Hearnes, six of whom played Test cricket for England or South Africa. Extensively researched, lovingly assembled and well illustrated.

Among the weightier books, **The Oxford Companion to Australian Cricket** (Oxford/Australian Society for Sports History

£30) runs to over 600 pages and is a landmark publication. Entries are not confined to players – or even males – and the quality of writing is high: Ian Chappell on captaincy; though Geoff Lawson's essay on fast bowling is historically flawed. Alex Buzo's satire on ex-players in the media is brilliant, and there are interesting entries on television, sponsorship, barracking and much else. There are laughs too: Mick Raymer's assault on the ferocious Alan Walker when he mistook his grunts for no-ball calls.

Humour adds too to the attraction of **Australian Cricket Anecdotes**, collected by Gideon Haigh (Oxford £16.99). Wrapped by a pleasing John Spooner montage, the contents embrace all the familiar names and many unfamiliar stories. Very good for the health, apart from the seizure risk should one laugh too heartily. 'You bat left-handed, don't you son?' asked a Victorian opener and skipper to his new partner. 'No,' replied the nervous youngster, 'but I'll try.'

The Penguin Book of Australian Sporting Anecdotes edited by Richard Smart (Penguin) contains 140 pages of cricket quotes, selected by Phil Derriman, some of them two-liners, others longer and gripping: Banjo Paterson on the young Bradman, and O'Reilly deploring kissing on the field: 'I most probably would have put my knee up.'

An especially worthy publication is Brian Bassano's update of **South African Cricket** (from 15 Hylands Road, Epsom KT18 9ED, £14.50 inc. p&p), this fourth volume (1947–1960) extending the earlier three volumes by Luckin and Duffus. Domestic and international seasons are summarised, and the pictorial content renders it an outstanding contribution to a cricket library.

The long-awaited history of Pakistan cricket emerged in Shuja Ud-din and Salim Parvez's **Babes of Cricket to World Champion** (from Martin Wood, 2 St John's Road, Sevenoaks TN13 3LW, £16.75 inc. p&p). It pulls no punches. The numerous squabbles and the intrigue are dealt with squarely, the raw material a soap-opera writer's dream.

There are squirms aplenty to be induced by **Tampering with Cricket**, umpire Don Oslear and Jack Bannister's inside story of deception, petulance and pusillanimous behaviour (Collins Willow £14.99). One of those books which 'authority' and many a reviewer seemed to regard as being a bad smell, it burrows deep into the matter of ball-tampering. Slightly depressing, but as significant as anything published in recent years.

The revised **Cricket Umpiring and Scoring** by the late Tom Smith (Weidenfeld £9.99) ought to be studied by every umpire, scorer and player, and is not altogether fancifully referred to as the 'bible' for the men in white coats.

In **Sobers: The Changing Face of Cricket** (Ebury £16.99), the greatest of cricketers expresses his views on many aspects of the game with characteristic frankness and a touch of autobiography. It serves to heighten the frustration at the reality that he can be seen no longer out in the middle.

In contrast, writers, some of them anyway, can seemingly go on for ever. **Last Over**, the latest collection of E. W. Swanton's writings over 70 years, gathered by David Rayvern Allen (Cohen £18.99), sustains a beautifully dated style and covers much familiar territory. The tussle with Ray Illingworth, chaired by Robin Day, is inconclusive but still a hoot, but the real strength lies in the enthralling descriptions of life in Japanese captivity.

Opinion – airing it or challenging it – is for many cricket-lovers the main motive for rising each morning. Words, words, words. There are another 75,000 of them in **Six of the Best** (Hodder £14.99), in which Bob Willis analyses the foremost cricketers of the world from these last two or three decades.

The Guinness Book of Cricket Blunders (Guinness £9.99) is an exquisite collection that should cheer up anyone inclined to take the game too seriously. Blofeld's gibberish, Bailey's mixed metaphors and even a few verbal blunders by Benaud interthread merrily with on-field disasters, of which there has never been a shortage.

No two enthusiasts would be likely to select the same 28 out-standing Tests from the 1300-odd now played, but Rick Smith has combed and come up with a readable collection in **Great Days in Test Cricket** (ABC Books). The first is the first (Melbourne 1877) and the last two are Zimbabwe's first Test win and the exciting Manchester Test of 1995, Cork hat-trick and all.

The Australian Cricket Book 1996 (ABC Books) records the destabilisation of Australia's cricket relations with Sri Lanka and Pakistan, and Ian Chappell proposes a formula for identifying the world's Test champions. The accent is on international cricket, culminating in the World Cup, and women's cricket receives its due.

Twice the size is **The Australian Cricket Almanac 1996** (Ironbark), which reaches to the furthest areas – club, country and junior – besides gathering together full statistical detail for all Australia's international and domestic matches in 1995–96.

Similarly, **Allan's Australian Cricket Annual 1996** edited by Allan Miller (from Sport-in-Print, 3 Radcliffe Road, West Bridgford NG2 5FF, £17 inc. p&p) is wideranging. It is also attractively presented and meticulously compiled, with much material unnoticed elsewhere, refreshingly relaxed match descriptions, a useful player directory, and plenty of illustrations, none sadder than the one showing the Sri Lankans refusing to shake hands with Mark Taylor.

Windows into the cricket world of long ago are provided by **Willows Publishing** (17 The Willows, Stone ST15 0DE), who continue to print well-crafted facsimiles of early *Wisdens* for just under £50 apiece, a fraction of the cost of originals, which are sometimes too fragile to read with peace of mind. The Willows series has just entered the 20th century, and if Albert Trott's bowling of L. G. Wright round his legs with a huge legbreak suggests there is nothing new in the game, not even from Shane Warne, then closer study will suggest otherwise on many of those historic pages.

Wisden Cricketers' Almanack's 134th edition, edited by Matthew Engel (£26), has a trendiness about it now that is aimed at capturing and retaining a younger readership. The broadening of the game puts pressure on space, but the fattest book of all continues to cope. The 1997 edition further broke with tradition by selecting a player (Jayasuriya) as a Cricketer of the Year purely on overseas performance.

Playfair Cricket Annual (Headline £4.99), edited by Bill Frindall, was published for the 50th time, another item of reference widely regarded as indispensable, though the cut-off date for printing makes overseas Test career figures awkward to update evenly.

At the other end of the English season, **Benson & Hedges Cricket Year** (Bloomsbury £20), edited by David Lemmon, is a bulky blend of stats, text and pictures that continues to amaze by its speed of arrival following the final ball of the season.

VIDEO

Cricket has never experienced such broad and heavy coverage as it does today, and it was inevitable that the visual global aspect would be addressed in the shape of a topical videotape series. This, ongoing, has been capably cornered by **Cover Point** (113 Upper Tulse Hill, London SW2 2RD, 10 tapes annually for £89.99; £120 outside UK), which presents footage from all the Test spots together with talking heads of anyone who is anyone in cricket. Stablemates include all manner of other features: Bradman, modern 'Superstars', county digests, etc.

★　★　★

The reviewer's own book **England v Australia: A Pictorial History of the Test Matches Since 1877** (BBC Books £16.99) was re-released for the 1997 Ashes series, and his autobiography, **Caught England, Bowled Australia** (Eva Press, Clifford Frost Ltd, Lyon Road, Wimbledon SW19 2SE, £19.99 inc. p&p), is also to be published this summer.

Obituaries

The following Test cricketers died during the Test match year which started May 1, 1996:

Keith David Boyce b. *St Peter, Barbados, Oct. 11, 1943; d. Barbados, Oct. 11, 1996.* 21 Tests for West Indies 1971–76: 657 runs at 24.33, 60 wickets at 30.02. Exciting allrounder: fast bowler, lithe action, hurricane hitter, and endowed with a long, flat throw. Headed West Indies bowling in 1973 Tests in England (19 at 15.47). Served Essex 1966–77: especially effective in one-day game. Highest score in Tests 95 not out, Adelaide, 1975–76; best bowling 6 for 77, Oval 1973 (11 for 147 in match: West Indies' first victory in 21 Tests). Member of West Indies' World Cup-winning side in 1975. Overcame drink problem, break-up of marriage and loss of house in hurricane and was coaching Barbados youngsters.

Leonard John Coldwell b. *Newton Abbot, Devon, Jan. 10, 1933; d. Teignmouth, Aug. 6, 1996.* Seven Tests for England 1962–64. Heavily-built medium-fast swing bowler: 22 wickets at 27.73. Best bowling 6 for 85 v Pakistan, Lord's, 1962 (debut Test: he took a wicket – Imtiaz Ahmed – with his fifth ball). Toured Australia and New Zealand 1962–63. Worcestershire 1955–69. Took 1076 first-class wickets at 21.18.

Denis Charles Scott Compton CBE b. *Hendon, May 23, 1918; d. Windsor, April 23, 1997.* Unrivalled darling of English cricket until knee problem forced retirement in 1957. In 78 Tests made 5807 runs (50.06), 17 centuries (HS 278 v Pakistan, Trent Bridge, 1954). Carefree manner disguised a serious approach. Holds record for most runs (3816) and centuries (18) in a season (1947), usually with Bill Edrich as partner. Made fastest triple-century (181 mins., MCC v NE Transvaal 1948–49). Record stands with Edrich of 370 (Eng. v SA, Lord's, 1947) and 424 (Middx v Somerset, Lord's, 1948). Made 38,942 f-c runs at 51.85, with 123 hundreds; took 622 wickets with slow left-arm. Popularity never waned in retirement. Stand named after him at Lord's.

Cecil (Sam) Cook b. *Tetbury, Gloucs., Aug. 23, 1921; d. Sept. 4, 1996.* One Test for England, v South Africa, Trent Bridge, 1947: 0 for 127. Slow left-arm bowler: 1782 first-class wickets at 20.53. Best bowling 9 for 42 v Yorkshire, Bristol, 1947. Later became umpire.

Frederick Eric Fisher b. *Johnsonville, Wellington, July 28, 1924; d. Palmerston North, June 19, 1996.* One Test for New Zealand, v South Africa, Wellington, 1952–53: 1 for 78, scored 9 and 14. Dropped McGlew (255 not out) twice. Left-arm seam bowler.

Gerald (Gerry) Ethridge Gomez b. *Belmont, Port-of-Spain, Oct. 10, 1919; d. Aug. 6, 1996.* 29 Tests for West Indies 1939–54: 1243 runs at 30.32, 58 wickets at 27.41, 18 catches. Captain in one Test. Member of 1950 West Indies side in England, which won for first time (Lord's): Gomez 70 in second innings, adding 211 with C.L. Walcott. One Test century: 101, Delhi, 1948–49. Test best bowling 7 for 55, Sydney, 1951–52, when he swung the ball either way. Stand of 434 with J.B. Stollmeyer for Trinidad, 1947. Best bowling 9 for 24 v South Zone, Madras, 1948–49, second-best figures ever by a West Indian. Managed successful 1960–61 tour of Australia. Eminent administrator, and founder of West Indies' Umpires Association.

Sridharan Jeganathan b. *Colombo, July 11, 1951; d. May 14, 1996.* Two Tests for Sri Lanka in New Zealand, 1982–83: 19 runs at 4.75, 0 for 12 with slow left-arm. Played in 1987 World Cup, having been in Sri Lanka team which won inaugural ICC Trophy, in England, 1979. Became Malaysia national coach. First Sri Lanka Test cricketer to die.

Donald Kenyon MBE b. *Wordsley, Staffs., May 15, 1924; d. Worcester, Nov. 12, 1996.* Eight Tests for England 1951–55: 192 runs at 12.80. Poor return for one so prolific and highly regarded in county cricket (37,002 first-class runs at 33.64, 74 centuries). Highest score in Tests 87 v South Africa, Trent Bridge, 1955 (91 with T.W. Graveney for first wicket). Dismissed by Lindwall in three of his four innings in the 1953 Tests v Australia. Captained Worcestershire to the county's first Championships (1964–65). England selector through successful period 1965–72.

Gorgumal Kishenchand b. *Karachi, April 14, 1925; d. Baroda, April 16, 1997.* 5 Tests, 4 in Australia 1947–48, when he made 0 in each of the second innings. Immortality came as the bowler off whom Bradman made the 100th run of his 100th century (Australian XI v Indians, Sydney). Test HS 44 on a difficult pitch at SCG. Only 89 runs (8.90) in his 10 Test innings.

Raymond Russell Lindwall MBE b. *Mascot, Sydney, Oct. 3, 1921; d. Brisbane, June 22, 1996.* 61 Tests for Australia 1946–60: 228 wickets at 23.03; 1502 runs at 21.15, 26 catches. Possibly the finest of all fast bowlers. Smooth, rhythmic run-up, low-slung action, master of variation, having bowled at express speed in younger days. Best-remembered performance 6 for 20 as England were humbled for 52 in 1948 Oval Test. He formed with K.R. Miller one of the most-feared new-ball attacks, with W.A. Johnston's sharp left-arm swing in support. Scored two Test hundreds, and led Australia in one Test in India in 1956–57. His 794 first-class wickets cost only 21.36 apiece. Also a noted Rugby League player.

Lawrence Somerville Martin Miller b. *New Plymouth, March 31, 1923; d. Porirua, Dec. 17, 1996.* Left-hander whose career was held back by rural (Taranaki) residence. Test debut at almost 30. Appalling run in South Africa 1953–54 after being hospitalised, coughing blood, from body blow from Adcock: 0, 0, 0, 0, 2. Came back as opener 1955–56 to make 47 and 25 in New Zealand's first-ever Test win, v West Indies, Auckland. Wretched time in 1958 Tests in England, though he top-scored with 26 out of 67 at Leeds. In 13 Tests he scored 346 runs at 13.84. Distinguished rugby player.

Rusi Sheriyar Modi b. *Bombay, Nov. 11, 1924; d. May 17, 1996.* 10

Tests for India 1946–53: 736 runs at 46.00, with one century (112 v West Indies, Bombay, 1948–49). Studious, highly-strung, slimly-built. Scored record centuries in seven consecutive matches in India 1943–45. First to make 1000 runs in Ranji Trophy season. Fell to his death from third floor of CCI pavilion, Brabourne Stadium.

Nazar Mohammad *b. Lahore, March 5, 1921; d. July 12, 1996.* Five Tests for Pakistan 1952–53 series: 277 runs at 39.57. These were Pakistan's first Test matches, and, having faced the first ball in the first, he carried his bat through the innings in the second, at Lucknow, for 124 not out (515 mins), becoming the first player to be on the field throughout a Test match. His son, Mudassar Nazar, became the second to carry his bat for Pakistan 30 years later. Forced to retire a year later after his arm was broken in an accident. Became Pakistan's coach.

Sir Jack Newman *b. Brightwater, Nelson, July 3, 1902; d. Sept. 23, 1996.* Three Tests for New Zealand 1932–33; 2 wickets for 254, 33 runs at 8.25. Oldest surviving Test player at time of death: Lionel Birkett (West Indies, b. April 14, 1904) succeeded him. Left-arm medium-pacer from rural Nelson who eventually received Test recognition via Wellington: 2 for 76 on debut v South Africa, 1931–32; then 0 for 178 in two Tests against visiting England (Hammond 227 in first, 336 not out in second). Hit for three successive sixes in latter record innings at Auckland. Later Test selector, and president of NZ Cricket Council.

Leo Patrick Joseph O'Brien *b. West Melbourne, July 2, 1907; d. Melbourne, March 13, 1997.* Allround sportsman: left-hand bat, played five Tests for Australia, two in 1932–33 Bodyline series, scoring 61 at Sydney, fifth Test. Toured South Africa 1935–36. Last Test v England, Sydney, 1936–37: 211 runs in career at 26.38. Shared Victoria fourth-wicket record, 301, with Len Darling. Dispensed slightly varying versions of Australian captain's tongue-lashing of England manager during Adelaide Bodyline Test. Was Australia's oldest Test survivor, position bequeathed to Sir Don Bradman.

Narotam (Tom) Puna *b. Surat, India, Oct. 28, 1929; d. June 7, 1996.* Three Tests for New Zealand v England 1965–66: 4 wickets at 60.00, 31 runs at 15.50. Emigrated as a child. Switched to offspin in late twenties; became Northern Districts' leading wicket-taker. Underused in third Test, when England were holding on for a draw at Auckland.

Alphonso (Alfie) Theodore Roberts *b. Kingstown, St Vincent, Sept. 18, 1937; d. Montreal, Canada, July 24, 1996.* One Test for West Indies, v New Zealand, Auckland, 1955–56 (New Zealand's first-ever Test victory). Scored 28 and 0. First Test player from St Vincent.

John (Jack) David Benbow Robertson *b. Chiswick, Feb. 22, 1917; d. Oct. 13, 1996.* 11 Tests for England 1947–52: 881 runs at 46.37, 2 centuries, 2 wickets at 29.00. Elegant opening batsman (Middlesex 1937–59: 31,914 first-class runs at 37.50, 67 centuries). Highest score 331 not out v Worcs., 1949 (Middlesex record). Made Test hundreds at Trinidad and Lord's (v New Zealand, 1949, his final

home Test appearance). Would have played more Tests but for the establishment of Hutton and Washbrook as England's openers. Was later Middlesex coach.

Nyalchand Shah *b. Dhangadhra, Sept. 14, 1919; d. Junagadh, Jan. 4, 1997.* Left-arm medium-pacer for Saurashtra: one Test, v Pakistan, Lucknow, 1952–53: 3 for 97 off 64 overs, on jute matting. India lost by an innings. Had represented India in 'unofficial Tests' previously.

David Charles Humphery Townsend *b. Norton-on-Tees, April 20, 1912; d. Stockton, Jan. 27, 1997.* Three Tests in West Indies, 1934–35, having played no county cricket apart from minor county Durham. Son of 1899 Test player C.L. Townsend. Top-scored (36 out of 107) at Trinidad in second Test innings, and saw fellow opener R.E.S. Wyatt have his jaw broken by a bouncer in Jamaica Test.

Leslie Watt *b. Waitati, Otago, Sept. 17, 1924; d. Dunedin, Nov. 15, 1996.* One Test for New Zealand, v England, Dunedin, 1954–55: 0 and 2 batting No. 6. Dour right-hander, opening partner to Bert Sutcliffe for Otago. Their opening stand of 373 against Auckland in 1950–51 is a NZ record. Had been 12th man for New Zealand when England visited in 1950–51.

Among others, not Test players, who passed on during this twelve-month, but who had a significant involvement with the international game, were **Alan McGilvray**, the Australian radio commentator, who died on July 16, 1996, aged 86, and **Gilbert Mant**, who reported the Bodyline series for Reuter. He died on Feb. 16, 1997, aged 94. Both were highly respected for their integrity and style, McGilvray, a former captain of the NSW XI, broadcasting cricket for almost half a century with impartiality, insight and a pleasing voice, while Mant, professionally muzzled during the 1932–33 Test series, gave his frank opinion in a book written 60 years later, and was still writing in his nineties, notably about the 1942 fall of Singapore, a first-hand account.

Another former broadcaster, **Alan Gibson**, died on April 10, 1997, aged 73. His polished diction and wordpower placed him in the top rank of commentators, but his predilection for a tipple finally exhausted his producer's patience. His final Test broadcast was at Headingley in 1975, a match coincidentally ruined by pitch damage inflicted by supporters of a jailed man. Gibson led a full life: lecturer, preacher, writer, all in his brilliantly distinctive style.

Former Test umpire **Mel McInnes** died on July 23, 1996, aged 80. It is the destiny of many an umpire to be remembered for crucial errors, particularly in the modern era of television replays. McInnes had the misfortune to commit a few blunders during the 1958–59 Ashes series, which was the first to be televised in Australia. He was also held responsible by some for doing nothing to curb the spread of very dubious bowling actions, as well as dragging which saw bowlers' front boots coming down a long way in front of the popping crease. Withal, McInnes was a distinguished cricket administrator and had happy memories of the 1954–55 series, when he officiated in all five Tests.